THE OFFICIAL RED BOOK
OF UNITED STATES COINS

1987

A GUIDE BOOK
of
UNITED STATES COINS

By R. S. YEOMAN

40th Revised Edition

Fully Illustrated

Catalog and Valuation List — 1616 to Date

Edited by Kenneth Bressett

A BRIEF HISTORY OF AMERICAN COINAGE
EARLY AMERICAN COINS AND TOKENS
EARLY MINT ISSUES   REGULAR MINT ISSUES
PRIVATE, STATE AND TERRITORIAL GOLD
SILVER AND GOLD COMMEMORATIVE ISSUES
PROOFS

 Whitman Coin Products

Copyright © MCMLXXXVI by
WESTERN PUBLISHING COMPANY, INC.
RACINE, WISCONSIN 53404

All Rights Reserved

Library of Congress Catalog Card No.: 47-22284

THE SPANISH MILLED DOLLAR
The Coin of Our Nation's Founders

The Spanish milled dollar valued at 8 *reales,* otherwise known as the "pillar dollar" or "piece of eight," has been given a place in romantic fiction unequaled by any other coin.

This time-honored piece and its fractional parts of ½ and 1 *real,* 2 and 4 *reales* were the principal coins of the American colonists, and were the forerunners of our own silver dollar and its fractional divisions.

The coin shown above bears the M̃ mint mark for Mexico City. Similar pieces with other mint marks were struck in Bolivia, Chile, Colombia, Guatemala and Peru. For details see listings in Whitman's *Coins of the World 1750-1850* by W. D. Craig and *Silver Dollars of North and South America* by Wayte Raymond. Average value for an 8 *reales* of common date and mint is about $125 in Fine to Very Fine condition. Dates range from 1732 to 1772.

Note: Many modern copies of the 8 *reales* exist. These are produced mostly as souvenirs and have little or no value.

THE PURPOSE OF THIS BOOK

Coin values listed in the Guide Book are averaged from data supplied by contributors several months before publication. The coin market is so active in some categories that values can easily change during this period. Prices are shown as a guide and are not intended to serve as a price-list for any dealer's stock. A dash appearing in a price column indicates the existence of coins in that grade, whose current values cannot be determined. It does not necessarily mean that such coins are excessively rare. Italicized prices indicate unsettled values. A number of listings of rare coins do not have prices or dashes in certain grades. This indicates that they are not available or known in those grades.

Prices rise when: 1. The economic trend is inflationary. 2. The number of collectors increases, while coin supplies remain stationary or decrease through attrition or melting. 3. Dealers replace their stocks of coins only from collectors or other dealers, who expect a profit over what they originally paid.

Prices decline when: 1. Changes in collecting habits may alter demand for certain coins. 2. Speculators buy and sell in large quantities. 3. Hoards or large holdings are suddenly released and cannot be quickly absorbed by the normal market. 4. Bullion gold and silver prices decline sharply.

Those who edit, contribute to, and publish this book advocate the collecting of coins for pleasure and educational benefits. A secondary consideration is that of investment, the profits from which are realized over the long term based on intelligent purchases.

The *Handbook of United States Coins* by R. S. Yeoman, Western Publishing Company, Inc. Racine, WI. containing average prices dealers will pay for these coins, is obtainable at most hobby dealers.

CONTRIBUTORS TO THE FORTIETH EDITION

JOYCE RESS, *Project Coordinator*

Burl Armstrong	Ronald J. Gillio	David Leventhal
Michael Aron	Harry Gittelson	Ed Leventhal
Richard A. Bagg	Ira Goldberg	Stuart Levine
Robert F. Batchedler	Kenneth M. Goldman	Dana Linett
Aubrey E. Bebee	David Hall	Denis W. Loring
Thomas Becker	James Halperin	Robert T. McIntire
Lee J. Bellisario	David J. Hendrickson	Raymond N. Merena
Philip E. Benedetti, Sr.	Leon E. Henderickson	Bob Merrill
Neil S. Berman	Gene Henry	Bill Mertes
George H. Blenker	C. Edward Hipps	Sylvia Novack
Brad Bohnert	Ed Hipps, Jr.	Paul B. Nugget
Q. David Bowers	Karl Hirtzinger	Sid Nusbaum
Philip Bressett	Ron Howard	Robert M. Paul
Hy Brown	John Hunter	William P. Paul
Mike Brownlee	Jesse Iskowitz	Joe Person
Joel Buzanowski	Curtis Iversen	Joel D. Rettew
Judy Cahn	Steve Ivy	Jack H. Robinson
James Carr	Robert H. Jacobs	Maurice Rosen
Bill Causey	Floyd O. Janney	Earl Schill
J. H. Cline	James J. Jelinski	Robert R. Shaw
Alan R. Cohen	A. M. Kagin	Michael Sherman
Jerome Cohen	Donald H. Kagin	James A. Simek
John Dannreuther	Paul S. Kagin	William J. Spencer
Larry Demerer	Stanley Kesselman	Leonard W. Stark
Kurt Eckstein	Jack Klausen	Maurice A. Storck, Sr.
Dennis J. Forgue	Mike Kliman	Charles Surasky
Michael Fuljenz	Paul Koppenhaver	Anthony Terranova
Chuck Furjanic	Abner Kreisberg	Russel P. Vaughn
Dorothy Gershenson	Greg Lauderdale	Douglas A. Winter
Dennis M. Gillio	Julian Leidman	Gary L. Young

Special credit is due to the following for service and data in this book:

Herbert Bergen, Harry X Boosel, Walter Breen, Dan Brown, Malcolm O. E. Chell-Frost, Ted F. Clark, Roger S. Cohen, Jr., Mike Danish, Tom DeLorey, Bill Fivaz, George Fuld, Natalie Halpern, V. M. Hanks, Jr., James A. Haxby, Herbert Hicks, Robert W. Julian, Jerry Kimmell, Lonesome John, Lester Merkin, Ed Metzger, Raymond D. Munde, Eric P. Newman, Mary Sauvain, Neil Shafer, Norman Shultz, Arlie Slabaugh, Anthony Swiatek, Thomas Underwood, Holland Wallace, Stewart P. Witham, John Wright, and Leo A. Young.

Those now deceased, but whose contributions have been a part of this book since early editions, include:

Kamal M. Ahwash, David M. Bullowa, William L. Clark, Carl Curcio, Ben M. Douglas, Ben Dreiske, Charles E. Green, Abe Kosoff, Steve Kosoff, Kenneth W. Lee, Ken Nichols, Jerome Nusbaum, Al C. Overton, Richard Picker, Hubert L. Polzer, Lewis M. Reagan, and Sidney Smith.

Auction price data furnished by "Auction Prices Realized: U.S. Coins," 1986 Edition, Krause Publications, Inc., and often reflect prices realized without commission adjustments.

CONDITION OF COINS

Essential elements of the A.N.A. grading system

PROOF — A specially made coin distinguished by sharpness of detail and usually with a brilliant mirrorlike surface. Proof refers to the method of manufacture and is not a condition, but normally the term implies perfect mint state unless otherwise noted and graded as below. See page 60 for details.

MINT STATE — The terms Mint State (MS) and Uncirculated (Unc.) are interchangeably used to describe coins showing no trace of wear. Such coins may vary to some degree because of blemishes, toning or slight imperfections as described in the following subdivisions.

PERFECT UNCIRCULATED (MS-70) — Perfect new condition, showing no trace of wear. The finest quality possible, with no evidence of scratches, handling or contact with other coins. Very few regular issue coins are ever found in this condition.

CHOICE UNCIRCULATED (MS-65) — An above average Uncirculated coin which may be brilliant or lightly toned and has very few contact marks on the surface or rim. MS-67 or MS-63 indicates a slightly higher or lower grade of preservation.

UNCIRCULATED (MS-60) — Has no trace of wear but may show a number of contact marks, and surface may be spotted or lack some luster.

CHOICE ABOUT UNCIRCULATED (AU-55) — Barest evidence of light wear on only the highest points of the design. Most of the mint luster remains.

ABOUT UNCIRCULATED (AU-50) — Has traces of light wear on many of the high points. At least half of the mint luster is still present.

CHOICE EXTREMELY FINE (EF-45) — Light overall wear shows on highest points. All design details are very sharp. Some of the mint luster is evident.

EXTREMELY FINE (EF-40) — Design is lightly worn throughout, but all features are sharp and well defined. Traces of luster may show.

CHOICE VERY FINE (VF-30) — Light even wear on the surface and highest parts of the design. All lettering and major features are sharp.

VERY FINE (VF-20) — Shows moderate wear on high points of design. All major details are clear.

FINE (F-12) — Moderate to considerable even wear. Entire design is bold with overall pleasing appearance.

VERY GOOD (VG-8) — Well worn with main features clear and bold although rather flat.

GOOD (G-4) — Heavily worn with design visible but faint in areas. Many details are flat.

ABOUT GOOD (AG-3) — Very heavily worn with portions of lettering, date and legends worn smooth. The date may be barely readable.

IMPORTANT: Damaged coins, such as those which are bent, corroded, scratched, holed, nicked, stained, or mutilated, are worth less than those without defects. *Flawless uncirculated coins are generally worth more than values quoted in this book.* Slightly worn coins ("sliders") which have been cleaned and conditioned ("whizzed") to simulate uncirculated luster are worth considerably less than perfect pieces.

Unlike damage inflicted after striking, manufacturing defects do not always lessen values. Examples are: Colonial coins with planchet flaws and weakly struck designs; early silver and gold with weight adjustment "file marks" (parallel cuts made prior to striking); and coins with "lint marks" (dust or other foreign matter which may mar the surface during striking).

Brief guides to grading are placed before each major coin type in this book. For those readers who desire more detailed descriptions of all coin grades, we recommend OFFICIAL A.N.A. GRADING STANDARDS FOR UNITED STATES COINS, by the American Numismatic Association.

AN INTRODUCTION TO UNITED STATES COINS

Money of the Early Americans

The story of American money, which occupies a period of over three centuries, began when the early settlers in New England carried on their fur trade with the Indians through the use of wampum, which had been fashioned from mussel shells in the form of "beads." Beaver skins, wampum, and in Virginia, tobacco, soon became the commonly accepted media of exchange for all other available commodities. The immigrants, in fact, had little use for coined money at first, but when traders arrived from foreign lands, coins were usually demanded in payment for goods. Any foreign coins were usually accepted, such as French louis, English guineas, German thalers, Dutch ducats, and various Spanish coins, including doubloons and particularly the Spanish milled dollar, or piece of eight. The piece of eight continued to be a standard money unit throughout the entire colonial period. Even after the Revolutionary War, the Spanish dollar and its fractional parts circulated in this country with official sanction until 1857. One *real* equaled 12½ cents and was known as a "bit." A quarter of the dollar thus became known as "two bits," a term still in use.

England consistently ignored the plight of the colonists and made no effort to provide gold or silver coins, or a small-change currency for them. Although coins known as "Hogge Money" were provided for the Sommer Islands, now known as the Bermudas, about the year 1616, the first coins minted in America were minted by John Hull in the Massachusetts Bay Colony. The General Court of the colony granted him authority to begin coinage. Starting in 1652 the Boston mint provided the famous N.E., pine tree, and similar shillings, with their fractional parts, for the hardpressed colonists. Other colonies tried similar projects but failed.

As time went by, coins and tokens of many types were introduced and employed by the colonists in their daily course of business. Lord Baltimore in Maryland was responsible for a series of silver pieces, which were probably struck in England in 1658. Mark Newby introduced a piece known as St. Patrick's Halfpence into the province of New Jersey in 1682. Coins dated 1722 to 1724, known as Rosa Americana and Hibernia coppers, were produced by William Wood in England and were widely circulated in America. The Carolina and New England Elephant tokens were current in the years following 1694. There were also a few issues of uncertain date and origin, such as the New Yorke Token, which circulated among the Dutch settlers and was probably sent over from Holland.

Enterprising American individuals were responsible for some of the copper pieces that circulated during the eighteenth century. The Gloucester Token, about which little is known, was one of these. John Higley of Granby, Connecticut, made an interesting series of threepence pieces during the period from 1737 to 1739. J. Chalmers, a goldsmith in Annapolis, Maryland, issued silver shillings, sixpence, and threepence pieces in 1783. In 1787 Ephraim Brasher, a New York goldsmith, struck a gold piece of the value of a doubloon (about $16.00). Standish Barry of Baltimore, Maryland, made a curious silver token threepence in 1790.

Still other tokens, struck in England, reached our shores in Revolutionary times and were for the most part speculative ventures. These much-needed, small-denomination coppers were readily circulated because of the great scarcity of fractional coins. Included in this category were the Nova Constellatio coppers and the Bar cent.

During the period of confederation following the War of Independence, still more English tokens were added to the great variety of coins and tokens employed in the new nation. In 1787 the Nova Eboracs, known as New York Coppers, the Georgius Triumpho, the Auctori Plebis, and later the Kentucky, Myddelton and Franklin Press tokens were introduced.

Another interesting series, historically important because of its close association with our first president, consists of those tokens bearing the portrait of Washington. Although most of these pieces are dated from 1783 to 1795, many of them were made in England around the turn of the century.

Coinage of the States

The Articles of Confederation, adopted March 1, 1781, provided that Congress should have the sole right to regulate the alloy and value of coin struck by its own authority or by that of the respective states.

Each state, therefore, had the right to coin money, but Congress served as a regulating authority. New Hampshire was the first state to consider coinage, but few if any coins were placed in circulation. The only specimens known bear the date 1776.

Vermont, Connecticut, and New Jersey granted coining privileges to companies or individuals. Massachusetts erected its own mint in which copper coins were produced. A number of interesting varieties of these state issues, most of which were struck in fairly large quantities, can still be acquired, and form the basis for many present day collections of early American coins.

The Beginnings of United States Coinage

Throughout the Colonial years, Americans had become accustomed to the use of the Spanish dollar and its fractional parts, the *real,* the medio (half- *real*), etc. It was only natural, therefore, that when a national coinage was under consideration the dollar was mentioned most frequently. In earlier years currency statutes in many of the colonies had given first consideration to the Spanish dollar. Connecticut, Massachusetts, and Virginia, particularly, passed laws making Spanish coins a legal tender. The first issue of Continental paper money May 10, 1775, offers further evidence that the dollar was to be our basic money unit, for it provided that the notes should be payable in "Spanish Milled dollars or the value thereof in gold or silver."

The Assistant Financier of the Confederation, Gouverneur Morris, proposed a decimal coinage ratio, and his plan was incorporated in a report presented by Robert Morris, Superintendent of Finance, to the Congress, January 15, 1782. Plans for a mint were advanced, and a uniform national currency to relieve the confused money conditions was outlined. Morris's unit, 1/1440 of a dollar, was calculated to agree without a fraction with all the different valuations of the Spanish milled dollar in the various States. Although a government mint was approved February 21, 1782, no immediate action was taken. During 1784 Thomas Jefferson, then a member of the House of Representatives, brought in a report concerning the plan, and expressed disagreement with Morris' complicated money unit. He advocated the simple dollar unit because he believed the dollar was already as familiar and convenient a unit of value as the British pound. He favored the decimal system and remarked that, "The most easy ratio of multiplication and division is that of ten. George Washington referred to it as 'a measure, which in my opinion, has become indispensibly necessary.'"

The Grand Committee in May 1785 recommended a gold five-dollar piece; a dollar of silver with fractional coins, of the same metal, in denominations of half, quarter, tenth, and twentieth parts of a dollar; and copper pieces valued at one-hundredth and one two-hundredth of a dollar.

In 1783 Robert Morris submitted a series of pattern pieces in silver which were designed by Dudley to carry out the decimal idea for United States money. These are known as the Nova Constellatio Patterns and consist of the "Mark" or 1,000 units, the "Quint" or 500 units, the "Bit" or 100 units, and a copper "five". The unit was to be a quarter grain of silver. This was not the first attempt at a dollar coin, for the Continental currency piece of dollar size, dated

1776, had been struck in such metals as brass, pewter, and silver. The variety in silver probably saw limited service as a dollar.

Congress gave formal approval to the basic dollar unit and decimal coinage ratio in its resolution of July 6, 1785, but other more pressing matters delayed further action. Not until the Constitutional Convention had placed the country on firm ground and the new nation had elected George Washington President, did the Congress again turn attention to the subject of currency, a mint, and a coinage system.

The Massachusetts cents and half cents struck in 1787 and 1788 were the first official coins to bear a stated value in terms of decimal parts of the dollar unit in this country. The cent represented a hundredth part of a Spanish dollar.

The first federally authorized coin was the Fugio Cent, sometimes called the Franklin Cent, as he was supposed to have supplied the design and composed the legends. This piece, similar in design to the Continental Currency dollar of 1776, was privately struck in 1787 by contract with the Government.

Alexander Hamilton, then Secretary of the Treasury, reported his views on monetary matters January 21, 1791. He concurred in all essentials with the decimal subdivisions and multiples of the dollar contained in the earlier resolutions and urged the use of both gold and silver in our standard money.

Congress passed a resolution March 3, 1791, that a mint be established, and authorized the President to engage artists and procure machinery for the making of coins. No immediate steps were taken, but when Washington delivered his third annual address, he recommended immediate establishment of a mint.

On April 2, 1792, a bill was finally passed providing "that the money of account of the United States should be expressed in dollars or units, dismes or tenths, cents or hundredths, and milles or thousandths; a disme being the tenth part of a dollar, a cent the hundredth part of a dollar, a mille the thousandth part of a dollar ... "

Denominations specified in the act were as follows:

	Value of	Grains Pure	Grains Standard
Gold Eagle	$10.00	247 - 4/8	270
Gold Half Eagle	5.00	123 - 6/8	135
Gold Quarter Eagle	2.50	61 - 7/8	67 - 4/8
Silver Dollar	1.00	371 - 4/16	416
Silver Half Dollar.	.50	185 - 10/16	208
Silver Quarter Dollar	.25	92 - 13/16	104
Silver Disme (dime).	.10	37 - 2/16	41 - 3/5
Silver Half Disme	.05	18 - 9/16	20 - 4/5
Copper Cent.	.01	11 pennyweights	
Copper Half Cent.	.005	5½ pennyweights	

The word "pure" meant unalloyed metal; "standard" meant, in the case of gold, 11/12 fine or 11 parts pure metal to one part alloy, which was mixed with the pure metal to improve the wearing qualities of the coins. The fineness for silver coins was 1485/1664 or approximately 892.43 thousandths, in contrast with the gold coins of 22 karats, or 916 2/3 thousandths fine.

The law also provided for free coinage of gold and silver coins at the fixed ratio of 15 to one, and a token coinage of copper cents and half cents. Under the free coinage provision no charge was to be made for converting gold or silver bullion into coins "weight for weight." At the depositor's option, however, he could demand an immediate exchange of coins for his bullion, for which privilege a deduction of one-half of one per cent was to be imposed.

Washington appointed David Rittenhouse, a well-known philosopher and scientist, as the first Director of the Mint. Construction began on a mint building nearly four months after the passage of the Act of April 2, 1792. The building was located on Seventh Street near Arch in Philadelphia.

The first coin struck by the government was the half disme. Fifteen hundred of these pieces were produced during the month of July 1792 before the mint was completed. Washington supplied some of his own silver to the value of about one hundred dollars for those first coins. Dismes also were probably struck at this time or a short while later. The portrait on these pieces may have been modeled by Martha Washington.

Copper for cents and half cents was covered in the Act of May 8, 1792 when the purchase of not over 150 tons was authorized. On September 11, 1792, six pounds of old copper were purchased, this being the first purchase of copper for coinage, which was probably used for the striking of patterns.

Planchets with upset rims for cents and half cents were purchased from Boulton of Birmingham, England from 1798 to 1838.

Several pattern coins were prepared in 1792 before regular mint operations commenced. These included the silver center cent by Henry Voigt, a smaller piece than that of regular issue. The small plug of silver, worth about three-quarters of a cent, was evidently intended to bring the intrinsic value of the coin up to the value of one cent and permit production of a coin of more convenient size. Alexander Hamilton had mentioned a year before that the proposed "intrinsic value" cent would be too large, and suggested that the amount of copper could be reduced and a trace of silver added. The pattern cent with a silver center may have been designed to conform to this recommendation.

The cents by Robert Birch are equally interesting. These patterns are identified by their legends which read "LIBERTY PARENT OF SCIENCE AND INDUSTRY" and "TO BE ESTEEMED BE USEFUL." The quarter with an eagle on the reverse side belongs among the early patterns devised before regular issues were struck.

The Bank of Maryland deposited the first silver, sending $80,715.73½ in French coins to the mint July 18, 1794. Moses Brown, a Boston merchant, deposited the first gold in the form of ingots, February 12, 1795, amounting to $2,276.22, receiving silver coin in payment. The first coins transferred to the Treasurer consisted of 11,178 cents on March 1, 1793. The first return of coined silver was made on October 15, 1794, and the first gold coins, 744 half eagles, were delivered July 31, 1795.

File marks on early U. S. coins are a result of the mint process of weight adjustment.

Regular Mint Issues

Cents and half cents exclusively were coined during the year 1793, and by 1799 approximately $50,000 in these coins had been placed in circulation. This amount proved insufficient for the requirements of commerce, and small denomination coins of the states and of foreign countries continued in use during the first few years of the nineteenth century.

One of the most serious problems confronting the commercial interests during the early years was the failure of the government to provide a sufficient volume of circulating coins. The fault, contrary to popular opinion at the time, did not lie with any lack of effort on the part of the mint. Other circumstances tended to interfere with the expected steady flow of new coinage into the channels of trade.

Free circulation of United States gold and silver coins was greatly hindered by speculators. For example, worn Spanish dollars of reduced weight and value were easily exchanged for U. S. silver dollars, which meant the export of most of the new dollars as fast as they were minted, and a complete loss to American trade channels.

Gold coins failed to circulate for similar reasons. The ratio of 15 to 1 between gold and silver was close to the world ratio when Hamilton recommended it, but by 1799 the ratio in European commercial centers had reached 15¾ to 1. At this rate the undervalued gold coins tended to flow out of the country, or were reduced for bullion. After 1800, therefore, United States gold coins were rarely seen in general circulation. As no remedy could be found, coinage of the

Eagle and the silver dollar was suspended by President Jefferson in 1804 and 1806 respectively. It is generally conceded that the silver dollar was discontinued in 1804, although the last coins minted for the period were dated 1803.

Lacking gold coins and silver dollars, the half dollar became the desirable coin for large transactions, bank reserves, and foreign payments. Until 1830, in fact, half dollars circulated very little as they were mainly transferred from bank to bank. This will account for the relatively good supply of half dollars of this period which are still available to collectors in better than average condition. A senate committee of 1830 reported that United States silver coins were considered so much bullion and were accordingly "lost to the community as coins."

There was only a negligible coinage of quarters, dimes, and half dimes from 1794 to 1834. It has been estimated that there was less than one piece for each person in the country in the year 1830. This period has been described as one of nondescript currency made up of banknotes, underweight foreign gold coins, foreign silver coins of many varieties, and domestic fractional silver coins. Notes of "wildcat banks" flooded the country before 1830 and were much more common than silver coins.

On June 28, 1834, a new law was passed reducing the weight of standard gold, which had the effect of placing our money on a gold standard. Trade and finance were greatly benefited by this act, which also proved a boon to the gold mines of Georgia and North Carolina. Branch mints in Dahlonega, Georgia, and Charlotte, North Carolina, were established two or three years later to handle the newly mined gold at the source. The Templeton Reid and Bechtler issues of private gold coins were struck in this area.

The law of January 18, 1837, completely revised and standardized the mint and coinage laws. Legal standards, mint charges, legal tender, mint procedure, tolerance in coin weights, accounting methods, a bullion fund, standardization of gold and silver coins to 900 thousandths fine, and other desirable regulations were covered by the new legislation. Results of importance to the collector were the changes in type for the various coin denominations and the resumption of coinage of the Eagle shortly thereafter.

The political and financial elements underwent a crisis at about this time. The familiar "Jackson Tokens" and fractional notes of banks and commercial establishments completely eclipsed the circulation of metallic currency. This was the era of "shinplasters."

The California gold discovery in 1848 was responsible for an interesting series of private, state, and territorial gold issues in the Western states, culminating in the establishment of a branch mint at San Francisco in 1854.

Two new regular gold issues were adopted in 1849. In that year the double Eagle and gold dollar joined our American family of coins. The California gold fields greatly influenced the world gold market, making the exportation of silver profitable. For example, the silver in two half dollars was worth $1.03½ in gold. The newly introduced gold dollars soon took over the burden and hastened the disappearance of silver coins from trade channels. This was the situation when the new three cent postage rate brought about the bill authorizing the coinage of the silver three cent piece in 1851. This was our country's first subsidiary coin, for its value was intrinsically 86% of its face value, an expedient designed to prevent its withdrawal from circulation.

The three dollar gold piece was authorized by the act of February 21, 1853. Never a popular or necessary coin, it nevertheless was issued regularly until 1889.

On February 21, 1853, fractional silver coins were made subsidiary resulting from the fact that the weight of all silver pieces, excepting the dollar, was reduced. As the coins were now worth less than their face value free coinage of silver was prohibited, and the mint was authorized to purchase its silver requirements on its own account using the bullion fund of the mint, and, according to law, "the profit of said coinage shall be, . . . transferred to the account of the treasury of the United States."

Arrows were placed at the date on all silver coins except three cent pieces and dollars, and on the quarters and half dollars rays were added on the reverse side to denote the change of weight. In 1854 the rays were removed, and in 1856 the arrows disappeared. Production of silver coins in large quantities during this period greatly relieved the demands on gold dollars and three cent pieces. Consequently for the first time in our nation's history there was a sufficient supply of fractional coins in general circulation.

The law of 1857 was designed primarily to reform the copper coinage. No matter how interesting and valuable the large cents and half cents may have become in the eyes of the modern collector, they were very unpopular with the people and cost the mint too much to produce.

The new law abolished the half cent piece, and reduced the size and changed the design of the cent. The new Flying Eagle cent contained 88% copper and 12% nickel. Several hundred experimental cents were stamped from dies bearing the date 1856 although no authority for the issue existed before 1857. Other important effects of the law were the retirement of the Spanish silver coins from circulation, and dispersal of the new cents in such excessive quantities as to create a nuisance to business houses, particularly in the eastern cities. The Indian head device replaced the Eagle in 1859, and in 1864 the weight of the cent was further reduced and its composition changed to a proportion of 95% copper and 5% tin and zinc. This bronze composition was the standard for our cent except for the years 1943, and 1944 to 1946. In 1962 the alloy was changed to 95% copper and 5% zinc. In 1982 the composition was changed to 97.5% zinc and 2.5% copper.

Both Jefferson and Hamilton had contended in their day that the currency of money of small value benefits society. The history of our cent and its daily use proves the soundness of this principle.

Abundance turned to scarcity following the outbreak of the Civil War. Anticipation of a scarcity and depreciation of the paper money was sufficient to induce hoarding. The large volume of greenbacks in circulation caused a premium on gold, and subsidiary silver as a result of the sudden depreciation quickly vanished in the North. Resort was soon made to postage stamps for small change. All types of fractional notes were put out at this time by municipalities and the government. "Postage currency" became widely used, and in 1863 a great variety of tokens appeared to help fill the vacuum. Like the tokens of 1837 they were of two general classes, tradesmen's coins and imitations of legal cents. Many of the latter were political or patriotic in character, carried slogans typical of the times, and were usually produced at a profit.

The Law of 1864, which effected changes in the cent, provided also for the new bronze two cent piece. The act, moreover, provided legal tender status for these two coins up to ten times their value. The two cent piece was the first coin to bear the motto IN GOD WE TRUST. The new coin was readily accepted by the people but proved an unnecessary denomination, going out of fashion and being discontinued only nine years later.

Secretary Chase had issued a great many currency notes of three cent denomination early in 1865. The nickel interests seized upon this circumstance to fight for a new three cent coin for redemption of the paper money. A law was quickly passed and signed by the president as of March 3, 1865, providing for a three cent coin of 75-25 copper-nickel composition. Our country now possessed two types of three cent pieces. The nickel three cent piece was struck continuously until 1889; the three cent silver until 1873.

The new copper-nickel alloy ratio was selected for the five cent coin, adopted May 16, 1866, to be thereafter known as a "nickel." Again the people had a coin value available in two forms. The silver half dime, like the three cent piece, was retired from service in 1873.

The Carson City Mint was established in 1870 as a convenient depository for the miners in that area and operated until 1893.

The Law of March 3, 1871, was a redemption measure and was passed to provide a means for the disposal to the United States Treasury of millions of minor coins which had accumulated in the hands of postmasters, newsdealers, and others. Small-denomination coins as a result of this new law were placed on an equal footing and could be redeemed when presented in lots of twenty dollars.

There was a general revision of the coinage laws in 1873. Several years of study and debate preceded the final enactment. The legislative history of the bill occupies hundreds of pages of the Congressional Globe, and the result was considered by many a clumsy attempt and a failure. The law has sometimes been referred to as the "Crime of '73." One consequence of the bill, which achieved final enactment February 12, 1873, was the elimination of the silver dollar. In its stead the Trade dollar of greater weight was provided for use in commerce with the Orient in competition with the Mexican dollar. The legal tender provision, which unintentionally gave the Trade dollar currency within our borders, was repealed the following year.

The charge for converting standard gold bullion into coin was reduced by the act to one-fifth of one per cent. The same rate was imposed on silver bullion for coining Trade dollars only.

It may be a surprise to some collectors to learn that the silver dollar had not circulated to any great extent in the United States after 1803. The coin had been turned out steadily since 1840, but for various reasons such as exportation, melting, and holding in bank vaults, the dollar was virtually an unknown coin. The Law of 1873 in effect demonetized silver and committed our country to a gold standard. The silver mining interests came to realize what had occurred a little later, and the ensuing quarter century of political and monetary history was filled with their voluble protests. There was a constant bitter struggle for the return to bimetallism.

From an economic point of view the inadequate supply of gold was responsible for a gradual decline in prices throughout the world. This brought about a gradual business depression in our country, particularly in the South and Middle-West. Private silver interests influenced great sections of the West for bimetallism as a remedy for the failing price level. Authorities have concluded that a world-wide adoption of bimetallism would have improved economic conditions, but the United States alone proceeding to place its money on a double standard at the old 16 to 1 ratio would have led only to a worse situation.

Of particular importance to collectors, however, were those features of the Law of 1873 which affected the status and physical properties of the individual coins. The weight of the half dollar, quarter, and dime, was slightly changed and arrows were placed at the date for the ensuing two years to indicate the difference in weight. Silver three cent pieces, half dimes, and two cent pieces were abolished by the act, and the manufacture of minor coins was restricted to the Mint at Philadelphia.

The short-lived twenty cent piece was authorized March 3, 1875. It was created for the Western states where the Spanish "bit" had become equivalent to a U. S. dime. The five cent piece did not circulate there, so when a quarter was offered for a "bit" purchase, only a dime change was returned. However, it was confused with the quarter dollar and was discontinued after 1878.

The Bland-Allison Act of February 28, 1878, gave the Secretary authority to purchase two to four million dollars worth of silver bullion each month to be coined into silver dollars. The coin, never popular, was produced in minimum quantitites. This was not a bimetallic law, nor was it a free coinage act. Strictly speaking it was a subsidiary coinage law, called by some "a wretched compromise."

The North and East so disliked the silver dollars that they did not actively circulate there and eventually found their way back to the Treasury, mostly through tax payments. Secretary Manning transferred ownership to the people and removed them from Treasury holdings by the simple expedient of issuing silver certificates in small bills to effect a wide circulation.

The Bland-Allison Act was repealed in 1890 and the Sherman Act took its place. Under this new law 4,500,000 ounces of silver per month could be paid for with Treasury Notes that were to be legal tender, and redeemable in gold or silver dollars coined from the bullion purchased. Important in this case was the fact that the notes were constantly being redeemed for gold which was mainly exported. The measure was actually a government subsidy for the silver miners and as such it was marked for failure, and was hastily repealed. The Bland-Allison Act and the Sherman Act gave a total of 570 million silver dollars to our monetary stocks.

The "Gold Standard Act" of 1900 gave our country a single standard, but reaffirmed the fiction that the silver dollar was a standard coin. It still enjoyed unlimited legal tender, but was as much a subsidiary coin, practically speaking, as the dime, for its value in terms of standard gold, even before the gold surrender executive order, was far below its face value.

The lapse in coinage after 1904 and until 1921 was due to lack of bullion. Legislation authorizing further metal supplies for silver dollars was not forthcoming until 1918 when the Pittman Act provided silver for the new dollars.

Before the first World War the value of gold was equal to the value of gold coined into money. In order to encourage a steady flow of gold to the mints the government (with the exception of the period 1853-1873) had adopted a policy of gratuitous coinage. The cost of converting gold into coin had generally been considered an expense chargeable to the government.

In practice the mint made fine bars for commercial use or mint bars for coinage at its discretion. The bars in later years were stored in vaults and gold or silver certificates issued in place of the coins.

On March 6, 1933 President Roosevelt issued an order prohibiting banks from paying out gold and gold certificates without permission, and gold currency was thus kept for reserve purposes. Gold imports and newly mined domestic gold could be sold only to the government. Gold bullion and coins may now be collected and saved by anyone as all restrictions were removed in 1975.

Under the Coinage Act of 1965, the composition of dimes, quarters and half dollars was changed to eliminate or reduce the silver content of these coins. The "clad" dimes and quarters were composed of an outer layer of copper-nickel (75% copper and 25% nickel) bonded to an inner core of pure copper. Starting 1971 the half dollar and dollar composition was changed to that of the dime and quarter. All silver clad coins have an outer layer of 80% silver bonded to an inner core of 21% silver, with a total content of 40% silver.

By the Law of September 26, 1890, changes in designs of United States coins cannot be made more often than once every twenty-five years. Since that date, there have been design changes in all denominations and there have been many gold and silver commemorative issues. These factors are largely responsible for the ever increasing interest in coin collecting.

QUANTITIES OF COINS STRUCK

Collectors are cautioned that mint reports are not always reliable for estimating the rarity of coins. In the early years of the mint, dies of previous years were often used until they became worn or broken.

It should also be emphasized that quantities reported, particularly for gold and silver, cover the number of coins struck and have no reference to the quantity reaching actual circulation. Many issues were deposited in the treasury as backing for paper currency and were later melted.

The rarity of gold pieces struck before 1834, particularly half eagles, can be traced to the fact that the gold content was reduced in 1834, making previous issues greater in value than face, causing melting and reminting.

The quantities reported by the mint of three dollar gold pieces from 1873 to 1877 and half cents from 1832 to 1836 are subject to doubt.

Coinage figures shown for 1964 through 1966 are for coins bearing those dates. Some of them were struck in more than one year and at various mints, both with and without mint marks.

Mint quantities are shown adjacent to each date throughout the book. Figures shown in *italic* are estimates based on the most accurate information available. PROOF TOTALS ARE SHOWN IN PARENTHESES.

I. THE BRITISH COLONIES IN AMERICA
SOMMER ISLANDS (Bermuda)

This coinage, the first struck for the English colonies in America, was issued about 1616. The coins were known as "Hogge Money" or "Hoggies."

The pieces were made of copper lightly silvered, in four denominations; shilling, sixpence, threepence and twopence, indicated by Roman numerals. The hog is the main device and appears on the obverse side of each. SOMMER ISLANDS is inscribed within beaded circles. The reverse shows a full-rigged galleon with the flag of St. George on each of four masts.

The islands were named for Sir George Sommers who was shipwrecked there in 1609 while enroute to the Virginia Plantations. Shakespeare's *The Tempest* was possibly based on this incident.

The Bermuda Islands, as they are known today, were named for Juan Bermudez who is believed to have stopped there in 1515. A few hogs which he carried for delivery to the West Indies were left behind. When Somers and his party arrived, the islands were overrun with the animals which served as a welcome source of food for the expedition.

Twopence   Threepence

Sixpence   Large Portholes   Small Portholes

Shilling ★

	Small Sail		Large Sail	
	Good	V. Good	Fine	V. Fine
Twopence	$1,500	$2,250	$3,500	$6,000
Threepence (V. Rare)	——	——	——	
Sixpence, small portholes.........	1,200	2,000	3,000	4,500
Sixpence, large portholes.........	1,000	1,900	3,000	4,500
Shilling, small sail	1,500	2,100	3,500	6,000
Shilling, large sail	1,750	2,400	3,750	7,000

★Star throughout colonial section indicates that struck copies exist

Copies of certain American issues were made after 1850 to provide facsimiles of rarer issues which would otherwise be unobtainable. A star has been placed adjacent to those pieces of which deceptive copies exist. Many crude imitations have also been made in recent years, as well as forgeries intended to deceive collectors. The specimens illustrated are genuine.

MASSACHUSETTS
"NEW ENGLAND" COINAGE (1652)

The earliest medium of exchange in the New England settlements was wampum. The General Court of Massachusetts in 1637 ordered "that wampamege should passe at 6 a penny for any sume under 12 d." Wampum consisted of shells of various colors ground to the size of a grain of corn. A hole was drilled through each piece so they could be strung on leather thongs for convenience and adornment.

Corn, pelts, and bullets were frequently used in lieu of coins, which were rarely available. Silver and gold coins brought over from England, Holland and other countries tended to flow back across the Atlantic to purchase needed supplies. The colonists thus left to their own resources dealt with the friendly Indians in kind. In 1661 the law making wampum legal tender was repealed.

Agitation for a standard coinage reached its height in 1651. England, with a civil war pending between the Puritans and Royalists, ignored the colonists, who took matters into their own hands in 1652.

The General Court in 1652 ordered the first metallic currency to be struck in the English Americas (the Spaniards had established a mint in Mexico City in 1535), the New England silver threepence, sixpence, and shilling. Silver bullion was procured principally from the West Indies. Joseph Jenks made the punches for the first coins at his Iron Works in Saugus, Massachusetts, close to Boston where the mint was located. John Hull was appointed mintmaster; his assistant was Robert Sanderson (or Saunderson). Mintmaster Hull received one shilling threepence for every twenty shillings coined as his compensation. This fee was adjusted several times during his term as mintmaster.

NE Threepence (1652)   **NE Sixpence (1652) ★**

Note: Early American coins are rare in conditions better than listed and valued much higher.

NE Shilling (1652)★

	V. Good	Fine	V. Fine
NE Threepence *(2 known)*	—	—	—
NE Sixpence *(7 known)*— Garrett Sale 1980. . .	—	—	$75,000
NE Shilling	$5,000	$8,500	18,000

[14]

MASSACHUSETTS
WILLOW TREE COINAGE (1653-1660)

The simplicity of the design on the N.E. coins invited counterfeiting and clipping of the edges. Therefore, they were soon replaced by the Willow, Oak and Pine Tree series. The Willow Tree coins were struck from 1653 to 1660, the Oak Trees 1660 to 1667, and the Pine Trees 1667 to 1682. All of them (with the exception of the Oak Tree twopence) bore the date 1652, however. This evasion was to give them the appearance of having been struck during the English civil war, when Cromwell was in power.

The coinage was abandoned in 1682; a proposal to renew coinage in 1686 was rejected by the General Court.

Many varieties of all of these coins exist.

Threepence

Sixpence

Shilling

	Fair	Good	Fine	E. Fine
Willow Tree Threepence 1652 *(3 known)*	—	—	—	—
Willow Tree Sixpence 1652 —				
Garrett Sale 1980	—	—	—	$46,000
Willow Tree Shilling 1652	$2,250	$5,000	$14,000	32,000

OAK TREE COINAGE (1660-1667)

Twopence ★

Threepence

	Good	V. Good	Fine	V. Fine
Oak Tree Twopence 1662	$250.00	$450.00	$850.00	$1,600
Oak Tree Threepence 1652	300.00	650.00	1,200	2,300

MASSACHUSETTS

Sixpence

Shilling ★

	Good	V. Good	Fine	V. Fine
Oak Tree Sixpence 1652...........	$225.00	$500.00	$1,000	$2,250
Oak Tree Shilling 1652............	225.00	500.00	1,000	2,250

PINE TREE COINAGE (1667-1682)

The first pine tree coins were minted on the same size planchets as the Oak Tree pieces. Subsequent issues of the shilling were narrower and thicker to conform to the size of English coins.

Threepence ★

Sixpence ★

**Shilling,
Large Planchet
(1667-1674) ★**

**Shilling,
Small Planchet
(1675-1682)**

	Good	V. Good	Fine	V. Fine
Pine Tree Threepence 1652..............	200.00	400.00	550.00	1,400
Pine Tree Sixpence 1652	250.00	450.00	800.00	1,600
Pine Tree Shilling, large planchet 1652...	275.00	450.00	800.00	1,800
Pine Tree Shilling, small planchet 1652...	250.00	425.00	700.00	1,700

MARYLAND

In 1658 Cecil Calvert, the second Lord Baltimore and "Lord Proprietor of Maryland," had coinage struck in England for use in Maryland.

There were four denominations: shillings, sixpence, and fourpence (groat) in silver, and a copper penny (denarium). The silver coins have the bust of Lord Baltimore on the obverse, and the Baltimore family Arms with the denomination in Roman numerals and the legend CRESCITE ET MULTIPLICAMINI (Increase and be multiplied) on the reverse. The obverse of the penny is similar, but the reverse has a ducal coronet with two pennants and the inscription DENARIUM, TERRAE-MARIAE (Penny, Maryland). Numerous die varieties and patterns exist in this series.

Fourpence (groat)

Lord Baltimore Shilling

Sixpence

Penny (denarium) ★

	Good	V. Good	Fine	V. Fine
Penny (Copper) (Ex. Rare)	—	—	—	—
Fourpence	$900.00	$1,500	$4,000	$6,000
Sixpence	850.00	1,400	3,000	4,250
Shilling	1,000	1,900	4,200	6,500

NEW JERSEY
ST. PATRICK OR MARK NEWBY COINAGE

Mark Newby, who came to America from Dublin, Ireland, in November 1681, brought copper pieces believed by numismatists to have been struck in England c. 1650. These are called St. Patrick Halfpence.

The coin received wide currency in the New Jersey Province, having been authorized to pass as legal tender by the General Assembly in May 1682.

These have a brass insert at the crown so that when the coin was struck it would appear as though it were a golden crown. On some pieces this insert has been removed or does not show.

The smaller piece, known as a farthing, was never authorized for circulation in the Colonies. The obverses show a crowned king kneeling playing a harp. The legend FLOREAT REX (May the King prosper) is separated by a crown. The reverse side of the halfpence shows St. Patrick with a crozier in his left hand and a trefoil in his right, surrounded by people. At his left is a shield. The legend is ECCE GREX (Behold the flock).

The farthing reverse shows St. Patrick driving away reptiles and serpents, as he holds a Metropolitan cross in his left hand. The legend reads QUIESCAT PLEBS (May the people be at ease). Numerous die variations exist.

NEW JERSEY

St. Patrick Farthing

St. Patrick Halfpenny

	V. Good	Fine	V. Fine
St. Patrick "Farthing"	$80.00	$175.00	$475.00
St. Patrick "Farthing" — Silver pattern	900.00	1,800	3,000
St. Patrick "Farthing" — Gold pattern			(Unique)
St. Patrick "Halfpenny"...........................	150.00	300.00	650.00

II. COINAGE AUTHORIZED BY ROYAL PATENT
AMERICAN PLANTATIONS TOKEN

These tokens struck in nearly pure tin were the first authorized coinage for the British colonies in America. They were made under a franchise granted in 1688 to John Holt. Bright, unblemished specimens are more valuable. Restrikes were made about 1828 from original dies.

(1688) James II Plantation Token farthing,	Fine	E. Fine	Unc.
1/24 PART REAL — Tin	$250.00	$600.00	$2,100
1/24 PART REAL — Tin. Sidewise 4 in 24....	600.00	2,100	——
Restrike	175.00	350.00	800.00

COINAGE OF WILLIAM WOOD
ROSA AMERICANA COINS

William Wood, an Englishman, obtained a patent from George I to make tokens for Ireland and the American Colonies.

The first pieces struck were undated; others bear the dates 1722, 1723, 1724 and 1733. The Rosa Americana pieces were issued in three denominations, halfpenny, penny and twopence, and were intended for America. This type had

ROSA AMERICANA

a full-blown rose on the reverse with the words ROSA AMERICANA UTILE DULCI (American Rose — useful and pleasant).

The obverse, common to both Rosa Americana and Hibernia pieces, shows the head of George I and the legend GEORGIUS D:G: MAG: BRI: FRA: ET. HIB: REX. (George, by the Grace of God, King of Great Britain, France and Ireland) or abbreviations thereof. Rosa Americana tokens, however, were rejected by the American colonists. The coins are made of a composition of 75% copper, 24.7% zinc, and .3% silver known as Bath metal.

	V. Good	Fine	V. F.	E. Fine
Twopence (no date) (illustrated)...................	$90.00	$200.00	$400.00	$600.00
Twopence (no date) motto without label (*3 known*) ..	—	—	—	—

1722 Halfpenny VTILE DVLCI......................	1,000	2,500	—	—
1722 Halfpenny D. G. REX ROSA AMERI.				
UTILE DULCI................................	90.00	200.00	400.00	625.00
1722 Halfpenny DEI GRATIA REX UTILE DULCI........	75.00	150.00	250.00	475.00

1722 Penny GEORGIVS............................				—
1722 Penny VTILE DVLCI.........................	75.00	150.00	250.00	500.00
1722 Penny UTILE DULCI.........................	65.00	125.00	200.00	450.00

ROSA AMERICANA

	V. Good	Fine	V. Fine	E. Fine
1722 Twopence, period after REX...........	$90.00	$200.00	$325.00	$575.00
1722 Twopence, no period after REX........	90.00	200.00	325.00	600.00

| 1723 Halfpenny, uncrowned rose .... | 1,500 | 2,500 | —— | —— |
| 1723 Halfpenny .... | 75.00 | 150.00 | 250.00 | 500.00 |

| 1723 Penny .... | 75.00 | 125.00 | 200.00 | 425.00 |
| 1723 Twopence (illustrated) .... | 100.00 | 200.00 | 375.00 | 625.00 |

1724, 4 over 3 Penny (Pattern) DEI GRATIA....................	5,000
1724, 4 over 3 Penny (Pattern) D GRATIA	5,000
1724 Penny (undated) ROSA: SINE: SPINA. (*3 known*)...........	5,000

ROSA AMERICANA

1724 Twopence (Pattern) $5,000

1733 Twopence (Pattern) Proof 16,000

The 1733 twopence is a pattern piece and bears the bust of George II facing to the left. Issued by the successors to the coinage patent, since William Wood had died in 1730.

WOOD'S HIBERNIA COINAGE

The type intended for Ireland had a seated figure with a harp on the reverse side and the word HIBERNIA. Denominations struck were halfpenny and farthing with dates 1722, 1723 and 1724. Hibernia coins were unpopular in Ireland, so many of them were sent to the American colonies.

	First Type	Second Type	1723 over 22

	V. Good	V. Fine	E. Fine
1722 Farthing, D: G: REX	$150.00	$300.00	$650.00
1722 Halfpenny, D: G: REX, rocks at right (Pattern) . .			
1722 Halfpenny, first type, harp at left	25.00	80.00	200.00
1722 Halfpenny, second type, harp at right	25.00	80.00	200.00
1723 Farthing — D.G.REX.	75.00	125.00	400.00
1723 Farthing — Silver pattern.	600.00	1,500	2,000
1723 Farthing — DEI. GRATIA. REX	20.00	50.00	175.00

WOOD'S HIBERNIA COINAGE

1723 Hibernia Farthing

1724 Hibernia Halfpenny

	V. Good	Fine	V. Fine	E. Fine
1723 over 22 Halfpenny	$50.00	$80.00	$150.00	$275.00
1723 Halfpenny	20.00	30.00	50.00	175.00
1723 Halfpenny — Silver pattern	—	—	—	
1724 Farthing	50.00	80.00	135.00	250.00
1724 Halfpenny	40.00	60.00	80.00	225.00

VIRGINIA HALFPENNY

In 1773 coinage of a copper halfpenny was authorized for Virginia by the Crown. The pattern in proof struck on a large planchet with wide milled border is often referred to as a penny.

The silver piece dated 1774 is referred to as a shilling, but may have been a pattern or trial for a halfpenny or a guinea.

Red uncirculated pieces without spots are worth considerably more.

	V. Good	Fine	V. Fine	Unc.
1773 Halfpenny, period after GEORGIVS	$40.00	$60.00	$85.00	$625.00
1773 Halfpenny, no period after GEORGIVS	50.00	80.00	125.00	700.00

	Proof
1773 "Penny"	$5,000

Proof
1774 "Shilling" (*6 known*) $16,500

III. EARLY AMERICAN TOKENS
Struck in America or England for use by American Merchants

LONDON ELEPHANT TOKENS

Struck c. 1664-1666 during the reign of Charles II, the London Token, an early historian states, was produced during the great plague raging in London. The legend on this piece relates directly to that crisis. It has also been stated that the London Token was to have been current in Tangier, Africa, but was never used in that locality. No date appears on this token.

It is unlikely that many ever circulated in America. They are associated with the 1694 pieces through use of a common obverse die.

	V. Good	Fine	V. Fine	E. Fine
(1664) Halfpenny GOD PRESERVE LONDON (Thick planchet)	$ 75.00	$150.00	$225.00	$500.00
(1664) Halfpenny GOD PRESERVE LONDON (Thin planchet)	100.00	200.00	275.00	600.00
(1664) Halfpenny GOD PRESERVE LONDON (Diagonals in center of shield)	175.00	275.00	375.00	800.00
(1664) Halfpenny, similar. Variety with sword in second quarter of shield instead of first....	—	—	—	—
(1664) Halfpenny LON DON.....................	400.00	1,000	1,600	2,500

CAROLINA AND NEW ENGLAND ELEPHANT TOKENS

Although no law is known authorizing coinage for Carolina, two very interesting pieces known as Elephant Tokens were made with the date 1694. These copper tokens were of halfpenny denomination. The reverse reads GOD PRESERVE CAROLINA AND THE LORDS PROPRIETERS. 1694.

The second and more common variety has the last word spelled PROPRIETORS. The correction was made on the original die, for the E shows plainly beneath the O. The elephant's tusks nearly touch the milling on the second variety.

The Carolina pieces were probably struck in England and perhaps intended only as tokens, or possibly as advertising to heighten interest in the Carolina Plantation.

Like the Carolina Tokens, the New England Elephant Tokens were believed to have been struck in England as a promotional piece to increase interest in the American Colonies.

CAROLINA ELEPHANT TOKENS

★

	V. Good	V. Fine
1694 PROPRIETERS..		$7,000
1694 PROPRIETORS, O OVER E	$1,000	$2,500

NEW ENGLAND ELEPHANT TOKEN

★

1694 NEW ENGLAND...................................	16,000	30,000

THE NEW YORKE TOKEN

Little is known about the origin of this token. The style of design and execution seem to be Dutch, and it is probable that the dies were prepared in Holland. There is no date on the piece which evidently belongs to the period between 1664, when the name New Yorke was first adopted, and the 1770's after which it was rarely spelled that way.

UNDATED

	V. Good	Fine
Brass	$2,750	$5,000
Pewter...........	3,000	6,000

GLOUCESTER TOKENS

S. S. Crosby, in his book "The Early Coins of America" stated that this coin appears to have been intended as a pattern for a shilling; a private coinage by Richard Dawson of Gloucester (county), Virginia. The only specimens known are struck in brass.

The denomination XII indicates that a silver coinage (one shilling) was planned but never issued. The only known specimens are imperfect and the full legend cannot be discerned. The obverse appears to read RIGHAVLT.DAWSON.

The building may represent some public building, possibly the court house. The legend on the reverse may have read GLOUCESTER COURT HOUSE VIRGINIA.

GLOUCESTER TOKENS

1714 Shilling Brass $25,000

HIGLEY OR GRANBY COPPERS

Dr. Samuel Higley owned a private copper mine near Granby, Connecticut. He worked the mine as an individual, smelting his own ore and making his own dies for the coins that he issued. After his death in 1737 his brother John continued the coinage.

The Higley coppers were never officially authorized. All the tokens were made of pure copper. There were seven obverse and four reverse dies. The first issue, in 1737, bore the legend THE VALUE OF THREEPENCE. After a time the quantity exceeded the local demand, and a protest arose against the value of the piece. Higley, a resourceful individual, promptly created a new design, still with the Roman III, but with the inscription VALUE ME AS YOU PLEASE. On the reverse appeared the words I AM GOOD COPPER.

(Electrotypes and Casts Exist)

★

	Good	Fine
1737 THE • VALVE • OF • THREE • PENCE. — 3 Hammers — CONNECTICVT	$4,000	$8,000
1737 THE • VALVE • OF • THREE • PENCE. — 3 Hammers — I • AM • GOOD • COPPER	5,000	10,000
1737 VALUE • ME • AS • YOU • PLEASE — 3 Hammers — I • AM • GOOD • COPPER	4,000	8,000

1737 VALVE • ME • AS • YOU • PLEASE — 3 Hammers — I • AM • GOOD • COPPER	(Ex. Rare)	
(1737) VALUE • ME • AS • YOU • PLEASE — Broad Axe — J • CUT • MY • WAY • THROUGH	4,500	9,000
(1737) THE • WHEELE • GOES • ROUND •, Rev. as above (Unique)................................		40,000
1739 VALUE • ME • AS • YOU • PLEASE — Broad Axe — J • CUT • MY • WAY • THROUGH	6,000	12,000

HIBERNIA-VOCE POPULI

These coins, struck in the year 1760, were prepared by one Roche, of King Street, Dublin, who was at that period engaged in the manufacture of buttons for the army, for which he held a contract with home government. Like other Irish tokens, some of these pieces found their way to Colonial America. The piece apparently dated 1700 is from a defective die. They possibly circulated in Colonies with numerous other counterfeit halfpence and "Bungtown Tokens."

Farthing 1760   Halfpenny 1760

Halfpenny "1700".   VOOE POPULI

	Good	V. Fine	E. Fine
1760 Farthing, large letters (illustrated)............	$125.00	$425.00	$1,100
1760 Farthing, small letters	300.00	1,200	2,500
1700 Halfpenny	—	—	—
1760 Halfpenny	35.00	120.00	235.00
1760 Halfpenny VOOE POPULI	40.00	125.00	300.00
1760 Halfpenny, P below bust	65.00	175.00	350.00
1760 Halfpenny, P in front of face	65.00	175.00	350.00

PITT TOKENS

William Pitt, who endeared himself to America, is the subject of these pieces, probably intended as commemorative medalets. The halfpenny served as currency during a shortage of regular coinage. The reverse legend refers to Pitt's efforts to have the stamp act repealed. The Pitt farthing-size token, struck in brass or copper on cast planchets, is rare.

1766 Farthing...... E.F. $5,000

1766 Halfpenny .... (illustrated)

V. Good	Fine	E. Fine
$125.00	$275.00	$800.00

RHODE ISLAND SHIP MEDAL

Although this medal has a Dutch inscription, the spelling and design indicate an English or Anglo-American origin. The satirical theme depicts the retreat from Rhode Island by Continental troops. Specimens are known in brass, copper, tin and pewter.

1778-1779
Rhode Island
Ship Medal

★

	V. Fine	E. Fine
		$12,000
VLUGTENDE (fleeing) below ship		
Wreath below ship	$500.00	800.00
Without wreath below ship	400.00	750.00

J. CHALMERS — Annapolis, Maryland

John Chalmers, a goldsmith, struck a series of silver tokens at Annapolis in 1783. The shortage of change and the refusal of the people to use underweight cut Spanish coins, or "bits," prompted the issuance of these pieces.

The shilling with rings on the reverse is very rare. The common type shilling has two clasped hands on the obverse. The reverse shows two doves competing for a worm.

The sixpence has a star within a wreath on the obverse, and a cross with hands clasped on the reverse. The threepence has the clasped hands on the obverse side, and the reverse shows a branch encircled by a wreath.

	V. Good	V. Fine
1783 Threepence	$550.00	$1,700
1783 Sixpence, small date	750.00	2,000
1783 Sixpence, large date	600.00	1,800

1783 Shilling — Birds, long worm	500.00	1,950
1783 Shilling — Birds, short worm (illustrated)	475.00	1,850
1783 Shilling — Rings — Roper Sale, 1983	—	24,200

IV. THE FRENCH COLONIES

None of the coins of the French regime is strictly American. They were all general issues for the French colonies of the New World. The coinage of 1670 was authorized by an edict of Louis XIV dated February 19, 1670, for use in New France, Acadia, the French settlements in Newfoundland, and the French West Indies. The copper of 1717 to 1722 was authorized by edicts of 1716 and 1721 for use in New France, Louisiana, and the French West Indies.

ISSUE OF 1670

The coinage of 1670 consisted of silver 5 and 15 sols. A copper 2 deniers was also authorized but never struck. A total of 200,000 of the 5 sols was struck, and 40,000 of the 15 sols, at Paris. Nantes was to have coined the copper, but did not; the reasons for this may never be known, since the archives of the Nantes mint before 1700 were destroyed. The only known specimen is a pattern struck at Paris. The silver coins were raised in value by a third in 1672 to keep them circulating, but in vain. They rapidly disappeared, and by 1680 none was to be seen. Later they were restored to their original value.

	V. Good	Fine	V. Fine	E. Fine	Unc.
5 Sols 1670 (200,000) ..	$175.00	$375.00	$850.00	$1,400	——
15 Sols 1670 (40,000) ...	5,000	9,000	17,500	——	——

COINAGE OF 1717-1720

The copper 6 and 12 deniers of 1717 were authorized by an edict of Louis XV dated December 1716, to be struck at Perpignan. The order could not be carried out, for the supply of copper was too brassy. A second attempt in 1720 also failed, probably for the same reason. All these coins are extremely rare.

"COLONIES" and no crowned arms on reverse

Copper

6 Deniers 1717	Ex. Rare
12 Deniers 1717	Ex. Rare

Crowned arms on reverse

6 Deniers 1720 — Garrett Sale, 1980	$4,250

BILLON COINAGE

The piece of 30 deniers was called a *mousquetaire*, and was coined at Metz and Lyon. The 15 deniers was coined only at Metz. The sou marque and half were coined at almost every French mint, those of Paris being commonest. The half sou of 1740 is the only commonly available date. Specimens of the sou marque dated after 1760 were not used in North America.

FRENCH COLONIES
BILLON COINAGE

	V. Good	Fine	V. Fine	E. Fine
15 Deniers 1711-1713AA	$100.00	$175.00	$300.00	$600.00
30 Deniers 1709-1713AA	70.00	125.00	200.00	350.00
30 Deniers 1709-1713D.................	70.00	125.00	200.00	350.00
Half sou marque 1738-1748.............	40.00	75.00	150.00	300.00
Sou marque 1738-1760, various mints	20.00	35.00	65.00	150.00

COINAGE OF 1721-1722

The copper coinage of 1721-1722 was authorized by an edict of Louis XV dated June 1721. The coins were struck on copper blanks imported from Sweden. Rouen and La Rochelle struck pieces of 9 deniers in 1721 and 1722. New France received 534,000 pieces, mostly from the mint of La Rochelle, but only 8,180 were successfully put into circulation as the colonists disliked copper. In 1726 the rest of the issue was sent back to France.

COPPER SOU OR NINE DENIERS

	V. Good	Fine
1721-B (Rouen) ...	$85.00	$200.00
1721-H		
(La Rochelle) ...	40.00	100.00
1722-H	40.00	100.00
1722-H, 2 over 1 ..	80.00	150.00

FRENCH COLONIES IN GENERAL

Coined for use in the French colonies and only unofficially circulated in Louisiana along with other foreign coins and tokens. Most were counterstamped RF (République Française) for use in the West Indies.

	V. Good	V. Fine	E. Fine
1767 French Colonies, Sou	$45.00	$135.00	$325.00
1767 French Colonies, Sou. Counterstamped RF	30.00	100.00	225.00

V. SPECULATIVE ISSUES, TOKENS & PATTERNS

THE CONTINENTAL DOLLAR

The Continental Dollars were probably a pattern issue only and never reached general circulation. It was the first silver dollar size coin ever proposed for the United States. The dies were engraved by someone whose initials were E. G. (possibly Elisha Gallaudet). Some of them have his signature "EG FECIT" on the obverse. The coins were probably struck in Philadelphia. The link design was suggested by Benjamin Franklin.

Varieties result from differences in the spelling of the word CURRENCY and the addition of EG FECIT. These coins were struck in silver, pewter and brass, those in silver probably having done service as a dollar. Pewter coins in original bright uncirculated condition are worth an additional premium.

Copies were struck in various metals for the 1876 Centennial Exposition in Philadelphia and also restruck from hubbed copy dies circa 1961.

"CURRENCY"   "CURENCY"

	Good	Fine	E. Fine	Unc.
1776 CURENCY — Pewter (2 varieties)	$800.00	$1,700	$4,000	$9,000
1776 CURENCY — Brass (2 varieties)......	——	——	——	——
1776 CURENCY — Silver — Garrett Sale, 1980	95,000			
1776 CURENCY — Pewter...............	1,000	1,900	5,500	12,000
1776 CURENCY — Pewter, EG FECIT......	800.00	1,750	4,500	10,000
1776 CURENCY — Silver, EG FECIT.......	——	——	——	——
1776 CURRENCEY — Pewter.............	——	——	——	——

★Star throughout colonial section indicates that struck copies exist

NOVA CONSTELLATIO COPPERS

The Nova Constellatio pieces were struck supposedly by order of Gouverneur Morris who had been Assistant Financier of the Confederation. The tokens

NOVA CONSTELLATIO COPPERS

were turned out in fairly large quantities and dated 1783 and 1785. Evidence indicates that they were all struck in Birmingham in 1785 from dies made there by George Wyon, and imported for American circulation as a private business venture by Gouverneur Morris.

1783
"CONSTELLATIO"
Pointed Rays, Small U.S.

V. Good	$40.00
Fine................	85.00
V. Fine.............	150.00
Ex. Fine............	350.00

1783
"CONSTELLATIO"
Pointed Rays, Large U.S.

V. Good	$50.00
Fine................	100.00
V. Fine.............	200.00
Ex. Fine............	400.00

1783
"CONSTELATIO"
Blunt Rays

V. Good	$45.00
Fine................	90.00
V. Fine.............	170.00
Ex. Fine............	375.00

1785
"CONSTELATIO"
Blunt Rays

V. Good	$50.00
Fine................	125.00
V. Fine.............	225.00
Ex. Fine............	475.00

1785
"CONSTELLATIO"
Pointed Rays

V. Good	$45.00
Fine................	90.00
V. Fine.............	175.00
Ex. Fine............	400.00

1786 (Similar).......	V. Rare

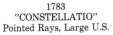

NOVA CONSTELLATIO PATTERNS (Silver)

These Nova Constellatio pieces undoubtedly represent the first patterns for a coinage of the United States. They were designed by Benjamin Dudley for Gouverneur Morris to carry out his ideas for a decimal coinage system. The 1000 unit designation he called a "mark," the 500 a "quint." These denominations, together with the small 100 unit piece, were designed to standardize the many different coin values among the several States. These pattern pieces represent the first attempt at a decimal ratio, and were the forerunners of our present system of money values. Neither the proposed denominations nor the coins advanced beyond the pattern stage. These unique pieces are all dated 1783. There are two types of the "quint." The enigmatic copper "five" was first brought to the attention of collectors in 1980.

★Sets of
Electrotypes
Exist

BIT 100 Units

QUINT Type 1   Reverse   QUINT Type 2

MARK

1783 (Five) "5," Copper	unique
1783 (Bit) "100," Silver (2 varieties) — Garrett Sale, 1979	$97,500
1783 (Quint) "500," Silver — Type 1 — Garrett Sale, 1979	165,000
1783 (Quint) "500," Silver — Type 2 — Garrett Sale, 1979	55,000
1783 (Mark) "1000," Silver — Garrett Sale, 1979	190,000

IMMUNE COLUMBIA PIECES

These are considered experimental or pattern pieces. No laws describing them are known. There are several types with the seated figure of Justice device. These dies were possibly the work of George Wyon.

1785 Copper, 13 stars........	$7,000
1785 Silver, 13 stars.........	12,000

IMMUNE COLUMBIA PIECES

1785 Ptd. Rays CONSTELLATIO
Copper. Extra star in legend $6,000
1785 Blunt Rays CONSTELATIO
Copper....... (*2 known*) $15,000
Gold .... (*Unique*)   ——
A gold specimen in the National Coin
Collection was acquired from Stickney
in exchange for an 1804 dollar.

1785
George III Obverse
Good...... $1,000 Fine...... $2,000

1785
Vermon Auctori Obverse
Good...... $1,000 Fine..... $2,000

1787
IMMUNIS COLUMBIA
Eagle Reverse
Dies by James Atlee

V. Good..............	$225.00
Fine.................	450.00
V. Fine	1,000
Ex. Fine	2,000

CONFEDERATIO COPPERS

The Confederatio Coppers are experimental or pattern pieces. This will explain why the die with the CONFEDERATIO legend was combined with other designs such as bust of George Washington, Libertas et Justitia of 1785, Immunis Columbia of 1786, the New York "Excelsiors," Inimica Tyrannis Americana and others. There were in all thirteen dies struck in fourteen combinations. Some of the dies are believed to have been made by George Wyon of Birmingham, England.

There are two types of the Confederatio reverse. In one instance the stars are contained in a small circle; in the other larger stars are in a larger circle.

Typical Obverse   **Small Circle Reverse**   **Large Circle Reverse**

Fine

1785 Stars in small circle — various obverses........................ $10,000
1785 Stars in large circle — various obverses........................ 10,000

SPECULATIVE PATTERNS

The motto and shield design used on some of these patterns was later adopted for use on the New Jersey copper coins.

1786 IMMUNIS COLUMBIA　　　**Eagle Reverse**　　　**Shield Reverse**

1786 IMMUNIS COLUMBIA, eagle rev. $25,000
1786 IMMUNIS COLUMBIA, shield rev. — Garrett Sale, 1980 17,000

1786 (No date) Washington obv., shield reverse — Garrett Sale, 1980 50,000
1786 Eagle obverse, shield reverse — Garrett Sale, 1980 37,500
1786 Washington obverse, eagle reverse (*Unique*) . . . . ——

VI. COINAGE OF THE STATES
NEW HAMPSHIRE

New Hampshire was the first of the states to consider the subject of coinage following the Declaration of Independence.

William Moulton was empowered to make a limited quantity of coins of pure copper authorized by the State House of Representatives in 1776. Although cast patterns were prepared, it is believed that they were not approved. Little of the proposed coinage was ever actually circulated.

Other purported patterns are of doubtful origin. These include a unique engraved piece and a rare struck piece with large initials WM on the reverse.

V. Good

1776 New Hampshire copper — Garrett Sale, 1980 . . . . $13,000

MASSACHUSETTS
MASSACHUSETTS UNOFFICIAL COPPERS

Nothing is known regarding the origin of the Pine Tree piece dated 1776. The obverse has a crude pine tree with the letters 1d LM at its base; Inscription, MASSACHUSETTS STATE. The reverse has a figure probably intended to represent the Goddess of Liberty, seated on a globe and holding a liberty cap and staff. A dog sits at her feet. The legend LIBERTY AND VIRTUE surrounds the figure.

1776 Pine Tree copper (*Unique*) .... ——

A similar piece, probably from the same source, has an Indian with bow on the obverse, and seated figure on the reverse.

1776 Indian copper (*Unique*) .... ——

This piece is sometimes called the "Janus Copper." There are three heads facing left, front and right on the obverse with the inscription STATE OF MASSA. ½ D. The reverse shows the Goddess of Liberty facing right, resting against a globe inscribed GODDESS LIBERTY 1776.

1776 Halfpenny, 3 heads on obverse (*Unique*) — Garrett Sale, 1979 .... $40,000

MASSACHUSETTS AUTHORIZED ISSUES

An "Act for establishing a mint for the coinage of gold, silver and copper" was passed by the Massachusetts General Court October 17, 1786. The next year the Council directed that the design should incorporate "the figure of an Indian with a bow and arrow and a star at one side, with the word 'Commonwealth,' the reverse, a spread eagle with the words 'of Massachusetts A.D. 1787'."

MASSACHUSETTS

The coinage of Massachusetts copper cents and half cents in 1787 and 1788 was under the direction of Joshua Witherle. These were the first coins bearing the denomination Cent as established by Congress. Many varieties exist, the most valuable being that with arrows in the eagle's right talon.

Most of the dies for these coppers were made by Joseph Callender. Jacob Perkins of Newburyport also engraved some of the dies.

The mint was abandoned early in 1789 in compliance with the newly ratified constitution.

1787 Half Cent	
Good	$40.00
Fine....................	100.00
V. Fine	185.00
Ex. Fine	450.00

Obverse   **Arrows in Eagle's Right Talon**   **Arrows in Left Talon**

	Good	*Fine*	*V. Fine*	*E. Fine*
1787 Cent, arrows in right talon—				
Garrett Sale, 1979	——	$5,500	——	——
1787 Cent, arrows in left talon............	$32.00	80.00	$185.00	$450.00
1787 Cent, "horn" (die break) from				
eagle's head	32.00	80.00	195.00	485.00

1788 Half Cent	
Good	$45.00
Fine.............	110.00
Very Fine........	225.00
Ex. Fine	500.00

1788 Cent
Period after Massachusetts

Good	32.00
Fine.............	80.00
V. Fine	200.00
Ex. Fine	450.00

No period after Massachusetts

Good	45.00
Fine.............	110.00
V. Fine	225.00
Ex. Fine	500.00

CONNECTICUT

Authority for establishing a mint near New Haven was granted by the State to Samuel Bishop, Joseph Hopkins, James Hillhouse and John Goodrich in 1785.

Available records indicate that most of the Connecticut coppers were coined under a sub-contract by Samuel Broome and Jeremiah Platt, former New York merchants. Abel Buel and James Atlee were the principal die-sinkers.

1785 Copper
Bust Facing Right
Good............ $40.00
V. Good........ 50.00
Fine 90.00
V. Fine......... 275.00

1785 Copper
African Head
Good........... $45.00
V. Good....... 75.00
Fine 150.00
V. Fine........ 400.00

1785 Copper
Bust Facing Left
Good............ 125.00
V. Good......... 175.00
Fine 300.00
V. Fine.......... 525.00

1786 Copper
ETLIB INDE
Good 45.00
V. Good 70.00
Fine.............. 140.00
V. Fine............ 325.00

1786 Copper
Large Head Facing Right
Good............ 55.00
V. Good......... 120.00
Fine 250.00
V. Fine......... 550.00

[37]

CONNECTICUT

1786 Copper
Mailed Bust Facing Left
Good $27.50
V. Good............ 45.00
Fine 100.00
V. Fine 220.00

1786 Copper
Mailed Bust Facing Left
Hercules Head
Good.......... $60.00
V. Good........ 100.00
Fine 225.00
V. Fine......... 500.00

1786 Copper
Draped Bust
Good........... 55.00
V. Good 90.00
Fine............ 185.00
V. Fine......... 400.00

The Connecticut coppers, especially those dated 1787 and 1788, were usually crudely struck and on imperfect planchets.

1787 Copper
Mailed Bust Facing Left
IND ET LIB
1787 over 1788
Good $65.00
V. Good 110.00
Fine............... 250.00
V. Fine 500.00

1787 Copper
Small Head Facing Right
ETLIB INDE
Good 65.00
V. Good 100.00
Fine............... 200.00
V. Fine 450.00

1787 Copper
Mailed Bust Facing Right
INDE ET LIB

Good.................... 70.00
V. Good................ 125.00
Fine 250.00
V. Fine................. 800.00

1787 Muttonhead Variety
Good.................... 65.00
V. Good................ 110.00
Fine 200.00
V. Fine................. 375.00

CONNECTICUT

	Good	V.G.	Fine	V. Fine
1787 Mailed bust facing left	$25.00	$45.00	$75.00	$200.00
1787 Similar, laughing head variety	30.00	50.00	85.00	225.00
1787 Similar, Hercules head (see 1786)......	175.00	250.00	450.00	825.00
1787 Similar, dated 1787 over 1877	50.00	90.00	170.00	400.00

1787 Similar, horned bust variety...........	25.00	45.00	100.00	225.00
1787 Similar, CONNECT variety.............	40.00	75.00	150.00	325.00

1787 Draped bust facing left (many varieties)	25.00	40.00	60.00	150.00
1787 Similar, AUCIORI variety..............	25.00	45.00	70.00	185.00
1787 Similar, AUCTOPI variety	25.00	45.00	80.00	200.00
1787 Similar, AUCTOBI variety	30.00	45.00	100.00	225.00
1787 Similar, CONNFC variety..............	25.00	45.00	70.00	185.00
1787 Similar, CONNLC variety..............	50.00	75.00	135.00	275.00
1787 Similar, FNDE variety	30.00	45.00	70.00	185.00
1787 Similar, ETLIR variety................	25.00	40.00	70.00	185.00
1787 Similar, ETIIB variety	25.00	40.00	70.00	185.00

1788 Mailed bust facing right..............	30.00	45.00	100.00	250.00
1788 Similar, small head (see picture page 38)	150.00	275.00	600.00	1,000

CONNECTICUT

	Good	V.G.	Fine	V. Fine
1788 Mailed bust facing left...............	$25.00	$35.00	$85.00	$225.00
1788 Mailed bust left CONNLC	30.00	40.00	100.00	250.00

1788 Draped bust facing left...............	25.00	35.00	85.00	225.00
1788 Similar, CONNLC variety..............	50.00	75.00	150.00	275.00
1788 Similar, INDL ET LIB variety	40.00	70.00	125.00	250.00

NEW YORK
THE BRASHER DOUBLOON

Perhaps the most famous pieces coined before the establishment of the U.S. Mint at Philadelphia were those produced by a well-known goldsmith and jeweler, Ephraim Brasher (pronounced BRAYzher), neighbor of George Washington, in New York.

Brasher produced a gold piece weighing about 408 grains, approximately equal in value to a Spanish doubloon (about $16.00).

The punch-mark EB appears in either of two positions as illustrated. This mark is found on some foreign gold coins as well, and probably was so used by Brasher as evidence of his testing of their value.

★

1787 Doubloon, punch on breast. Gold (*Unique*) — Garrett Sale, 1981....	$625,000
1787 Doubloon, punch on wing. Gold } Garrett Sale, 1979.........	725,000
Auction '79 Sale, 1979.....	430,000

Pieces with the design of a Spanish-American gold doubloon of Lima, dated 1742, with the name BRASHER and EB punch-mark, are currently being studied by numismatists to determine their origin and use.

NEW YORK

No coinage was authorized for New York following the Revolutionary War although several propositions were considered. The only coinage laws passed were those regulating coins already in use.

A partnership headed by Thomas Machin was formed in 1787 for the purpose of striking copper coins, near Newburgh. The establishment was called a "Manufactory of hardware," but the operations there were conducted in secret and looked upon as illegal.

Subsequently, Reuben Harmon, Jr., who operated the mint at Rupert, Vermont, and William Coley were listed as copartners "in such trades and merchandizing and in the coinage of copper for the states of Vermont, Connecticut and New York, for their most benefit advantage and profit."

Many of the pieces classified as Connecticut coins, the Vermon Auctori with the Britannia reverse, and the counterfeit George III halfpence, were products of this "hardware manufactory" known as Machin's Mills.

COPPER COINAGE

1786
NON VI VIRTUTE VICI

(Believed to be the bust of Washington.)

Good	$1,750
Fine	3,000
V. Fine	5,000

★

★

	Good	Fine	V. Fine
1787 EXCELSIOR copper, eagle on globe facing right....	$700.00	$1,500	$3,200
1787 EXCELSIOR copper, eagle on globe facing left	600.00	1,400	3,000

1787 Large Eagle on Reverse—Arrows and branch
transposed —Garrett Sale, 1979 .... $26,000

[41]

NEW YORK

1787 George Clinton
Good $3,500
Fine. 7,000
V. Fine 12,000

★

1787
Indian and N.Y. Arms
Good $2,000
Fine 4,000
V. Fine 6,000

★

1787
Indian and Eagle
on Globe
Good 3,250
Fine. 6,000
V. Fine 9,000

★

1787 Indian and George III
Reverse (*3 known*) $8,000

MACHIN'S MILLS COINAGE (1786-1789)

The most prevalent Machin's Mills coins are lightweight imitations of the British halfpenny, with bust obverse and Britannia seated reverse. These can be distinguished by their crude die work and single outline in the crosses of Britannia's shield. Dates used are 1747, 1771, 1772, 1774-1776, 1778, 1787, and 1788. These pieces are not to be confused with other American, or English-made George III counterfeits, some of which have identical dates, or genuine George III British halfpence, which were dated 1770 to 1775.

	Good	V. Good	Fine	V. Fine
Machin's Mills Copper, various dates				
GEORGIUS III REX/BRITANNIA	$45.00	$75.00	$160.00	$275.00

NEW YORK
THE NOVA EBORACS

1787
NOVA EBORAC
Reverse Seated
Figure Facing Right

Fair	$22.00
Good	75.00
Fine	200.00
V. Fine	400.00

1787
NOVA EBORAC
Reverse Seated
Figure Facing Left

Fair	$20.00
Good...........	77.00
Fine	185.00
V. Fine..........	350.00

1787
NOVA EBORAC
Small Head

Fair	400.00
Good...........	900.00
Fine	——
V. Fine..........	——

1787
NOVA EBORAC
Large Head

Fair..............	$50.00
Good	225.00
Fine..............	500.00
V. Fine...........	1,200

NEW JERSEY

On June 1, 1786, the New Jersey Colonial legislature granted to Thomas Goadsby, Albion Cox and Walter Mould authority to coin some three million coppers weighing six pennyweight and six grains apiece, not later than June 1788, on condition that they delivered to the Treasurer of the State, "one-tenth part of the full sum they shall strike and coin," in quarterly installments. These coppers were to pass current at 15 to the shilling.

In an operation of this kind the contractors purchased the metal and assumed all expenses of coining. The difference between these expenses and the total face value of the coins issued represented the profit.

NEW JERSEY

Later Goadsby and Cox asked authority to coin two-thirds of the total independently. Their petition was granted November 22, 1786. Mould was known to have produced his coins at Morristown, while Cox (and probably Goadsby) operated in Rahway. Coins were also minted in Elizabethtown and Newburgh, New York.

The series offers many varieties. The obverse shows a horse's head with plow and the legend NOVA CAESAREA (New Jersey). The reverse has a United States shield and legend E PLURIBUS UNUM (One composed of many).

1786 Date Under Draw Bar   **1786 No Coulter**

	Good	Fine	V. Fine
1786 Date under draw bar — Garrett Sale, 1980 (Ex. F)			$52,000
1786 No coulter	$135.00	$400.00	750.00

Narrow Shield   **Wide Shield**

1786 Narrow shield..............................	30.00	90.00	200.00
1786 Wide shield	35.00	100.00	225.00
1786 Similar, bridle variety	35.00	100.00	200.00

Pluribs Variety, Lg. Planchet   **Small Planchet**   **Outlined Shield**

1787 Pronounced outline to shield	30.00	100.00	200.00
1787 Small planchet, plain shield	30.00	100.00	200.00
1787 Large planchet, plain shield	30.00	100.00	200.00
1787 Similar, PLURIBS variety.....................	50.00	150.00	350.00

NEW JERSEY

Serpent Head

Fox Variety

	Good	Fine	V. Fine
1787 Serpent head variety......................	$37.50	$150.00	$350.00
1788 Horse's head facing right..................	30.00	100.00	200.00
1788 Similar, running fox before legend	50.00	175.00	400.00
1788 Horse's head facing left	125.00	350.00	650.00

VERMONT

Reuben Harmon, Jr., of Rupert, Vermont, was granted permission to coin copper pieces for a period of two years beginning July 1, 1785. The well-known Vermont plow coppers were first produced in that year. The franchise was extended for eight years in 1786.

Harmon's mint was located in the northeast corner of Rupert near a stream known as Millbrook. Col. William Coley, a New York goldsmith, made the first dies.

Some of the late issues were made near Newburgh, N.Y. by the Machin's Mills coiners.

1785 IMMUNE COLUMBIA

1785 VERMONTS

	Good	Fine		Good	Fine
1785 IMMUNE COLUMBIA...	$1,000	$2,000	1785 VERMONTS ...	$125.00	$475.00

1785 VERMONTIS

1786 VERMONTENSIUM

1785 VERMONTIS ..	185.00	500.00	1786 VERMON-TENSIUM	100.00	400.00

VERMONT

1786 Baby Head

	Good	Fine
1786 Baby head ..	$150.00	$550.00

1787 BRITANNIA

	Good	Fine
1787 BRITANNIA...	$50.00	$185.00

Reverse of this coin is always weak.

1786 Bust Left

1786 Bust left	85.00	450.00

1788 (Several Varieties)

1788 (Several var.)	65.00	225.00
1788 VERMON AUOTORI	—	—
1788 *ET LIB* *INDE	125.00	450.00

1787 Bust Left

1787 Bust left	—	—

1788 GEORGIVS III REX

1788 GEORGIVS III REX	150.00	550.00

This piece should not be confused with the common English halfpence with similar design and reverse legend BRITANNIA.

Most Vermont coppers are struck on poor and defective planchets. Well struck coins on smooth full planchets command higher prices.

1787 Bust Right

1787 Bust right (Several var.)	75.00	225.00

VII. PRIVATE TOKENS AFTER CONFEDERATION
NORTH AMERICAN TOKEN

This piece was struck in Dublin, Ireland. The obverse shows the seated figure of Hibernia facing left. The date of issue is believed to have been much later than that shown on the token.

Like many Irish tokens, this issue found its way to America in limited quantities and was accepted near the Canadian border.

Copper or Brass

	V. Good	Fine	V. Fine
1781..	$20.00	$40.00	$110.00

THE BAR "COPPER"

The Bar "Copper" is undated and of uncertain origin. It has thirteen parallel and unconnected bars on one side. On the other side is the large roman letter USA monogram. The design was supposedly copied from a Continental button.

The significance of the design is clearly defined by its extreme simplicity. The separate thirteen states (bars) unite into a single entity as symbolized by the interlocking letters (USA).

This coin is believed to have been issued at the same time as the Nova Constellatio coppers by Thomas Wyon at Birmingham, England, for America. It first circulated in New York during November, 1785.

On the less valuable struck copy made by J. A. Bolen c. 1862 the A passes under, instead of over, the S.

★

	V. Good	Fine	V. Fine	E. Fine
Undated (about 1785) Bar "Copper".......	$200.00	$350.00	$500.00	$900.00

AUCTORI PLEBIS TOKEN

This token is sometimes included with the coins of Connecticut as it greatly resembles issues of that state. It was struck in England by an unknown maker, possibly for use in America.

1787
AUCTORI PLEBIS

Good..............	$30.00
V. Good	60.00
Fine....................	100.00
V. Fine............	200.00

THE MOTT TOKEN

This was one of the first tradesman's tokens issued in America. Manufactured in England, they were issued by Messrs. Mott of New York in 1789. The firm was composed of William and John Mott, located at 240 Water Street, a fashionable section of New York at that time.

	V. Good	Fine	V. Fine	E. Fine
1789 Mott Token, thick planchet..............	$80.00	$150.00	$250.00	$500.00
1789 Mott Token, thin planchet...............	110.00	175.00	300.00	600.00
1789 Mott Token, entire edge engrailed	135.00	350.00	500.00	1,100

STANDISH BARRY, BALTIMORE, MARYLAND

Standish Barry, a Baltimore silversmith, circulated a silver threepence in 1790. He was a watch and clockmaker, engraver and later a silversmith. The tokens were believed to have been an advertising venture at a time when small change was scarce. The precise date, July 4, 90, on this piece may indicate that Barry intended to commemorate Independence Day, but there are no records to substantiate this belief. The head shown on the obverse is probably that of George Washington. The legend BALTIMORE TOWN JULY 4, 90 appears in the border. STANDISH BARRY THREE PENCE is on the reverse.

	Fine	V. Fine
1790 Threepence...	$2,500	$6,500

ALBANY CHURCH PENNY

The First Presbyterian Church of Albany, New York authorized an issue of one thousand copper uniface tokens in 1790. These passed at twelve to a shilling and were used to stop contributions of worn and counterfeit coppers. Two varieties were made, one with the addition of a large D above the word CHURCH.

	V. Good	Fine
(1790) Without D............	$1,750	$3,500
(1790) With D added........	1,500	3,000

KENTUCKY TOKEN

These tokens were struck in England about 1792-94. Each star in the triangle represents a state, identified by its initial letter. These pieces are usually called Kentucky Cents because the letter K (for Kentucky) happens to be at the top. Some of the edges are plain; others are engrailed with an oblique reeding, and some have the edge lettered: "PAYABLE IN LANCASTER LONDON OR BRISTOL," or "PAYABLE AT BEDWORTH NUNEATON OR HINKLEY."

	V. Good	V. Fine	E. Fine	Unc.
Cent, (1792-94) plain edge	$45.00	$100.00	$225.00	$600.00
Cent, engrailed edge		250.00	400.00	1,200
Cent, lettered edge PAYABLE AT BEDWORTH, etc.	—	—	—	—
Cent, lettered edge PAYABLE IN LANCASTER, etc.	50.00	110.00	250.00	700.00
Cent, lettered edge PAYABLE AT I. FIELDING, etc.	—	—	—	—

FRANKLIN PRESS

This piece is an English tradesman's token but, being associated with Benjamin Franklin, has accordingly been included in American collections.

1794 Franklin Press Token	45.00	100.00	250.00	600.00

TALBOT, ALLUM & LEE CENTS

Talbot, Allum & Lee, engaged in the India trade and located at 241 Pearl Street, New York, placed a large quantity of English-made coppers in circulation during 1794 and 1795. ONE CENT appears on the 1794 issue, and the legend PAYABLE AT THE STORE OF on the edge. The denomination is not found on the 1795 reverse but the edge legend was changed to read: WE PROMISE TO PAY THE BEARER ONE CENT. Rare plain edge specimens of both dates exist.

1794 Cent with NEW YORK	
V. Good	$35.00
V. Fine	125.00
Unc..	725.00

1794 Cent Without NEW YORK	
V. Good	200.00
V. Fine	625.00
Unc..	2,000

TALBOT, ALLUM & LEE CENTS

1795 Cent		
V. Good		$35.00
V. Fine		110.00
E. Fine		250.00
Unc................		700.00

MYDDELTON TOKENS

These tokens were struck at the Soho Mint of Boulton and Watt near Birmingham, England. They are unsurpassed in beauty and design by any piece of this period.

1796
Myddelton Token

	Proof
Copper........	$5,500
Silver.........	4,500

COPPER COMPANY OF UPPER CANADA

The obverse of this piece is the same as the Myddelton token. The new reverse legend was apparently intended for Canadian circulation, or it was used to give the token credibility.

1796 Copper ...... $\quad$ *Proof* $3,000

THE CASTORLAND MEDAL

This medal is dated 1796 and alludes to a proposed French settlement known as Castorland in Carthage, New York, at the time of the French Revolution.

1796 Silver original. (Reeded edge)...................................... $4,000
1796 Copper original. (Reeded edge, unbroken dies) 2,000
Copy dies are still available and have been used at the Paris Mint for restriking throughout the years. Restrikes are thinner and usually have more modern letters.

NEW YORK THEATRE TOKEN

Token penny issued by Skidmore illustrating the Park Theatre, New York c. 1797.

	E. Fine	Proof
Penny, THE • THEATRE • AT • NEW YORK • AMERICA.........	$2,000	$5,000

NEW SPAIN (TEXAS) JOLA

These tokens were authorized by the military governor of San Antonio in 1818. Eight thousand pieces were coined by Jose Antonio de la Garza (JAG). Large and small planchet varieties exist, and all are very rare.

1818 ½ Real...................... Fine $1,600

NORTH WEST COMPANY TOKEN

These tokens were probably valued at one beaver and struck in Birmingham in 1820 by John Walker & Co. All but two known specimens are holed, and most have been found in the region of the lower Columbia River valley in Oregon.

V. Good

1820 Copper or brass ... $500.00

VIII. WASHINGTON PIECES

An interesting series of coins and tokens dated from 1783 to 1795 bear the portrait of George Washington. The likenesses in most instances were faithfully reproduced and were designed to honor Washington. Many of these pieces were of English origin and made later than the dates indicate.

The legends generally signify a strong unity among the states and a marked display of patriotism which pervaded the new nation during that period. We find among these tokens an employment of what were soon to become our official coin devices, namely, the American eagle, the United States shield and stars. The denomination One Cent is used in several instances, while on some of the English pieces Halfpenny will be found. Several of these pieces were private patterns for proposed coinage contracts.

GEORGIUS TRIUMPHO TOKEN

Although the head shown on this token bears a strong resemblance to that upon some coins of George III, many collectors consider the Georgius Triumpho (Triumphant George) a token intended to commemorate the successful termination of the Revolutionary War — a triumph justly claimed for Washington.

The reverse side shows the Goddess of Liberty behind a framework of thirteen bars and fleur de lis. She holds an olive branch in her right hand and staff of liberty in her left. VOCE POPOLI (By the Voice of the People) 1783.

1783 GEORGIUS TRIUMPHO

V. Good.............	$40.00
Fine................	125.00
V. Fine	300.00

WASHINGTON PIECES

Military Bust

Large Military Bust
Point of Bust Close to W
(illustrated)

	Fine	V. Fine	E. Fine
1783 Large military bust	$40.00	$85.00	$200.00
1783 Small military bust, plain edge	45.00	90.00	235.00
1783 Small military bust, engrailed edge	60.00	130.00	275.00

1783 Draped bust, no button (illustrated)	40.00	80.00	200.00
1783 Draped bust, with button on drapery at neck ..	75.00	135.00	300.00

	Proof
1783 Draped bust. Copper restrike, plain edge	$350.00
1783 Draped bust. Copper restrike, engrailed edge	250.00
1783 Draped bust. Silver restrike, engrailed edge	600.00

UNITY STATES
V. Good	$30.00
V. Fine	100.00
Ex. Fine	200.00

Undated Double Head Cent
Fine................	$50.00
V. Fine.............	100.00
Ex. Fine............	200.00

Satirical Medal presumably of
American origin.
1784 Ugly head —
    Roper Sale, 1983 ..... $14,850

WASHINGTON PIECES

1791 Cent
Edge Lettered: UNITED STATES OF AMERICA

	Fine	E. Fine	Unc.
1791 Cent, small eagle	$175.00	$475.00	$1,200
1791 Cent, large eagle..........................	175.00	475.00	1,200

1791 Liverpool
Halfpenny
Lettered Edge

Fine	$350.00
Ex. Fine.......	700.00
Unc.	1,500

1792 Eagle with Stars

Copper...........	—
Silver............	—
Gold (*Unique*)....	—

(1792) Undated Cent
"WASHINGTON BORN VIRGINIA"

1792 Cent
"WASHINGTON PRESIDENT"

	Fine			Fine
Copper..................	$1,750	Plain edge		$2,500
Silver....................	—	Lettered edge		—

Uniface restrike of Obverse exists, made by Albert Collis, 1959.

WASHINGTON PIECES

★

	V. Good	Fine
1792 Small eagle. Silver..................................	—	—
1792 Small eagle. Copper................................	$2,000	$3,500
1792 Same. Ornamented edge (circles and squares)........	—	—
1792 Same. Silver.......................................	—	—
1792 Lg. eagle. Silver (unknown origin) — Garrett Sale, 1981 (Ex. F.)		$16,500

1792 Cent
Roman Head

Lettered Edge:
**UNITED STATES OF
AMERICA**
Proof $10,000

1793 Ship
Halfpenny

Lettered Edge

Fine	$ 95.00
V. Fine...........	175.00
Ex. Fine..........	325.00
Plain edge (Rare) ..	—

1795 Halfpenny
Grate Token
(Large coat buttons
variety illustrated.)

	V. Fine	E. Fine	Unc.
1795 Large buttons, lettered edge................	$300.00	$550.00	$1,200
1795 Large buttons, reeded edge.................	100.00	175.00	500.00
1795 Small buttons, reeded edge	125.00	300.00	650.00

WASHINGTON PIECES

LIBERTY AND SECURITY TOKENS

	Fine	V. Fine	E. Fine
1795 Halfpenny, plain edge........................	$85.00	$150.00	$425.00
1795 Halfpenny, LONDON edge	70.00	110.00	325.00
1795 Halfpenny, BIRMINGHAM edge.................	75.00	125.00	425.00
1795 Halfpenny, ASYLUM edge	150.00	300.00	700.00
1795 Penney, ASYLUM edge	——	——	

Liberty and
Security Penny
Undated (1795)

Fine	$125.00
V. Fine...........	200.00
Ex. Fine..........	350.00
Unc.	1,400

SUCCESS MEDALS

	Fine	V. Fine	E. Fine
SUCCESS medal, large. Plain or reeded edge	$125.00	$200.00	$400.00
SUCCESS medal, small. Plain or reeded edge	125.00	200.00	450.00

Specimens with full silvering are extremely rare and more valuable.

NORTH WALES HALFPENNY

	Good	Fine
1795 NORTH WALES		
Halfpenny .	$65.00	$150.00
Lettered edge	300.00	700.00
Two stars at each		
side of harp....	750.00	2,000

IX. THE FUGIO CENTS

The first coins issued by authority of the United States were the "Fugio" cents. Entries in the Journal of Congress supply interesting information about proceedings relating to this coinage.

"Saturday, April 21, 1787. . . .

"That the board of treasury be authorized to contract for three hundred tons of copper coin of the federal standard, agreeable to the proposition of Mr. James Jarvis, . . . That it be coined at the expense of the contractor, etc."

On Friday, July 6, 1787, there was "Resolved, that the board of treasury direct the contractor for the copper coinage to stamp on one side of each piece the following device, viz: thirteen circles linked together, a small circle in the middle, with the words 'United States,' around it; and in the centre, the words 'We are one'; on the other side of the same piece the following device, viz: a dial with the hours expressed on the face of it; a meridian sun above on one side of which is the word 'Fugio,' (The meaning is, 'time flies') and on the other the year in figures '1787', below the dial, the words 'Mind Your Business.' "

The legends have been credited to Benjamin Franklin, and the coin, as a consequence, has been referred to as the Franklin Cent.

These cents were coined in New Haven, Conn., and possibly elsewhere. Most of the copper used in this coinage came from military stores. It is believed to have been the copper bands which held together the powder kegs sent to us by the French. The dies were made by Abel Buel of New Haven.

1787 WITH POINTED RAYS

	V. Good	V. Fine	E. Fine	Unc.
Obv. no cinquefoils. Cross after date. Rev. label with raised rims		(Ex. Rare)		
Same obv., rev. STATES UNITED	$275.00	$900.00	——	——
Same obv., rev. UNITED STATES	250.00	800.00	——	——

Note: The following types with pointed rays have regular obverses punctuated with four cinquefoils.

	V. Good	V. Fine	E. Fine	Unc.
STATES UNITED. Label with raised rims (simply two concentric circles). Large letters in WE ARE ONE	135.00	500.00	$1,600	——
STATES UNITED. 8-pointed stars on label	120.00	350.00	900.00	——
UNITED above, STATES below. (Rare)	——	——	——	——

THE FUGIO CENTS

	V. Good	Fine	V. Fine	E. Fine	Unc.
STATES UNITED at sides of circle.					
Cinquefoils (small, five-bladed clover design) on label..................	$85.00	$175.00	$300.00	$450.00	$900.00
STATES UNITED. at sides of circle.....	80.00	150.00	275.00	400.00	800.00
STATES UNITED, 1 over horizontal 1 ..	80.00	150.00	350.00	650.00	

1787 WITH CLUB RAYS

	V. Good	Fine	V. Fine
Club Rays. Rounded ends	$110.00	$250.00	$600.00
Club Rays. Concave ends to rays:			
FUCIO (c instead of G). (Ex. Rare)......	1,200	—	—
Club Rays. Concave ends. FUGIO UNITED STATES ...	1,200	—	—
Club Rays. Similar, STATES UNITED Rev.	—	—

American Congress Pattern

New Haven "Restrike", note narrow rings

	E. Fine	Unc.
Reverse with rays and AMERICAN CONGRESS....... $18,000	Gold (*2 known*)		
	Silver..............	$250.00	$550.00
	Copper or Brass	125.00	270.00

New Haven "restrikes" were supposedly struck from dies discovered by the fourteen-year-old C. Wyllys Betts in 1858 on the site of the Broome & Platt Store in New Haven, Conn., where the originals were made. Three pairs of dies were reportedly found and are still extant. Actually, the "restrikes" were made from copy dies c. 1860.

BIBLIOGRAPHY

Baker, W. S. *Medallic Portraits of Washington.* Philadelphia 1885 (reprinted 1965).
Crosby, S. S. *The Early Coins of America.* Boston 1875 (reprinted 1945, 1965, 1975).
Dickeson, M. W. *The American Numismatic Manual.* Philadelphia 1859, 1860, 1865.
Kessler, Alan. *The Fugio Cents.* Newtonville, Massachusetts 1976.
Maris, Edward. *A Historic Sketch of the Coins of New Jersey.* Philadelphia 1881 (reprinted 1925).
Miller, Henry C. and Hillyer Ryder. *The State Coinages of New England.* New York 1920.
Nelson, Philip. *The Coinage of William Wood 1722-1733.* London 1903 (reprinted 1959).
Newman, Eric P. *Coinage for Colonial Virginia.* New York 1957.
    Studies on Money in Early America. American Numismatic Society. New York, 1976.
Noe, Sydney P. *The New England and Willow Tree Coinage of Massachusetts.* New York 1943. *The Oak Tree Coinage of Massachusetts.* New York 1947, and *The Pine Tree Coinage of Massachusetts.* New York 1952. (all reprinted 1973).
Wurtzbach, Carl. *Massachusetts Colonial Silver Money.* 1937.

FIRST UNITED STATES MINT ISSUES

Many members of the House favored a representation of the President's head on the obverse of each coin. Others considered the idea a monarchical practice. Washington is believed to have expressed disapproval of the use of his portrait on our coins.

The majority considered a figure emblematic of Liberty more appropriate and the Senate finally concurred in this opinion. Robert Birch was an engraver employed at designing proposed devices for our coins. He, perhaps together with Adam Eckfeldt, engraved the dies for the disme and half disme. He has also been associated with a large copper cent of unusual design known as the Birch Cent.

1792 SILVER CENTER CENT

Cent. Silver Center — Garrett Sale, 1981 (Unc.)...................... $95,000
Cent. No silver center — Garrett Sale, 1981 (V. Fine) 28,000

1792 BIRCH CENT

Copper — Garrett Sale, 1981 (Unc.).................................. 200,000
G.W. PT. (George Washington President) below wreath, white metal —
Garrett Sale, 1981 (*Unique*) 90,000

1792 HALF DISME

	Good	Fine	V. Fine
Silver	$1,200	$3,500	$6,250
Copper			(*Unique*)

FIRST UNITED STATES MINT ISSUES

1792 DISME

	E. Fine	*Unc.*
Silver (*3 known*)	—	—
Copper — Garrett Sale, 1981 (A.U.)		$54,000

1792 PATTERN QUARTER DOLLAR

Copper.......	(*2 known*)
White Metal.....	(*Unique*)

MINTS AND MINT MARKS

Mint marks are small letters designating where coins were made. Coins struck at Philadelphia before 1979 (except 1942-1945 five-cent pieces) do not have a mint mark. Starting in 1979 a letter P was used on the dollar, and thereafter on all other denominations except the cent. Mint mark position is on the reverse of nearly all coins prior to 1965 (the cent is an exception), and on the obverse after 1967. Letters used are as follows:

C — Charlotte, North Carolina (gold coins only). 1838-1861.
CC — Carson City, Nevada. 1870-1893.
D — Dahlonega, Georgia (gold coins only). 1838-1861.
D — Denver, Colorado. 1906 to date.
O — New Orleans, Louisiana. 1838-1909.
P — Philadelphia, Pennsylvania. 1793 to date.
S — San Francisco, California. 1854 to date.
W — West Point. 1984.

All dies for United States coins are made at the Philadelphia Mint. Dies for use at branch mints are hand stamped with the appropriate mint mark before they are shipped from Philadelphia. Because of this hand operation, the exact positioning and size of the mint mark may vary slightly, depending on where and how deeply the punch was impressed. This also accounts for double-punched and superimposed mint marks such as the 1938 D over D, and D over S Buffalo nickels. Polishing of dies may also alter the apparent size of fine details. Occasionally the mint mark is inadvertently left off a die sent to a branch mint, as was the case with some of the recent proof dimes. Similarly, some 1982 dimes without mint mark were made as business strikes.

Prior to 1900, punches for mint marks varied greatly in size. This is particularly noticeable in the 1850 to 1880 period in which the letters range from very small to very large. An attempt to standardize sizes started in 1892 with the Barber series, but exceptions are seen in the 1892 O half dollar and 1905 O

MINTS AND MINT MARKS

dime, both of which have normal and "microscopic" mint marks. A more or less standard size small mint mark was used on all minor coins starting in 1909, and on all dimes, quarters and halves after the Barber series was replaced in 1916. Slight variations in mint mark size occur through 1940 with notable differences in 1928, when small and large S mint marks were used.

In recent years a single D or S punch has been used to mark all branch mint dies. The change to the larger D for Denver coins occurred in 1933. Dimes, half dollars and dollars of 1934 exist with either the old, smaller size mint mark or the new, larger size D. All other denominations of 1934 and after are standard. The San Francisco mint mark was changed to larger size during 1941 and, with the exception of the half dollar, all 1941 S coins are known with either small or large size mint mark. Halves were not changed until 1942, and the 1942 S and 1943 S pieces exist both ways. The 1945 S dime with "microscopic" S is an unexplained abnormality. In 1979 the punches were replaced. Varieties of some 1979 coins appear with either the old or new shaped S or D. The S punch was again replaced in 1982 with a more distinct letter.

PROOF COINS

A "proof" is a specimen striking of coinage for presentation, souvenir, exhibition, or numismatic purposes. Pre-1968 proofs were made only at the Philadelphia Mint. Current proofs are made at San Francisco and West Point.

The term "proof" refers to the method of manufacture and not the condition of a coin. Regular production coins in mint state have coruscating, frosty luster, soft details, and minor imperfections. Proof coins can usually be distinguished by their sharpness of detail, high wire edge, and extremely brilliant, mirrorlike surface. All proofs are originally sold by the mint at a premium.

Very few proof coins were made prior to 1856. Because of their rarity and infrequent sales, they are not all listed in this catalog.

Frosted proofs were issued prior to 1936 and starting again in the late 1970's. These have a brilliant mirrorlike field with contrasting dull or frosted design.

Matte proofs have a granular "sandblast" surface instead of the mirror finish. Matte proof cents, nickels, and gold coins were issued from 1908 to 1916; a few 1921 and 1922 silver dollars were also struck this way.

Brilliant proofs have been issued from 1936 to date. These have a uniformly brilliant mirrorlike surface and sharp, high relief details.

"Prooflike" coins are occasionally seen. These are specimens from the first few impressions of regular coinage dies from any mint. They are not true proofs, but may have most of the characteristics of a proof coin and generally command a premium. Collectors should beware of coins that have been buffed to look like proofs; magnification will reveal polishing lines and lack of detail.

How A Proof Coin Is Made . . .

Selected dies are inspected for perfection and are highly polished and cleaned. They are again wiped clean or polished after every 15 to 25 impressions and are replaced frequently to avoid imperfections from worn dies. Coinage blanks are polished and cleaned to assure high quality in striking. They are then hand fed into the coinage press one at a time, each blank receiving two or more blows from the dies to bring up sharp, high relief details. The coinage operation is done at slow speed with extra pressure. Finished proofs are individually inspected and are handled by gloves or tongs. They also receive a final inspection by packers before being sonically sealed in special plastic cases.

After a lapse of twenty years, proof coins were struck at the Philadelphia Mint from 1936 to 1942 inclusive. In 1942, when the composition of the five-cent piece was changed, there were two types of this denomination available to collectors. The striking of proof coins was temporarily suspended from 1943 to 1949, and again from 1965 to 1967; during the latter period special mint sets

PROOF SETS

were struck. Proof sets were resumed in 1968. They are available only during the year of issue from: Bureau of the Mint, 55 Mint Street, San Francisco, Calif. 94175. Sets from 1936 through 1972 include the cent, nickel, dime, quarter and half; from 1973 through 1981 the dollar was also included.

Figures in parentheses represent the total number of full sets minted.

1936 (3,837)	$5,000	1970S with sm. date 1c......	$95.00
1937 (5,542)	3,500	1970S 10c without mint mark	
1938 (8,045)	1,550	(estimated 2,200)......	600.00
1939 (8,795)	1,450	1971S (3,220,733)	4.00
1940 (11,246)	1,200	1971S 5c without mint mark	
1941 (15,287)	1,050	(estimated 1,655)......	800.00
1942 both nickels	1,250	1972S (3,260,996)	4.00
1942 one nickel } (21,120)	1,050	1973S (2,760,339)	7.00
1950 (51,386)	550.00	1974S (2,612,568)	7.00
1951 (57,500)	310.00	1975S (2,909,369)	8.00
1952 (81,980)	215.00	1975S 10c without mint mark	——
1953 (128,800)	135.00	1976S (4,149,730)	7.50
1954 (233,300)	75.00	1976S three pc. set (3,295,714)	15.00
1955 box pack } (378,200)	65.00	1977S (3,251,152)	6.50
1955 flat pack	67.00	1978S (3,127,781)	7.50
1956 (669,384)	45.00	1979S filled S } (3,677,175)	12.50
1957 (1,247,952)............	24.00	1979S clear S	100.00
1958 (875,652)..............	36.00	1980S (3,554,806)	11.00
1959 (1,149,291)............	23.00	1981S (4,063,083)	11.00
1960 (1,691,602 both kinds)		1982S (3,857,479)	6.50
with lg. date 1c	21.50	1983S (3,138,765)	13.50
1960 with sm. date 1c......	27.00	1983S incl. Olympic dollar	
1961 (3,028,244)............	19.00	(140,361)	60.00
1962 (3,218,019)............	19.00	1983S 10c without mint mark	775.00
1963 (3,075,645)............	19.00	1984S.....................	13.50
1964 (3,950,762)............	15.00	1984S incl. Olympic dollar	
1968S (3,041,506)	7.00	(316,680)	60.00
1968S 10c without mint mark	——	1985S.....................	13.50
1969S (2,934,631)	7.00	1986S.....................	13.50
1970S (2,632,810)	8.00	1986S incl. Commemoratives	55.00

Original issue prices: 1936 thru 1942, $1.89; 1950 thru 1964, $2.10; 1968S thru 1972S, $5.00; 1973S thru 1976S, $7.00; 1977S thru 1979S, $9.00; 1980S, $10.00; 1981S to date, $11.00.

UNCIRCULATED MINT SETS

Official Mint Sets are specially packaged by the government for sale to collectors. They contain uncirculated specimens of each year's coins for every denomination issued from each mint. Unlike the proof sets, these are normal coins intended for circulation and are not minted with any special consideration for quality. Coins struck only as proofs are not included.

Uncirculated sets sold by the Treasury from 1947 through 1958 contained two examples of each regular issue coin. These were packaged in cardboard holders that did not protect the coins from tarnish. Nicely preserved early sets generally command a 10 to 20 percent premium above listed values. No official mint sets were produced in 1950, 1982 or 1983.

UNCIRCULATED MINT SETS

Since 1959 sets have been sealed in a protective plastic envelope. In 1965, 1966 and 1967, Special Mint Sets of higher than normal quality were packaged in hard plastic holders as a substitute for proof sets which were not made during that period.

Privately assembled mint sets, and souvenir sets produced for sale at the Philadelphia or Denver mints, or for special occasions, are valued according to the individual pieces they contain. Only the official government sealed full sets are included in the following list.

Current year sets may be ordered from The United States Mint, 55 Mint Street, San Francisco, CA 94175.

Year Minted	Sets Sold	Issue Price	Face Value	Current Value
1947 P-D-S		$4.87	$4.46	$850.00
1948 P-D-S		4.92	4.46	250.00
1949 P-D-S		5.45	4.96	800.00
1951 P-D-S	8,654	6.75	5.46	425.00
1952 P-D-S	11,499	6.14	5.46	300.00
1953 P-D-S	15,538	6.14	5.46	250.00
1954 P-D-S	25,599	6.19	5.46	125.00
1955 P-D-S	49,656	3.57	2.86	75.00
1956 P-D	45,475	3.34	2.64	60.00
1957 P-D	34,324	4.40	3.64	85.00
1958 P-D	50,314	4.43	3.64	75.00
1959 P-D	187,000	2.40	1.82	35.00
1960 P-D	260,485	2.40	1.82	27.50
1961 P-D	223,704	2.40	1.82	27.50
1962 P-D	385,285	2.40	1.82	24.00
1963 P-D	606,612	2.40	1.82	21.00
1964 P-D	1,008,108	2.40	1.82	15.00
1968 P-D-S	2,105,128	2.50	1.33	3.50
1969 P-D-S	1,817,392	2.50	1.33	3.50
1970 P-D-S Lg. Date	2,038,134	2.50	1.33	23.00
1970 P-D-S Sm. Date	Incl. above	2.50	1.33	34.00
1971 P-D-S	2,193,396	3.50	1.83	3.00
1972 P-D-S	2,750,000	3.50	1.83	3.00
1973 P-D-S	1,767,691	6.00	3.83	15.00
1974 P-D-S	1,975,981	6.00	3.83	5.25
1975 P-D	1,921,488	6.00	3.82	5.25
1776-1976 (3 pieces)	3,400,000	9.00	1.75	10.00
1976 P-D	1,892,513	6.00	3.82	5.50
1977 P-D	2,006,869	7.00	3.82	5.50
1978 P-D	2,162,609	7.00	3.82	5.50
1979 P-D*	2,526,000	8.00	3.82	5.50
1980 P-D-S	2,815,066	9.00	4.82	7.00
1981 P-D-S	2,908,145	11.00	4.82	15.00
1984 P-D		7.00	1.82	4.00
1985 P-D		7.00	1.82	9.00
1986 P-D		7.00	1.82	9.00

*S mint dollar not included.

SPECIAL MINT SETS

1965 (2,360,000)....... $4.00   1966 (2,261,583)..... $5.00   1967 (1,863,344) $6.50

UNITED STATES REGULAR ISSUES
HALF CENTS — 1793-1857

From the standpoint of face value the half cent is the smallest coin struck by the United States. All half cents are scarce, but the series has never enjoyed the popularity of some of the other series, hence the more common dates and varieties are reasonably priced.

There were various intermissions in coinage, and during most of the period 1836 to 1849 the coinage was very small, causing a very noticeable lapse in the series for the average collector. While 1796 is the most valuable date, the originals and restrikes of 1831, 1836 and 1840 through 1849, and rare varieties are all difficult to obtain.

The half cent was authorized to be coined April 2, 1792. Originally the weight was to have been 132 grains, but this was changed to 104 grains by the Act of January 14, 1793, before coinage commenced. The weight was again changed to 84 grains January 26, 1796 by presidential proclamation in conformity with the Act of March 3, 1795. Coinage was discontinued by the Act of February 21, 1857. All were coined at the Philadelphia Mint.

TYPE COIN VALUES

	G-4	F-12	EF-40	AU-50	MS-60	MS-63	MS-65	PF-60	PF-63	PF-65
Flowing Hair 1793	$1,300	$2,300	$6,300	$12,000	$22,500	$30,000	$45,000			
Liberty Cap 1794-1797	165.00	475.00	1,800	2,700	4,500	9,000	14,000			
Draped Bust 1800-1808	23.00	45.00	170.00	375.00	725.00	1,800	5,200			
Classic Head 1809-1835	19.00	30.00	75.00	125.00	300.00	700.00	3,000	$2,250	$3,000	$5,500
Braided Hair 1840-1857	25.00	35.00	75.00	125.00	300.00	700.00	3,000	2,250	3,200	5,500

LIBERTY CAP TYPE 1793-1797

AG-3 ABOUT GOOD—*Clear enough to identify.*
G-4 GOOD—*Outline of bust clear, no details. Date readable. Reverse lettering incomplete.*
VG-8 VERY GOOD—*Some hair details. Reverse lettering complete.*
F-12 FINE—*Most of hair detail shows. Leaves worn but all visible.*
VF-20 VERY FINE—*Hair near ear and forehead worn, other areas distinct. Some details in leaves show.*
EF-40 EXTREMELY FINE—*Light wear on highest parts of head and wreath.*

Head Facing Left 1793

Designer, possibly Adam Eckfeldt; weight 6.74 grams; composition: copper; approx. diameter 22 mm; edge: TWO HUNDRED FOR A DOLLAR.

	Quan. Minted	AG-3	G-4	VG-8	F-12	VF-20	EF-40
1793	35,334	$550.00	$1,300	$1,800	$2,300	$3,600	$6,300

HALF CENTS
Head Facing Right 1794-1797

1794 — Designer Robert Scot; weight 6.74 grams; composition: copper; approx. diameter 23.5 mm; edge: TWO HUNDRED FOR A DOLLAR.

1795 — Designer John Smith Gardner; weight 6.74 grams; composition: copper; approx. diameter 23.5 mm; edge: TWO HUNDRED FOR A DOLLAR.

1795-1797 (thin planchet) — Weight 5.44 grams; composition: copper; approx. diameter 23.5 mm; edge: plain (some 1797 are either lettered or gripped).

	Quan. Minted	AG-3	G-4	VG-8	F-12	VF-20	EF-40
1794	81,600	$75.00	$250.00	$400.00	$700.00	$1,000	$2,000

Pole to Cap	**Punctuated Date**	**No Pole to Cap**

	Quan. Minted	AG-3	G-4	VG-8	F-12	VF-20	EF-40
1795 All kinds	139,690						
1795 Lettered edge, with pole		70.00	175.00	275.00	500.00	900.00	1,900
1795 Lettered edge, punctuated date		65.00	165.00	250.00	475.00	850.00	1,800
1795 Plain edge, punctuated date		70.00	175.00	275.00	500.00	900.00	1,900
1795 Plain edge, no pole		70.00	175.00	275.00	500.00	900.00	1,900
1796 With pole*		1,200	2,400	4,200	7,000	11,000	——
1796 No pole	1,390	2,000	4,000	7,500	13,000	22,000	——

*The deceptive "Dr. Edwards" struck copy of this coin has a different head and larger letters.

1797 Plain Edge	**1797, 1 above 1, Plain Edge**

	Quan. Minted	AG-3	G-4	VG-8	F-12	VF-20	EF-40
1797 All kinds	127,840						
1797 Lettered edge		200.00	375.00	600.00	1,200	2,300	——
1797 Plain edge		70.00	175.00	250.00	450.00	800.00	1,700
1797 Gripped edge		800.00	1,200	3,500	——	——	——
1797, 1 above 1, plain edge		70.00	175.00	250.00	450.00	800.00	1,700

HALF CENTS
DRAPED BUST TYPE 1800-1808

AG-3 ABOUT GOOD—*Clear enough to identify.*
G-4 GOOD—*Bust outline clear, few details, date readable. Reverse lettering worn and incomplete.*
VG-8 VERY GOOD—*Some drapery shows. Date and legends complete.*
F-12 FINE—*Shoulder drapery and hair over brow worn smooth.*
VF-20 VERY FINE—*Only slight wear in above areas. Slight wear on reverse.*
EF-40 EXTREMELY FINE—*Light wear on highest parts of head and wreath.*

Designer Robert Scot: weight 5.44 grams; composition: copper; diameter 23.5 mm; plain edge.

A modified reverse design was introduced during 1802, and used through 1808.

	Quan. Minted	AG-3	G-4	VG-8	F-12	VF-20	EF-40
1800	202,908	$18.00	$25.00	$35.00	$50.00	$85.00	$200.00
1802, 2 over 0, rev. of 1800.....	20,266	500.00	1,500	2,750	4,750		
1802, 2 over 0, 2nd rev.		85.00	185.00	350.00	675.00	1,500	3,600
1803	92,000	17.50	25.00	35.00	50.00	85.00	250.00

Plain 4	**Crosslet 4**	**Stemless Wreath**	**Stems to Wreath**

		AG-3	G-4	VG-8	F-12	VF-20	EF-40
1804 Plain 4, stems ..		17.50	25.00	35.00	50.00	85.00	225.00
1804 Pl. 4, stemless .		15.00	23.00	32.00	45.00	75.00	170.00
1804 Cr. 4, stems ...	1,055,312	15.00	23.00	32.00	45.00	75.00	170.00
1804 Cr. 4, stemless..		15.00	23.00	32.00	45.00	75.00	170.00
1804 "Spiked chin" ..		20.00	27.50	37.50	60.00	100.00	300.00

	Small 5	**Medium 5**	**Large 5**

1804 "Spiked Chin"

		AG-3	G-4	VG-8	F-12	VF-20	EF-40
1805 Med. 5, stemless		15.00	23.00	32.00	45.00	75.00	170.00
1805 Small 5, stems .	814,464	50.00	100.00	150.00	375.00	725.00	——
1805 Large 5, stems..		15.00	23.00	32.00	45.00	75.00	170.00

HALF CENTS

| **Small 6** | **Large 6** | **1808, 8 over 7** | **Normal Date** |

	Quan. Minted	AG-3	G-4	VG-8	F-12	VF-20	EF-40
1806 Small 6, stems. }		$25.00	$50.00	$80.00	$150.00	$250.00	$420.00
1806 Sm. 6, stemless .. } 356,000		15.00	23.00	32.00	45.00	75.00	170.00
1806 Large 6, stems.. }		15.00	23.00	32.00	45.00	75.00	170.00
1807 476,000		15.00	23.00	32.00	45.00	75.00	170.00
1808, 8 over 7 .... } 400,000		45.00	55.00	90.00	160.00	450.00	850.00
1808 Normal date..... }		15.00	23.00	32.00	45.00	85.00	210.00

CLASSIC HEAD TYPE 1809-1836

Designer John Reich. Standards same as previous issue.

G-4 GOOD—*LIBERTY only partly visible on hair band. Lettering, date, stars, worn but visible.*
VG-8 VERY GOOD—*LIBERTY entirely visible on hair band. Lower curls worn.*
F-12 FINE—*Only part wear on LIBERTY and hair at top worn in spots.*
VF-20 VERY FINE—*Lettering clear-cut. Hair only slightly worn.*
EF-40 EXTREMELY FINE—*Light wear on highest points of hair and leaves*
MS-60 UNCIRCULATED—*Typical brown to red surface. No trace of wear.*

| **1809 Normal Date** | **1809, 9 over 6** | **1809 Circle Inside 0** |

	Quan. Minted	G-4	VG-8	F-12	VF-20	EF-40	MS-60
1809 Circle inside 0. }		$20.00	$25.00	$35.00	$60.00	$100.00	$525.00
1809 9 over 6..... } 1,154,572		20.00	25.00	35.00	60.00	100.00	450.00
1809 Normal date .. }		20.00	25.00	35.00	60.00	100.00	450.00
1810 215,000		25.00	35.00	50.00	90.00	175.00	1,200
1811 63,140		70.00	100.00	200.00	700.00	1,200	2,500
1811 Rev. of 1802. Unofficial restrike. (*Extremely Rare.*)							—
1825 63,000		23.00	30.00	40.00	60.00	90.00	360.00
1826 234,000		19.00	23.00	33.00	50.00	70.00	350.00

Brilliant red uncirculated half cents are worth more than prices shown.

| **13 Stars** | | **12 Stars** | |

		G-4	VG-8	F-12	VF-20	EF-40	MS-60
1828, 13 Stars ...... }		19.00	23.00	33.00	50.00	70.00	350.00
1828, 12 Stars .... } 606,000		22.00	28.00	38.00	60.00	90.00	600.00
1829 487,000		19.00	23.00	33.00	50.00	70.00	350.00

HALF CENTS

**Reverse
1831-1836**

**Reverse
1840-1857**

Beginning in 1831 new coinage equipment and modified dies produced a raised rim on each side of these coins. Proofs and restrikes were made at the mint for sale to collectors. Restrikes are believed to have been struck c. 1858-59.

	Quan. Minted	EF-40	MS-60	Proof-63
1831 Original. (Beware of altered date)............ 2,200		$5,000	——	$10,000
1831 Restrike. Lg. berries (Rev. of 1836)				6,000
1831 Restrike. Sm. berries (Rev. of 1840-1857)				10,000

	Quan. Minted	VG-8	F-12	VF-20	EF-40	MS-60	Proof-63
1832 .... 154,000*		$25.00	$30.00	$40.00	$75.00	$300.00	$3,000
1833 .... 120,000*		25.00	30.00	40.00	75.00	300.00	3,000
1834 .... 141,000*		25.00	30.00	40.00	75.00	300.00	3,000
1835 .... 398,000*		25.00	30.00	40.00	75.00	300.00	3,000
1836 Original...................							6,000
1836 Restrike. (Rev. of 1840-1857)							7,500

*The figures given here are thought to be correct, although official mint records report these quantities for 1833-36 rather than 1832-35.

No half cents were struck in 1837. Because of the great need for small change, however, a large number of tokens similar in size to current half cents and large cents were issued privately by businessmen who needed them in commerce. One of the most popular pieces is listed and illustrated below.

	G-4	VG-8	F-12	VF-20	EF-40	MS-60
1837 Token (not a coin)	$20.00	$27.50	$40.00	$85.00	$120.00	$400.00

BRAIDED HAIR TYPE 1840-1857

HALF CENTS

Designer Christian Gobrecht; weight 5.44 grams; composition: copper; diameter 23 mm; plain edge.

VG-8 VERY GOOD—*Beads uniformly distinct. Hairlines show in spots.*
F-12 FINE—*Hairlines above ear worn. Beads sharp.*
VF-20 VERY FINE—*Lowest curl shows wear, hair otherwise distinct.*
EF-40 EXTREMELY FINE—*Light wear on highest points of hair and leaves.*
MS-60 UNCIRCULATED—*No trace of wear, light blemishes.*

Both originals and restrikes use reverse of 1840-1857. Originals have large berries, restrikes have small berries in wreath.

	Proof-63		*Proof-63*
1840 Original..............	$3,300	1845 Original..............	$4,500
1840 Restrike	3,200	1845 Restrike	4,000
1841 Original..............	3,300	1846 Original..............	4,100
1841 Restrike	3,200	1846 Restrike	3,300
1842 Original..............	3,500	1847 Original..............	3,300
1842 Restrike	3,200	1847 Restrike	3,300
1843 Original..............	3,400	1848 Original..............	3,300
1843 Restrike	3,300	1848 Restrike	3,300
1844 Original..............	4,500	1849 Original. Small date ...	3,900
1844 Restrike	3,300	1849 Restrike. Small date ...	3,900

Small Date,   **Large Date**

Brilliant or red uncirculated half cents are worth more than prices shown.

	Quan. Minted	VG-8	F-12	VF-20	EF-40	MS-60	Proof-63
1849 Large date 39,864		$35.00	$40.00	$60.00	$85.00	$400.00	——
1850 39,812		35.00	40.00	60.00	85.00	400.00	
1851 147,672		30.00	35.00	50.00	75.00	300.00	——
1852 restrike							$3,750
1853 129,694		30.00	35.00	50.00	75.00	300.00	
1854 55,358		30.00	35.00	50.00	75.00	300.00	4,000
1855 56,500		30.00	35.00	50.00	75.00	300.00	4,000
1856 40,430		35.00	40.00	55.00	85.00	325.00	4,000
1857 35,180		37.50	42.50	65.00	100.00	375.00	4,000

BIBLIOGRAPHY

Breen, Walter, *Walter Breen's Encyclopedia of United States Half Cents 1793-1857*. South Gate, California, 1983.
Cohen, Roger S., Jr. *American Half Cents—The "Little Half Sisters"*. 2nd Edition, 1982.
Crosby, S. S. *United States Coinage of 1793—Cents and Half Cents*. Boston, 1897.
Frossard, Edward. *United States Cents and Half Cents 1793-1857*. Irvington, New York, 1879.
Gilbert, Ebenezer, *United States Half Cents*. New York, 1916. Hewitt Reprint, Chicago.

LARGE CENTS — 1793-1857

Cents and half cents were the first coins struck under the authority of the United States Government. Coinage began in 1793 with laws specifying that the cent should weigh exactly twice as much as the half cent. Large cents were coined every year from 1793 to 1857 with the exception of 1815, when a lack of copper prevented production. All were coined at the Philadelphia Mint. Mintage records in some cases may be inaccurate, as many of the early pieces were struck later than the dates shown on the coins. Varieties listed are those most significant to collectors. Numerous other die varieties may be found because each of the early dies was individually made. Values of varieties not listed in this guide depend on collector interest, rarity and demand. Proof large cents were first made in 1817; all proofs are rare, as they were not made available to the general public before the mid-1850's.

TYPE COIN VALUES

	G-4	F-12	EF-40	AU-50	MS-60	MS-63	MS-65	PF-60	PF-63	PF-65
Chain 1793	1,600	3,250	13,000	25,000	45,000	—	—			
Wreath 1793	750.00	1,500	6,000	10,000	17,000	25,000	40,000			
Liberty Cap 1793-1796	90.00	250.00	1,300	2,500	6,000	11,000	18,000			
Draped Bust 1796-1807	20.00	70.00	425.00	900.00	2,600	4,500	13,000			
Classic Head 1808-1814	22.50	75.00	600.00	1,100	2,700	6,500	18,000			
Coronet Head 1816-1839	8.00	12.00	75.00	140.00	325.00	600.00	3,000	—		
Braided Hair 1840-1857	7.00	10.00	50.00	110.00	275.00	550.00	2,750	3,000	4,000	6,000

FLOWING HAIR, CHAIN TYPE REVERSE 1793

Designer Henry Voigt; weight 13.48 grams; composition: copper; approx. diameter 26-27 mm; edge: bars and slender vine with leaves.

AG-3 ABOUT GOOD—*Date and devices clear enough to identify.*

G-4 GOOD—*Lettering worn but readable. Bust has no detail.*

VG-8 VERY GOOD—*Date and lettering distinct, some details of head visible.*

F-12 FINE—*About half of hair, etc. details show.*

VF-20 VERY FINE—*Ear visible. Most of details can be seen.*

EF-40 EXTREMELY FINE—*Highest points of hair and back of temple show wear.*

Values shown for Fine and better copper coins are for those with attractive surfaces and color that are consistent with the amount of normal wear. Coins that are porous, corroded, or similarly defective are worth significantly lower prices.

Obverse	AMERI. Reverse		AMERICA Reverse		
Quan. Minted	*AG-3*	*G-4*	*VG-8*	*F-12*	*VF-20*	*EF-40*

	Quan. Minted	AG-3	G-4	VG-8	F-12	VF-20	EF-40
1793 Chain	36,103						
1793 AMERI. in legend		$900.00	$1,800	$2,750	$3,500	$6,000	$14,500
1793 AMERICA*		800.00	1,600	2,500	3,250	5,500	13,000

*Varieties with or without periods after date and LIBERTY.

FLOWING HAIR, WREATH TYPE REVERSE 1793

The reverse of this type bears a "single-bow" wreath, as distinguished from the wreath tied with a double bow on the following type. A three-leaf sprig appears above the date on the obverse, and both sides have borders of small beads.

LARGE CENTS

Introduction of this reverse answered criticism of the chain design, but the stronger modeling of the face and hair still failed to gain acceptance as representative of Liberty. After three months' production the design was abandoned in favor of the Liberty Cap type.

Instead of the normal sprig above the date, the rare "strawberry leaf" variety has a spray of trefoil leaves and a small blossom. The trefoils match those found on the normal wreath reverse. It is not clear why this variety was created. All known specimens are badly worn.

Designer Adam Eckfeldt; weight 13.48 grams; composition: copper; approx. diameter 26-28 mm; edge: vine and bars, or lettered ONE HUNDRED FOR A DOLLAR followed by either a single or double leaf.

		Wreath Type			Strawberry Leaf Var.	
	Quan. Minted	*AG-3*	*G-4*	*VG-8*	*F-12*	*VF-20*	*EF-40*
1793 Wreath ...	63,353						
1793 Vine/bars edge ..		$400.00	$750.00	$1,000	$1,500	$2,800	$6,000
1793 Lettered Edge ...		450.00	850.00	1,200	1,600	3,000	6,500
1793 Strawberry leaf..				*(4 known)*			

LIBERTY CAP TYPE 1793-1796

Another major change was made in 1793 to satisfy continuing objections to the obverse portrait. This version appears to have been more successful, as it was continued into 1796. The 1793 pieces had beaded borders, but a border of denticles or "teeth" was adopted in 1794. A famous 1794 variety is the probably whimsical "starred" reverse, with a border of 94 tiny 5-pointed stars under the denticles.

Portrait variations listed below for 1794 are the result of several changes of die engravers. The so-called "Jefferson head" of 1795 is now thought to be a sample for a proposed coinage contract by a private manufacturer, John Harper.

Planchets became too thin for edge lettering after the weight reduction ordered late in 1795. The variety with reeded edge was probably an experimental substitute, rejected in favor of a plain edge.

1793-1795 (thick planchet) — Designer Joseph Wright; weight 13.48 grams; composition: copper; approx. diameter 29 mm; edge: ONE HUNDRED FOR A DOLLAR followed by a single leaf.
1795-1796 (thin planchet) — Designer John Smith Gardner; weight 10.89 grams; composition: copper; approx. diameter 29 mm; plain edge.

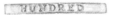

1793 Vine and Bar edge
Chain and Wreath Type Only

Lettered edge 1793-1795
ONE HUNDRED FOR A DOLLAR

Beaded Border, 1793 Only

LARGE CENTS

1793-1794	1794 Only	1794-1796

"Head of 1793"	"Head of 1794"	"Head of 1795"
Head is in high	Well defined hair,	Head in low relief,
rounded relief	hook on lowest curl	no hook on lowest curl

	Quan. Minted	AG-3	G-4	VG-8	F-12	VF-20	EF-40
1793 Lib. Cap ..	11,056	$500.00	$1,200	$2,000	$3,000	$5,500	$16,000
1794 All kinds.	918,521						
1794 "Head of 1793"..		150.00	250.00	425.00	1,000	2,500	7,500
1794 "Head of 1794"...		50.00	110.00	150.00	275.00	600.00	1,600
1794 "Head of 1795"..		50.00	110.00	150.00	275.00	600.00	1,600
1794 Starred rev......		1,600	3,000	4,250	8,000	22,500	——
1795 Ltd. ed....	37,000	50.00	110.00	175.00	300.00	650.00	1,750
1795 Plain ed..	501,500	35.00	90.00	140.00	250.00	550.00	1,300

Reeded Edge

1795 Reeded edge				*(6 known)*		
1795 Jefferson Head (not a regular mint issue)						
Plain edge.......	1,200	2,000	3,500	6,000	15,000	
Lettered edge....			*(3 known)*			
1796 Lib. Cap .	109,825	45.00	100.00	160.00	300.00	700.00	1,700

Obverse 1796-1807

This head was modified slightly in 1798. See page 73 for details.

1794 Starred Reverse   **"Jefferson Head"**

DRAPED BUST TYPE 1796-1807

Designer Robert Scot; weight 10.89 grams; composition: copper; approx. diameter 29 mm; plain edge.

AG-3 ABOUT GOOD—*Clear enough to identify.*
G-4 GOOD—*Lettering worn, but clear; date clear. Bust lacks details.*
VG-8 VERY GOOD—*Drapery partly visible. Less wear in date and lettering.*
F-12 FINE—*Hair over brow is smooth, some detail showing in other parts of hair.*
VF-20 VERY FINE—*Hairlines slightly worn. Hair over brow better defined.*
EF-40 EXTREMELY FINE—*Hair above forehead and left of eye outlined and detailed. Only slight wear on olive leaves.*

LARGE CENTS

1794-1796

1795-1798

1796-1807

"Reverse of 1794"
Note double leaf at top
right; 14-16 leaves left,
16-18 leaves right.

"Reverse of 1796"
Note single leaf at top
right; 17-21 leaves left,
16-20 leaves right.

"Reverse of 1797"
Note double leaf at top
right; 16 leaves left,
19 leaves right.

	Quan. Minted	*AG-3*	*G-4*	*VG-8*	*F-12*	*VF-20*	*EF-40*
1796 Dr. Bust...	363,375						
1796 reverse of 1794 ...		$35.00	$70.00	$125.00	$190.00	$500.00	$1,200
1796 reverse of 1796 ...		37.50	75.00	150.00	225.00	550.00	1,450
1796 reverse of 1797 ...		40.00	80.00	160.00	250.00	600.00	1,550
1796 LIHERTY error.....		50.00	90.00	175.00	325.00	750.00	2,500

**LIHERTY
error**

Gripped Edge

Stems   **Stemless**

1797 All kinds .. 897,510						
1797 Gr. Ed., '96 rev....	21.00	37.50	90.00	175.00	400.00	900.00
1797 Pl. edge, '96 rev...	21.00	40.00	100.00	190.00	450.00	1,000
1797, '97 rev., Stems ...	17.00	35.00	70.00	125.00	300.00	700.00
1797, '97 rev., Stemless.	28.00	55.00	125.00	250.00	600.00	1,550

LARGE CENTS

1798, 8 over 7

Style 1 Hair   Style 2 Hair

Style 1 hair appears on all 1796-97, many 1798 varieties and 1800 over 1798. Style 2 hair, used 1798-1807, is most easily recognized by the extra curl near the shoulder.

Quan. Minted	AG-3	G-4	VG-8	F-12	VF-20	EF-40
1798 All kinds 1,841,745						
1798, 8 over 7	$25.00	$40.00	$100.00	$225.00	$550.00	$1,200
1798, reverse of 1796...	22.50	37.50	80.00	175.00	475.00	1,100
1798, 1st hair style.....	12.50	25.00	45.00	100.00	275.00	600.00
1798, 2nd hair style....	12.50	25.00	45.00	100.00	275.00	550.00

1799, 9 over 8,   1800 over 1798   1800, 80 over 79

1799, 9 over 8*	300.00	625.00	1,100	2,400	5,000	——
1799 Nor. date .. 42,540	265.00	600.00	1,000	2,100	4,300	——
1800 All kds... 2,822,175						
1800 over 1798, Style 1 hair	10.00	23.00	32.50	75.00	250.00	650.00
1800, 80 over 79, Style 2 hair	9.00	20.00	30.00	70.00	225.00	450.00
1800 Normal date	9.00	20.00	30.00	70.00	225.00	450.00

*Mintage for 1799, 9 over 8 variety is included with the 1798 figure.

Fraction 1/000   Corrected Fraction   1801 Reverse, 3 Errors

Error-fraction dies appear on cents of 1801, 1802, and 1803, but all of these dies originated in 1801, possibly all by the same blunderer.

[73]

LARGE CENTS

	Quan. Minted	AG-3	G-4	VG-8	F-12	VF-20	EF-40
1801 All kds...	1,362,837						
1801 Normal rev.......		$9.00	$20.00	$30.00	$70.00	$225.00	$450.00
1801, 3 errors: 1/000, one							
stem & IINITED......		17.50	40.00	75.00	175.00	425.00	1,250
1801 Fraction 1/000....		11.00	22.00	40.00	90.00	250.00	600.00
1801, 1/100 over 1/000.		11.00	25.00	50.00	100.00	300.00	675.00
1802 All kds...	3,435,100						
1802 Normal rev.......		9.00	20.00	30.00	70.00	200.00	425.00
1802 Fraction 1/000....		11.00	23.00	35.00	80.00	250.00	475.00
1802 Stemless wreath..		9.00	20.00	30.00	70.00	200.00	450.00

1803 Sm. Date, Blunt 1   **1803 Large Date, Pointed 1**   **Small Fraction**   **Large Fraction**

All small date varieties have a blunt 1 in date. Large dates have pointed 1 and noticeably larger 3.

1803 All kds..	3,131,691						
1803 Sm. dt., sm. fract.		9.00	20.00	30.00	70.00	200.00	425.00
1803 Sm. dt., lg. fract..		9.00	20.00	30.00	70.00	200.00	425.00
1803 Lg. dt., sm. fract..		350.00	650.00	1,100	2,000	3,750	
1803 Lg. dt., lg. fract...		25.00	45.00	80.00	160.00	325.00	1,000
1803, 1/100 over 1/000.		11.00	24.00	50.00	90.00	250.00	550.00
1803 Stemless wreath..		10.00	22.00	45.00	80.00	235.00	525.00

1804 With Normal or Broken Dies

Broken Dies

All genuine 1804 Cents have a crosslet 4 in the date and a large fraction. The 0 in the date is in line with the O in OF on the reverse of the coin.

1804	96,500	185.00	325.00	650.00	1,000	2,000	4,700

LARGE CENTS

Restrike of 1804 Cent

A fake 1804 was manufactured from discarded mint dies. An altered 1803 die was used for the obverse and a die of the 1820 cent used for the reverse. They were struck about the year 1860 to satisfy the demand for this rare date. Known as the "restrike," it was a patchwork job and is easily distinguished from a genuine 1804 cent.

Quan. Minted	AG-3	G-4	VG-8	F-12	VF-20	EF-40
1804 Unofficial restrike of 1860 (Uncirculated)						$325.00
1805 941,116	$9.00	$20.00	$30.00	$75.00	$225.00	500.00
1806 348,000	11.00	25.00	55.00	125.00	300.00	750.00

Sm. 1807, 7 over 6, blunt 1

Lg. 1807, 7 over 6, pointed 1

"Comet Variety"

1807 All kinds.. 829,221						
1807 Small 7 over 6,... Blunt 1...........	400.00	600.00	1,100	2,000	4,000	——
1807 Large 7 over 6 ...	9.00	20.00	30.00	75.00	225.00	500.00
1807 Small fraction....	10.00	22.00	45.00	100.00	250.00	600.00
1807 Large fraction....	9.00	20.00	30.00	75.00	225.00	500.00
1807 "Comet" variety (die break behind head)	10.00	22.00	45.00	100.00	250.00	650.00

CLASSIC HEAD TYPE 1808-1814

1808 to 1814 — This group does not compare in sharpness and quality to those struck before (1793-1807), nor to those struck after (1816 on). The copper used was "softer," having less metallic impurity. This impaired the wearing quality of the series. For this reason collectors find greater difficulty in obtaining these dates in choice condition.

Designer John Reich. Standards same as previous issue.

LARGE CENTS

AG-3 ABOUT GOOD—*Details clear enough to identify.*
G-4 GOOD—*Legends, stars, date worn, but plain.*
VG-8 VERY GOOD—*LIBERTY all readable. Ear shows. Details worn but plain.*
F-12 FINE—*Hair on forehead and before ear nearly smooth. Ear and hair under ear sharp.*
VF-20 VERY FINE—*All hairlines show some detail. Leaves on reverse show slight wear.*
EF-40 EXTREMELY FINE—*All hairlines sharp. Very slight wear on high points.*

	Quan. Minted	AG-3	G-4	VG-8	F-12	VF-20	EF-40
1808	1,007,000	$12.00	$24.00	$47.50	$85.00	$225.00	$625.00
1809	222,867	32.50	65.00	110.00	225.00	525.00	1,100

1810, 10 over 09   **Normal Date**   **1811, last 1 over 0**   **Normal Date**

		AG-3	G-4	VG-8	F-12	VF-20	EF-40
1810 All kds. . .	1,458,500						
1810, 10 over 09		11.00	22.50	40.00	75.00	225.00	600.00
1810 Normal date.		11.00	22.50	40.00	75.00	225.00	600.00
1811 All kds. . . .	218,025						
1811 Last 1 over 0		27.50	45.00	85.00	175.00	425.00	1,100
1811 Normal date.		25.00	42.50	80.00	165.00	400.00	900.00

1812 Small Date   **1812 Large Date**   **1814 Plain 4**   **1814 Crosslet 4**

		AG-3	G-4	VG-8	F-12	VF-20	EF-40
1812 Sm. dt. }		11.00	22.50	40.00	75.00	225.00	600.00
1812 Lg. dt. . . . . . }	1,075,500	11.00	22.50	40.00	75.00	225.00	600.00
1813	418,000	15.00	32.00	60.00	110.00	275.00	700.00
1814 Plain 4 }		11.00	22.50	40.00	75.00	225.00	600.00
1814 Crosslet 4 . . }	357,830	11.00	22.50	40.00	75.00	225.00	600.00

LARGE CENTS

CORONET TYPE 1816-1857

G-4 GOOD—*Head details partly visible. Even wear in date and legends.*
VG-8 VERY GOOD—*LIBERTY, date, stars, legends clear. Part of hair cord visible.*
F-12 FINE—*All hairlines show. Hair cords show uniformly.*
VF-20 VERY FINE—*Hair cords only slightly worn. Hairlines only partly worn, all well defined.*
EF-40 EXTREMELY FINE—*Both hair cords stand out sharply. All hairlines sharp.*
MS-60 UNCIRCULATED—*Typical brown to red surface. No trace of wear.*

Designer Robert Scot; weight 10.89 grams; composition: copper; approx. diameter 28-29 mm; plain edge.

MATRON HEAD 1816-1835

13 Stars   **15 Stars**

	Quan. Minted	G-4	VG-8	F-12	VF-20	EF-40	MS-60*
1816	2,820,982	$8.00	$10.00	$15.00	$35.00	$75.00	$325.00
1817, 13 stars. . . . . }	3,948,400	8.00	10.00	14.00	30.00	75.00	325.00
1817, 15 stars. . . . . . }		10.00	12.00	21.00	45.00	125.00	700.00
1818	3,167,000	8.00	10.00	14.00	30.00	75.00	325.00

1819, 9 over 8   **1819 Large Date**   **1819 Small Date**

1819, 9 over 8 . . . . }		9.00	12.00	20.00	35.00	90.00	400.00
1819 Large date . . . }	2,671,000	8.00	10.00	13.00	27.50	75.00	325.00
1819 Small date . . . . . }		8.00	10.00	13.00	27.50	75.00	325.00

1820, 20 over 19   **1820 Large Date**   **1820 Small Date**
Note 1 under 2.   **Note plain-topped 2.**   **Note curl-topped 2.**

*Values shown are for average condition. Red to bright red uncirculated large cents with attractive surface (not cleaned) command higher prices. Beware of slightly worn copper coins which have been cleaned and recolored to simulate uncirculated luster. Cents in VF or better condition with attractive surface and tone may also command higher prices than listed here.

LARGE CENTS

	Quan. Minted	G-4	VG-8	F-12	VF-20	EF-40	MS-60*
1820, 20 over 19 ...		$9.00	$10.00	$18.00	$30.00	$80.00	$350.00
1820 Large date .	4,407,550	8.00	10.00	12.00	25.00	75.00	325.00
1820 Small date ...		8.00	10.00	12.00	25.00	75.00	325.00
1821	389,000	15.00	25.00	40.00	87.50	250.00	1,300
1822	2,072,339	8.00	10.00	12.00	25.00	80.00	375.00

1823, 3 over 2

1823 Restrike

		G-4	VG-8	F-12	VF-20	EF-40	MS-60*
1823, 3 over 2	Included	25.00	37.50	75.00	150.00	425.00	—
1823 Normal date.....	with 1824	27.50	40.00	85.00	160.00	625.00	—
1823 Unofficial restrike, from broken obverse die						125.00	350.00

The 1823 unofficial restrike was made at the same time and by the same people as the 1804 restrike copy (qv), using a discarded 1823 obverse and an 1813 reverse die. The dies are heavily rusted (lumps on coin) and most examples have both dies cracked across.

1824, 4 over 2

1826, 6 over 5

		G-4	VG-8	F-12	VF-20	EF-40	MS-60*
1824, 4 over 2		12.00	20.00	40.00	90.00	275.00	—
1824 Normal date	1,262,000	9.00	12.00	18.00	35.00	150.00	900.00
1825	1,461,100	8.00	10.00	15.00	30.00	80.00	375.00
1826, 6 over 5		13.00	22.00	35.00	75.00	165.00	750.00
1826 Normal date	1,517,425	8.00	10.00	12.00	25.00	75.00	350.00
1827	2,357,732	8.00	10.00	12.00	25.00	75.00	325.00

This date size appears on cents before 1828.

This date size appears on cents after 1828.

		G-4	VG-8	F-12	VF-20	EF-40	MS-60*
1828 Lg. nar. date .	2,260,624	8.00	10.00	12.00	25.00	75.00	350.00
1828 Sm. wide date ...		9.00	12.00	18.00	35.00	80.00	400.00

*See footnote page 77.

LARGE CENTS

This letter size appears on cents of 1808-1834.

This letter size appears on cents of 1829-1837.

Note individual letter size and proximity.

Note isolation of letters. esp. STATES.

	Quan. Minted	G-4	VG-8	F-12	VF-20	EF-40	MS-60*
1829 Large letters ...	} 1,414,500	$8.00	$10.00	$14.00	$25.00	$75.00	$325.00
1829 Med. letters		10.00	15.00	25.00	60.00	125.00	——
1830 Large letters ...	} 1,711,500	8.00	10.00	14.00	25.00	75.00	325.00
1830 Med. letters		18.00	30.00	60.00	125.00	270.00	——
1831 Large letters ...	} 3,359,260	8.00	10.00	12.00	20.00	75.00	325.00
1831 Med. letters		8.00	10.00	12.00	20.00	65.00	325.00
1832 Large letters		8.00	10.00	12.00	20.00	75.00	325.00
1832 Med. letters	2,362,000	8.00	10.00	12.00	20.00	75.00	325.00
1833	2,739,000	8.00	10.00	12.00	20.00	75.00	325.00

Large 8 and Stars

Large 8, Small Stars

Small 8, Large Stars

1834 All kinds 1,855,100							
1834 Lg. 8, stars & rev. letters...		10.00	14.00	20.00	35.00	100.00	400.00
1834 Lg. 8 & stars, med. letters ..		20.00	35.00	50.00	90.00	190.00	——
1834 Lg. 8, sm. stars, med. let....		8.00	10.00	12.00	27.50	80.00	350.00
1834 Sm. 8, lg. stars, med. let. ...		8.00	10.00	12.00	27.50	80.00	350.00

Large 8 and Stars, Matron Head

Small 8 and Stars, Matron Head

"Head of 1836" 1835-1837 Slim Bust

1835 Lg. 8 & stars	} 3,878,400	9.00	12.00	15.00	30.00	85.00	375.00
1835 Sm. 8 & stars....		9.00	12.00	15.00	30.00	85.00	375.00
1835 "Head of 1836" ..		8.00	10.00	12.00	25.00	75.00	325.00
1836	2,111,000	8.00	10.00	12.00	25.00	75.00	325.00

*See footnote page 77.

[79]

LARGE CENTS

G-4 GOOD—*Considerably worn. LIBERTY readable.*
VG-8 VERY GOOD—*Hairlines smooth but visible, outline of ear clearly defined.*
F-12 FINE—*Hairlines at top of head and behind ear worn but visible. Braid over brow plain, ear clear.*
VF-20 VERY FINE—*All details more sharp. Hair over brow shows only slight wear.*
EF-40 EXTREMELY FINE—*Hair above ear detailed, but slightly worn.*
MS-60 UNCIRCULATED—*Typical brown to red surface. No trace of wear.*

Designer Christian Gobrecht; weight 10.89 grams; composition: copper; diameter 27.5 mm; plain edge.

1829-1837	**"Head of 1838"**	**1837-1839**
Medium letters,	Beaded Cords,	Small letters,
note proximity	note slim bust	note isolation
of letters.	with beaded cords.	of letters.

	Quan. Minted	G-4	VG-8	F-12	VF-20	EF-40	MS-60*
1837 Pl. crd., med. let ..	} 5,558,300	$8.00	$10.00	$12.00	$25.00	$75.00	$325.00
1837 Pl. crd., sm. let ...		8.50	10.00	15.00	35.00	80.00	350.00
1837 Head of 1838		8.00	10.00	12.00	20.00	75.00	325.00
1838	6,370,200	8.00	10.00	12.00	20.00	75.00	325.00

1839 over 1836	**Silly Head**	**Booby Head**
Note closed 9,	Note browlock	Note back tip of
plain cords.	at forehead.	shoulder exposed.

	Quan. Minted	G-4	VG-8	F-12	VF-20	EF-40	MS-60
1839 All kinds 3,128,661							
1839, 9 over 6, plain cords.......		85.00	150.00	275.00	525.00	1,500	——
1839 Head of 1838, beaded cords..		8.00	12.00	15.00	25.00	75.00	350.00
1839 Silly Head.................		9.00	13.00	20.00	35.00	90.00	470.00
1839 Booby Head...............		8.00	12.00	18.00	30.00	80.00	435.00
1839 Petite head................		8.00	12.00	15.00	25.00	75.00	375.00

The last two 1839 heads use a modified reverse which omits the line under CENT (see illustration of 1849).

*See footnote page 77.

LARGE CENTS

1840 Large Date   **1840 Small Date**   **Small Date over Large 18**

	Quan. Minted	G-4	VG-8	F-12	VF-20	EF-40	MS-60*
1840 Large date	⎱ 2,462,700	$8.00	$10.00	$12.00	$20.00	$60.00	$300.00
1840 Small date		8.00	10.00	12.00	20.00	60.00	300.00
1840 Sm. dt., lg. 18..	⎰	9.00	12.00	16.00	27.50	65.00	350.00
1841 Small date	1,597,367	8.00	10.00	12.00	20.00	60.00	325.00

1842 Small Date   **1842 Large Date**   **Small Letters 1839-1843**

1842 Small date ...	⎱ 2,383,390	7.50	9.00	11.00	20.00	60.00	300.00
1842 Large date .	⎰	7.50	9.00	11.00	20.00	60.00	300.00

"Head of 1840" Petite Head 1839-1843   **"Head of 1844" Mature Head 1843-1857**   **Large Letters 1843-1857**

1843 Petite, sm. let...	⎱	7.50	9.00	12.00	20.00	60.00	300.00
1843 Petite, lg. let....	⎬ 2,425,342	10.00	18.00	34.00	55.00	90.00	500.00
1843 Mature, lg. let ..	⎰	9.00	12.00	19.00	35.00	70.00	300.00
1844 Normal date....	⎱	7.50	9.00	11.00	18.00	60.00	300.00
1844 over 81 (error)..	⎰ 2,398,752	9.00	12.00	20.00	45.00	135.00	650.00
1845	3,894,804	7.00	8.00	10.00	16.00	50.00	275.00

*See footnote page 77.

LARGE CENTS

1846 Small Date
Note squat date
with closed 6.

1846 Medium Date
Note medium height
with ball-top 6.

1846 Tall Date
Note vertically stretched
date with open-mouthed 6.

	Quan. Minted	G-4	VG-8	F-12	VF-20	EF-40	MS-60*
1846 Small date		$7.00	$8.00	$10.00	$16.00	$50.00	$275.00
1846 Medium date	4,120,800	8.00	9.00	12.00	20.00	60.00	275.00
1846 Tall date		8.00	9.00	12.00	20.00	50.00	275.00
1847	6,183,669	7.00	8.00	10.00	16.00	50.00	275.00
1847, 7 over "sm." 7		9.00	11.00	20.00	37.50	80.00	325.00

1848	6,415,799	7.00	8.00	10.00	16.00	60.00	275.00
1849	4,178,500	7.00	8.00	10.00	16.00	70.00	275.00
1850	4,426,844	7.00	8.00	10.00	16.00	60.00	275.00

1844, 44 over 81

1851, 51 over 81

1847, 7 over "Small" 7

These are not true overdates, but are some of the more spectacular of several date-punch blunders of the 1844-1854 period. The so-called "overdates" of 1844 and 1851 each have the date punched upside-down, then corrected normally.

1851 Normal date	9,889,707	7.00	8.00	10.00	16.00	50.00	275.00
1851 over 81 (error)		9.00	11.00	17.00	40.00	80.00	350.00
1852	5,063,094	7.00	8.00	10.00	16.00	50.00	275.00
1853	6,641,131	7.00	8.00	10.00	16.00	50.00	275.00
1854	4,236,156	7.00	8.00	10.00	16.00	50.00	275.00

*See footnote page 77.

LARGE CENTS

1855 Upright 5's

1855 Slanting 5's

1855 Knob on ear

Original sketches of engraver James B. Longacre's work reveal that slanting 5's were a peculiarity of his work. The figure punch for an upright 5 was probably the work of an apprentice.

	Quan. Minted	G-4	VG-8	F-12	VF-20	EF-40	MS-60*
1855 All kinds.........	1,574,829						
1855 Upright 5's...............		$7.00	$8.00	$10.00	$16.00	$50.00	$275.00
1855 Slanting 5's...............		7.00	8.00	10.00	16.00	50.00	275.00
1855 Slanting 5's, knob on ear ...		8.00	10.00	14.00	30.00	60.00	300.00
1856 Upright 5 ... ⎫	2,690,463	7.00	8.00	10.00	16.00	50.00	275.00
1856 Slanting 5... ⎭		7.00	8.00	10.00	16.00	50.00	275.00

1857 Large Date

1857 Small Date

1857 Large date ... ⎫	333,456	22.50	30.00	40.00	50.00	70.00	300.00
1857 Small date . ⎭		25.00	35.00	45.00	55.00	80.00	335.00

*See footnote page 77.

Passing of the Large Cent and Half Cent

By 1857 the cost of making and distributing copper coins had risen. Mint Director Snowden reported that they "barely paid expenses." Both cents and half cents had become unpopular, in fact, they hardly circulated outside of the larger cities. The practice of issuing subsidiary silver coins which began in 1853, brought about a reform of the copper coinage. The half cent was abandoned and a smaller cent was introduced late in 1857.

The law of 1857 brought important benefits to the citizens. By its terms Spanish coins were redeemed and melted at the Mint in exchange for new small cents. The decimal system became popular and official thereafter, and the old method of reckoning in reals, medios, shillings, etc., was gradually given up, although the terms, "two bits" and "penny" are still commonly used. The new, convenient small cent won popular favor and soon became a useful instrument of retail trade and a boon to society generally.

BIBLIOGRAPHY

Sheldon, Wm. H. *Penny Whimsy (1793-1814)*. New York, 1958.
Newcomb, H.R. *United States Copper Cents 1816-1857*. New York, 1944.
PENNY-WISE, official publication of Early American Coppers, Inc. (EAC)

SMALL CENTS — 1856 to Date

TYPE COIN VALUES

	G-4	F-12	EF-40	AU-50	MS-60	MS-63	MS-65	PF-60	PF-63	PF-65
Flying Eagle 1857-1858	9.00	15.00	65.00	150.00	300.00	600.00	2,300	1,800	3,200	5,500
Indian CN 1859	4.25	10.00	60.00	150.00	300.00	600.00	2,000	1,200	1,500	3,000
Indian CN 1860-1864	3.25	5.00	17.50	38.00	130.00	300.00	1,100	400.00	900.00	2,500
Indian 1864-1909	.75	1.30	7.00	12.00	34.00	75.00	375.00	125.00	375.00	800.00
Lincoln 1909-V.D.B.	2.25	3.00	4.00	5.50	13.00	27.50	55.00	800.00	1,800	2,400

FLYING EAGLE TYPE 1856-1858

The Act of February 21, 1857 provided for the coinage of the small cent, and made uncurrent the coins of other countries, particularly the Spanish and Mexican dollars. The new cents weighed 72 grains. Composition, 88% copper, 12% nickel.

The 1856 Eagle cent was not an authorized mint issue, as the law governing the new size coin was enacted after the date of issue. It is believed that about 1,000 of these pieces were struck. They are properly referred to as patterns. Collectors are advised to inspect any 1856 Flying Eagle cent carefully.

A few tests will aid in establishing genuineness of this cent, as follows: If the lower half of the 6 is thick it is probably an altered 1858. A magnifying glass will often reveal poor workmanship.

The figure 5 slants slightly to the right on a genuine 1856. The vertical bar points to the center of the ball just beneath. On the 1858, this bar points *outside* the ball.

The 1858 cent is found in two minor varieties. The A and M in the word AMERICA are joined in the large letter variety and separated in the small letter variety. The reverse design of the eagle cents is dominated by a wreath of corn, wheat, cotton and tobacco.

G-4 GOOD—*All details worn, but readable.*

VG-8 VERY GOOD—*Feather details and eye of eagle are evident, but worn.*

F-12 FINE—*Eagle head details and feather tips sharp.*

VF-20 VERY FINE—*Feathers in right wing and tail show considerable detail.*

EF-40 EXTREMELY FINE—*Slight wear, all details sharp.*

MS-60 UNCIRCULATED—*No trace of wear. Light blemishes.*

Designer James B. Longacre; weight 4.67 grams; composition: .880 copper, .120 nickel; diameter 19 mm; plain edge. All coined at Philadelphia Mint.

1858, 8 over 7

Large Letters

Small Letters

	Quan. Minted	G-4	VG-8	F-12	VF-20	EF-40	MS-60	Proof-63
1856	est. *1,000*	$1,300	$1,600	$2,000	$2,300	$2,600	$3,500	$4,000
1857	*(485)* 17,450,000	9.00	11.00	15.00	27.50	65.00	300.00	3,200
1858 Lg. let .. *(80)*	} 24,600,00	9.00	11.00	15.00	27.50	65.00	300.00	3,200
1858 Sm. let. *(200)*		9.00	11.00	15.00	27.50	65.00	300.00	3,200
1858, 8 over 7			50.00	125.00	250.00	500.00	1,000	

SMALL CENTS
INDIAN HEAD TYPE 1859-1909

The small cent was redesigned in 1859, and a representation of an Indian princess was adopted as the obverse device. The 1859 reverse was also changed to represent a laurel wreath. In 1860 the reverse was modified to display an oak wreath with a small shield at the top. The weight and composition of the coin were not changed.

Designer James B. Longacre; weight 4.67 grams; composition: .880 copper, .120 nickel; diameter 19 mm; plain edge. All coined at Philadelphia Mint.

G-4 GOOD—*No LIBERTY visible.*
VG-8 VERY GOOD—*At least three letters of LIBERTY readable on head band.*
F-12 FINE—*LIBERTY completely visible.*
VF-20 VERY FINE—*Slight but even wear on LIBERTY.*
EF-40 EXTREMELY FINE—*LIBERTY sharp. All other details sharp. Only slight wear on ribbon end.*
MS-60 UNCIRCULATED—*No trace of wear. Light blemishes.*

Without Shield at Top of Wreath	**With Shield on Reverse**
1859 Only	**1860 to 1909**

Variety 1 — Copper-nickel, Laurel Wreath Reverse 1859

Spotted, cleaned or discolored uncirculated pieces are worth less than values shown.

	Quan. Minted	G-4	VG-8	F-12	VF-20	EF-40	MS-60	Proof-63
1859 .... (800)	36,400,000	$4.25	$5.75	$10.00	$23.00	$60.00	$300.00	$1,500

Variety 2 — Copper-nickel, Oak Wreath with Shield 1860-1864

	Quan. Minted	G-4	VG-8	F-12	VF-20	EF-40	MS-60	Proof-63
1860 .. (1,000)	20,566,000	3.75	5.00	8.75	14.00	27.50	160.00	1,100
1861 .. (1,000)	10,100,000	8.50	11.50	17.50	25.00	37.50	235.00	1,100
1862 .... (550)	28.075,000	3.25	4.25	5.00	8.00	17.50	130.00	900.00
1863 .... (460)	49,840,000	3.25	4.25	5.00	8.00	17.50	130.00	900.00
1864 .... (370)	13,740,000	7.00	9.00	15.00	20.00	30.00	175.00	1,200

Variety 3 — Bronze 1864-1909

During the year 1864 the alloy of the cent was changed to 95% copper and 5% tin and zinc. The weight was reduced to 48 grains, resulting in a thinner coin than the so-called "white" cents of 1856-1864. The design remained unchanged. Before 1864 cents did not have the designer's initial L on the bonnet ribbon; late in that year the letter appeared on only a small quantity. The initial appeared on all dates of Indian cents thereafter. Consult the illustration details.

Indian Head Cent with "L"

If the coin is turned slightly (so Indian faces observer) the highlighted details of the "L" will appear to better advantage. The point of the bust is pointed on the variety with "L"; rounded without "L." The "L" is the initial of the engraver, Longacre.

SMALL CENTS

Designer James B. Longacre; weight 3.11 grams; composition: .950 copper, .050 tin and zinc; diameter 19 mm; plain edge; mints: Philadelphia, San Francisco.

Choice brilliant Unc. and Proof small cents command higher prices. Spotted, cleaned or discolored pieces are worth less.

	Quan. Minted	G-4	VG-8	F-12	VF-20	EF-40	MS-60	Proof-63
1864 All kinds..	39,233,714							
1864 No L............ *(150)*		$3.50	$5.50	$8.50	$17.50	$27.50	$85.00	$1,100
1864 L must show ..... *(20)*		25.00	35.00	55.00	90.00	130.00	340.00	10,000
1865* . *(500+)*	35,429,286	3.25	4.50	7.50	15.00	25.00	70.00	600.00
1866 .. *(725+)*	9,826,500	20.00	25.00	33.00	50.00	75.00	185.00	600.00
1867 .. *(625+)*	9,821,000	20.00	25.00	33.00	50.00	75.00	185.00	600.00
1868 .. *(600+)*	10,266,500	20.00	25.00	33.00	50.00	75.00	185.00	600.00
1869 over 8* ⎫	6,420,000	50.00	75.00	150.00	300.00	450.00	950.00	
1869 .. *(600+)* ⎭		30.00	37.00	65.00	100.00	150.00	350.00	800.00
1870 *(1,000+)*	5,275,000	23.00	30.00	50.00	70.00	95.00	225.00	600.00
1871 .. *(960+)*	3,929,500	30.00	40.00	70.00	95.00	130.00	275.00	700.00
1872 .. *(950+)*	4,042,000	43.00	50.00	80.00	120.00	165.00	350.00	725.00

*One variety of 1865 appears to show traces of a 4 under the 5 in the date. The 9 is doubled on some varieties of the 1869, on others it appears to be over an 8, although it is probably only a doubled 9.

On coins 1859-1886 the last feather of the headdress points between I and C of AMERICA; from mid-1886 to 1909 it points between C and A.

Closed 3   **Open 3**

1873 All Kinds 11,676,500								
1873 Closed 3 *(1,100+)*.		9.00	11.00	17.00	27.00	47.00	125.00	525.00
1873 Doubled LIBERTY ..				150.00	300.00	500.00	1,200	
1873 Open 3...........		9.00	11.00	17.00	27.00	47.00	125.00	
1874 *(700+)*	14,187,500	9.00	11.00	17.00	27.00	47.00	115.00	500.00
1875 *(700+)*	13,528,000	9.00	11.00	17.00	27.00	47.00	100.00	500.00
1876 *(1,150+)*	7,944,000	12.00	15.00	28.00	40.00	65.00	135.00	500.00
1877 *(900+)*	852,500	225.00	250.00	325.00	500.00	725.00	1,500	2,850
1878 . *(2,350)*	5,799,850	14.00	17.00	28.00	40.00	65.00	135.00	450.00
1879 . *(3,200)*	16,231,200	3.50	4.25	7.00	13.00	21.00	55.00	425.00
1880 . *(3,955)*	38,964,955	1.50	2.25	3.50	5.75	14.00	45.00	400.00
1881 . *(3,575)*	39,211,575	1.50	2.25	3.50	5.75	14.00	45.00	400.00
1882 . *(3,100)*	38,581,100	1.50	2.25	3.50	5.75	14.00	45.00	400.00
1883 . *(6,609)*	45,598,109	1.50	2.25	3.50	5.75	14.00	45.00	400.00
1884 . *(3,942)*	23,261,742	1.75	2.75	5.00	8.00	15.00	55.00	425.00
1885 . *(3,790)*	11,765,384	3.75	6.00	9.00	15.00	27.50	75.00	450.00
1886 . *(4,290)*	17,654,290	2.10	3.25	6.00	10.00	20.00	60.00	400.00
1887 . *(2,960)*	45,226,483	1.00	1.25	2.00	3.50	10.00	40.00	400.00

On coins 1859-1886 the last feather of the headdress points between I and C of AMERICA; from mid-1886 to 1909 it points between C and A.

1888, last 8 over 7

1888 over 7 ⎫	37,494,414			—	—	—	—	
1888 .. *(4,582)* ⎭		1.00	1.25	2.00	3.50	10.00	40.00	400.00
1889 .. *(3,336)*	48,869,361	1.00	1.25	2.00	3.50	8.00	40.00	375.00

SMALL CENTS

	Quan. Minted	G-4	VG-8	F-12	VF-20	EF-40	MS-60	Proof-63
1890 .. (2,740)	57,182,854	$1.00	$1.25	$2.00	$3.50	$8.00	$40.00	$375.00
1891 .. (2,350)	47,072,350	1.00	1.25	2.00	3.50	8.00	40.00	375.00
1892 .. (2,745)	37,649,832	1.00	1.25	2.00	3.50	8.00	40.00	375.00
1893 .. (2,195)	46,642,195	1.00	1.25	2.00	3.50	8.00	40.00	375.00
1894 .. (2,632)	16,752,132	1.50	3.00	5.00	9.00	15.00	50.00	400.00
1895 .. (2,062)	38,343,636	.75	1.00	1.60	2.75	7.00	37.00	375.00
1896 .. (1,862)	39,057,293	.75	1.00	1.60	2.75	7.00	37.00	375.00
1897 .. (1,938)	50,466,330	.75	1.00	1.60	2.75	7.00	35.00	375.00
1898 .. (1,795)	49,823,079	.75	1.00	1.60	2.75	7.00	35.00	375.00
1899 .. (2,031)	53,600,031	.75	1.00	1.60	2.75	7.00	35.00	375.00
1900 .. (2,262)	66,833,764	.75	.90	1.30	2.30	7.00	34.00	375.00
1901 .. (1,985)	79,611,143	.75	.90	1.30	2.30	7.00	34.00	375.00
1902 .. (2,018)	87,376,722	.75	.90	1.30	2.30	7.00	34.00	375.00
1903 .. (1,790)	85,094,493	.75	.90	1.30	2.30	7.00	34.00	375.00
1904 .. (1,817)	61,328,015	.75	.90	1.30	2.30	7.00	34.00	375.00
1905 .. (2,152)	80,719,163	.75	.90	1.30	2.30	7.00	34.00	375.00
1906 .. (1,725)	96,022,255	.75	.90	1.30	2.30	7.00	34.00	375.00
1907 .. (1,475)	108,138,618	.75	.90	1.30	2.30	7.00	34.00	375.00

**Location of mint mark S
on reverse of Indian cent
(1908 and 1909 only).**

		G-4	VG-8	F-12	VF-20	EF-40	MS-60	Proof-63
1908 .. (1,620)	32,327,987	.75	.90	1.30	2.30	7.00	35.00	400.00
1908S	1,115,000	21.00	24.00	27.50	32.00	45.00	155.00	
1909 .. (2,175)	14,370,645	.85	1.25	2.00	3.00	8.00	45.00	425.00
1909S	309,000	100.00	125.00	150.00	175.00	225.00	400.00	

LINCOLN TYPE, WHEAT EARS REVERSE 1909-1958

Victor D. Brenner designed this cent which was issued to commemorate the
hundredth anniversary of Lincoln's birth. The designer's initials VDB appear
on the reverse of a limited quantity of cents of 1909. The initials were restored,
in 1918, to the obverse side as illustrated below. The Lincoln type was the first
cent to have the motto IN GOD WE TRUST.

Matte proof coins were made for collectors from 1909 through 1916, and an
exceptional specimen dated 1917 is also known to exist.

Designer Victor D. Brenner; weight 3.11 grams; composition: .950 copper, .050 tin and zinc; diameter
19 mm; plain edge; mints: Philadelphia, Denver, San Francisco, West Point.

G-4 GOOD—*Date worn but apparent. Lines in wheat ears missing. Full rims.*

VG-8 VERY GOOD—*Half of lines show in upper wheat ears.*

F-12 FINE—*Wheat lines worn but visible.*

VF-20 VERY FINE—*Cheek and jaw bones worn but separated. No worn spots on wheat ears.*

EF-40 EXTREMELY FINE—*Slight wear. All details sharp.*

MS-60 UNCIRCULATED—*No trace of wear. Light blemishes or discoloration.*

MS-63 SELECT UNCIRCULATED—*No trace of wear. Slight blemishes.*

MS-65 CHOICE UNCIRCULATED—*No trace of wear. Barely noticeable blemishes.*

*Choice brilliant uncirculated cents command higher prices. Discolored or weak-
ly struck pieces are worth less.*

SMALL CENTS

Location of designer's initials V.D.B. on 1909 only.

No V.D.B. on reverse 1909-1958.

Location of mint mark.

Variety 1 — Bronze 1909-1942

	Quan. Minted	G-4	VG-8	F-12	VF-20	EF-40	MS-60	MS-63
1909 V.D.B.	27,995,000	$2.25	$2.65	$3.00	$3.25	$4.00	$13.00	$27.50
1909 V.D.B. Matte prf.	(420)							1,800
1909S, V.D.B......	484,000	225.00	250.00	285.00	325.00	375.00	500.00	700.00
1909	72,702,618	.50	.60	.75	1.00	1.75	12.00	25.00
1909 Matte proof ...	(2,198)							375.00
1909S	1,825,000	40.00	43.00	50.00	55.00	85.00	175.00	250.00
1909S, S over horiz. S.....		40.00	43.00	50.00	60.00	90.00	185.00	275.00
1910	146,801,218	.20	.30	.45	.80	1.75	13.00	23.00
1910 Matte proof ...	(2,405)							375.00
1910S.............	6,045,000	8.00	9.00	10.00	11.00	18.00	95.00	150.00
1911	101,177,787	.20	.30	.60	1.25	3.75	18.00	30.00
1911 Matte proof ...	(1,733)							375.00
1911D..........	12,672,000	3.50	4.25	6.00	10.00	25.00	100.00	170.00
1911S.............	4,026,000	11.00	13.00	15.00	18.00	30.00	115.00	240.00
1912	68,153,060	.25	.40	1.35	3.50	6.50	25.00	45.00
1912 Matte proof ...	(2,145)							375.00
1912D..........	10,411,000	4.00	5.00	6.00	12.00	31.00	110.00	175.00
1912S.............	4,431,000	10.00	11.00	13.00	17.00	35.00	110.00	200.00
1913	76,532,352	.20	.35	1.00	2.25	8.00	20.00	35.00
1913 Matte proof ...	(2,848)							375.00
1913D..........	15,804,000	2.00	2.50	4.50	7.00	17.50	70.00	145.00
1913S.............	6,101,000	8.00	9.00	10.00	13.00	23.00	100.00	225.00
1914	75,238,432	.20	.40	1.25	2.50	6.00	65.00	90.00
1914 Matte proof ...	(1,365)							550.00
1914D*...........	1,193,000	70.00	80.00	100.00	135.00	350.00	1,000	1,650
1914S.............	4,137,000	9.00	10.00	12.00	18.00	31.00	165.00	425.00
1915	29,092,120	.80	1.50	3.25	6.00	22.00	110.00	175.00
1915 Matte proof ...	(1,150)							750.00
1915D..........	22,050,000	.60	1.00	1.50	3.00	10.00	45.00	110.00
1915S.............	4,833,000	7.75	8.50	9.00	12.00	22.00	100.00	200.00
1916	131,833,677	.20	.25	.35	.75	1.50	12.00	25.00
1916 Matte proof ...	(1,050)							1,000
1916D..........	35,956,000	.20	.35	.75	1.85	6.00	50.00	125.00
1916S..........	22,510,000	.75	1.25	1.75	2.25	7.50	60.00	125.00
1917	196,429,785	.20	.25	.30	.85	1.50	12.00	25.00
1917 Matte proof								—
1917D..........	55,120,000	.25	.35	.65	1.50	5.00	50.00	100.00
1917S..........	32,620,000	.25	.35	.65	1.50	5.00	55.00	125.00

*Beware of altered date or mint mark. No VDB on shoulder of genuine 1914D cent.

SMALL CENTS

**Designer's initials restored
starting 1918.**

	Quan. Minted	G-4	VG-8	F-12	VF-20	EF-40	MS-60	MS-63
1918	288,104,634	$ .20	$ .25	$ .40	$ .80	$ 1.50	$13.00	$25.00
1918D	47,830,000	.25	.35	.65	1.50	5.00	50.00	105.00
1918S	34,680,000	.25	.35	.65	1.50	5.00	55.00	120.00
1919	392,021,000	.15	.25	.40	.60	1.50	11.00	20.00
1919D	57,154,000	.25	.30	.45	1.30	4.00	40.00	80.00
1919S	139,760,000	.15	.25	.40	.80	2.50	30.00	65.00
1920	310,165,000	.15	.25	.35	.40	1.50	10.00	20.00
1920D	49,280,000	.25	.35	.60	1.00	4.00	50.00	90.00
1920S	46,220,000	.25	.35	.60	1.00	4.00	65.00	120.00
1921	39,157,000	.20	.35	.60	1.00	3.00	40.00	70.00
1921S	15,274,000	.60	.85	1.50	3.00	10.00	125.00	300.00
1922D	} 7,160,000	4.75	6.00	7.00	9.50	19.00	80.00	150.00
1922 Plain†		175.00	225.00	300.00	400.00	750.00	3,100	——
1923	74,723,000	.15	.20	.35	.50	1.50	10.00	20.00
1923S	8,700,000	1.50	2.00	3.00	4.75	13.00	175.00	350.00
1924	75,178,000	.15	.20	.35	.50	2.00	22.00	40.00
1924D	2,520,000	10.00	12.00	14.00	18.00	40.00	235.00	375.00
1924S	11,696,000	.60	.80	1.25	2.50	6.00	110.00	185.00
1925	139,949,000	.15	.25	.35	.50	1.50	10.00	22.50
1925D	22,580,000	.20	.30	.40	1.00	4.00	50.00	80.00
1925S	26,380,000	.20	.25	.35	.75	4.00	60.00	120.00
1926	157,088,000	.15	.20	.30	.45	1.25	8.00	16.00
1926D	28,020,000	.25	.35	.60	1.30	5.00	50.00	85.00
1926S	4,550,000	3.00	3.60	5.00	6.00	12.00	100.00	170.00
1927	144,440,000	.15	.20	.30	.55	1.25	8.00	16.00
1927D	27,170,000	.25	.35	.50	.85	2.75	26.00	60.00
1927S	14,276,000	.40	.55	.90	1.65	4.00	65.00	135.00
1928	134,116,000	.15	.20	.30	.55	1.25	8.00	16.00
1928D	31,170,000	.20	.30	.40	.80	2.00	22.00	50.00
1928S*	17,266,000	.25	.35	.60	1.25	3.50	45.00	100.00
1929	185,262,000	.15	.20	.30	.60	1.35	7.50	13.00
1929D	41,730,000	.15	.25	.35	.65	1.35	18.00	40.00
1929S	50,148,000	.15	.25	.35	.60	1.25	9.00	18.00
1930	157,415,000	.10	.15	.25	.40	.90	5.50	11.00
1930D	40,100,000	.15	.20	.30	.45	1.50	12.00	26.00
1930S	24,286,000	.15	.20	.30	.50	1.00	9.00	16.00
1931	19,396,000	.25	.35	.45	.85	1.80	17.00	40.00
1931D	4,480,000	2.25	2.50	3.50	4.25	7.50	55.00	125.00
1931S	866,000	31.00	35.00	40.00	45.00	50.00	90.00	135.00
1932	9,062,000	1.50	1.75	2.00	2.50	3.00	18.00	40.00
1932D	10,500,000	.60	.80	1.20	1.75	2.50	16.00	33.00
1933	14,360,000	.75	.90	1.25	1.50	2.75	18.50	40.00
1933D	6,200,000	1.75	2.00	2.25	3.00	4.00	25.00	50.00
1934	219,080,000	......	.10	.15	.30	.60	4.00	7.00
1934D	28,446,000	.15	.25	.30	.45	1.00	23.00	40.00
1935	245,388,000	......	.10	.15	.20	.40	2.00	3.50
1935D	47,000,000	......	.10	.15	.25	.40	4.00	8.00
1935S	38,702,000	......	.10	.20	.30	.60	12.00	25.00

†The 1922 without D caused by defective die. Beware removed mint mark.
*Large and small mint mark varieties, see pages 59-60.

SMALL CENTS

	Quan. Minted	G-4	VG-8	F-12	VF-20	EF-40	MS-65	Proof-63
1936 .. (5,569)	309,637,569	$ .10	$ .15	$ .20	$ .30	$4.00	$250.00
1936D.........	40,620,000		.10	.20	.30	.45	7.00
1936S.........	29,130,000		.10	.25	.40	.55	8.00
1937 .. (9,320)	309,179,320			.10	.15	.30	4.00	100.00
1937D.........	50,430,000		.10	.15	.25	.35	5.00
1937S.........	34,500,000		.10	.20	.30	.40	6.00
1938 . (14,734)	156,696,734		.10	.15	.20	.30	4.00	60.00
1938D.........	20,010,000	$ .15	.20	.30	.45	.65	6.00
1938S.........	15,180,000	.25	.35	.45	.55	.75	7.00
1939 . (13,520)	316,479,520			.10	.15	.25	2.00	40.00
1939D.........	15,160,000	.35	.45	.55	.65	.85	9.00
1939S.........	52,070,000	.10	.15	.20	.30	.40	6.00
1940 . (15,872)	586,825,872				.10	.20	2.00	37.50
1940D.........	81,390,000			.10	.15	.25	3.50
1940S*........	112,940,000			.10	.15	.25	4.00
1941 . (21,100)	887,039,100				.10	.20	2.00	30.00
1941D.........	128,700,000				.10	.25	6.00
1941S*........	92,360,000			.10	.15	.30	9.00
1942 . (32,600)	657,828,600				.10	.20	1.75	30.00
1942D.........	206,698,000				.10	.20	2.00
1942S.........	85,590,000	.10	.15	.25	.30	.45	13.00

*Large and small mint mark varieties, see pages 59-60.

Variety 2 — Zinc-coated Steel 1943, Only

Owing to a shortage of copper during the critical war year 1943, the Treasury Department resorted to the use of zinc-coated steel for our cents. No bronze cents were officially issued in 1943. A few specimens struck on bronze planchets by error are known to exist. Through a similar error, a few of the 1944 cents were struck on steel planchets.

1943 — Weight 2.70 grams; composition: steel, coated with zinc; diameter 19 mm; plain edge.

	Quan. Minted.	F-12	VF-20	EF-40	MS-65	Proof-65
1943......................	684,628,670	$ .15	$ .25	$ .30	$3.50	
1943D.....................	217,660,000	.15	.25	.30	5.00	
1943S.....................	191,550,000	.30	.45	.55	9.00	

Variety 1 Resumed 1944-1958

1944D, D over S

Cartridge cases were salvaged for coinage of 1944 through 1946. Although the color was slightly different for uncirculated specimens, the coins proved satisfactory in every respect. The original alloy of 1864-1942 was resumed in 1947.

1944-1946 — Weight 3.11 grams; composition: .950 copper, .050 zinc; diameter 19 mm; plain edge.

	Quan. Minted	VF-20	EF-40	MS-65	Proof-65
1944...........................	1,435,400,000	$ .10	$ .20	$ .75	
1944D....................		.10	.15	1.25	
1944D, D over S.........	} 430,578,000	100.00	150.00	*250.00	
1944S.....................	282,760,000	.10	.20	.65	
1945...........................	1,040,515,000	.10	.15	.40	
1945D.....................	266,268,000	.10	.20	1.00	
1945S.....................	181,770,000	.10	.20	.75	

*Value is for MS-60 uncirculated.

SMALL CENTS

	Quan. minted	VF-20	EF-40	MS-65	Proof-65
1946	991,655,000	$ .10	$ .15	$ .40	
1946D	315,690,000	.10	.20	.50	
1946S	198,100,000	.10	.20	.90	
1947	190,555,000	.10	.20	1.25	
1947D	194,750,000	.10	.20	.60	
1947S	99,000,000	.15	.25	1.10	
1948	317,570,000	.10	.20	1.00	
1948D	172,637,500	.10	.20	1.00	
1948S	81,735,000	.15	.30	1.50	
1949	217,775,000	.10	.20	1.75	
1949D	153,132,500	.10	.20	1.35	
1949S	64,290,000	.20	.30	4.00	
1950 (51,386)	272,686,386	.10	.20	1.50	$65.00
1950D	334,950,000	.10	.20	.50	
1950S	118,505,000	.10	.25	1.25	
1951 (57,500)	284,633,500	.10	.25	1.50	40.00
1951D	625,355,000	.10	.15	.60	
1951S	136,010,000	.15	.25	2.25	
1952 (81,980)	186,856,980	....	.15	.75	30.00
1952D	746,130,000		.15	1.00	
1952S	137,800,004	....	.20	1.25	
1953 (128,800)	256,883,800	....	.10	.50	18.00
1953D	700,515,000	....	.10	.70	
1953S	181,835,000	....	.15	.80	
1954 (233,300)	71,873,350	.25	.35	1.00	13.00
1954D	251,552,500	....	.10	.40	
1954S	96,190,000	....	.20	.45	

1955 Doubled Die Error

The 1955 doubled die error coins were made from improperly prepared dies that show full-doubled outline of date and legend. Do not confuse with less valuable pieces showing only minor traces of doubling.

		VF	EF	MS	Proof
1955 Doubled die obv........ ⎫		350.00	450.00	*3,250	
1955 .... (378,200) ⎬	330,958,200		.10	.25	9.00
1955D .... ⎭	563,257,500	....	.10	.25	
1955S	44,610,000	.30	.40	.70	
1956 (669,384)	421,414,384	....		.35	3.50
1956D	1,098,201,100	....		.20	
1957 (1,247,952)	283,787,952	....		.20	2.50
1957D	1,051,342,000	....		.15	
1958 (875,652)	253,400,652	....		.15	3.00
1958D	800,953,300	....		.15	

*Value for MS-60 Uncirculated is $675.00; MS-63 is $1,200.

SMALL CENTS
LINCOLN TYPE, MEMORIAL REVERSE 1959 TO DATE

Frank Gasparro designed the Lincoln Memorial reverse which was introduced in 1959 on the 150th anniversary of Lincoln's birth.

1959-1962 — Designer: Obv. V. D. Brenner, Rev. Frank Gasparro; weight 3.11 grams; composition: .950 copper, .050 tin and zinc; diameter 19 mm; plain edge; mints: Philadelphia, Denver, San Francisco, 1962-1982-composition changed to: .950 copper, .050 zinc. 1982-composition changed to: copper plated zinc. Core is 99.2% zinc, 0.8% copper, with a plating of pure copper. Total content is 97.5% zinc, 2.5% copper. Weight 2.5 grams. Both types issued in 1982.

	Quan. Minted		MS-65	Proof-65
1959 . . . . (1,149,291)	610,864,291		$ .10	$1.50
1959D	1,279,760,000		.10	

Small Date   **Large Date**

	Quan. Minted		MS-65	Proof-65
1960 Large date . . . } (1,691,602)	. . . .		.10	1.10
1960 Sm. date . . .	588,096,602		3.00	15.00
1960D Large date . . . . }	. . . .		.10	
1960D Small date	1,580,884,000		.25	
1961 . . . . (3,028,244)	756,373,244		.10	1.00
1961D	1,753,266,700		.10	
1962 . . . . (3,218,019)	609,263,019		.10	1.00
1962D	1,793,148,400		.10	
1963 . . . . (3,075,645)	757,185,645		.10	1.00
1963D	1,774,020,400		.10	
1964 . . . . (3,950,762)	2,652,525,762		.10	1.00
1964D	3,799,071,500		.10	
1965	1,497,224,900		.10	
1966	2,188,147,783		.10	
1967	3,048,667,100		.10	
1968	1,707,880,970		.15	
1968D	2,886,269,600		.10	
1968S . . . . (3,041,506)	261,311,510		.10	1.00

In 1969, the dies were modified to strengthen the design, and Lincoln's head was made slightly smaller. In 1973, dies were further modified and engraver's initials FG made larger. The initials were reduced slightly in 1974. During 1982 the dies were again modified and the bust, lettering and date made slightly smaller. One variety of the 1984 cent shows Lincoln's ear doubled.

SMALL CENTS

1969S Doubled Die Error

	Quan. Minted	MS-65	Proof-65
1969	1,136,910,000	$ .60	
1969D	4,002,832,200	.15	
1969S Doubled die obv....	——		
1969S (2,934,631)			
	547,309,631	.15	$1.00
1970	1,898,315,000	.50	
1970D	2,891,438,900	.10	

Small Date   Large Date,

	Quan. Minted	MS-65	Proof-65
1970S (2,632,810)			
	693,192,814		
1970S Sm. date		11.00	90.00
1970S Lg. date (low 7)		.15	1.00
1971	1,919,490,000	.30	
1971D	2,911,045,600	.15	
1971S (3,220,733)			
	528,354,192	.35	1.00

1972 Doubled Die Error

		MS-65	
1972 Doubled die obv.		300.00	
1972	2,933,255,000	.10	
1972D	2,665,071,400	.15	

	Quan. Minted	MS-65	Proof-65
1972S (3,260,996)			
	380,200,104	$ .10	$1.00
1973	3,728,245,000	.10	
1973D	3,549,576,588	.10	
1973S (2,760,339)			
	319,937,634	.10	1.00
1974	4,232,140,523	.10	
1974D	4,235,098,000	.10	
1974S (2,612,568)			
	412,039,228	.15	1.00
1975	5,451,476,142	.10	
1975D	4,505,275,300	.10	
1975S Proof	(2,845,450)		5.00
1976	4,674,292,426	.10	
1976D	4,221,592,455	.10	
1976S Proof	(4,149,730)		3.25
1977	4,469,930,000	.10	
1977D	4,194,062,300	.10	
1977S Proof	(3,251,152)		3.25
1978	5,558,605,000	.10	
1978D	4,280,233,400	.10	
1978S Proof	(3,127,781)		3.50
1979	6,018,515,000	.10	
1979D	4,139,357,254	.10	
1979S Proof	(3,677,175)		
Filled S			3.50
Clear S			6.00
1980	7,414,705,000	.10	
1980D	5,140,098,660	.10	
1980S Proof	(3,554,806)		3.00
1981	7,491,750,000	.10	
1981D	5,373,235,677	.10	
1981S Proof	(4,063,083)		3.00
1982	10,712,525,000		
Lg. Date		.10	
Sm. Date		.15	
1982D	6,012,979,368		
Lg. date		.10	
1982S Proof	(3,857,479)		4.00

Copper Plated Zinc

Large Date   **Small Date**

1982 Lg. Date ....⎫	inc. above	.10
1982 Sm. Date ⎭		.10

1982D Lg. Date ⎫	inc. above	.25
1982D Sm. Date ⎭		.10

SMALL CENTS

1983 Doubled Die Rev.

	Quan. Minted	MS-65	Proof-65
1983 Doubled die Rev....	$175.00		
1983.........	7,752,355,000	.10	
1983D	6,467,199,428	.10	
1983S Proof....	(3,228,648)		$7.00
1984.........	8,151,079,000	.10	
1984D	5,569,238,906	.10	
1984S Proof.............			6.00

	Quan. Minted	MS-65	Proof-65
1985........	*5,648,489,887	$.10	
1985D	5,287,399,926	.10	
1985S Proof.............			$6.00
1986....................		.10	
1986D		.10	
1986S Proof.............			5.00

*696,585,000 of these were manufactured at West Point

TWO-CENT PIECES — 1864-1873

		TYPE COIN VALUES							
	G-4	F-12	EF-40	AU-50	MS-60	MS-63	MS-65	PF-60	PF-63	PF-65
1864-1873	4.50	7.00	30.00	60.00	175.00	450.00	1,200	375.00	950.00	2,200

The Act of April 22, 1864, which changed the weight and composition of the cent, included a provision for the bronze two cent piece. The weight was specified as 96 grains, the alloy being the same as for the cent.

The two cent piece is one of the short-lived issues of United States coinage. The motto "In God We Trust" appeared for the first time on the new coin due largely to the increased religious sentiment during the Civil War Crisis.

There are two varieties for the first year of issue, 1864: the small motto which is scarce and the large motto. See illustrations below.

1864 Small Motto   **1864 Large Motto**

On the obverse the D in GOD is narrow on the large motto. The stem to the leaf shows plainly on the small motto variety. There is no stem on the large motto.

The first T in TRUST touches ribbon crease at left on the small motto variety; there is a 1mm gap on the large motto variety.

It will be noted that the shield device is very similar to the nickel five cent piece introduced in 1866. Proof mintage totals are unknown.

Designer James B. Longacre; weight 6.22 grams; composition: .950 copper, .050 tin and zinc; diameter 23 mm; plain edge. All coined at Philadelphia Mint.

G-4 GOOD— *At least IN GOD visible.*

VG-8 VERY GOOD— *WE weakly visible.*

F-12 FINE— *Complete motto visible. WE weak.*

EF-40 EXTREMELY FINE— *WE is bold.*

MS-60 UNCIRCULATED— *No trace of wear. Light blemishes.*

MS-63 SELECT UNCIRCULATED— *No trace of wear. Nice color, few blemishes.*

Brilliant red choice uncirculated and proof coins command higher prices. Spotted, cleaned or discolored pieces are worth less.

	Quan. Minted	G-4	F-12	EF-40	MS-60	MS-63	Proof-63
1864 Sm. motto.....		$60.00	$100.00	$250.00	$525.00	$1,100	——
1864 Lg. motto *(100+)*	19,847,500	4.50	7.00	30.00	175.00	450.00	$1,000
1865* .... *(500+)*	13,640,000	4.50	7.00	30.00	175.00	450.00	1,000
1866 .... *(725+)*	3,177,000	4.50	7.00	30.00	175.00	450.00	950.00
1867 .... *(625+)*	2,938,750	4.50	7.00	30.00	175.00	450.00	950.00
1867 Doubled die		——	——	——	——	——	——
1868 .... *(600+)*	2,803,750	4.50	7.00	30.00	175.00	450.00	950.00
1869, 9 over 8	1,546,500	100.00	200.00	600.00			
1869 ..... *(600+)*		6.00	10.00	35.00	225.00	500.00	1,000
1870 .... *(1,000+)*	861,250	7.00	15.00	50.00	325.00	575.00	1,200
1871 .... *(960+)*	721,250	8.00	19.00	75.00	350.00	650.00	1,350
1872 .... *(950+)*	65,000	75.00	145.00	325.00	875.00	1,800	2,000
1873 Closed 3. Proofs only (Est. 600). (See illustration on page 86)..............							2,750
1873 Open 3. Restrike (Est. 500)							3,000

*One variety appears to show traces of a 4 under the 5 in the date.

BIBLIOGRAPHY

Kliman, Myron M. *The Two Cent Piece and Varieties. 1977.*

SILVER THREE-CENT PIECES 1851-1873

	G-4	F-12	EF-40	AU-50	MS-60	MS-63	MS-65	PF-60	PF-63	PF-65
TYPE COIN VALUES										
Variety I 1851-1853	9.00	14.00	55.00	110.00	270.00	650.00	3,500			
Variety II 1854-1858	11.00	22.00	80.00	200.00	450.00	1,000	4,700	950.00	2,100	7,500
Variety III 1859-1873	11.00	21.00	55.00	115.00	275.00	650.00	3,100	500.00	1,000	4,000

This smallest of United States silver coins was authorized by Congress March 3, 1851. The first three-cent silver pieces had no lines bordering the six-pointed star. From 1854 through 1858 there were three lines, while issues of the last fifteen years show only two lines. Issues from 1854 through 1873 have an olive sprig over the III and a bundle of three arrows beneath.

1851-1853 — Designer James B. Longacre; weight .80 gram; composition: .750 silver, .250 copper; diameter 14 mm; plain edge; mints: Philadelphia, New Orleans.

1854-1873 — Weight .75 gram; composition: .900 silver, .100 copper; diameter 14 mm; plain edge. All coined at Philadelphia Mint.

mint mark
o

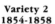

G-4 GOOD— Star worn smooth. Legend and date readable.

VG-8 VERY GOOD— Outline of shield defined. Legend and date clear.

F-12 FINE— Only star points worn smooth.

VF-20 VERY FINE— Only partial wear on star ridges.

EF-40 EXTREMELY FINE— Ridges on star points show.

MS-60 UNCIRCULATED— No trace of wear. Light blemishes.

Variety 1, 1851-1853

	Quan. Minted	G-4	VG-8	F-12	VF-20	EF-40	MS-60	Proof-63
1851 Var. 1....	5,447,440	$ 9.00	$12.00	$15.00	$27.50	$55.00	$270.00	——
1851O.........	720,000	13.00	20.00	30.00	55.00	100.00	500.00	
1852	18,663,500	9.00	11.00	14.00	25.00	55.00	270.00	——
1853	11,400,000	9.00	11.00	14.00	25.00	55.00	270.00	

Variety 2
1854-1858

Well struck specimens command higher prices.

1854 Var. 2.....	671,000	13.50	17.50	24.00	40.00	85.00	450.00	——
1855	139,000	16.00	22.00	32.00	50.00	135.00	700.00	$3,000
1856	1,458,000	11.00	16.00	22.00	35.00	80.00	450.00	2,500
1857	1,042,000	11.00	16.00	22.00	35.00	80.00	450.00	2,500
1858	1,604,000	11.00	16.00	22.00	35.00	80.00	450.00	2,100

Variety 3
1859-1873

1862,
2 over 1

1859 Var. 3 (800)	365,000	11.00	15.00	21.00	32.00	55.00	275.00	1,000
1860 .. (1,000)	287,000	11.00	15.00	21.00	32.00	55.00	275.00	1,000
1861 .. (1,000)	498,000	11.00	15.00	21.00	32.00	55.00	275.00	1,000
1862, 2 over 1	343,550 {	15.00	20.00	30.00	60.00	120.00	325.00	
1862 .... (550)		11.00	15.00	21.00	32.00	55.00	275.00	1,000
1863, 3 over 2	21,460 {	....	....	....	....	....	....	1,500
1863 .... (460)		....	....	....	....	....	500.00	1,100
1864 .... (470)	12,470	....	....	....	....	....	600.00	1,100

SILVER THREE-CENT PIECES

	Quan. Minted	G-4	VG-8	F-12	VF-20	EF-40	MS-60	Proof-63
1865 .... (500)	8,500						$700.00	$1,100
1866 .... (725)	22,725						700.00	1,100
1867 .... (625)	4,625						700.00	1,100
1868 .... (600)	4,100						700.00	1,100
1869, 9 over 8	} 5,100						—	—
1869 .... (600)							700.00	1,100
1870 .. (1,000)	4,000						700.00	1,100
1871 .... (960)	4,360						700.00	1,100
1872 .... (950)	1,950						750.00	1,100
1873 .... (600)	600 (Closed 3, proof only)							2,200

NICKEL THREE-CENT PIECES 1865-1889

TYPE COIN VALUES

	G-4	F-12	EF-40	AU-50	MS-60	MS-63	MS-65	PF-60	PF-63	PF-65
1865-1889	4.25	6.50	16.00	40.00	150.00	350.00	1,600	350.00	700.00	2,300

The three cent pieces struck in nickel composition were designed to replace the silver three cent coins. Composition is 75% copper and 25% nickel. All were coined at Philadelphia and have plain edges.

Designer James B. Longacre; weight 1.94 grams; composition: .750 copper, .250 nickel; diameter 17.9 mm; plain edge. All coined at Philadelphia Mint.

G-4 GOOD—*Date and legends complete though worn. III smooth.*

VG-8 VERY GOOD—*III is half worn. Rims complete.*

F-12 FINE—*Hair curls well defined.*

EF-40 EXTREMELY FINE—*Slight, even wear.*

MS-60 UNCIRCULATED—*No trace of wear. Light blemishes.*

	Quan. Minted	G-4	VG-8	F-12	EF-40	MS-60	Proof-63
1865 .... (500+)	11,382,000	$4.25	$5.50	$6.50	$16.00	$150.00	$1,500
1866 .... (725+)	4,801,000	4.25	5.50	6.50	16.00	150.00	700.00
1867 .... (625+)	3,915,000	4.25	5.50	6.50	16.00	150.00	700.00
1868 .... (600+)	3,252,000	4.25	5.50	6.50	16.00	150.00	700.00
1869 .... (600+)	1,604,000	4.25	5.50	6.50	16.00	150.00	700.00
1870 .... (1,000+)	1,335,000	5.25	6.00	8.00	17.00	160.00	700.00
1871 .... (960+)	604,000	5.25	6.50	9.00	20.00	175.00	700.00
1872 .... (950+)	862,000	5.25	6.50	9.00	20.00	175.00	700.00
1873 Closed 3 (1,100+)	390,000	5.25	6.50	9.00	20.00	175.00	
1873 Open 3	783,000	5.25	6.50	9.00	20.00	175.00	
1874 .... (700+)	790,000	5.25	6.50	9.00	20.00	175.00	700.00
1875 .... (700+)	228,000	8.00	10.00	12.00	24.00	200.00	700.00
1876 .... (1,150+)	162,000	8.00	10.00	13.00	30.00	200.00	700.00
1877 (Prfs. only) (510+)	510				1,400		2,200
1878 (Prfs. only) (2,350)	2,350				700.00		1,400
1879 .... (3,200)	41,200	40.00	45.00	55.00	80.00	275.00	750.00
1880 .... (3,955)	24,955	55.00	65.00	75.00	110.00	300.00	750.00
1881 .... (3,575)	1,080,575	4.25	5.50	6.50	16.00	150.00	725.00
1882 .... (3,100)	25,300	55.00	65.00	75.00	120.00	300.00	850.00
1883 .... (6,609)	10,609	100.00	125.00	160.00	250.00	400.00	1,000
1884 .... (3,942)	5,642	225.00	275.00	325.00	450.00	575.00	1,150
1885 .... (3,790)	4,790	350.00	400.00	450.00	600.00	875.00	1,400
1886 (Prfs. only) (4,290)	4,290				700.00		1,400
1887 All kinds } (2,960)	7,961	225.00	275.00	325.00	450.00	575.00	1,400
1887, 7 over 6 }					700.00		1,400
1888 .... (4,582)	41,083	40.00	45.00	55.00	75.00	300.00	700.00
1889 .... (3,436)	21,561	55.00	65.00	75.00	110.00	325.00	700.00

NICKEL FIVE-CENT PIECES — 1866 to Date

	G-4	F-12	EF-40	AU-50	MS-60	MS-63	MS-65	PF-60	PF-63	PF-65
Shield-Rays 1866-1867	11.25	20.00	75.00	150.00	375.00	750.00	3,500	1,800	2,500	6,000
Shield-No Rays 1867-1883	7.50	12.00	27.50	50.00	175.00	450.00	2,000	325.00	700.00	2,600
Liberty Head-NC 1883	2.50	4.00	8.00	11.00	47.50	85.00	475.00	325.00	750.00	3,000
Liberty Head-WC 1883-1912	.60	2.50	18.00	40.00	125.00	300.00	1,700	275.00	550.00	2,300
Buffalo Variety I 1913	3.00	4.25	12.00	18.00	35.00	75.00	425.00	1,100	2,300	3,000
Buffalo Variety II 1913-1938	.30	.40	1.50	3.00	12.00	23.00	45.00	600.00	1,500	3,000
Jefferson Wartime 1942-1945	.50	.50	1.00	1.75	3.00	4.00	5.50	125.00	200.00	350.00

SHIELD TYPE 1866-1883

The shield type nickel was made possible by the Act of May 16, 1866. Its weight was set at 77-16/100 grains with the same composition as the nickel three-cent piece which was authorized in 1865. In 1866 the coin was designed with rays between the stars on the reverse. Some of the pieces minted in 1867 have the same details, but later the rays were eliminated creating two varieties for that year. There was no further change in the type until it was replaced by the Liberty head device in 1883. Only proof pieces were struck in 1877 and 1878.

Designer James B. Longacre; weight 5 grams; composition: .750 copper, .250 nickel; diameter 20.5 mm; plain edge. All coined at Philadelphia Mint.

G-4 GOOD—*All letters in motto readable.*

VG-8 VERY GOOD—*Motto stands out clearly. Rims worn slightly but even. Part of shield lines visible.*

F-12 FINE—*Half of each olive leaf is smooth.*

EF-40 EXTREMELY FINE—*Leaf tips show slight wear. Cross over shield slightly worn.*

MS-60 UNCIRCULATED—*No trace of wear. Light blemishes.*

**Rays Between Stars
1866-1867**

Sharply struck uncirculated coins are valued higher than the prices shown here.

	Quan. Minted	G-4	VG-8	F-12	EF-40	MS-60	Proof-63
1866 Rays..... *(125+)*	14,742,500	$11.25	$14.50	$20.00	$75.00	$375.00	$2,500
1867 Rays...... *(25+)*	2,019,000	13.50	18.00	29.00	85.00	425.00	8,000

**Typical Example of 1883, 3 over 2.
Other varieties exist
as well as those with recut 3.**

Without Rays 1867-1883

1867 No rays.. *(600+)*	28,890,500	7.50	9.00	12.00	27.50	175.00	700.00
1868 .... *(600+)*	28,817,000	7.50	9.00	12.00	27.50	175.00	700.00
1869 .... *(600+)*	16,395,000	7.50	9.00	12.00	27.50	200.00	700.00
1870 ....*(1,000+)*	4,806,000	7.50	10.00	13.00	35.00	210.00	700.00
1871 .... *(960+)*	561,000	30.00	40.00	50.00	95.00	300.00	850.00
1872 .... *(950+)*	6,036,000	7.50	10.00	13.00	35.00	200.00	700.00
1873 Closed 3 *(1,100+)*	436,050	8.00	10.00	13.00	35.00	210.00	700.00
1873 Open 3..........	4,113,950	8.00	10.00	13.00	35.00	210.00	
1874 .... *(700+)*	3,538,000	10.00	12.00	15.00	40.00	200.00	700.00
1875 .... *(700+)*	2,097,000	11.00	13.50	20.00	50.00	250.00	750.00

NICKEL FIVE-CENT PIECES

	Quan. Minted	G-4	VG-8	F-12	EF-40	MS-60	Proof-63
1876 .... (1,150+)	2,530,000	$11.00	$13.50	$20.00	$50.00	$225.00	$725.00
1877 (Prfs. only) (510+)	510				1,500		2,400
1878 (Prfs. only) (2,350)	2,350				750.00		1,600
1879 .... (3,200) ⎰	29,100	210.00	265.00	325.00	475.00	625.00	1,100
1879, 9 over 8 .... ⎱							‾‾‾
1880 .... (3,955)	19,955	225.00	300.00	350.00	500.00	700.00	1,200
1881 .... (3,575)	72,375	175.00	210.00	275.00	375.00	550.00	1,100
1882 .... (3,100)	11,476,000	7.50	9.00	12.00	27.50	175.00	700.00
1883 .... (5,419) ⎰	1,456,919	7.50	9.00	12.00	27.50	175.00	700.00
1883, 3 over 2 ⎱				40.00	55.00	125.00	375.00

LIBERTY HEAD TYPE 1883-1913

In 1883 the type was changed to the familiar "Liberty head." This type first appeared without the word CENTS on the coin, merely a large letter "V." These "centless" coins were goldplated and passed for five dollars. Later in that year the word CENTS was added.

Five 1913 Liberty head nickels were originally owned by Col. E. H. R. Green (son of the famous Hetty Green). These have since been dispersed and are now held in individuals' collections. These were not a regular issue and were never placed in circulation.

Designer Charles E. Barber; weight 5 grams; composition: .750 copper, .250 nickel; diameter 21.2 mm; plain edge; mints: Philadelphia, Denver, San Francisco.

Sharply struck uncirculated coins are valued higher than the prices shown; dull or weakly struck pieces are worth less.

Variety 1 — Without CENTS 1883 Only

G-4 GOOD— *No details in head. LIBERTY obliterated.*

VG-8 VERY GOOD— *At least 3 letters in LIBERTY readable.*

F-12 FINE— *All letters in LIBERTY show.*

VF-20 VERY FINE— *LIBERTY bold, including letter I.*

EF-40 EXTREMELY FINE— *LIBERTY sharp. Corn grains at bottom of wreath show, on reverse.*

MS-60 UNCIRCULATED— *No trace of wear. Light blemishes.*

	Quan. Minted	G-4	VG-8	F-12	VF-20	EF-40	MS-60	Proof-63
1883 without CENTS								
(5,219)	5,479,519	$2.50	$3.00	$4.00	$6.00	$8.00	$47.50	$750.00

Variety 2 — With CENTS 1883-1913

Location of mint mark.

	Quan. Minted	G-4	VG-8	F-12	VF-20	EF-40	MS-60	Proof-63
1883 with CENTS								
(6,783)	16,032,983	5.50	8.00	12.00	20.00	30.00	185.00	625.00
1884 (3,942)	11,273,942	6.75	9.50	15.00	24.00	35.00	225.00	625.00
1885 (3,790)	1,476,490	250.00	275.00	400.00	550.00	700.00	1,200	1,600
1886 (4,290)	3,330,290	50.00	60.00	100.00	140.00	225.00	500.00	1,000
1887 (2,960)	15,263,652	4.50	6.00	15.00	20.00	30.00	175.00	575.00
1888 (4,582)	10,720,483	6.00	9.00	17.00	25.00	37.50	200.00	575.00
1889 (3,336)	15,881,361	4.00	5.00	14.00	20.00	30.00	175.00	575.00

NICKEL FIVE-CENT PIECES

	Quan. Minted	G-4	VG-8	F-12	VF-20	EF-40	MS-60	Proof-63
1890 (2,740)	16,259,272	$4.00	$5.00	$14.00	$20.00	$30.00	$200.00	$575.00
1891 (2,350)	16,834,350	3.50	5.00	14.00	20.00	30.00	175.00	575.00
1892 (2,745)	11,699,642	3.50	5.00	14.00	20.00	30.00	200.00	575.00
1893 (2,195)	13,370,195	3.50	5.00	14.00	20.00	30.00	175.00	575.00
1894 (2,632)	5,413,132	5.50	8.00	17.00	25.00	40.00	200.00	575.00
1895 (2,062)	9,979,884	3.00	4.50	14.00	17.50	25.00	160.00	575.00
1896 (1,862)	8,842,920	3.50	5.00	15.00	20.00	30.00	160.00	575.00
1897 (1,938)	20,428,735	1.00	2.00	5.00	7.50	20.00	140.00	575.00
1898 (1,795)	12,532,087	1.00	2.00	5.00	7.50	20.00	140.00	575.00
1899 (2,031)	26,029,031	1.00	2.00	5.00	7.50	20.00	140.00	575.00
1900 (2,262)	27,255,995	.60	1.00	2.50	6.00	18.00	125.00	550.00
1901 (1,985)	26,480,213	.60	1.00	2.50	6.00	18.00	125.00	550.00
1902 (2,018)	31,489,579	.60	1.00	2.50	6.00	18.00	125.00	550.00
1903 (1,790)	28,006,725	.60	1.00	2.50	6.00	18.00	125.00	550.00
1904 (1,817)	21,404,984	.60	1.00	2.50	6.00	18.00	125.00	550.00
1905 (2,152)	29,827,276	.60	1.00	2.50	6.00	18.00	125.00	550.00
1906 (1,725)	38,613,725	.60	1.00	2.50	6.00	18.00	125.00	550.00
1907 (1,475)	39,214,800	.60	1.00	2.50	6.00	18.00	125.00	550.00
1908 (1,620)	22,686,177	.60	1.00	2.50	6.00	18.00	125.00	550.00
1909 (4,763)	11,590,526	.75	1.25	2.75	7.00	19.00	130.00	550.00
1910 (2,405)	30,169,353	.60	1.00	2.50	6.00	18.00	125.00	550.00
1911 (1,733)	39,559,372	.60	1.00	2.50	6.00	18.00	125.00	550.00
1912 (2,145)	26,236,714	.60	1.00	2.50	6.00	18.00	125.00	550.00
1912D.........	8,474,000	1.00	1.50	4.00	10.00	45.00	300.00	
1912S..........	238,000	45.00	55.00	75.00	175.00	375.00	675.00	
1913 Liberty Head (5 known)							1985 Buss Sale $385,000	

INDIAN HEAD or BUFFALO TYPE 1913-1938

These pieces are known as Buffalo, Bison or Indian Head nickels. In the first year of issue, 1913, there were two distinct varieties, the first showing the bison on a mound, and the second with the base redesigned to a thinner, straight line.

James E. Fraser designed this nickel employing three different Indians as models. His initial F is beneath the date. The bison was modeled after "Black Diamond" in the New York Zoological Gardens.

Matte proof coins were made for collectors from 1913 to 1917.

Designer James Earle Fraser; weight 5 grams; composition: .750 copper, .250 nickel; diameter 21.2 mm; plain edge; mints: Philadelphia, Denver, San Francisco.

G-4 GOOD—Legends and date readable. Horn worn off.
VG-8 VERY GOOD—Half horn shows.
F-12 FINE—Three-quarters of horn shows. Obv. rim intact.
VF-20 VERY FINE—Full horn shows. Indian's cheekbone worn.
EF-40 EXTREMELY FINE—Full horn. Slight wear on Indian's hair ribbon.
MS-63 SELECT UNCIRCULATED—No trace of wear. Light blemishes. Attractive mint luster.

Variety 1 — FIVE CENTS on Raised Ground

NICKEL FIVE-CENT PIECES

	Quan. Minted	G-4	VG-8	F-12	VF-20	EF-40	MS-63	Matte Proof-63
1913 Var. 1								
(1,250)	30,993,520	$3.00	$3.50	$4.25	$6.75	$12.00	$75.00	$2,300
1913D Var. 1 ...	5,337,000	6.00	7.00	8.50	12.50	22.50	125.00	
1913S Var. 1 ...	2,105,000	9.00	11.00	16.00	24.00	40.00	200.00	

Variety 2 — FIVE CENTS in Recess

Mint mark below
FIVE CENTS

1916 Doubled Die Obverse

1918D, 8 over 7

	Quan. Minted	G-4	VG-8	F-12	VF-20	EF-40	MS-63	Matte Proof-63
1913 Var. 2								
(1,514)	29,858,700	3.00	3.50	4.25	6.75	13.00	80.00	1,500
1913D Var. 2 ...	4,156,000	40.00	45.00	55.00	70.00	100.00	325.00	
1913S Var. 2 ...	1,209,000	70.00	85.00	125.00	150.00	200.00	550.00	
1914 .. (1,275)	20,665,738	3.75	4.50	5.75	7.25	15.00	130.00	1,500
1914D.........	3,912,000	27.50	32.50	42.50	60.00	100.00	425.00	
1914S.........	3,470,000	4.50	6.00	9.00	16.00	37.50	250.00	
1915 .. (1,050)	20,987,270	1.75	2.50	3.75	6.50	12.50	125.00	1,600
1915D.........	7,569,000	6.00	7.50	13.00	35.00	55.00	275.00	
1915S.........	1,505,000	10.00	12.00	20.00	55.00	100.00	600.00	
1916 .... (600)	63,498,066	.75	1.00	1.75	2.50	5.00	90.00	2,500
1916 Doubled die obv.....		500.00	750.00	1,000	1,400	2,200	———	
1916D.........	13,333,000	4.50	5.50	8.00	25.00	45.00	275.00	
1916S.........	11,860,000	3.00	4.00	6.00	17.50	42.50	260.00	
1917	51,424,019	.85	1.25	1.90	3.00	8.00	110.00	———
1917D.........	9,910,000	4.50	6.00	11.00	37.50	85.00	365.00	
1917S.........	4,193,000	3.50	5.50	10.00	35.00	70.00	390.00	
1918	32,086,314	.85	1.35	2.50	5.50	15.00	180.00	
1918D, 8 over 7 ⎫	8,362,000	415.00	525.00	725.00	1,100	2,500	15,000	
1918D......... ⎭		4.50	6.00	12.00	60.00	85.00	550.00	
1918S.........	4,882,000	3.50	5.00	9.50	37.50	75.00	475.00	
1919	60,868,000	.65	.85	1.50	3.00	7.50	85.00	
1919D†........	8,006,000	4.00	6.00	11.50	70.00	100.00	650.00	
1919S†........	7,521,000	2.50	4.50	9.00	45.00	80.00	525.00	
1920	63,093,000	.65	.85	1.50	3.00	7.50	90.00	
1920D†........	9,418,000	3.00	4.50	8.75	55.00	100.00	700.00	
1920S.........	9,689,000	1.75	2.75	6.25	26.00	75.00	500.00	
1921	10,663,000	.85	1.25	3.00	6.75	17.00	190.00	
1921S†........	1,557,000	12.00	17.00	38.00	125.00	300.00	1,000	
1923	35,715,000	.45	.65	1.25	2.75	7.00	90.00	
1923S†........	6,142,000	1.50	2.50	5.50	22.50	60.00	400.00	
1924	21,620,000	.45	.65	1.25	3.50	8.00	135.00	
1924D.........	5,258,000	2.25	3.00	8.00	45.00	85.00	450.00	
1924S.........	1,437,000	4.50	6.50	14.50	125.00	275.00	1,450	
1925	35,565,100	.45	.65	1.25	2.75	7.00	90.00	
1925D†........	4,450,000	3.50	5.50	11.00	55.00	90.00	550.00	
1925S.........	6,256,000	2.25	3.50	6.75	20.00	55.00	450.00	
1926	44,693,000	.40	.60	.95	1.50	5.00	80.00	
1926D†........	5,638,000	2.00	3.75	9.00	45.00	90.00	425.00	

†Uncirculated pieces with full sharp details are worth considerably more.

NICKEL FIVE-CENT PIECES

	Quan. Minted	G-4	VG-8	F-12	VF-20	EF-40	MS-63	Proof-65
1926S	970,000	$5.50	$8.50	$14.00	$60.00	$240.00	$1,300	
1927	37,981,000	.40	.60	.95	1.50	5.00	75.00	
1927D	5,730,000	1.00	1.75	3.00	10.00	35.00	250.00	
1927S	3,430,000	1.00	1.75	3.00	13.00	60.00	325.00	
1928	23,411,000	.40	.60	.95	1.50	4.50	75.00	
1928D	6,436,000	.75	1.00	2.25	4.50	11.00	110.00	
1928S	6,936,000	.75	1.00	1.50	3.00	10.00	175.00	
1929	36,446,000	.40	.50	.85	1.50	4.00	65.00	
1929D	8,370,000	.60	.80	1.40	3.50	10.00	125.00	
1929S	7,754,000	.55	.75	1.00	2.25	7.00	90.00	
1930	22,849,000	.40	.50	.85	1.50	4.00	65.00	
1930S	5,435,000	.50	.75	1.00	2.00	6.75	125.00	
1931S	1,200,000	3.50	4.50	5.50	6.50	10.00	125.00	
1934	20,213,003	.30	.45	.60	1.50	3.50	60.00	
1934D	7,480,000	.45	.60	.85	1.50	5.00	115.00	
1935	58,264,000	.30	.35	.45	.75	2.00	35.00	
1935D	12,092,000	.35	.45	.60	1.75	3.50	110.00	
1935S	10,300,000	.35	.40	.50	1.00	2.50	50.00	
1936 . (4,420)	119,001,420	.30	.35	.40	.75	1.50	25.00	$3,200
1936D	24,814,000	.30	.40	.50	1.00	2.00	35.00	
1936S	14,930,000	.30	.40	.50	1.00	1.90	37.50	
1937 . (5,769)	79,485,769	.30	.35	.45	.75	1.50	23.00	3,000

1937D "3-Legged" Variety

1938 D over S

	Quan. Minted	G-4	VG-8	F-12	VF-20	EF-40	MS-63
1937D All Kinds	17,826,000	.30	.40	.55	1.00	1.75	25.00
1937D 3-Legged		90.00	110.00	135.00	175.00	250.00	1,250
1937S	5,635,000	.40	.45	.55	1.00	1.75	25.00
1938D	7,020,00	.40	.45	.55	1.00	1.75	23.00
1938D, D over S‡				5.00	7.50	10.00	40.00

‡Varieties exist.

JEFFERSON TYPE 1938 to Date

This nickel was designed by Felix Schlag. He won an award of $1,000 in a competition with some 390 artists. It established the definite public approval of portrait and pictorial rather than symbolic devices on our coinage.

Designer Felix Schlag; weight 5 grams; composition: 1938-1942, 1946- , .750 copper, .250 nickel; 1942-1945, .560 copper, .350 silver, .090 manganese; diameter 21.2 mm; plain edge; mints: Philadelphia, Denver, San Francisco. Net weight 1942-1945: .05626 oz. pure silver.

VG-8 VERY GOOD—*Second porch pillar from right nearly gone, other three still visible but weak.*

F-12 FINE—*Cheekbone worn flat. Hairlines and eyebrow faint. Second pillar weak, especially at bottom.*

VF-20 VERY FINE—*Second pillar plain and complete on both sides.*

EF-40 EXTREMELY FINE—*Cheekbone, hairlines, eyebrow slightly worn but well defined. Base of triangle above pillars visible but weak.*

MS-65 CHOICE UNCIRCULATED—*No trace of wear. Barely noticeable blemishes.*

NICKEL FIVE-CENT PIECES

Uncirculated pieces with fully struck steps are valued higher.

	Quan. Minted	VG-8	F-12	VF-20	EF-40	MS-65	Proof-65
1938 .... (19,365)	19,515,365	$ .15	$ .25	$ .40	$ .55	$3.00	$120.00
1938D	5,376,000	1.10	1.45	1.65	2.25	8.00	
1938S	4,105,000	2.00	2.25	3.00	3.50	10.00	
1939 .... (12,535)	120,627,535	.15	.25	.35	.50	1.75	140.00
1939 Doubled MONTICELLO and FIVE CENTS		7.50	10.00	25.00	50.00	——	
1939D	3,514,000	4.00	4.50	5.50	9.00	55.00	
1939S	6,630,000	.70	.90	1.25	2.30	40.00	
1940 .... (14,158)	176,499,158			.20	.35	1.50	100.00
1940D	43,540,000			.25	.40	3.50	
1940S	39,690,000			.30	.60	3.50	
1941 .... (18,720)	203,283,720			.15	.30	1.25	85.00
1941D	53,432,000			.20	.35	4.25	
1941S†	43,445,000			.25	.45	5.75	
1942 .... (29,600)	49,818,600			.25	.40	2.00	85.00
1942D		.40	.75	1.00	2.00	35.00	
1942D over horiz. D }	13,938,000					35.00	

†Large and small mint mark varieties, see pages 59-60.

Wartime Alloy Variety 1942-1945

On October 8, 1942, the wartime five-cent piece composed of copper (56%), silver (35%) and manganese (9%) was introduced to eliminate nickel, a critical war material. A larger mint mark was placed above the dome. Letter P (Philadelphia) was used for the first time, indicating the change of alloy.

Location of mint mark

1943, 3 over 2

		VG-8	F-12	VF-20	EF-40	Proof-65
1942P .... (27,600)	57,900,600	.50	.80	1.25	17.00	350.00
1942S	32,900,000	.50	.85	1.50	16.00	
1943P, 3 over 2 ..... }	271,165,000	65.00	100.00	200.00	850.00	
1943P		.50	.80	1.00	5.50	
1943D	15,294,000	.50	.80	1.00	8.00	
1943S	104,060,000	.50	.80	1.10	6.50	
1944P*	119,150,000	.50	.80	1.00	6.50	
1944D	32,309,000	.50	.80	1.25	12.00	
1944S	21,640,000	.50	.80	1.25	11.00	
1945P	119,408,100	.50	.80	1.00	7.50	
1945D	37,158,000	.50	.80	1.15	7.50	
1945S	58,939,000	.50	.80	1.10	5.50	

*1944 nickels without mint marks are counterfeits. Genuine pieces of other dates struck in nickel by error are known to exist.

Prewar composition and mint mark style resumed 1946-1964

	Quan. Minted	VF-20	EF-40	MS-65	Proof-65
1946	161,116,000		$.20	$.85	
1946D	45,292,200	$.20	.30	.90	
1946S	13,560,000	.25	.35	1.00	
1947	95,000,000		.20	.50	
1947D	37,822,000		.25	1.00	
1947S	24,720,000	.25	.35	.80	

NICKEL FIVE-CENT PIECES

	Quan. Minted	VF-20	EF-40	MS-65	Proof-65
1948	89,348,000		$ .20	$ .70	
1948D	44,734,000	$ .25	.40	1.25	
1948S	11,300,000	.35	.40	1.25	
1949	60,652,000	.15	.25	1.35	
1949D	} 36,498,000		.30	1.25	
1949D, D over S		35.00	65.00	400.00	
1949S	9,716,000	.40	.75	2.25	
1950 (51,386)	9,847,386	.40	.70	2.00	$70.00
1950D	2,630,030	8.00	9.00	12.00	
1951 (57,500)	28,609,500	.20	.30	1.25	60.00
1951D	20,460,000	.20	.30	1.25	
1951S	7,776,000	.50	.90	3.00	
1952 (81,980)	64,069,980		.20	.80	40.00
1952D	30,638,000	.30	.65	2.00	
1952S	20,572,000	.20	.30	.75	
1953 (128,800)	46,772,800		.20	.30	25.00
1953D	59,878,600		.20	.30	
1953S	19,210,900	.20	.30	.50	

**1954S,
S over D**

**1955D
D over S***

	Quan. Minted	VF-20	EF-40	MS-65	Proof-65
1954 (233,300)	47,917,350		.15	.30	12.00
1954D	117,183,060		.15	.30	
1954S	} 29,384,000	.15	.20	.30	
1954S, S over D		5.00	12.00	40.00	
1955 (378,200)	8,266,200	.50	.60	1.00	10.00
1955D	} 74,464,100		.15	.25	
1955D, D over S*		6.00	15.00	70.00	
1956 (669,384)	35,885,384		.15	.25	2.50
1956D	67,222,940		.15	.25	
1957 (1,247,952)	39,655,952		.15	.25	2.00
1957D	136,828,900		.15	.20	
1958 (875,652)	17,963,652		.20	.35	2.50
1958D	168,249,120		.15	.20	
1959 (1,149,291)	28,397,291		.15	.30	1.25
1959D	160,738,240			.15	
1960 (1,691,602)	57,107,602			.15	1.00
1960D	192,582,180			.15	
1961 (3,028,144)	76,668,244			.15	1.00
1961D	229,342,760			.15	
1962 (3,218,019)	100,602,019			.15	1.00
1962D	280,195,720			.15	
1963 (3,075,645)	178,851,645			.15	1.00
1963D	276,829,460			.15	
1964 (3,950,762)	1,028,622,762			.15	1.00
1964D	1,787,297,160			.15	
1965	136,131,380			.15	

*Varieties exist. Value is for that illustrated.

NICKEL FIVE-CENT PIECES

The designer's initials FS were added below the bust starting in 1966, and dies were further remodeled to strengthen the design in 1971, 1972, 1977 and 1982. Mint mark position was moved to the obverse starting in 1968.

Quan. Minted	MS-65	Proof-65	Quan. Minted	MS-65	Proof-65
1966 156,208,283	$ .15	——†	1977D 297,313,422	$ .20	
1967 107,325,800	.15		1977S Proof (3,251,152)		$1.50
1968D 91,227,880	.15		1978 391,308,000	.10	
1968S (3,041,506)			1978D 313,092,780	.10	
..... 103,437,510	.15	$ .75	1978S Proof (3,127,781)		1.50
1969D 202,807,500	.15		1979 463,188,000	.10	
1969S (2,934,631)			1979D 325,867,672	.10	
..... 123,009,631	.15	.75	1979S Proof (3,677,175)		
1970D 515,485,380	.15		Filled S		1.50
1970S (2,632,810)			Clear S		3.00
..... 241,464,814	.15	.75	1980P..... 593,004,000	.10	
1971 106,884,000	.40		1980D 502,323,448	.10	
1971D 316,144,800	.15		1980S Proof (3,554,806)		1.25
1971S Proof*			1981P..... 657,504,000	.10	
...... (3,220,733)		1.75	1981D 364,801,843	.10	
1972 202,036,000	.10		1981S Proof (4,063,083)		1.00
1972D 351,694,600	.10		1982P..... 292,355,000	.10	
1972S Proof (3,260,996)		1.75	1982D 373,726,544	.10	
1973 384,396,000	.10		1982S Proof (3,857,479)		2.00
1973D 261,405,000	.10		1983P..... 561,615,000	.10	
1973S Proof (2,760,339)		1.75	1983D 536,726,276	.10	
1974 601,752,000	.10		1983S Proof (3,228,648)		1.50
1974D 277,373,000	.20		1984P..... 746,769,000	.10	
1974S Proof (2,612,568)		2.00	1984D 517,675,146	.10	
1975 181,772,000	.20		1984S Proof..........		1.50
1975D 401,875,300	.20		1985P..... 647,114,962	.10	
1975S Proof (2,845,450)		2.00	1985D 459,747,446	.10	
1976 367,124,000	.10		1985S Proof..........		1.50
1976D 563,964,147	.10		1986P.....	.10	
1976S Proof (4,149,730)		1.50	1986D	.10	
1977 585,376,000	.10		1986S Proof..........		1.50

*1971 proof nickels without mint mark were made in error. See pages 59-60.
†Two presentation pieces were struck in proof.

HALF DIMES 1794-1873

The half dime types present the same general characteristics as larger United States silver coins. Authorized by the Act of April 2, 1792, they were not coined until February, 1795, although dated 1794. At first the weight was 20.8 grains, and fineness 892.4. By the Act of January 18, 1837, the weight was slightly reduced to 20 5/8 grains and the fineness changed to .900. Finally the weight was reduced to 19.2 grains by the Act of February 21, 1853. Both half dimes and dimes offer many varieties in the early dates.

TYPE COIN VALUES

	G-4	F-12	EF-40	AU-50	MS-60	MS-63	MS-65	PF-60	PF-63	PF-6
Flowing Hair 1794-1795	700.00	1,200	2,700	4,000	7,500	12,000	30,000			
Drpd Bust, SE 1796-1797	700.00	1,200	2,700	4,000	7,500	15,000	36,000			
Drpd Bust, HE 1800-1805	600.00	1,000	2,500	3,200	7,500	13,000	30,000			
Cap Bust 1829-1837	13.00	25.00	115.00	250.00	650.00	1,200	5,500			
Lib Seated-NS 1837-1838	27.50	50.00	235.00	350.00	800.00	1,200	5,500			
Lib. Seat-Stars 1838-1859	5.00	9.00	40.00	115.00	325.00	800.00	4,000	1,000	2,200	6,0
Lib. Seat-Arr. 1853-1855	5.00	9.00	45.00	125.00	350.00	850.00	4,200	3,000	4,500	8,0
Lib. Seat-Leg. 1860-1873	5.00	8.00	30.00	70.00	275.00	700.00	3,000	375.00	900.00	4,0

FLOWING HAIR TYPE 1794-1795

Designer Robert Scot; weight 1.35 grams; composition: .8924 silver, .1076 copper; approx. diameter 16.5 mm; reeded edge. All coined at Philadelphia Mint.

AG-3 ABOUT GOOD—*Details clear enough to identify.*

G-4 GOOD—*Eagle, wreath, bust outlined but lack details.*

VG-8 VERY GOOD—*Some details remain on face. All lettering readable.*

F-12 FINE—*Hair ends show. Hair at top smooth.*

VF-20 VERY FINE—*Hairlines at top show. Hair about ear defined.*

EF-40 EXTREMELY FINE—*Hair above forehead and at neck well defined but shows some wear.*

MS-60 UNCIRCULATED—*No trace of wear. Light blemishes.*

	Quan. Minted	AG-3	G-4	VG-8	F-12	VF-20	EF-40	MS-60
1794 ...	} 86,416	$350.00	$750.00	$900.00	$1,500	$2,250	$3,250	$9,000
1795 ...		325.00	700.00	800.00	1,200	1,800	2,700	7,500

DRAPED BUST TYPE, SMALL EAGLE REVERSE 1796-1797

AG-3 ABOUT GOOD—*Details clear enough to identify.*

G-4 GOOD—*Date, stars, LIBERTY readable. Bust outlined but no details.*

VG-8 VERY GOOD—*Some details show.*

F-12 FINE—*Hair and drapery lines worn, but visible.*

VF-20 VERY FINE—*Only left of drapery indistinct.*

EF-40 EXTREMELY FINE—*All hairlines show details.*

MS-60 UNCIRCULATED—*No trace of wear. Light blemishes.*

	Quan. Minted	AG-3	G-4	VG-8	F-12	VF-20	EF-40	MS-60
1796, 6 over 5		$450.00	$750.00	$1,100	$1,400	$2,250	$3,500	$9,000
1796 Nor. dt.	} 10,230	425.00	725.00	1,000	1,300	2,100	3,250	8,500
1796 LIKERTY		425.00	725.00	1,000	1,300	2,100	3,500	10,000
1797, 15 Stars		325.00	700.00	800.00	1,200	1,800	2,700	7,500
1797, 16 stars	} 44,527	325.00	700.00	800.00	1,200	1,800	2,700	7,500
1797, 13 stars		325.00	700.00	800.00	1,200	1,800	3,000	9,000

HALF DIMES
DRAPED BUST TYPE, HERALDIC EAGLE REVERSE 1800-1805

1800 LIBEKTY

	Quan. Minted	AG-3	G-4	VG-8	F-12	VF-20	EF-40	MS-60
1800	24,000	$180.00	$600.00	$700.00	$1,000	$1,500	$2,500	$7,000
1800 LIBEKTY	16,000	180.00	600.00	700.00	1,000	1,500	2,500	7,500
1801	27,760	180.00	600.00	700.00	1,000	1,600	2,600	8,000
1802	3,060	2,000	3,750	4,500	9,000	15,000	40,000	——
1803 Large 8	} 37,850	180.00	600.00	700.00	1,000	1,500	2,500	7,000
1803 Small 8		180.00	600.00	700.00	1,000	1,600	2,600	8,000
1805	15,600	200.00	625.00	750.00	1,100	1,800	3,250	——

CAPPED BUST TYPE 1829-1837

Designer William Kneass; weight 1.35 grams; composition: .8924 silver, .1076 copper; approx. diameter 15.5 mm; reeded edge. All coined at Philadelphia Mint.

G-4 GOOD—*Bust outlined, no detail. Date and legend readable.*
VG-8 VERY GOOD—*Complete legend and date plain. At least 3 letters of LIBERTY show clearly.*
F-12 FINE—*All letters in LIBERTY show.*
VF-20 VERY FINE—*Full rims. Ear and shoulder clasp show plainly.*
EF-40 EXTREMELY FINE—*Ear very distinct, eyebrow and hair well defined.*
MS-60 UNCIRCULATED—*No trace of wear. Light blemishes.*

	Quan. Minted	G-4	VG-8	F-12	VF-20	EF-40	MS-60
1829	1,230,000	$13.00	$18.00	$25.00	$45.00	$115.00	$675.00
1830	1,240,000	13.00	18.00	25.00	45.00	115.00	650.00
1831	1,242,700	13.00	18.00	25.00	45.00	115.00	650.00
1832	965,000	13.00	18.00	25.00	45.00	115.00	650.00
1833	1,370,000	13.00	18.00	25.00	45.00	115.00	650.00
1834	1,480,000	13.00	18.00	25.00	45.00	115.00	650.00
1835 All kinds	2,760,000						
1835 Lg. date and 5c		13.00	18.00	25.00	45.00	115.00	650.00
1835 Lg. date, sm. 5c		13.00	18.00	25.00	45.00	115.00	650.00
1835 Sm. date, lg. 5c		13.00	18.00	25.00	45.00	115.00	650.00
1835 Sm. date and 5c		13.00	18.00	25.00	45.00	115.00	650.00
1836 Small 5c	} 1,900,000	13.00	18.00	25.00	45.00	115.00	650.00
1836 Large 5c		13.00	18.00	25.00	45.00	115.00	650.00
1837 Small 5c	} 871,000	18.00	25.00	35.00	75.00	150.00	1,275
1837 Large 5c		13.00	18.00	25.00	45.00	115.00	650.00

LIBERTY SEATED TYPE 1837-1873
Variety 1 — No Stars on Obverse 1837-1838

Designer Christian Gobrecht; weight 1.34 grams; composition: .900 silver, .100 copper; diameter 15.5 mm; reeded edge; mints: Philadelphia, New Orleans.

G-4 GOOD—*LIBERTY on shield smooth. Date and letters readable.*
VG-8 VERY GOOD—*At least 3 letters in LIBERTY are visible.*
F-12 FINE—*Entire LIBERTY visible, weak spots.*
VF-20 VERY FINE—*Entire LIBERTY strong and even.*
EF-40 EXTREMELY FINE—*LIBERTY and scroll edges distinct.*
MS-60 UNCIRCULATED—*No trace of wear. Light blemishes.*

1837 Sm. date	} 1,405,000	30.00	40.00	60.00	100.00	250.00	900.00
1837 Lg. date		27.50	35.00	50.00	90.00	235.00	800.00
1838O No stars	70,000	60.00	85.00	150.00	300.00	750.00	4,000

HALF DIMES

No Drapery from Elbow 1837-1840

Drapery from Elbow Starting 1840

From 1838 through 1859 mint mark is located above bow on reverse. Large, medium or small mint mark varieties occur for several dates.

Variety 2 — Stars on Obverse 1838-1853

	Quan. Minted	G-4	VG-8	F-12	VF-20	EF-40	MS-60
1838 No drpy...	} 2,225,000	$7.00	$8.25	$12.50	$27.50	$55.00	$525.00
1838 Small stars		8.00	10.00	15.00	35.00	75.00	900.00
1839 No drpy....	1,069,150	7.00	8.25	12.50	27.50	55.00	550.00
1839O No drpy ...	1,034,039	9.00	12.50	17.50	30.00	60.00	600.00
1840 No drapery..	1,034,000	7.00	8.25	12.50	27.50	55.00	500.00
1840O No drapery .	695,000	8.00	11.00	17.50	40.00	80.00	625.00
1840 Drapery......	310,085	10.00	20.00	40.00	70.00	150.00	700.00
1840O Drapery	240,000	25.00	40.00	75.00	150.00	300.00	——
1841	1,150,000	5.00	6.00	9.00	17.50	40.00	325.00
1841O.............	815,000	10.00	13.00	20.00	35.00	80.00	650.00
1842	815,000	5.00	6.00	9.00	17.50	40.00	325.00
1842O.............	350,000	20.00	30.00	50.00	100.00	200.00	——
1843	1,165,000	5.00	6.00	9.00	17.50	40.00	325.00
1844	430,000	5.00	6.00	9.00	17.50	40.00	325.00
1844O.............	220,000	55.00	85.00	140.00	325.00	800.00	——
1845	1,564,000	5.00	6.00	9.00	17.50	40.00	325.00
1846	27,000	125.00	175.00	250.00	475.00	900.00	——
1847	1,274,000	5.00	6.00	9.00	17.50	40.00	325.00
1848 Med. date	} 668,000	5.00	6.00	9.00	17.50	40.00	325.00
1848 Lg. date		5.50	7.00	10.00	19.00	50.00	450.00
1848O.............	600,000	12.00	20.00	27.50	60.00	100.00	500.00
1849, 9 over 6 .		8.00	12.00	20.00	30.00	75.00	500.00
1849, 9 over 8	} 1,309,000	9.00	14.00	22.00	35.00	80.00	525.00
1849 Nor. date..		5.00	6.00	9.00	17.50	40.00	325.00
1849O.............	140,000	30.00	45.00	85.00	225.00	450.00	——
1850	955,000	5.00	6.00	9.00	17.50	40.00	325.00
1850O.............	690,000	12.00	20.00	27.50	60.00	110.00	750.00
1851	781,000	5.00	6.00	9.00	17.50	40.00	325.00
1851O.............	860,000	12.00	17.00	25.00	40.00	80.00	650.00
1852	1,000,500	5.00	6.00	9.00	17.50	40.00	325.00
1852O.............	260,000	26.00	35.00	65.00	125.00	250.00	——
1853 No arrows....	135,000	24.00	32.50	60.00	100.00	175.00	650.00
1853O No arrows ..	160,000	125.00	175.00	250.00	400.00	750.00	——

Variety 3 — Arrows at Date 1853-1855

Weight 1.24 grams; composition: .900 silver, .100 copper; diameter 15.5 mm; reeded edge; mints: Philadelphia, New Orleans, San Francisco.

As on the dimes, quarters and halves, arrows were placed at the sides of the date for a short period starting in 1853. They were placed there to denote the reduction of weight under the terms of the Act of February 21, 1853.

	Quan. Minted	G-4	VG-8	F-12	VF-20	EF-40	MS-60	Proof-63
1853	13,210,020	$5.00	$6.00	$9.00	$17.50	$45.00	$350.00	
1853O........	2,200,000	7.00	10.00	14.00	25.00	75.00	425.00	
1854	5,740,000	5.00	6.00	9.00	17.50	45.00	350.00	
1854O........	1,560,000	6.50	8.50	11.00	23.00	50.00	650.00	

HALF DIMES

	Quan. Minted	G-4	VG-8	F-12	VF-20	EF-40	MS-60	Proof-63
1855	1,750,000	$5.00	$6.00	$9.00	$17.50	$45.00	$350.00	$4,500
1855O	600,000	12.00	15.00	25.00	40.00	100.00	750.00	

Variety 2 Resumed 1856-1859

1858 over Inverted Date

1856	4,880,000	5.00	6.00	9.00	17.50	40.00	325.00	2,750
1856O	1,100,000	6.50	8.50	11.00	22.00	45.00	600.00	
1857	7,280,000	5.00	6.00	9.00	17.50	40.00	325.00	2,500
1857O	1,380,000	6.50	8.50	11.00	22.00	45.00	600.00	
1858		5.00	6.00	9.00	17.50	40.00	325.00	2,200
1858 over inverted date }	3,500,000	30.00	35.00	67.50	110.00	200.00	700.00	
1858O	1,660,000	6.50	8.50	11.00	22.00	45.00	550.00	
1859O	560,000	10.00	17.50	25.00	40.00	75.00	600.00	
1859	340,000	10.00	17.50	25.00	40.00	75.00	400.00	2,200

New die 1859 Philadelphia Mint. Stars hollow in center. Arms slimmer.

In the years 1859 and 1860 interesting half dime patterns were made which do not bear our nation's identity. These are transitional pieces, not made for circulation, but struck at the time the inscription UNITED STATES OF AMERICA was being transferred from the reverse to the obverse.

1859 Obv. of 59, rev. of 60		10,000
1860 Obv. of 59, rev. of 60 (With stars) 100	2,750	

Variety 4 — Legend on Obverse 1860-1873

Mint Mark below bow 1860-1869, 1872-1873.

Mint Mark above bow 1870-1872.

1860 Legend (1,000)	799,000	5.00	6.00	8.00	14.00	30.00	300.00	1,000
1860O	1,060,000	5.00	6.00	9.00	15.00	32.50	375.00	
1861 . (1,000)	3,361,000	5.00	6.00	8.00	12.00	30.00	275.00	900.00
1861, 1 over 0		—	—	—	—	—	—	
1862 ... (550)	1,492,550	5.00	6.00	8.00	12.00	30.00	275.00	900.00
1863 ... (460)	18,460	60.00	80.00	125.00	160.00	275.00	600.00	1,000
1863S	100,000	12.50	17.50	25.00	50.00	110.00	675.00	
1864 ... (470)	48,470	175.00	250.00	325.00	400.00	600.00	1,500	1,700
1864S	90,000	22.50	30.00	65.00	100.00	200.00	825.00	
1865 ... (500)	13,500	125.00	150.00	200.00	250.00	325.00	650.00	1,000
1865S	120,000	12.50	17.50	25.00	50.00	110.00	675.00	
1866 ... (725)	10,725	125.00	150.00	225.00	300.00	425.00	700.00	1,000
1866S	120,000	12.50	17.50	25.00	50.00	110.00	650.00	

HALF DIMES

	Quan. Minted	G-4	VG-8	F-12	VF-20	EF-40	MS-60	Proof-63
1867 . . . (625)	8,625	$150.00	$200.00	$275.00	$350.00	$500.00	$800.00	$1,000
1867S	120,000	12.50	17.50	25.00	50.00	110.00	650.00	
1868 . . . (600)	89,200	30.00	45.00	70.00	110.00	225.00	525.00	900.00
1868S	280,000	8.00	11.50	15.00	25.00	50.00	300.00	
1869 . . . (600)	208,600	6.00	8.00	12.00	17.50	35.00	275.00	900.00
1869S	230,000	8.00	11.50	15.00	25.00	50.00	325.00	
1870 . (1,000)	536,000	5.00	6.00	8.00	12.00	30.00	275.00	900.00
1870S	Unique			Auction sale 1985			176,000.	
1871 . . . (960)	1,873,960	5.00	6.00	8.00	12.00	30.00	275.00	900.00
1871S	161,000	10.00	15.00	30.00	50.00	90.00	425.00	
1872 . . . (950)	2,947,950	5.00	6.00	8.00	12.00	30.00	275.00	900.00
1872S All kinds. 837,000								
1872S mm. above bow. .		5.00	6.00	8.00	12.00	30.00	275.00	
1872S mm. below bow. .		5.00	6.00	8.00	12.00	30.00	275.00	
1873 (Closed 3 only)								
. . . . (600)	712,600	5.00	6.00	8.00	12.00	30.00	275.00	900.00
1873S (Closed 3 only)								
. . . . 324,000		5.00	6.00	8.00	12.00	30.00	275.00	

BIBLIOGRAPHY

Ahwash, Kamal M. *Encyclopedia of United States Liberty Seated Dimes 1837-1891.* Kamal Press, 1977.
Breen, Walter. *United States Half Dimes: A Supplement.* New York, 1958.
Davis, David. et al. *Early United States Dimes 1796-1837.* Ypsilanti, Michigan, 1984.
Kosoff, A. *United States Dimes from 1796.* New York, 1945.
Nagengast, Bernard. *The Jefferson Nickel Analyst.* Sidney, Ohio, 1979.
Newlin, H. P. *The Early Half-Dimes of the United States.* Philadelphia, 1883 (reprinted 1933).
Valentine, D. W. *The United States Half Dimes.* New York, 1931

DIMES — 1796 to Date

The designs of the dimes, first coined in 1796, follow closely those of the half dimes up through the Liberty seated type. The dimes in each instance weigh twice as much as the half dimes.

TYPE COIN VALUES										
	G-4	F-12	EF-40	AU-50	MS-60	MS-63	MS-65	PF-60	PF-63	PF-65
Drpd Bust, SE 1796-1797	850.00	1,500	3,250	4,250	9,000	15,000	35,000			
Drpd Bust, HE 1798-1807	500.00	1,000	1,900	2,500	5,000	9,000	22,000			
Cap Bust lg. 1809-1828	14.00	25.00	300.00	675.00	1,350	3,000	10,000			
Cap Bust sm. 1828-1837	12.00	20.00	200.00	375.00	775.00	2,400	8,000			
Lib Seated-NS 1837-1838	25.00	50.00	300.00	600.00	1,100	2,400	6,500			
Lib. Seat-Stars 1838-1860	4.00	7.50	30.00	90.00	325.00	900.00	4,700	1,000	2,220	7,200
Lib. Seat-Arr. 1853-1855	5.00	8.00	45.00	115.00	375.00	900.00	5,200	3,500	6,000	7,500
Lib. Seat-Leg. 1860-1891	4.00	6.50	22.50	55.00	235.00	550.00	3,000	350.00	850.00	4,000
Lib. Seat-Arr. 1873-1874	8.00	18.50	100.00	275.00	750.00	2,000	5,500	850.00	2,200	5,200
Barber 1892-1916	1.25	3.00	18.00	37.50	150.00	400.00	2,300	350.00	850.00	3,750
Mercury 1916-1945	1.00	1.00	3.00	4.00	6.00	12.00	25.00	175.00	250.00	650.00
Roosevelt 1946-1964	.70	.80	1.00	1.10	1.15	1.25	2.00	1.50	1.75	2.25

DRAPED BUST TYPE, SMALL EAGLE REVERSE 1796-1797

AG-3 ABOUT GOOD—*Details clear enough to identify.*

G-4 GOOD—*Date readable. Bust outlined, but no detail.*

VG-8 VERY GOOD—*All but deepest drapery folds worn smooth. Hairlines nearly gone and curls lack detail.*

F-12 FINE—*All drapery lines visible. Hair partly worn.*

VF-20 VERY FINE—*Only left side of drapery is indistinct.*

EF-40 EXTREMELY FINE—*Hair well outlined and shows details.*

MS-60 UNCIRCULATED—*No trace of wear. Light blemishes.*

Designer Robert Scot; weight 2.70 grams; composition: .8924 silver, .1076 copper; approx. diameter 19 mm; reeded edge. All coined at Philadelphia Mint.

DIMES

1797, 16 Stars   **1797, 13 Stars**

	Quan. Minted	AG-3	G-4	VG-8	F-12	VF-20	EF-40	MS-60
1796	22,135	$550.00	$950.00	$1,300	$1,800	$2,500	$3,500	$10,000
1797 16 stars ⎫		500.00	850.00	1,100	1,500	2,250	3,250	9,000
1797 13 stars ⎬	25,261	500.00	850.00	1,100	1,500	2,250	3,250	11,000

DRAPED BUST TYPE, HERALDIC EAGLE REVERSE 1798-1807

	AG-3	G-4	VG-8	F-12	VF-20	EF-40	MS-60
1798 All kinds 27,550							
1798 over 97, 16 stars on rev.	200.00	500.00	650.00	1,000	1,400	1,900	6,000
1798 over 97, 13 stars			1,200	1,700	3,200	——	
1798	200.00	500.00	650.00	1,000	1,400	1,900	6,000
1798 Small 8	250.00	625.00	800.00	1,400	2,000	2,500	
1800 21,760	200.00	500.00	650.00	1,000	1,400	1,900	5,750
1801 34,640	200.00	500.00	650.00	1,000	1,400	1,900	5,750
1802 10,975	200.00	500.00	650.00	1,000	1,400	1,900	5,750
1803 33,040	200.00	500.00	650.00	1,000	1,400	1,900	5,750
1804 All kinds . 8,265							
1804 13 stars on rev.	450.00	900.00	1,500	2,000	3,250	6,000	——
1804 14 stars on rev.	450.00	900.00	1,500	2,000	3,250	6,000	8,000
1805 4 ber. ⎫	200.00	500.00	650.00	1,000	1,400	1,900	5,000
1805 5 ber. ⎬ 120,780	200.00	500.00	650.00	1,000	1,500	3,000	8,000
1807 165,000	200.00	500.00	650.00	1,000	1,400	1,900	5,000

CAPPED BUST TYPE 1809-1837

AG-3 ABOUT GOOD—*Details clear enough to identify.*
G-4 GOOD—*Date, letters and stars discernible. Bust outlined, no details.*
VG-8 VERY GOOD—*Legends and date plain. Minimum of 3 letters in LIBERTY.*
F-12 FINE—*Full LIBERTY. Ear and shoulder clasp visible. Part of rim shows both sides.*
VF-20 VERY FINE—*LIBERTY distinct. Full rim. Ear and clasp plain and distinct.*
EF-40 EXTREMELY FINE—*LIBERTY sharp. Ear distinct. Hair above eye well defined.*
MS-60 UNCIRCULATED—*No trace of wear. Light blemishes.*

Designer John Reich; weight 2.70 grams; composition: .8924 silver, .1076 copper; approx. diameter 18.8 mm; reeded edge. All coined at Philadelphia Mint.

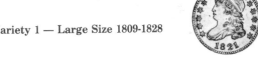

Variety 1 — Large Size 1809-1828

1809 51,065	35.00	70.00	100.00	150.00	250.00	400.00	3,750
1811 over 9. . . 65,180	25.00	50.00	75.00	90.00	150.00	325.00	3,500

DIMES

1814 Small Date

1814 Large Date

	Quan. Minted	G-4	VG-8	F-12	VF-20	EF-40	MS-60
1814 Sm. date . ⎫		$50.00	$75.00	$90.00	$175.00	$350.00	$3,500
1814 Lg. date ⎬	421,500	25.00	30.00	45.00	125.00	325.00	1,750
1814 STATESOFAMERICA		25.00	30.00	45.00	125.00	325.00	2,000
1820 STATESOFAMERICA		25.00	30.00	45.00	125.00	3 25.00	2,000

1820 Large 0

Small Date

Large Date

		G-4	VG-8	F-12	VF-20	EF-40	MS-60
1820 Lg. 0 . . . . . ⎫		14.00	18.00	25.00	90.00	300.00	1,350
1820 Sm. 0 . . . . ⎬	942,587	14.00	18.00	25.00	90.00	300.00	1,350
1821 Sm. date . ⎫		14.00	18.00	25.00	90.00	300.00	1,350
1821 Lg. date . . ⎬	1,186,512	14.00	18.00·	25.00	90.00	300.00	1,350
1822	100,000	70.00	120.00	200.00	350.00	750.00	3,500

1823, 3 over 2   **Small E's**   **Large E's**

		G-4	VG-8	F-12	VF-20	EF-40	MS-60
1823, 3 over 2, All kinds	440,000						
1823, 3 over 2, sm. E's		14.00	18.00	25.00	90.00	300.00	1,750
1823, 3 over 2, lg. E's		14.00	18.00	25.00	90.00	300.00	1,750

1824, 4 over 2   **Large Date**   **Small Date**

		G-4	VG-8	F-12	VF-20	EF-40	MS-60
1824, 4 over 2 . ⎫		25.00	30.00	45.00	125.00	325.00	1,750
1825 . . . . ⎬	510,000	14.00	18.00	25.00	90.00	300.00	1,350
1827	1,215,000	14.00	18.00	25.00	90.00	300.00	1,350
1827, 7 over 5 . . . . (rare)							
1828 Both vars	125,000						
1828 Lg. date, curl base 2 . .		30.00	40.00	70.00	150.00	350.00	1,750

Variety 2 — Reduced Size 1828-1837

New mint equipment was used to make the small date 1828 dimes and subsequent issues. Unlike earlier coinage, these have beaded borders and a uniform diameter. Large date has curl base knob 2; small date has square base knob 2.

1829 Small 10c

Large 10c

Curl Base 2

1830, 30 over 29

DIMES

	Quan. Minted	G-4	F-12	VF-20	EF-40	MS-60
1828 Small date, sq. base 2		$25.00	$50.00	$80.00	$225.00	$1,100
1829 Curl base 2.....		——	——			
1829 Small 10c		12.00	20.00	50.00	200.00	800.00
1829 Medium 10c....	770,000	12.00	20.00	50.00	200.00	775.00
1829 Large 10c		14.00	25.00	60.00	210.00	800.00
1830, 30 over 29		——	125.00	200.00	425.00	2,000
1830 Large 10c......	510,000	12.00	20.00	50.00	200.00	775.00
1830 Small 10c		12.00	20.00	50.00	200.00	775.00
1831	771,350	12.00	20.00	50.00	200.00	775.00
1832	522,500	12.00	20.00	50.00	200.00	775.00
1833		12.00	20.00	50.00	200.00	775.00
1833 Last 3 high.....	485,000	12.00	20.00	50.00	200.00	800.00
1834 Small 4		12.00	20.00	50.00	200.00	900.00
1834 Large 4	635,000	12.00	20.00	50.00	200.00	800.00
1835	1,410,000	12.00	20.00	50.00	200.00	775.00
1836	1,190,000	12.00	20.00	50.00	200.00	775.00
1837	359,500	12.00	20.00	50.00	200.00	775.00

LIBERTY SEATED TYPE 1837-1891

Variety 1 — No Stars on Obverse 1837-1838

Designer Christian Gobrecht; weight 2.67 grams; composition: .900 silver, .100 copper; diameter 17.9 mm; reeded edge; mints: Philadelphia, New Orleans.

G-4 GOOD—*LIBERTY* on shield smooth. Date and letters readable.
F-12 FINE—*Entire LIBERTY visible, weak spots.*
VF-20 VERY FINE—*Entire LIBERTY strong and even.*
EF-40 EXTREMELY FINE—*LIBERTY and scroll edges distinct.*
MS-60 UNCIRCULATED—*No trace of wear. Light blemishes.*

No Drapery from Elbow
No Stars on Obverse

Mint marks on Liberty seated dimes are placed on the reverse within, or below, the wreath. Size of mint mark varies on many dates.

1837 Large date		25.00	50.00	125.00	300.00	1,100
1837 Small date	682,500	25.00	50.00	135.00	325.00	1,200
1838O.................	406,034	40.00	100.00	225.00	450.00	2,800

Variety 2 — Stars on Obverse 1838-1853

No Drapery from Elbow
Tilted Shield

1838 Small Stars   **1838 Large Stars**

1838 Small stars		15.00	35.00	60.00	120.00	1,600
1838 Large stars......	1,992,500	8.00	12.50	20.00	50.00	500.00
1838 Partial drapery ..		15.00	32.50	55.00	110.00	1,400
1839	1,053,115	5.50	10.00	18.00	50.00	425.00
1839O................	1,323,000	6.50	14.00	27.50	65.00	500.00
1840	981,500	5.50	10.00	18.00	40.00	425.00
1840O................	1,175,000	7.00	15.00	30.00	65.00	1,200
1841 Proof, see page 114.						

DIMES

**Drapery from Elbow
Upright Shield**

	Quan. Minted	G-4	F-12	VF-20	EF-40	MS-60	Proof-63
1840	377,500	$25.00	$65.00	$120.00	$400.00	——	
1841	1,622,500	4.75	9.00	18.00	35.00	$350.00	——*
1841O	2,007,500	7.00	15.00	25.00	65.00	1,200	
1842	1,887,500	4.75	9.00	18.00	35.00	350.00	
1842O	2,020,000	4.75	10.00	20.00	75.00	——	
1843	1,370,000	4.75	9.00	18.00	35.00	350.00	
1843O	150,000	35.00	90.00	235.00	625.00	——	
1844	72,500	30.00	80.00	160.00	375.00	2,000	
1845	1,755,000	4.75	9.00	18.00	35.00	350.00	
1845O	230,000	15.00	40.00	150.00	600.00	——	
1846	31,300	75.00	125.00	300.00	700.00	——	
1847	245,000	10.00	30.00	55.00	150.00	1,000	
1848	451,500	8.00	20.00	40.00	90.00	400.00	
1849	839,000	4.75	9.00	18.00	35.00	375.00	
1849O	300,000	10.00	20.00	85.00	275.00	——	
1850	1,931,500	4.75	9.00	17.00	32.50	350.00	
1850O	510,000	8.00	15.00	60.00	175.00	1,000	
1851	1,026,500	4.75	9.00	17.00	45.00	375.00	
1851O	400,000	10.00	20.00	60.00	175.00	1,400	
1852	1,535,500	4.75	9.00	17.00	45.00	375.00	
1852O	430,000	13.00	30.00	90.00	200.00	1,600	
1853 No arrows	95,000	35.00	60.00	110.00	250.00	1,100	

*Termed "no drapery" because excessive polishing of the proof die removed most of the drapery and reduced the size of the stars. Unique. 1973 M.A.N.A. sale $52,000.

Variety 3 — Arrows at Date 1853-1855

Weight 2.49 grams; composition: .900 silver, .100 copper; diameter 17.9 mm, reeded edge; mints: Philadelphia, New Orleans. Also San Francisco and Carson City after 1855.

Arrows at Date					**Small Date, Arrows Removed**	
1853 With arrows	12,078,010	5.00	8.00	16.00	45.00	375.00	
1853O	1,100,000	6.00	9.00	25.00	85.00	675.00	
1854	4,470,000	5.00	8.00	16.00	45.00	375.00	$10,000
1854O	1,770,000	6.00	9.00	22.50	80.00	675.00	
1855	2,075,000	5.00	8.00	16.00	45.00	375.00	6,000

Variety 2 Resumed 1856-1860

1856 Lg. date		4.25	8.00	15.00	35.00	350.00	
1856 Sm. date	5,780,000	4.25	8.00	15.00	35.00	325.00	2,600
1856O	1,180,000	4.25	8.00	18.00	45.00	350.00	
1856S	70,000	45.00	90.00	200.00	400.00	——	

[114]

DIMES

	Quan. Minted	G-4	F-12	VF-20	EF-40	MS-60	Proof-63
1857	5,580,000	$4.00	$7.50	$14.00	$30.00	$325.00	$2,400
1857O	1,540,000	4.00	7.75	15.00	45.00	350.00	
1858	1,540,000	4.00	7.50	14.00	30.00	325.00	2,300
1858O	290,000	10.00	30.00	75.00	165.00	800.00	
1858S	60,000	45.00	100.00	200.00	450.00	——	
1859	(800) 430,000	5.00	9.00	20.00	50.00	325.00	2,200
1859O	480,000	5.00	15.00	40.00	80.00	350.00	
1859S	60,000	60.00	125.00	225.00	450.00	2,000	
1860S	140,000	13.00	40.00	80.00	185.00	——	

In 1859 an interesting dime pattern was made which does not bear our nation's identity. It is a "transitional" piece, not made for circulation, but struck at the time the inscription UNITED STATES OF AMERICA was being transferred from the reverse to the obverse.

1859 15,000

Variety 4 — Legend on Obverse 1860-1873

	Quan. Minted	G-4	F-12	VF-20	EF-40	MS-60	Proof-63
1860	(1,000) 607,000	4.00	7.50	12.50	25.00	250.00	900.00
1860O	40,000	325.00	650.00	1,050	2,000	——	
1861*	(1,000) 1,884,000	4.00	7.50	12.50	25.00	250.00	900.00
1861S	172,500	15.00	35.00	80.00	175.00	750.00	
1862	(550) 847,550	4.00	7.50	12.50	25.00	250.00	900.00
1862S	180,750	15.00	30.00	70.00	150.00	800.00	
1863	(460) 14,460	80.00	135.00	225.00	350.00	800.00	1,100
1863S	157,500	18.00	40.00	75.00	175.00	950.00	
1864	(470) 11,470	100.00	200.00	300.00	400.00	800.00	1,100
1864S	230,000	12.00	30.00	60.00	140.00	850.00	
1865	(500) 10,500	75.00	150.00	225.00	400.00	900.00	1,100
1865S	175,000	12.00	30.00	60.00	140.00	850.00	
1866	(725) 8,725	125.00	300.00	450.00	650.00	1,100	1,100
1866S	135,000	15.00	30.00	60.00	150.00	1,250	
1867	(625) 6,625	175.00	325.00	500.00	750.00	1,500	1,200
1867S	140,000	12.50	27.50	55.00	125.00	1,100	
1868	(600) 464,600	5.00	10.00	30.00	70.00	400.00	900.00
1868S	260,000	10.00	20.00	60.00	125.00	325.00	
1869	(600) 256,000	5.00	10.00	30.00	70.00	325.00	900.00
1869S	450,000	8.00	15.00	33.00	80.00	350.00	
1870	(1,000) 471,500	4.00	7.50	17.50	35.00	250.00	900.00
1870S	50,000	50.00	100.00	200.00	425.00	2,750	
1871	(960) 907,710	4.00	7.50	12.50	25.00	250.00	900.00
1871CC	20,100	350.00	850.00	1,200	2,400	——	
1871S	320,000	11.00	30.00	50.00	110.00	750.00	
1872	(950) 2,396,450	4.00	7.50	12.50	25.00	225.00	900.00
1872CC	35,480	200.00	500.00	800.00	1,500	——	
1872S	190,000	20.00	50.00	100.00	200.00	800.00	
1873 Closed 3	(1,100) 1,508,000	4.00	7.50	12.50	25.00	325.00	900.00
1873 Open 3	60,000	23.00	45.00	85.00	160.00	350.00	
1873CC (Unique)	12,400					——	

*Dies modified slightly during 1861. First variety with only five vertical lines in top of shield is scarcer than the later variety.

DIMES
Variety 5 — Arrows at Date 1873-1874

Weight 2.50 grams; composition: .900 silver, .100 copper; diameter 17.9 mm; reeded edge; mints: Philadelphia, New Orleans, San Francisco, Carson City.

In 1873 the dime was increased in weight to 2.50 grams. Arrows at date in 1873 and 1874 indicate this change.

	Quan. Minted	G-4	F-12	VF-20	EF-40	MS-60	Proof-63
1873 .... (800)	2,378,500	$8.00	$18.50	$45.00	$100.00	$750.00	$2,200
1873CC	18,791	450.00	900.00	1,350	2,500	——	
1873S	455,000	16.00	32.50	60.00	100.00	900.00	
1874 .... (700)	2,940,000	8.00	18.50	45.00	100.00	750.00	2,200
1874CC	10,817	650.00	1,500	2,200	3,250	——	
1874S	240,000	25.00	60.00	100.00	175.00	1,000	

Variety 4 Resumed 1875-1891

		G-4	F-12	VF-20	EF-40	MS-60	Proof-63
1875 .... (700)	10,350,700	4.00	6.50	12.00	22.50	225.00	900.00
1875CC Below bow							
All kinds 4,645,000		4.50	8.50	16.00	25.00	300.00	
1875CC Above bow		4.00	6.50	12.00	35.00	300.00	
1875S Below bow							
All kinds 9,070,000		4.00	6.50	12.00	22.50	225.00	
1875S Above bow		4.00	6.50	12.00	30.00	300.00	
1876 .. (1,150)	11,461,150	4.00	6.50	12.00	22.50	235.00	900.00
1876CC 8,270,000		4.00	6.50	12.00	22.50	250.00	
1876S 10,420,000		4.00	6.50	12.00	22.50	235.00	
1877 .... (510)	7,310,510	4.00	6.50	12.00	22.50	235.00	1,000
1877CC 7,700,000		4.00	6.50	12.00	22.50	250.00	
1877S 2,340,000		4.00	6.50	12.00	22.50	250.00	
1878 .... (800)	1,678,000	4.00	6.50	12.00	22.50	235.00	900.00
1878CC	200,000	30.00	80.00	115.00	200.00	650.00	
1879 .. (1,100)	15,100	125.00	250.00	300.00	400.00	650.00	1,000
1880 .. (1,355)	37,355	60.00	125.00	200.00	300.00	500.00	1,000
1881 .... (975)	24,975	75.00	175.00	250.00	350.00	550.00	1,000
1882 .. (1,100)	3,911,100	4.00	6.50	12.00	22.50	235.00	900.00
1883 .. (1,039)	7,675,712	4.00	6.50	12.00	22.50	235.00	900.00
1884 .... (875)	3,366,380	4.00	6.50	12.00	22.50	235.00	900.00
1884S	564,969	11.00	20.00	40.00	60.00	400.00	
1885 .... (930)	2,533,427	4.00	6.50	12.00	22.50	235.00	900.00
1885S	43,690	125.00	225.00	325.00	500.00	2,000	
1886 .... (886)	6,377,570	4.00	6.50	12.00	22.50	235.00	850.00
1886S	206,524	11.00	20.00	40.00	75.00	450.00	
1887 .... (710)	11,283,939	4.00	6.50	12.00	22.50	235.00	850.00
1887S 4,454,450		4.00	6.50	12.00	22.50	235.00	
1888 .... (832)	5,496,487	4.00	6.50	12.00	22.50	235.00	850.00
1888S 1,720,000		4.00	6.50	12.00	22.50	225.00	
1889 .... (711)	7,380,711	4.00	6.50	12.00	22.50	235.00	850.00
1889S	972,678	11.00	20.00	45.00	80.00	400.00	
1890 .... (590)	9,911,541	4.75	6.50	12.00	22.50	235.00	900.00
1890S 1,423,076		4.00	9.00	18.00	30.00	275.00	
1891 .... (600)	15,310,600	4.00	6.50	12.00	22.50	235.00	900.00
1891O	4,540,000	4.00	6.50	20.00	35.00	270.00	
1891S 3,196,116		4.00	6.50	12.00	22.50	250.00	

DIMES
BARBER or LIBERTY HEAD TYPE 1892-1916

Designed by Charles E. Barber, Chief Engraver of the Mint. He also designed the 25 and 50-cent pieces. His initial B is at the truncation of the neck.

Designer Charles E. Barber; weight 2.50 grams; composition: .900 silver, .100 copper; diameter 17.9 mm; reeded edge; mints: Philadelphia, Denver, New Orleans, San Francisco. Net weight: .07234 oz. pure silver.

G-4 GOOD—Date and letters plain. LIBERTY is obliterated.
VG-8 VERY GOOD—At least 3 letters visible in LIBERTY.
F-12 FINE—All letters in LIBERTY visible, though some are weak.
VF-20 VERY FINE—All letters of LIBERTY evenly plain.
EF-40 EXTREMELY FINE—All letters in LIBERTY are sharp, distinct. Headband edges are distinct.
MS-60 UNCIRCULATED—No trace of wear. Light blemishes.

Mint mark location is on the reverse below the wreath.

Note: Prices in italic are based on silver bullion at $8.00 per ounce.

	Quan. Minted	G-4	VG-8	F-12	VF-20	EF-40	MS-60	Proof-63
1892 . (1,245)	12,121,245	$2.35	$4.00	$5.50	$8.50	$25.00	$160.00	$850.00
1892O.........	3,841,700	4.50	6.00	8.00	13.00	28.00	180.00	
1892S.........	990,710	23.00	30.00	37.50	60.00	80.00	235.00	
1893, 3 over 2 ⎫							150.00	385.00	900.00
1893 ... (792) ⎬	3,340,792	4.50	5.50	7.50	11.00	25.00	160.00	850.00
1893O.........	1,760,000	12.00	15.00	25.00	32.50	45.00	225.00	
1893S.........	2,491,401	6.00	8.00	12.00	19.00	32.00	200.00	
1894 ... (972)	1,330,972	7.00	9.00	13.00	25.00	45.00	210.00	850.00
1894O...........	720,000	32.00	37.50	65.00	100.00	225.00	1,000	
1894S................. 24				Buss Auction '85			50,600	
1895 ... (880)	690,880	55.00	62.50	80.00	120.00	175.00	550.00	850.00
1895O...........	440,000	150.00	175.00	200.00	270.00	400.00	1,000	
1895S.........	1,120,000	14.00	18.00	25.00	35.00	60.00	225.00	
1896 ... (762)	2,000,762	5.00	6.00	10.00	18.00	35.00	170.00	850.00
1896O...........	610,000	42.50	48.00	65.00	85.00	135.00	550.00	
1896S.........	575,056	35.00	45.00	60.00	80.00	125.00	400.00	
1897 ... (731)	10,869,264	1.25	1.50	3.00	6.00	18.00	150.00	850.00
1897O...........	666,000	35.00	40.00	60.00	90.00	175.00	650.00	
1897S.........	1,342,844	7.00	9.00	15.00	30.00	50.00	225.00	
1898 ... (735)	16,320,735	1.25	1.50	3.00	6.00	18.00	150.00	850.00
1898O...........	2,130,000	3.25	6.00	10.00	22.00	45.00	285.00	
1898S.........	1,702,507	3.25	5.00	9.00	16.00	30.00	175.00	
1899 ... (846)	19,580,846	1.25	1.50	3.00	6.00	18.00	150.00	850.00
1899O.........	2,650,000	3.25	5.00	9.00	21.00	47.50	300.00	
1899S.........	1,867,493	3.25	5.00	8.00	15.00	30.00	175.00	
1900 ... (912)	17,600,912	1.25	1.50	3.00	6.00	18.00	150.00	850.00
1900O.........	2,010,000	4.50	8.00	15.00	30.00	65.00	325.00	
1900S.........	5,168,270	2.00	3.00	5.00	9.00	25.00	175.00	
1901 ... (813)	18,860,478	1.25	1.50	3.00	6.00	18.00	150.00	850.00
1901O.........	5,620,000	2.00	3.00	5.00	14.00	42.00	300.00	
1901S...........	593,022	32.50	50.00	80.00	130.00	200.00	800.00	
1902 ... (777)	21,380,777	1.25	1.50	3.00	6.00	18.00	150.00	850.00
1902O.........	4,500,000	2.00	3.00	5.00	10.00	27.50	225.00	
1902S.........	2,070,000	3.00	5.00	10.00	22.50	52.50	260.00	

DIMES

	Quan. Minted	G-4	VG-8	F-12	VF-20	EF-40	MS-60	Proof-63
1903 .. (755)	19,500,755	$1.25	$1.50	$3.00	$6.00	$18.00	$150.00	$850.00
1903O	8,180,000	2.00	3.00	4.00	8.00	25.00	225.00	
1903S	613,300	25.00	30.00	45.00	75.00	135.00	600.00	
1904 .. (670)	14,601,027	1.25	1.50	3.00	6.00	18.00	150.00	850.00
1904S	800,000	18.00	23.00	37.50	75.00	135.00	550.00	
1905 .. (727)	14,552,350	1.25	1.50	3.00	6.00	18.00	150.00	850.00
1905O*	3,400,000	1.75	3.00	6.00	12.00	25.00	200.00	
1905S	6,855,199	1.75	3.00	5.00	9.00	24.00	210.00	
1906 .. (675)	19,958,406	1.25	1.50	3.00	6.00	18.00	150.00	850.00
1906D	4,060,000	2.00	3.00	5.00	9.00	23.00	190.00	
1906O	2,610,000	2.00	4.50	8.50	15.00	30.00	200.00	
1906S	3,136,640	2.00	3.25	5.50	10.00	25.00	200.00	
1907 .. (575)	22,220,575	1.25	1.50	3.00	6.00	18.00	150.00	850.00
1907D	4,080,000	1.75	2.75	5.00	8.50	24.00	200.00	
1907O	5,058,000	1.75	2.75	5.00	8.50	23.00	160.00	
1907S	3,178,470	2.00	3.00	5.00	10.00	28.00	210.00	
1908 .. (545)	10,600,545	1.25	1.50	3.00	6.00	18.00	150.00	850.00
1908D	7,490,000	1.75	2.75	4.50	6.50	19.00	160.00	
1908O	1,789,000	2.25	3.75	8.00	17.50	35.00	220.00	
1908S	3,220,000	1.75	3.00	4.50	9.00	25.00	200.00	
1909 .. (650)	10,240,650	1.25	1.50	3.00	6.00	18.00	150.00	850.00
1909D	954,000	2.75	5.00	11.00	20.00	35.00	300.00	
1909O	2,287,000	2.25	3.00	5.50	12.00	27.50	175.00	
1909S	1,000,000	2.75	5.00	11.00	20.00	35.00	225.00	
1910 .. (551)	11,520,551	1.25	1.50	3.00	6.00	18.00	150.00	850.00
1910D	3,490,000	1.75	2.75	4.50	9.00	28.00	300.00	
1910S	1,240,000	1.75	2.75	6.75	13.00	28.00	200.00	
1911 .. (543)	18,870,543	1.25	1.50	3.00	6.00	18.00	150.00	850.00
1911D	11,209,000	1.25	1.50	3.00	6.00	18.00	150.00	
1911S	3,520,000	1.75	2.75	5.00	8.00	20.00	175.00	
1912 .. (700)	19,350,000	1.25	1.50	3.00	6.00	18.00	150.00	850.00
1912D	11,760,000	1.25	1.50	3.00	6.00	18.00	150.00	
1912S	3,420,000	1.75	2.75	5.00	8.00	20.00	175.00	
1913 .. (622)	19,760,622	1.25	1.50	3.00	6.00	18.00	150.00	850.00
1913S	510,000	6.50	9.00	24.00	60.00	150.00	325.00	
1914 .. (425)	17,360,655	1.25	1.50	3.00	6.00	18.00	150.00	850.00
1914D	11,908,000	1.25	1.50	3.00	6.00	18.00	150.00	
1914S	2,100,000	1.75	2.50	4.50	8.00	22.00	175.00	
1915 .. (450)	5,620,450	1.25	1.50	3.00	6.00	18.00	160.00	850.00
1915S	960,000	2.00	3.00	5.00	9.50	27.50	200.00	
1916	18,490,000	1.25	1.50	3.00	6.00	18.00	150.00	
1916S	5,820,000	1.25	1.50	3.00	6.00	18.00	150.00	

*Normal and "microscopic" mint mark varieties, see pages 59-60.

WINGED LIBERTY HEAD or "MERCURY" TYPE 1916-1945

Although this coin is commonly called the "Mercury Dime," the main device is in fact a representation of Liberty. The wings crowning her cap are intended to symbolize liberty of thought. The designer's monogram AW is right of neck.

Designer Adolph A. Weinman; weight 2.50 grams; composition: .900 silver, .100 copper; diameter 17.9 mm; reeded edge; mints: Philadelphia, Denver, San Francisco. Net weight: .07234 oz. pure silver.

G-4 GOOD—*Letters and date clear. Lines and bands in fasces are obliterated.*

VG-8 VERY GOOD—*One-half of sticks discernible in fasces.*

F-12 FINE—*All sticks in fasces are defined. Diagonal bands worn nearly flat.*

VF-20 VERY FINE—*The two crossing diagonal bands must show.*

EF-40 EXTREMELY FINE—*Diagonal bands show only slight wear. Braids and hair before ear show clearly.*

MS-63 SELECT UNCIRCULATED—*No trace of wear. Light blemishes. Attractive mint luster.*

MS-65—CHOICE UNCIRCULATED—*No trace of wear. Barely noticeable blemishes.*

DIMES

Mint mark location is on reverse, left of fasces.

Uncirculated values shown are for average pieces with minimum blemishes, those with sharp strikes and split bands on reverse are worth much more.

	Quan. Minted	G-4	VG-8	F-12	VF-20	EF-40	MS-63	Proof-65
1916	22,180,080	$1.75	$2.25	$3.50	$5.50	$8.00	$37.50	
1916D	264,000	375.00	475.00	750.00	1,000	1,400	2,800	
1916S	10,450,000	1.25	2.00	6.00	7.50	14.00	65.00	
1917	55,230,000	1.00	1.25	2.00	3.50	4.25	29.00	
1917D	9,402,000	2.75	4.00	7.00	12.00	30.00	190.00	
1917S	27,330,000	1.00	2.00	4.00	5.00	8.00	75.00	
1918	26,680,000	1.00	2.00	4.00	8.00	20.00	95.00	
1918D	22,674,800	1.00	2.25	4.00	7.50	19.00	125.00	
1918S	19,300,000	1.00	2.25	3.50	6.50	13.00	80.00	
1919	35,740,000	1.00	1.25	3.00	4.50	7.50	50.00	
1919D	9,939,000	2.75	3.50	5.50	14.00	30.00	200.00	
1919S	8,850,000	2.75	3.50	5.50	14.00	30.00	240.00	
1920	59,030,000	1.00	1.25	2.50	4.50	6.00	30.00	
1920D	19,171,000	1.25	2.00	3.00	5.50	12.00	125.00	
1920S	13,820,000	1.25	2.00	3.00	5.50	12.00	100.00	
1921	1,230,000	20.00	30.00	60.00	125.00	325.00	1,100	
1921D	1,080,000	30.00	40.00	85.00	160.00	350.00	1,100	
1923*	50,130,000	1.00	1.25	2.50	3.75	5.00	27.50	
1923S	6,440,000	1.25	2.00	4.00	6.50	18.00	150.00	
1924	24,010,000	1.00	1.25	2.50	4.00	6.50	65.00	
1924D	6,810,000	1.00	2.00	4.00	6.50	16.50	190.00	
1924S	7,120,000	1.00	2.00	4.00	6.00	15.00	200.00	
1925	25,610,000	1.00	1.25	2.50	4.00	6.00	55.00	
1925D	5,117,000	4.00	5.00	7.50	19.00	60.00	300.00	
1925S	5,850,000	1.00	2.00	4.00	6.50	16.50	250.00	
1926	32,160,000	1.00	1.25	3.00	4.00	5.00	25.00	
1926D	6,828,000	1.00	1.25	3.00	5.00	15.00	125.00	
1926S	1,520,000	8.00	10.00	15.00	27.50	85.00	625.00	
1927	28,080,000	1.00	1.25	2.00	3.50	5.00	25.00	
1927D	4,812,000	2.75	3.50	5.00	16.00	30.00	300.00	
1927S	4,770,000	1.75	2.25	3.00	5.00	13.50	150.00	
1928	19,480,000	1.00	1.25	2.00	3.50	4.25	25.00	
1928D	4,161,000	1.25	2.50	4.00	12.00	30.00	200.00	
1928S†	7,400,000	1.00	2.00	3.00	4.00	12.00	90.00	
1929	25,970,000	1.00	1.25	2.00	3.50	4.25	20.00	
1929D	5,034,000	1.00	2.00	3.00	4.00	6.00	65.00	
1929S	4,730,000	1.00	2.00	3.00	4.00	6.00	75.00	
1930*	6,770,000	1.00	1.25	2.00	3.50	4.50	30.00	
1930S	1,843,000	3.25	4.00	4.50	5.50	11.00	135.00	
1931	3,150,000	1.00	1.25	2.00	4.00	9.00	50.00	
1931D	1,260,000	7.50	9.00	11.00	16.00	27.50	150.00	
1931S	1,800,000	3.25	4.00	5.00	6.50	10.00	135.00	

*Dimes dated 1923D and 1930D are counterfeit.

DIMES

	Quan. Minted	F-12	VF-20	EF-40	MS-63	MS-65	Proof-65
1934	24,080,000	$1.25	$2.50	$3.00	$37.50	$55.00	
1934D*	6,772,000	1.25	2.50	5.50	45.00	90.00	
1935	58,830,000	1.25	2.50	3.00	25.00	40.00	
1935D	10,477,000	1.25	2.50	6.50	80.00	165.00	
1935S	15,840,000	1.25	2.50	4.25	37.50	55.00	
1936 .... (4,130)	87,504,130	1.25	2.50	3.00	24.00	37.00	$1,350
1936D	16,132,000	1.25	2.50	4.50	55.00	70.00	
1936S	9,210,000	1.25	2.50	3.00	30.00	45.00	
1937 .... (5,756)	56,865,756	1.25	2.50	3.00	22.00	35.00	1,000
1937D	14,146,000	1.25	2.50	3.00	37.50	60.00	
1937S	9,740,000	1.25	2.50	3.00	27.50	40.00	
1938 .... (8,728)	22,198,728	1.00	1.25	3.00	22.00	40.00	850.00
1938D	5,537,000	1.00	1.25	3.00	42.00	75.00	
1938S	8,090,000	1.00	1.25	3.00	30.00	45.00	
1939 .... (9,321)	67,749,321	1.00	1.25	3.00	20.00	30.00	750.00
1939D	24,394,000	1.00	1.25	3.00	21.00	31.00	
1939S	10,540,000	1.00	1.25	3.00	40.00	65.00	
1940 ... (11,827)	65,361,827	1.00	1.25	3.00	15.00	20.00	675.00
1940D	21,198,000	1.00	1.25	3.00	25.00	35.00	
1940S	21,560,000	1.00	1.25	3.00	16.00	25.00	
1941 ... (16,557)	175,106,557	1.00	1.25	3.00	12.00	20.00	650.00
1941D	45,634,000	1.00	1.25	3.00	25.00	35.00	
1941S*	43,090,000	1.00	1.25	3.00	20.00	30.00	

1942, 2 over 1   1942D, 2 over 1

	Quan. Minted	F-12	VF-20	EF-40	MS-63	MS-65	Proof-65
1942, 2 over 1	} 205,432,329	225.00	250.00	300.00	1,750	2,500	
1942 ...... (22,329)		1.00	1.25	3.00	12.00	20.00	650.00
1942D, 2 over 1	} 60,740,000	225.00	250.00	325.00	1,900	2,750	
1942D		1.00	1.25	3.00	20.00	30.00	
1942S	49,300,000	1.00	1.25	3.00	25.00	40.00	
1943	191,710,000	1.00	1.25	3.00	12.00	20.00	
1943D	71,949,000	1.00	1.25	3.00	16.00	25.00	
1943S	60,400,000	1.00	1.25	3.00	16.50	26.50	
1944	231,410,000	1.00	1.25	3.00	12.00	20.00	
1944D	62,224,000	1.00	1.25	3.00	13.00	22.00	
1944S	49,490,000	1.00	1.25	3.00	13.00	22.00	
1945	159,130,000	1.00	1.25	3.00	12.00	20.00	
1945D	40,245,000	1.00	1.25	3.00	13.00	22.00	
1945S Normal S ...	} 41,920,000	1.00	1.25	3.00	13.00	22.00	
1945S Micro S*		1.00	1.25	3.00		22.00	40.00

*Large and small mint mark varieties, see pages 59-60.

Note: Prices in italic are based on silver bullion valued at $8.00 per ounce.

DIMES

ROOSEVELT TYPE 1946 to Date

John R. Sinnock (whose initials JS are at the truncation of the neck) designed this dime showing a portrait of Franklin D. Roosevelt. The design has heavier lettering and a more modernistic character than preceding types.

Mint mark on reverse 1946-1964. **Mint mark on obverse starting 1968.**

Silver Coinage — 1946-1964

Designer John R. Sinnock; weight 2.50 grams; composition: .900 silver, .100 copper; diameter 17.9 mm; reeded edge; mints: Philadelphia, Denver, San Francisco. Net weight: .07234 oz. pure silver.

VF-20 VERY FINE— *Hair above ear slightly worn. All vertical lines on torch plain.*
EF-40 EXTREMELY FINE— *All lines of torch, flame and hair very plain.*
MS-60 UNCIRCULATED— *No trace of wear. Light blemishes.*
MS-63 SELECT UNCIRCULATED— *No trace of wear. Very light blemishes. Attractive mint luster.*
MS-65 CHOICE UNCIRCULATED— *No trace of wear. Barely noticeable blemishes.*

	Quan. Minted	EF-40	MS-63	MS-65	Proof-65
1946	255,250,000	*$1.00*	$2.00	$3.00	
1946D	61,043,500	*1.00*	2.50	3.75	
1946S	27,900,000	*1.00*	4.00	6.00	
1947	121,520,000	*1.00*	2.50	3.75	
1947D	46,835,000	*1.00*	5.00	7.50	
1947S	34,840,000	*1.00*	3.50	5.25	
1948	74,950,000	*1.00*	8.00	12.00	
1948D	52,841,000	*1.00*	6.50	9.00	
1948S	35,520,000	*1.00*	7.50	10.00	
1949	30,940,000	*1.25*	22.00	30.00	
1949D	26,034,000	*1.00*	8.00	12.00	
1949S	13,510,000	2.00	45.00	60.00	
1950 (51,386)	50,181,500	*1.00*	3.50	5.25	$75.00
1950D	46,803,000	*1.00*	3.00	4.50	
1950S	20,440,000	*1.00*	18.00	27.00	
1951 (57,500)	103,937,602	*1.00*	2.00	3.00	65.00
1951D	56,529,000	*1.00*	2.50	3.75	
1951S	31,630,000	*1.00*	13.00	20.00	
1952 (81,980)	99,122,073	*1.00*	2.50	3.50	40.00
1952D	122,100,000	*1.00*	3.00	4.00	
1952S	44,419,500	*1.00*	5.00	7.50	
1953 (128,800)	53,618,920	*1.00*	2.00	3.00	25.00
1953D	136,433,000	*1.00*	2.00	2.25	
1953S	39,180,000	*1.00*	2.85	2.50	
1954 (233,300)	114,243,503	*1.00*	2.00	2.50	13.00
1954D	106,397,000	*1.00*	2.00	2.50	
1954S	22,860,000	*1.00*	2.00	3.00	
1955 (378,200)	12,828,381	*1.00*	3.00	3.75	11.00
1955D	13,959,000	*1.00*	1.75	2.75	
1955S	18,510,000	*1.00*	1.75	2.75	
1956 (669,384)	109,309,384	*1.00*	*1.50*	2.00	3.50
1956D	108,015,100	*1.00*	*1.50*	2.00	
1957 (1,247,952)	161,407,952	*1.00*	*1.50*	2.00	2.75
1957D	113,354,330	*1.00*	1.75	2.50	

[121]

DIMES

	Quan. Minted	EF-40	MS-63	MS-65	Proof-65
1958 . . . . (875,652)	32,785,652	$1.00	$1.75	$2.50	$3.50
1958D.	136,564,600	1.00	1.50	2.00	
1959 . . . . (1,149,291)	86,929,291	1.00	1.50	2.00	2.75
1959D.	164,919,790	1.00	1.50	2.00	
1960 . . . . (1,691,602)	72,081,602	1.00	1.25	2.00	2.25
1960D.	200,160,400	1.00	1.25	2.00	
1961 . . . . (3,028,244)	96,758,244	1.00	1.25	2.00	2.25
1961D.	209,146,550	1.00	1.25	2.00	
1962 . . . . (3,218,019)	75,668,019	1.00	1.25	2.00	2.25
1962D.	334,948,380	1.00	1.25	2.00	
1963 . . . . (3,075,645)	126,725,645	1.00	1.25	2.00	2.25
1963D.	421,476,530	1.00	1.25	2.00	
1964* . . . . (3,950,762)	933,310,762	1.00	1.25	2.00	2.25
1964D*.	1,357,517,180	1.00	1.25	2.00	

*Variations of 9 in date have either pointed or straight tail.

Clad Coinage — 1965 to date

Weight 2.27 grams; composition: outer layers of copper-nickel (.750 copper, .250 nickel) bonded to inner core of pure copper; diameter 17.9 mm; reeded edge.

	Quan. Minted	MS-65	Proof-65
1965	1,652,140,570	$ .25	
1966	1,382,734,540	.25	
1967	2,244,007,320	.25	
1968	424,470,400	.25	
1968D	480,748,280	.25	
1968S Proof* . .	(3,041,506)		$ .85
1969	145,790,000	.50	
1969D	563,323,870	.25	
1969S Proof . . .	(2,934,631)		.85
1970	345,570,000	.25	
1970D	754,942,100	.25	
1970S Proof* . .	(2,632,810)		.85
1971	162,690,000	.25	
1971D	377,914,240	.25	
1971S Proof . . .	(3,220,733)		.85
1972	431,540,000	.25	
1972D	330,290,000	.25	
1972S Proof . . .	(3,260,996)		.85
1973	315,670,000	.25	
1973D	455,032,426	.25	
1973S Proof . . .	(2,760,339)		.85
1974	470,248,000	.25	
1974D	571,083,000	.25	
1974S Proof . . .	(2,612,568)		1.00
1975	585,673,900	.25	
1975D	313,705,300	.25	
1975S Proof* . .	(2,845,450)		1.00
1976	568,760,000	.25	
1976D	695,222,774	.25	
1976S Proof . . .	(4,149,730)		.85
1977	796,930,000	.25	
1977D	376,607,228	.25	
1977S Proof . . .	(3,251,152)		.85

	Quan. Minted	MS-65	Proof-65
1978	663,980,000	$ .25	
1978D	282,847,540	.25	
1978S Proof . . .	(3,127,781)		$1.00
1979	315,440,000	.30	
1979D	390,921,184	.35	
1979S Proof . . .	(3,677,175)		
Filled S			1.00
Clear S			2.00
1980P	735,170,000	.20	
1980D	719,354,321	.20	
1980S Proof . . .	(3,554,806)		1.00
1981P	676,650,000	.20	
1981D	712,284,143	.20	
1981S Proof . . .	(4,063,083)		1.00
1982 (no mint mark)		175.00	
1982P*	519,475,000	.20	
1982	542,713,584	.20	
1982S Proof . . .	(3,857,479)		1.00
1983P	647,025,000	.20	
1983D	730,129,224	.20	
1983S Proof* . .	(3,228,648)		1.50
1984P	856,669,000	.20	
1984D	704,803,976	.20	
1984S Proof			1.00
1985P	705,200,962	.20	
1985D	587,979,970	.20	
1985S Proof			1.00
1986P.		.20	
1986D		.20	
1986S Proof			1.00

*1968, 1970, 1975 and 1983 proof dimes without S mint mark were made in error. Some of the 1982 business strike dimes were also made without a mint mark. See pages 60-61.

TWENTY-CENT PIECES — 1875-1878

This short-lived coin was authorized by the Act of March 3, 1875. Soon after the appearance of the first twenty-cent pieces, the people complained about the similarity in design and size to the quarter dollar. The eagle is very similar to that used on the Trade Dollar. The edge of the coin is plain. Most of the 1876CC coins were melted at the mint and never released. Mint mark is on the reverse below the eagle.

TYPE COIN VALUES

	G-4	F-12	EF-40	AU-50	MS-60	MS-63	MS-65	PF-60	PF-63	PF-65
1875-1878	35.00	60.00	180.00	350.00	1,000	2,400	7,500	1,200	2,500	11,000

Designer William Barber; weight 5 grams; composition: .900 silver, .100 copper; diameter 22 mm; plain edge; mints: Philadelphia, Carson City, San Francisco.

G-4 GOOD—*LIBERTY on shield obliterated. Letters and date legible.*

VG-8 VERY GOOD—*One or two letters in LIBERTY may show. Other details will be bold.*

F-12 FINE—*At least 3 letters of LIBERTY show.*

VF-20 VERY FINE—*LIBERTY completely readable, but partly weak.*

EF-40 EXTREMELY FINE—*LIBERTY sharp. Only slight wear on high points of coin.*

MS-60 UNCIRCULATED—*No trace of wear. Light blemishes.*

	Quan. Minted	G-4	VG-8	F-12	VF-20	EF-40	MS-60	Proof-63
1875 ... (2,790)	39,700	$50.00	$60.00	$85.00	$125.00	$225.00	$1,200	$2,500
1875CC	133,290	45.00	55.00	75.00	115.00	225.00	1,200	
1875S	1,155,000	35.00	45.00	60.00	90.00	180.00	1,000	—
1876 ... (1,260)	15,900	75.00	100.00	135.00	185.00	300.00	1,400	2,700
1876CC	10,000						60,000	
1877 ..... (350)	350							3,700
1878 ..... (600)	600							3,600

QUARTER DOLLARS — 1796 to Date

Authorized in 1792, this denomination was not issued until four years later. The first coinage, dated 1796, follows the pattern of the early half-dimes and dimes by the absence of a mark of value. In 1804 the value "25c" was added to the reverse. Figures were used until 1838 when the term "QUAR. DOL." appeared. It was not until 1892 that the value was spelled out entirely.

The first type weighed 104 grains which remained standard until modified to 103⅛ grains by the Act of January 18, 1837. As with the dime and half dime, the weight was reduced and arrows placed at the date in 1853. Rays were placed in the field of the reverse during that year only.

The law of 1873 also affected the quarter, for the weight was slightly increased and arrows again placed at the date.

Proofs of some dates prior to 1856 are known to exist, and all are rare.

TYPE COIN VALUES

	G-4	F-12	EF-40	AU-50	MS-60	MS-63	MS-65	PF-60	PF-63	PF-65
Drpd Bust-SE 1796	$2,800	$4,600	$12,000	$15,000	$25,000	$32,000	$50,000			
Drpd Bust-HE 1804-1807	225.00	600.00	1,800	2,600	7,000	12,000	33,000			
Lg. Bust 1815-1828	40.00	80.00	550.00	1,100	2,100	4,250	14,500			
Sm. Bust 1831-1838	30.00	50.00	275.00	625.00	1,200	3,300	12,000			
Lib Seated-NM 1838-1865	8.00	14.00	50.00	125.00	450.00	1,000	5,500	500.00	1,100	6,000
Lib Seat-A&R 1853	8.00	16.00	100.00	300.00	1,100	2,400	9,000			
Lib. Seat-Arr. 1854-1865	8.00	13.00	70.00	225.00	800.00	1,700	5,750			
Lib. Seat-WM 1866-1891	7.00	11.00	45.00	115.00	500.00	1,000	4,500	450.00	1,000	5,000
Lib. Seat-Arr. 1873-1874	10.00	20.00	125.00	350.00	1,000	1,800	5,500	900.00	2,300	7,500
Barber 1892-1916	2.75	9.00	50.00	100.00	300.00	700.00	3,500	475.00	1,000	4,500
Stand Lib. I 1916-1917	9.00	16.00	60.00	100.00	265.00	550.00	2,750			
Stand Lib. II 1917-1930	2.75	9.00	25.00	55.00	100.00	225.00	1,250			
Washington 1932-1964	2.00	2.00	2.25	2.25	2.50	2.75	3.25	4.00	5.00	6.00

QUARTER DOLLARS
DRAPED BUST TYPE, SMALL EAGLE REVERSE 1796

Designer Robert Scot; weight 6.74 grams; composition: .8924 silver, .1076 copper; approx. diameter 27.5 mm; reeded edge. All coined at Philadelphia.

AG-3 ABOUT GOOD—*Details clear enough to identify.*
G-4 GOOD—*Date readable. Bust outlined, but no detail.*
VG-8 VERY GOOD—*All but deepest drapery folds worn smooth. Hairlines nearly gone and curls lack detail.*
F-12 FINE—*All drapery lines visible. Hair partly worn.*
VF-20 VERY FINE—*Only left side of drapery is indistinct.*
EF-40 EXTREMELY FINE—*Hair well outlined and detailed.*
MS-60 UNCIRCULATED—*No trace of wear. Light blemishes.*

	Quan. Minted	AG-3	G-4	VG-8	F-12	VF-20	EF-40	MS-60
1796	6,146	$1,400	$2,800	$3,500	$4,600	$8,000	$12,000	$25,000

DRAPED BUST TYPE, HERALDIC EAGLE REVERSE 1804-1807

	Quan. Minted	AG-3	G-4	VG-8	F-12	VF-20	EF-40	MS-60
1804	6,738	400.00	700.00	900.00	2,000	4,000	8,000	——
1805	121,395	125.00	225.00	300.00	600.00	1,100	1,800	7,000
1806 6 over 5	} 206,124	125.00	225.00	300.00	600.00	1,100	1,800	7,000
1806		125.00	225.00	300.00	600.00	1,100	1,800	7,000
1807	220,643	125.00	225.00	300.00	600.00	1,100	1,800	7,000

CAPPED BUST TYPE 1815-1838
Variety 1 — Large Size 1815-1828

AG-3 ABOUT GOOD—*Details clear enough to identify.*
G-4 GOOD—*Date, letters and stars readable. Hair under headband smooth. Cap lines worn smooth.*
VG-8 VERY GOOD—*Rim well defined. Main details visible. Full LIBERTY on cap. Hair above eye nearly smooth.*
F-12 FINE—*All hairlines show but drapery has only part details. Shoulder clasp distinct.*
VF-20 VERY FINE—*All details show, but some wear. Clasp and ear sharp.*
EF-40 EXTREMELY FINE—*All details show distinctly. Hair well outlined.*
MS-60 UNCIRCULATED—*No trace of wear. Light blemishes.*

Designer John Reich; weight 6.74 grams; composition: .8924 silver, .1076 copper; approx. diameter 27 mm; reeded edge. All coined at Philadelphia.

QUARTER DOLLARS

	Quan. Minted	AG-3	G-4	VG-8	F-12	VF-20	EF-40	MS-60
1815	89,235	$25.00	$50.00	$70.00	$100.00	$250.00	$700.00	$3,000
1818 8 over 5	} 361,174	25.00	45.00	65.00	95.00	250.00	700.00	2,750
1818 Normal date . .		25.00	45.00	65.00	95.00	210.00	600.00	2,100
1819 Small 9	} 144,000	25.00	45.00	65.00	95.00	210.00	600.00	2,100
1819 Large 9		25.00	45.00	65.00	95.00	210.00	600.00	2,100

1820 Small 0		**1820 Large 0**		**1822, 25 over 50c**

1820 Small 0	} 127,444	25.00	45.00	65.00	95.00	210.00	600.00	2,100
1820 Large 0		25.00	45.00	65.00	95.00	210.00	600.00	2,100
1821	216,851	25.00	45.00	65.00	95.00	210.00	600.00	2,100
1822 All kinds . .	64,080	25.00	45.00	65.00	95.00	210.00	625.00	2,500
1822, 25 over 50c		150.00	200.00	300.00	450.00	900.00	1,600	4,500
1823, 3 over 2 . .	17,800	1,200	2,500	5,250	9,000	13,000	20,000	——

1825, 5 over 2 (wide date)		**1825, 5 over 3 or 4 (close date)**

1824 4 over 2		30.00	50.00	70.00	100.00	275.00	650.00	3,000
1825 5 over 2	} 168,000	25.00	45.00	60.00	90.00	225.00	600.00	2,750
1825 5 over 3		21.00	40.00	55.00	80.00	200.00	550.00	2,100
1825 5 over 4		21.00	40.00	55.00	80.00	200.00	550.00	2,500
1827 Original (Curled base 2 in 25c) 4,000 Minted								60,000
1827 Restrike (Square base 2 in 25c)								25,000
1828 All kds . . .	102,000	21.00	40.00	55.00	80.00	200.00	550.00	2,100
1828, 25 over 50c		50.00	80.00	110.00	200.00	450.00	700.00	3,750

Variety 2 — Reduced Size, No Motto on Reverse 1831-1838

G-4 GOOD— *Bust well defined. Hair under headband smooth. Date, letters, stars readable. Scant rims.*

VG-8 VERY GOOD— *Details apparent but worn on high spots. Rims strong. Full LIBERTY.*

F-12 FINE— *All hairlines visible. Drapery partly worn. Shoulder clasp distinct.*

VF-20 VERY FINE— *Only top spots worn. Clasp sharp. Ear distinct.*

EF-40 EXTREMELY FINE— *Hair details and clasp are bold and clear.*

MS-60 UNCIRCULATED— *No trace of wear. Light blemishes.*

Designer William Kneass; weight 6.74 grams; composition: .8924 silver, .1076 copper; diameter 24.3 mm; reeded edge. All coined at Philadelphia.

QUARTER DOLLARS

Small Letters **Large Letters**

	Quan. Minted	G-4	VG-8	F-12	VF-20	EF-40	MS-60
1831 Small letters. ⎫		$30.00	$40.00	$50.00	$100.00	$275.00	$1,100
1831 Large letters .. ⎬	398,000	30.00	40.00	50.00	100.00	275.00	1,100
1832	320,000	30.00	40.00	50.00	100.00	275.00	1,100
1833	156,000	35.00	45.00	65.00	125.00	300.00	1,600
1834	286,000	30.00	40.00	50.00	100.00	275.00	1,100
1835	1,952,000	30.00	40.00	50.00	100.00	275.00	1,100
1836	472,000	30.00	40.00	50.00	100.00	275.00	1,100
1837	252,400	30.00	40.00	50.00	100.00	275.00	1,100
1838	366,000	30.00	40.00	50.00	100.00	275.00	1,100

LIBERTY SEATED TYPE 1838-1891
Variety 1 — No Motto Above Eagle 1838-1853

G-4 GOOD—*Scant rim. LIBERTY on shield worn off. Date and letters readable.*
VG-8 VERY GOOD—*Rim fairly defined, at least 3 letters in LIBERTY evident.*
F-12 FINE—*LIBERTY complete, but partly weak.*
VF-20 VERY FINE—*LIBERTY strong.*
EF-40 EXTREMELY FINE—*Complete LIBERTY and edges of scroll. Clasp shows plainly.*
MS-60 UNCIRCULATED—*No trace of wear. Light blemishes.*

Designer Christian Gobrecht; weight 6.68 grams; composition: .900 silver, .100 copper; diameter 24.3 mm; reeded edge; mints: Philadelphia, New Orleans.

No Drapery from Elbow

Drapery from Elbow

Mint mark location is on the reverse below the eagle.

1838 No drapery.......	466,000	10.00	15.00	25.00	50.00	160.00	1,800
1839 No drapery......	491,146	10.00	15.00	25.00	50.00	160.00	1,800
1840O No drapery	382,200	10.00	15.00	25.00	50.00	160.00	2,000
1840 Drapery..........	188,127	15.00	20.00	30.00	75.00	175.00	1,500
1840O Drapery	43,000	12.00	18.00	30.00	60.00	135.00	1,500
1841	120,000	30.00	40.00	100.00	160.00	250.00	1,000
1841O.................	452,000	12.00	18.00	30.00	60.00	150.00	1,000

Small Date					**Large Date**		

1842 Small Date .. ⎫						Proofs Only ——	
1842 Large date ⎬	88,000	60.00	80.00	125.00	250.00	400.00	1,600

QUARTER DOLLARS

	Quan. Minted	G-4	VG-8	F-12	VF-20	EF-40	MS-60
1842O Small date ... }	769,000	$200.00	$350.00	$700.00	$1,000	$2,000	——
1842O Large date ... }		15.00	20.00	30.00	50.00	100.00	$1,200
1843	645,600	12.00	16.00	20.00	40.00	80.00	800.00
1843O	968,000	15.00	25.00	40.00	70.00	200.00	——
1844	421,200	12.00	16.00	25.00	40.00	85.00	600.00
1844O	740,000	15.00	20.00	30.00	60.00	110.00	1,200
1845	922,000	12.00	16.00	20.00	35.00	75.00	600.00
1846	510,000	12.00	16.00	25.00	40.00	85.00	600.00
1847	734,000	12.00	16.00	20.00	35.00	75.00	600.00
1847O	368,000	20.00	30.00	50.00	90.00	190.00	1,000
1848	146,000	20.00	30.00	50.00	90.00	150.00	950.00
1849	340,000	15.00	20.00	35.00	50.00	125.00	750.00
1849O .... †incl. below		350.00	450.00	850.00	1,650	3,000	——
1850	190,800	15.00	25.00	35.00	60.00	100.00	900.00
1850O	412,000	25.00	35.00	50.00	70.00	125.00	1,000
1851	160,000	15.00	25.00	35.00	60.00	110.00	850.00
1851O	88,000	150.00	225.00	400.00	600.00	1,200	2,000
1852	177,060	20.00	30.00	45.00	65.00	110.00	900.00
1852O	96,000	210.00	300.00	450.00	750.00	1,200	2,500
1853* Recut date, no arrows or rays...........	44,200	150.00	200.00	300.00	425.00	600.00	3,000

†Coinage for 1849O included with 1850O.
*Beware of altered 1858.

Variety 2 — Arrows at Date, Rays Around Eagle 1853 Only

1853, 3 over 4

Weight 6.22 grams; composition: .900 silver, .100 copper; diameter 24.3 mm; reeded edge; mints: Philadelphia, New Orleans, San Francisco, Carson City.

The reduction in weight is indicated by the arrows at the date. Rays were added on the reverse side in the field around the eagle. The arrows were retained through 1855, but the rays were omitted after 1853.

	Quan. Minted	G-4	VG-8	F-12	VF-20	EF-40	MS-60
1853 .... }	15,210,000	8.00	12.00	16.00	35.00	100.00	1,100
1853, 3 over 4 .... }		70.00	125.00	300.00	400.00	800.00	2,500
1853O	1,332,000	10.00	13.00	20.00	50.00	140.00	1,350

Variety 3 — Arrows at Date, No Rays 1854-1855

	Quan. Minted	G-4	VG-8	F-12	VF-20	EF-40	MS-60
1854	12,380,000	8.00	10.00	13.00	30.00	70.00	800.00
1854O .... }	1,484,000	8.00	11.00	14.00	32.00	75.00	900.00
1854O Huge O.... }		60.00	80.00	150.00	250.00	500.00	——
1855	2,857,000	8.00	11.00	14.00	32.00	75.00	850.00
1855O	176,000	45.00	65.00	95.00	175.00	325.00	1,850
1855S	396,400	45.00	65.00	95.00	160.00	300.00	1,850

Variety 1 Resumed 1856-1865

	Quan. Minted	G-4	VG-8	F-12	VF-20	EF-40	MS-60	Proof-63
1856	7,264,000	$8.00	$10.00	$14.00	$20.00	$50.00	$450.00	$3,000
1856O	968,000	10.00	15.00	25.00	35.00	75.00	600.00	

QUARTER DOLLARS

	Quan. Minted	G-4	VG-8	F-12	VF-20	EF-40	MS-60	Proof-63
1856S........	} 286,000	$21.00	$30.00	$45.00	$100.00	$200.00	$1,100	
1856S, S over S.		25.00	50.00	100.00	250.00	400.00	———	
1857......... 9,644,000		8.00	10.00	14.00	20.00	50.00	450.00	$2,500
1857O........ 1,180,000		9.00	11.50	16.00	25.00	50.00	600.00	
1857S........... 82,000		45.00	70.00	100.00	235.00	500.00	1,500	
1858......... 7,368,000		8.00	10.00	14.00	20.00	50.00	450.00	2,000
1858O.......... 520,000		9.00	12.00	18.00	30.00	70.00	750.00	
1858S.......... 121,000		35.00	40.00	65.00	175.00	300.00	1,400	
1859..... (800) 1,344,000		8.00	10.00	14.00	20.00	50.00	450.00	1,100
1859O.......... 260,000		15.00	25.00	40.00	65.00	95.00	850.00	
1859S........... 80,000		55.00	90.00	150.00	250.00	450.00	1,800	
1860... (1,000) 805,400		8.00	10.00	14.00	20.00	50.00	450.00	1,100
1860O.......... 388,000		10.00	14.00	20.00	30.00	60.00	800.00	
1860S........... 56,000		80.00	125.00	225.00	400.00	800.00	2,000	
1861... (1,000) 4,854,600		8.00	10.00	14.00	20.00	50.00	450.00	1,100
1861S........... 96,000		25.00	35.00	75.00	200.00	300.00	2,000	
1862.... (550) 932,550		8.00	10.00	14.00	20.00	50.00	450.00	1,100
1862S........... 67,000		25.00	35.00	75.00	200.00	300.00	2,000	
1863..... (460) 192,060		16.00	20.00	30.00	45.00	85.00	750.00	1,200
1864..... (470) 94,070		25.00	35.00	65.00	100.00	175.00	900.00	1,200
1864S........... 20,000		100.00	175.00	275.00	450.00	1,000	———	
1865..... (500) 59,300		35.00	50.00	75.00	110.00	200.00	900.00	1,200
1865S........... 41,000		35.00	50.00	100.00	225.00	325.00	2,500	
1866.......... (Unique)								———

The 1866 proof quarter, half and dollar without motto are not mentioned in the Director's Report, and were not issued for circulation.

Variety 4 — Motto Above Eagle 1866-1873

The motto IN GOD WE TRUST was added to the reverse side in 1866. As on the half dollar and silver dollar the motto has been retained since that time.

1866..... (725)	17,525	175.00	225.00	325.00	450.00	650.00	1,550	1,350
1866S...........	28,000	80.00	120.00	200.00	325.00	550.00	1,900	
1867..... (625)	20,625	80.00	120.00	180.00	300.00	475.00	1,200	1,350
1867S...........	48,000	45.00	65.00	120.00	175.00	275.00	2,000	
1868..... (600)	30,000	50.00	75.00	150.00	200.00	300.00	900.00	1,350
1868S...........	96,000	30.00	50.00	90.00	125.00	200.00	1,500	
1869..... (600)	16,600	80.00	120.00	200.00	300.00	500.00	1,100	1,350
1869S...........	76,000	30.00	50.00	90.00	125.00	200.00	1,100	
1870... (1,000)	87,400	25.00	35.00	50.00	90.00	140.00	700.00	1,350
1870CC	8,340	1,000	1,500	2,500	3,500	4,750	———	
1871..... (960)	119,160	12.00	15.00	30.00	50.00	85.00	600.00	1,200
1871CC	10,890	450.00	700.00	1,100	1,900	2,750	———	
1871S...........	30,900	125.00	250.00	400.00	550.00	850.00	2,250	
1872..... (950)	182,950	10.00	20.00	27.50	50.00	75.00	500.00	1,200

QUARTER DOLLARS

	Quan. Minted	G-4	VG-8	F-12	VF-20	EF-40	MS-60	Proof-63
1872CC	22,850	$225.00	$350.00	$475.00	$750.00	$1,800	$4,500	
1872S...........	83,000	125.00	225.00	350.00	450.00	700.00	3,500	
1873 Cl. 3 (600)...	40,600	30.00	50.00	90.00	175.00	275.00	900.00	$1,200
1873 Open 3.....	172,000	10.00	20.00	30.00	50.00	115.00	500.00	
1873CC	4,000			Private Sale 1980		190,000		

Variety 5 — Arrows at Date 1873-1874

Arrows were placed at the date in the years 1873 and 1874 to denote the change of weight from 6.22 to 6.25 grams.

Weight 6.25 grams; composition: .900 silver, .100 copper; diameter 24.3 mm; reeded edge; mints: Philadelphia, San Francisco, Carson City.

		G-4	VG-8	F-12	VF-20	EF-40	MS-60	Proof-63
1873 .. (540)	1,271,700	10.00	16.00	20.00	50.00	125.00	1,000	2,300
1873CC	12,462	450.00	600.00	850.00	1,100	2,000	5,500	
1873S...........	156,000	18.00	21.00	40.00	80.00	200.00	1,200	
1874 .. (700)	471,900	10.00	16.00	20.00	50.00	125.00	1,000	2,300
1874S...........	392,000	18.00	21.00	40.00	80.00	200.00	1,200	

Variety 4 Resumed 1875-1891

1877S, S over horizontal S

		G-4	VG-8	F-12	VF-20	EF-40	MS-60	Proof-63
1875 .. (700)	4,293,500	7.00	9.00	11.00	20.00	40.00	375.00	1,000
1875CC	140,000	35.00	45.00	95.00	135.00	300.00	1,400	
1875S..........	680,000	8.00	12.00	20.00	35.00	65.00	600.00	
1876 (1,150)	17,817,150	7.00	9.00	11.00	20.00	45.00	375.00	1,000
1876CC*	4,944,000	8.00	11.00	15.00	30.00	60.00	500.00	
1876S.........	8,596,000	7.00	9.00	11.00	20.00	45.00	450.00	
1877 .. (510)	10,911,710	7.00	9.00	11.00	20.00	45.00	375.00	1,000
1877CC	4,192,000	8.00	11.00	15.00	30.00	60.00	500.00	
1877S.........	8,996,000	7.00	9.00	11.00	20.00	45.00	400.00	
1877S over horizontal S.	——	——		100.00	135.00	225.00	1,000	
1878 .. (800)	2,260,800	7.00	9.00	11.00	20.00	45.00	375.00	1,000
1878CC	996,000	9.00	12.00	16.00	26.00	60.00	550.00	
1878S..........	140,000	50.00	75.00	125.00	175.00	250.00	1,750	
1879 (1,100)	14,700	70.00	80.00	110.00	145.00	210.00	650.00	1,200
1880 (1,355)	14,955	70.00	80.00	110.00	145.00	210.00	650.00	1,200
1881 .. (975)	12,975	70.00	80.00	110.00	145.00	210.00	650.00	1,200

*Variety with fine edge reeding is scarcer than normal.

QUARTER DOLLARS

	Quan. Minted	G-4	VG-8	F-12	VF-20	EF-40	MS-60	Proof-63
1882 (1,100)	16,300	$70.00	$80.00	$110.00	$145.00	$210.00	$650.00	$1,200
1883 (1,039)	15,439	70.00	80.00	110.00	145.00	210.00	650.00	1,200
1884 .. (875)	8,875	80.00	95.00	125.00	165.00	250.00	725.00	1,200
1885 .. (930)	14,530	70.00	80.00	110.00	145.00	225.00	700.00	1,200
1886 .. (886)	5,886	90.00	110.00	140.00	190.00	300.00	725.00	1,200
1887 .. (710)	10,710	70.00	80.00	110.00	145.00	225.00	700.00	1,200
1888 .. (832)	10,833	70.00	80.00	110.00	145.00	225.00	700.00	1,200
1888S	1,216,000	10.00	12.00	14.00	22.00	40.00	375.00	
1889 .. (711)	12,711	65.00	75.00	100.00	125.00	175.00	700.00	1,200
1890 .. (590)	80,590	40.00	50.00	65.00	90.00	125.00	650.00	1,100
1891 .. (600)	3,920,600	7.00	9.00	11.00	20.00	45.00	450.00	1,000
1891O	68,000	110.00	125.00	200.00	325.00	550.00	2,100	
1891S	2,216,000	7.00	10.00	15.00	25.00	50.00	375.00	

BARBER or LIBERTY HEAD TYPE 1892-1916

Like other silver coins of this type the quarter dollars minted from 1892 to 1916 were designed by Charles E. Barber. His initial B is found at the truncation of the neck of Liberty. There are two varieties of the 1892 reverse: 1) Eagle's wing covers only half of E. 2) Eagle's wing covers most of E.

Designer Charles E. Barber; weight 6.25 grams; composition: .900 silver, .100 copper; diameter 24.3 mm; reeded edge; mints: Philadelphia, Denver, New Orleans, San Francisco. Net weight: .18084 oz. pure silver.

G-4 GOOD— *Date and legends readable. LIBERTY worn off headband.*
VG-8 VERY GOOD— *Minimum of 3 letters in LIBERTY readable.*
F-12 FINE— *LIBERTY completely readable but not sharp.*
VF-20 VERY FINE— *All letters in LIBERTY evenly plain.*
EF-40 EXTREMELY FINE— *LIBERTY bold, and its ribbon distinct.*
MS-60 UNCIRCULATED— *No trace of wear. Light blemishes.*

Mint mark location is on the reverse below the eagle.

	Quan. Minted	G-4	VG-8	F-12	VF-20	EF-40	MS-60	Proof-63
1892 (1,245)	8,237,245	$2.75	$3.50	$9.00	$16.00	$50.00	$325.00	$1,000
1892O	2,640,000	5.00	6.50	12.00	23.00	55.00	365.00	
1892S	964,079	15.00	18.00	27.50	45.00	80.00	450.00	
1893 .. (792)	5,444,815	2.75	3.50	9.00	16.00	50.00	300.00	1,000
1893O	3,396,000	2.75	3.50	11.00	25.00	55.00	375.00	
1893S	1,454,535	6.00	8.00	13.00	30.00	65.00	375.00	
1894 .. (972)	3,432,972	2.75	3.50	9.00	19.00	50.00	300.00	1,000
1894O	2,852,000	2.75	3.50	11.00	22.00	55.00	375.00	
1894S	2,648,821	2.75	3.50	11.00	22.00	55.00	375.00	
1895 .. (880)	4,440,880	2.75	3.50	9.00	16.00	50.00	300.00	1,000
1895O	2,816,000	2.75	3.50	11.00	22.00	55.00	450.00	
1895S	1,764,681	2.75	3.50	13.00	30.00	57.50	400.00	
1896 .. (762)	3,874,762	2.75	3.50	9.00	16.00	52.50	325.00	1,000
1896O	1,484,000	3.50	6.00	14.00	35.00	95.00	850.00	
1896S	188,039	235.00	265.00	550.00	900.00	1,500	3,500	
1897 .. (731)	8,140,731	2.75	3.50	9.00	16.00	50.00	300.00	1,000
1897O	1,414,800	6.00	9.00	15.00	40.00	100.00	850.00	

QUARTER DOLLARS

	Quan. Minted	G-4	VG-8	F-12	VF-20	EF-40	MS-60	Proof-63
1897S	542,229	$10.00	$14.00	$25.00	$42.00	$90.00	$450.00	
1898 . . (735)	11,100,735	2.75	3.50	9.00	16.00	50.00	300.00	$1,000
1898O	1,868,000	2.75	3.50	12.00	27.50	65.00	575.00	
1898S	1,020,592	2.75	3.50	10.00	25.00	55.00	400.00	
1899 . . (846)	12,624,846	2.75	3.50	9.00	16.00	50.00	300.00	1,000
1899O	2,644,000	4.00	6.00	12.00	25.00	55.00	400.00	
1899S	708,000	7.50	11.00	16.00	32.00	62.50	425.00	
1900 . . (912)	10,016,912	2.75	3.50	9.00	16.00	50.00	300.00	1,000
1900O	3,416,000	5.00	7.00	13.50	30.00	65.00	425.00	
1900S	1,858,585	2.75	3.50	9.00	21.00	52.50	350.00	
1901 . . (813)	8,892,813	2.75	3.50	9.00	16.00	50.00	300.00	1,000
1901O	1,612,000	10.00	15.00	30.00	60.00	120.00	800.00	
1901S	72,664	1,000	1,200	1,800	2,400	3,500	11,000	
1902 . . (777)	12,197,744	2.75	3.50	9.00	16.00	50.00	300.00	1,000
1902O	4,748,000	2.75	3.50	9.00	16.00	55.00	450.00	
1902S	1,524,612	6.00	10.00	14.00	30.00	75.00	425.00	
1903 . . (755)	9,670,064	2.75	3.50	9.00	16.00	50.00	300.00	1,000
1903O	3,500,000	2.75	3.50	10.00	25.00	60.00	375.00	
1903S	1,036,000	7.00	10.00	14.00	35.00	80.00	450.00	
1904 . . (670)	9,588,813	2.75	3.50	9.00	16.00	50.00	300.00	1,000
1904O	2,456,000	2.75	7.00	15.00	32.50	85.00	750.00	
1905 . . (727)	4,968,250	2.75	3.50	9.00	16.00	50.00	300.00	1,000
1905O	1,230,000	5.00	7.00	15.00	30.00	60.00	400.00	
1905S	1,884,000	5.00	3.50	9.00	23.00	55.00	375.00	
1906 . . (675)	3,656,435	2.75	3.50	9.00	16.00	50.00	300.00	1,000
1906D	3,280,000	2.75	3.50	9.00	20.00	50.00	350.00	
1906O	2,056,000	2.75	3.50	9.00	23.00	50.00	350.00	
1907 . . (575)	7,192,575	2.75	3.50	9.00	16.00	50.00	300.00	1,000
1907D	2,484,000	2.75	3.50	9.00	20.00	50.00	350.00	
1907O	4,560,000	2.75	3.50	9.00	19.00	50.00	325.00	
1907S	1,360,000	2.75	3.50	9.00	21.00	55.00	400.00	
1908 . . (545)	4,232,545	2.75	3.50	9.00	16.00	50.00	300.00	1,000
1908D	5,788,000	2.75	3.50	9.00	16.00	50.00	325.00	
1908O	6,244,000	2.75	3.50	9.00	16.00	50.00	325.00	
1908S	784,000	6.00	9.00	17.50	35.00	80.00	475.00	
1909 . . (650)	9,268,650	2.75	3.50	9.00	16.00	50.00	300.00	1,000
1909D	5,114,000	2.75	3.50	9.00	16.00	50.00	325.00	
1909O	712,000	9.00	13.00	30.00	55.00	130.00	650.00	
1909S	1,348,000	2.75	3.50	9.00	16.00	50.00	400.00	
1910 . . (551)	2,244,551	2.75	3.50	9.00	16.00	50.00	300.00	1,000
1910D	1,500,000	2.75	3.50	9.00	16.00	50.00	350.00	
1911 . . (543)	3,720,543	2.75	3.50	9.00	16.00	50.00	300.00	1,000
1911D	933,600	2.75	3.50	10.00	20.00	50.00	350.00	
1911S	988,000	2.75	3.50	10.00	20.00	50.00	400.00	
1912 . . (700)	4,400,700	2.75	3.50	9.00	16.00	50.00	300.00	1,000
1912S	708,000	2.75	3.50	10.00	20.00	52.50	375.00	
1913 . . (613)	484,613	10.00	14.00	40.00	100.00	350.00	1,400	1,300
1913D	1,450,800	2.75	3.50	9.00	16.00	50.00	325.00	
1913S	40,000	300.00	350.00	575.00	900.00	1,500	3,500	
1914 . . (380)	6,244,610	2.75	3.50	9.00	16.00	50.00	300.00	1,000
1914D	3,046,000	2.75	3.50	9.00	16.00	50.00	300.00	
1914S	264,000	13.00	18.00	40.00	90.00	235.00	725.00	
1915 . . (450)	3,480,450	2.75	3.50	9.00	16.00	50.00	300.00	1,000
1915D	3,694,000	2.75	3.50	9.00	16.00	50.00	300.00	
1915S	704,000	3.50	6.00	13.00	23.00	50.00	325.00	
1916	1,788,000	2.75	3.50	9.00	16.00	50.00	300.00	
1916D	6,540,888	2.75	3.50	9.00	16.00	50.00	300.00	

QUARTER DOLLARS
STANDING LIBERTY TYPE 1916-1930

This type quarter was designed by Hermon A. MacNeil. The left arm of Liberty is upraised bearing a shield in the attitude of protection, from which the cover is being drawn. The right hand bears the olive branch of peace. The designer's initial M is located above and to the right of the date.

There was a modification in 1917 because of public resentment to Liberty's exposed breast. The reverse has a new arrangement of the stars and the eagle is higher.

In 1925 a depression was made in the pedestal on which Liberty stands and which bears the date. On the first issues the dates wore off easily because they were too high and were not protected by other features of the coin. The new "recessed" dates proved more durable as a result of this change.

No proof coins of this type were officially issued, but specimens of the first variety, dated 1917, are known to exist.

G-4 GOOD— *Date and lettering readable. Top of date worn. Liberty's right leg and toes worn off. Left leg and drapery lines show much wear.*

VG-8 VERY GOOD— *Distinct date. Toes show faintly. Drapery lines visible above her left leg.*

F-12 FINE— *High curve of right leg flat from thigh to ankle. Left leg shows only slight wear. Drapery lines over right thigh seen only at sides of leg.*

VF-20 VERY FINE— *Garment line across right leg will be worn but show at sides.*

EF-40 EXTREMELY FINE— *Flattened only at high spots. Her toes are sharp. Drapery lines across right leg are evident.*

MS-63 SELECT UNCIRCULATED— *No trace of wear. Light blemishes. Attractive mint luster.*

(Some modifications must be made for grading variety 2.)

Designer Hermon A. MacNeil. Standards same as previous issue; mints: Philadelphia, Denver, San Francisco.

Uncirculated pieces with fully struck head of Liberty are worth more than double the prices listed below.

Variety 1

	Quan. Minted	G-4	VG-8	F-12	VF-20	EF-40	MS-63
1916	52,000	$1,000	$1,200	$1,500	$1,800	$2,200	$4,300
1917 Variety 1	8,740,000	9.00	12.00	16.00	30.00	60.00	550.00
1917D Variety 1	1,509,200	12.00	16.00	23.00	60.00	110.00	600.00
1917S Variety 1	1,952,000	12.00	16.00	23.00	60.00	110.00	650.00

1918S, 8 over 7

Variety 2

Mint mark location is on obverse at left of date.

	Quan. Minted	G-4	VG-8	F-12	VF-20	EF-40	MS-63
1917 Variety 2	13,880,000	10.00	14.00	18.00	25.00	40.00	225.00
1917D Variety 2	6,224,400	20.00	25.00	45.00	65.00	110.00	350.00
1917S Variety 2	5,552,000	18.00	23.00	32.00	50.00	85.00	350.00
1918	14,240,000	12.00	16.00	25.00	35.00	55.00	240.00

QUARTER DOLLARS

	Quan. Minted	G-4	VG-8	F-12	VF-20	EF-40	MS-63
1918D	7,380,000	$22.00	$26.00	$40.00	$60.00	$95.00	$385.00
1918S Norm. date	} 11,072,000	12.00	16.00	22.50	30.00	50.00	275.00
1918S 8 over 7.		1,000	1,300	1,700	2,300	3,500	15,000
1919	11,324,000	28.00	32.00	40.00	50.00	75.00	225.00
1919D	1,944,000	45.00	70.00	100.00	140.00	240.00	935.00
1919S	1,836,000	45.00	65.00	95.00	130.00	220.00	875.00
1920	27,860,000	10.00	15.00	18.00	22.50	37.50	225.00
1920D	3,586,400	25.00	35.00	50.00	75.00	125.00	425.00
1920S	6,380,000	12.50	18.00	24.00	30.00	50.00	250.00
1921	1,916,000	50.00	80.00	125.00	160.00	250.00	750.00
1923	9,716,000	10.00	15.00	19.00	25.00	40.00	250.00
1923S	1,360,000	100.00	150.00	210.00	275.00	400.00	825.00
1924	10,920,000	10.00	15.00	19.00	25.00	40.00	250.00
1924D	3,112,000	25.00	30.00	40.00	60.00	90.00	275.00
1924S	2,860,000	15.00	18.00	25.00	30.00	45.00	350.00

Recessed Date Style 1925-1930

	Quan. Minted	G-4	VG-8	F-12	VF-20	EF-40	MS-63
1925	12,280,000	2.75	3.50	9.00	15.00	25.00	225.00
1926	11,316,000	2.75	3.50	9.00	15.00	25.00	225.00
1926D	1,716,000	7.00	7.50	12.00	19.00	40.00	225.00
1926S	2,700,000	2.75	3.50	11.00	19.00	55.00	400.00
1927	11,912,000	2.75	3.50	9.00	15.00	25.00	225.00
1927D	976,000	8.00	10.00	15.00	30.00	60.00	300.00
1927S	396,000	12.00	22.00	65.00	160.00	600.00	2,500
1928	6,336,000	2.75	3.50	9.00	15.00	25.00	225.00
1928D	1,627,600	5.00	8.00	12.00	18.00	38.00	240.00
1928S*	2,644,000	4.00	6.00	10.00	16.00	30.00	240.00
1929	11,140,000	2.75	3.50	9.00	15.00	25.00	225.00
1929D	1,358,000	5.00	8.00	12.00	18.00	32.00	230.00
1929S	1,764,000	4.00	6.00	10.00	16.00	30.00	225.00
1930	5,632,000	2.75	3.50	9.00	15.00	25.00	225.00
1930S	1,556,000	2.75	3.50	9.00	15.00	28.00	225.00

*Large and small mint mark varieties, see pages 59-60.

WASHINGTON TYPE 1932 to Date

This type was intended to be a commemorative issue marking the two-hundredth anniversary of Washington's birth. John Flanagan, a New York sculptor, was the designer. The initials JF are found at the base of the neck. Mint mark is on reverse below wreath, 1932 to 1964.

VG-8 VERY GOOD—*Wing tips outlined. Rims are fine and even. Tops of letters at rim are flattened.*

F-12 FINE—*Hairlines about ear are visible. Tiny feathers on eagle's breast are faintly visible.*

VF-20 VERY FINE—*Most hair details show. Wing feathers are clear.*

EF-40 EXTREMELY FINE—*Hairlines sharp. Wear spots confined to top of eagle's legs and center of breast.*

MS-63 SELECT UNCIRCULATED—*No trace of wear. Light blemishes. Attractive mint luster.*

MS-65 CHOICE UNCIRCULATED—*No trace of wear. Barely noticeable blemishes.*

QUARTER DOLLARS
Silver Coinage — 1932-1964

	Quan. Minted	VG-8	F-12	VF-20	EF-40	MS-63	MS-65
1932	5,404,000	$2.50	$2.75	$8.00	$11.00	$60.00	$450.00
1932D	436,800	45.00	60.00	95.00	170.00	1,200	4,000
1932S	408,000	40.00	50.00	65.00	100.00	450.00	2,700
1934 Light motto		2.25	2.50	7.00	11.00	55.00	200.00
1934 Hvy. motto	31,912,052	2.25	2.50	6.50	10.00	45.00	175.00
1934 Doubled die				50.00	150.00	350.00	700.00
1934D	3,527,200	2.25	2.75	11.00	20.00	165.00	900.00
1935	32,484,000	2.25	2.50	6.50	9.00	40.00	100.00
1935D	5,780,000	2.25	2.50	10.00	18.00	160.00	825.00
1935S	5,660,000	2.25	2.50	8.00	12.00	125.00	525.00

	Quan. Minted	VF-20	EF-40	MS-63	MS-65	Proof-65
1936 ..... (3,837)	41,303,837	$2.25	$7.00	$30.00	$100.00	$1,400
1936D	5,374,000	14.00	30.00	350.00	1,600	
1936S	3,828,000	8.00	12.00	125.00	425.00	
1937 ..... (5,542)	19,701,542	2.25	7.00	30.00	100.00	425.00
1937D	7,189,600	7.00	10.00	60.00	325.00	
1937S	1,652,000	12.00	18.00	140.00	700.00	
1938 ..... (8,045)	9,480,045	10.00	14.00	75.00	325.00	400.00
1938S	2,832,000	8.00	12.00	75.00	325.00	
1939 ..... (8,795)	33,548,795	2.25	6.00	20.00	60.00	250.00
1939D	7,092,000	6.00	8.00	35.00	160.00	
1939S	2,628,000	9.00	12.00	70.00	325.00	
1940 .... (11,246)	35,715,246	2.25	6.00	20.00	40.00	200.00
1940D	2,797,600	10.00	14.00	85.00	325.00	
1940S	8,244,000	2.25	6.00	25.00	50.00	
1941 .... (15,287)	79,047,287	2.25	4.00	10.00	25.00	175.00
1941D	16,714,800	2.25	5.00	25.00	50.00	
1941S*	16,080,000	2.25	5.00	23.00	50.00	
1942 .... (21,123)	102,117,123	2.25	4.00	10.00	18.00	175.00
1942D	17,487,200	2.25	5.00	15.00	28.00	
1942S	19,384,000	2.25	7.00	90.00	150.00	
1943	99,700,000	2.25	4.00	8.00	14.00	
1943D	16,095,600	2.25	5.00	18.00	30.00	
1943S	21,700,000	2.25	6.00	50.00	85.00	
1943S Doubled die obverse ..		165.00	200.00	600.00	1,200	
1944	104,956,000	2.25	2.50	6.00	12.00	
1944D	14,600,800	2.25	2.50	12.00	25.00	
1944S	12,560,000	2.25	2.50	13.00	26.00	
1945	74,372,000	2.25	2.50	5.00	10.00	
1945D	12,341,600	2.25	2.50	10.00	15.00	
1945S	17,004,001	2.25	2.50	8.00	12.00	
1946	53,436,000	2.25	2.50	5.00	8.00	
1946D	9,072,800	2.25	2.50	7.00	10.00	
1946S	4,204,000	2.25	2.50	8.00	12.00	
1947	22,556,000	2.25	2.50	7.00	10.00	
1947D	15,338,400	2.25	2.50	8.00	12.00	
1947S	5,532,000	2.25	2.50	6.00	10.00	
1948	35,196,000	2.25	2.50	4.00	7.00	
1948D	16,766,800	2.25	2.50	6.00	9.00	
1948S	15,960,000	2.25	2.50	6.00	10.00	
1949	9,312,000	2.25	2.50	27.50	40.00	
1949D	10,068,400	2.25	2.50	10.00	15.00	
1950 .... (51,386)	24,971,512	2.25	2.50	5.00	8.00	150.00
1950D		2.25	2.50	5.00	9.00	
1950D, D over S	21,075,600	60.00	150.00	350.00	500.00	

*Large and small mint mark varieties, see pages 59-60.

QUARTER DOLLARS

	Quan. Minted	VF-20	EF-40	MS-63	MS-65	Proof-65
1950 S	} 10,284,004	$2.25	$2.50	$8.00	$13.00	
1950 S, S over D		60.00	165.00	475.00	600.00	
1951 . . . . (57,500)	43,505,602	2.25	2.25	4.00	6.00	$80.00
1951D	35,354,800	2.25	2.25	4.00	6.50	
1951S	9,048,000	2.25	2.25	9.00	14.50	
1952 . . . . (81,980)	38,862,073	2.25	2.25	4.00	7.00	60.00
1952D	49,795,200	2.25	2.25	5.00	7.50	
1952S	13,707,800	2.25	2.25	7.00	11.00	
1953 . . . (128,800)	18,664,920	2.25	2.25	5.00	7.50	30.00
1953D	56,112,400	2.25	2.25	3.75	5.00	
1953S	14,016,000	2.25	2.25	5.00	7.00	
1954 . . . (233,300)	54,645,503	2.25	2.25	3.50	5.00	16.00
1954D	46,305,500	2.25	2.25	3.50	5.00	
1954S	11,834,722	2.25	2.25	3.75	5.50	

	Quan. Minted	EF-40	MS-63	MS-65	Proof-65
1955 . . . . (378,200)	18,558,381	$2.25	$3.50	$5.25	$12.00
1955D	3,182,400	2.25	4.00	7.00	
1956 . . . . (669,384)	44,813,384	2.25	2.75	3.25	7.00
1956D	32,334,500	2.25	2.75	3.25	
1957 . . . . (1,247,952)	47,779,952	2.25	2.75	3.25	6.00
1957D	77,924,160	2.25	2.75	3.25	
1958 . . . . (875,652)	7,235,652	2.25	2.75	5.50	8.00
1958D	78,124,900	2.25	2.75	3.25	
1959 . . . . (1,149,291)	25,533,291	2.25	2.75	3.25	7.00
1959D	62,054,232	2.25	2.75	3.25	
1960 . . . . (1,691,602)	30,855,602	2.25	2.75	3.25	6.00
1960D	63,000,324	2.25	2.75	3.25	
1961 . . . . (3,028,244)	40,064,244	2.25	2.75	3.25	6.00
1961D	83,656,928	2.25	2.75	3.25	
1962 . . . . (3,218,019)	39,374,019	2.25	2.75	3.25	6.00
1962D	127,554,756	2.25	2.75	3.25	
1963 . . . . (3,075,645)	77,391,645	2.25	2.75	3.25	6.00
1963D	135,288,184	2.25	2.75	3.25	
1964 . . . . (3,950,762)	564,341,347	2.25	2.75	3.25	6.00
1964D	704,135,528	2.25	2.75	3.25	

Note: Prices in italic are based on silver bullion valued at $8.00 per ounce.

Clad Coinage — 1965 to Date

Proof coins from 1937 through 1972 were made from special dies with high relief and minor detail differences. Some of the circulation coins of 1956-1964 and 1969D-1972D were also made from reverse dies with these same features. A variety of the 1964D quarter occurs with the modified reverse normally found only on the clad coins.

Weight 5.67 grams; composition: outer layers of copper-nickel (.750 copper, .250 nickel) bonded to inner core of pure copper; diameter 24.3 mm; reeded edge.

Starting in 1968 mint mark is on obverse at right of ribbon.

QUARTER DOLLARS

	Quan. Minted	MS-65	Proof-65		Quan. Minted	MS-65	Proof-65
1965	1,819,717,540	$ .75		1971	109,284,000	$ .50	
1966	821,101,500	.75		1971D	258,634,428	.50	
1967	1,524,031,848	.75		1971S Proof	(3,220,733)		$1.00
1968	220,731,500	.75		1972	215,048,000	.50	
1968D	101,534,000	1.00		1972D	311,067,732	.50	
1968S Proof	(3,041,506)		$1.00	1972S Proof	(3,260,996)		1.00
1969	176,212,000	.50		1973	346,924,000	.50	
1969D	114,372,000	1.00		1973D	232,977,400	.50	
1969S Proof	(2,934,631)		1.00	1973S Proof	(2,760,339)		1.00
1970	136,420,000	.50		1974	801,456,000	.50	
1970D	417,341,364	.50		1974D	353,160,300	.50	
1970S Proof	(2,632,810)		1.00	1974S Proof	(2,612,568)		1.00

BICENTENNIAL COINAGE DATED 1776-1976

In October of 1973, the Treasury announced an open contest for the selection of suitable designs for the Bicentennial reverses of the quarter, half dollar and dollar, with $5,000 to be awarded to each winner. Twelve semifinalists were chosen, and from these the symbolic entry of Jack L. Ahr was selected for the quarter reverse. It features a Colonial drummer facing left, with a victory torch encircled by thirteen stars at the upper left. Except for a dual dating, 1776-1976, the obverse remained unchanged. Pieces with this dual dating were coined during 1975 and 1976. They were struck for general circulation and included in all the Mint's offerings of proof and uncirculated sets.

Designers John Flanagan and Jack L. Ahr. Silver issue: weight 5.75 grams; composition: outer layers of .800 silver, .200 copper bonded to inner core of .209 silver, .791 copper. Copper-nickel issue: weight 5.67 grams; composition: outer layers of .750 copper, .250 nickel bonded to inner core of pure copper. Diameter 24.3 mm; reeded edge. Net weight of silver issues: .0739 oz. pure silver.

	Quan. Minted	MS-65	Proof-65
1776-1976 Copper-nickel clad	809,784,016	$ .50	
1776-1976D Copper-nickel clad	860,118,839	.50	
1776-1976S Copper-nickel clad	(7,059,099)		$1.75
1776-1976S Silver clad	*11,000,000	2.50	
1776-1976S Silver clad	(*4,000,000)		4.00

*Approximate mintage.

Eagle Reverse Resumed (Dies slightly modified to lower relief)

	Quan. Minted	MS-65	Proof-65		Quan. Minted	MS-60	Proof-65
1977	468,556,000	$ .50		1979S Proof	(3,677,175)		
1977D	256,524,978	.50		Filled S			$1.00
1977S Proof	(3,251,152)		$1.00	Clear S			4.00
1978	521,452,000	.50		1980P	635,832,000	$ .50	
1978D	287,373,152	.50		1980D	518,327,487	.50	
1978S Proof	(3,127,781)		1.00	1980S Proof	(3,554,806)		1.00
1979	515,708,000	.50		1981P	601,716,000	.50	
1979D	489,789,780	.50		1981D	575,722,833	.50	

QUARTER DOLLARS

	Quan. Minted	MS-65	Proof-65
1981S Proof	(4,063,083)		$1.00
1982P	500,931,000	$ .75	
1982D	480,042,788	.50	
1982S Proof	(3,857,479)		1.00
1983P	673,535,000	.50	
1983D	617,806,446	.50	
1983S Proof	(3,228,648)		1.50
1984P	676,545,000	.50	
1984D	546,483,064	.50	

	Quan. Minted	MS-65	Proof-65
1984S Proof			$1.00
1985P	775,818,962	$.50	
1985D	519,962,888	.50	
1985S Proof			1.00
1986P		.50	
1986D		.50	
1986S Proof			1.00

BIBLIOGRAPHY

Browning, A. W. *The Early Quarter Dollars of the United States 1796-1838.* New York, 1925.
Cline, J. H. *Standing Liberty Quarters.* 1976.
Duphorne, R. *The Early Quarter Dollars of The United States.* 1975.
Haseltine, J. W. *Type Table of United States Dollars, Half Dollars and Quarter Dollars.* Philadelphia, 1881 (reprinted 1927, 1968).
Kelman, Keith N. *Standing Liberty Quarters,* N.H., 1976.

HALF DOLLARS — 1794 to Date

The half dollar, authorized by the Act of April 2, 1792, was not minted until December, 1794. The early types of this series have been extensively collected by die varieties, of which many exist for most dates. Valuations given below are in each case for the most common variety, scarcer ones as listed by Beistle and Overton (see bibliography) generally command higher prices.

The weight of the half dollar was 208 grains and its fineness .8924 when first issued. This standard was not changed until 1837 when the law of January 18, 1837 specified 206¼ grains, .900 fine, which continued in use until 1965.

Arrows at the date in 1853 indicate the reduction of weight to 192 grains, in conformity with the Act of February 21, 1853. During that year only, rays were added to the field on the reverse side. Arrows remained in 1854 and 1855.

The 1866 proof quarter, half and dollar without motto are not mentioned in the Director's Report, and were not issued for circulation.

In 1873 the weight was raised by law to 192.9 grains and arrows were again placed at the date, to be removed in 1875.

TYPE COIN VALUES

	G-4	F-12	EF-40	AU-50	MS-60	MS-63	MS-65	PF-60	PF-63	PF-65
Flowing Hair 1794-1795	475.00	725.00	2,400	4,500	12,500	20,000	50,000			
Drpd Bust, SE 1796-1797	9,000	16,000	32,000	40,000						
Drpd Bust, HE 1801-1807	70.00	150.00	725.00	1,200	5,000	9,500	25,000			
Cap Bust Type 1807-1836	27.00	37.50	115.00	225.00	775.00	1,700	8,000			
Cap Bust, RE 1836-1839	40.00	50.00	175.00	400.00	900.00	2,400	10,000			
Lib Seated-NM 1839-1866	16.00	24.00	70.00	140.00	525.00	1,200	6,500	625.00	1,400	7,000
Lib. Seat-A&R 1853	16.00	28.00	225.00	500.00	2,000	4,750	15,500			
Lib. Seat-Arr. 1854-1855	16.00	24.00	90.00	250.00	900.00	2,200	6,800			
Lib. Seated-WM 1866-1891	15.00	22.00	60.00	115.00	500.00	1,250	5,800	600.00	1,300	6,500
Lib. Seat-Arr. 1873-1874	20.00	30.00	175.00	375.00	1,000	2,300	6,500	1,200	2,500	8,000
Barber 1892-1915	5.50	20.00	130.00	225.00	575.00	1,300	5,500	650.00	1,600	7,000
Lib Walking 1916-1947	4.50	4.50	9.00	16.00	40.00	120.00	350.00	350.00	550.00	1,200

FLOWING HAIR TYPE 1794-1795

AG-3 ABOUT GOOD— *Clear enough to identify.*

G-4 GOOD— *Date and letters sufficient to be readable. Main devices outlined, but lack details.*

VG-8 VERY GOOD— *Major details discernible. Letters well formed but worn.*

F-12 FINE— *Hair ends distinguishable. Top hairlines show, but otherwise worn smooth.*

VF-20 VERY FINE— *Hair in center shows some detail. Other details more bold.*

EF-40 EXTREMELY FINE— *Hair above head and down neck detailed, with slight wear.*

Designer Robert Scot; weight 13.48 grams; composition: .8924 silver, .1076 copper; approx. diameter 32.5 mm; edge: FIFTY CENTS OR HALF A DOLLAR with decorations between words.

				2 Leaves under Wings			3 Leaves under Wings		
	Quan. Minted	*AG-3*	*G-4*	*VG-8*	*F-12*	*VF-20*	*EF-40*		
1794	23,464	$475.00	$1,000	$1,500	$2,500	$4,000	$6,500		
1795 All kinds	299,680	250.00	475.00	550.00	725.00	1,200	2,400		
1795 Recut date		250.00	500.00	575.00	750.00	1,300	2,600		
1795 3 leaves under each wing.	300.00	625.00	900.00	1,500	2,800	5,500			

Varieties of 1795 are known with final S in STATES over D, with A in STATES over E, and with Y in LIBERTY over a star.

[138]

HALF DOLLARS
DRAPED BUST TYPE, SMALL EAGLE REVERSE 1796-1797

AG-3 ABOUT GOOD— *Clear enough to identify.*
G-4 GOOD— *Date and letters sufficient to be readable. Main devices outlined, but lack details.*
VG-8 VERY GOOD— *Major details discernible. Letters well formed but worn.*
F-15 FINE— *Hair ends distinguishable. Top hairlines show, but otherwise worn smooth.*
VF-20 VERY FINE— *Right side of drapery slightly worn. Left side to curls is smooth.*
EF-40 EXTREMELY FINE— *All lines in drapery on bust will show distinctly around to hair curls.*

1796, 15 Stars

1796, 16 Stars

	Quan. Minted	AG-3	G-4	VG-8	F-12	VF-20	EF-40
1796, 15 stars.........	} 3,918	$6,200	$9,000	$12,000	$16,000	$22,000	$32,000
1796, 16 stars.........		6,200	9,000	12,000	16,000	22,000	32,000
1797, 15 stars.........		6,200	9,000	12,000	16,000	22,000	32,000

DRAPED BUST TYPE, HERALDIC EAGLE REVERSE
1801-1807

	Quan. Minted	G-4	VG-8	F-12	VF-20	EF-40	MS-60
1801	30,289	$150.00	$225.00	$400.00	$750.00	$1,300	$8,500
1802	29,890	125.00	200.00	350.00	600.00	1,000	7,000
1803 Small 3	} 188,234	115.00	160.00	250.00	550.00	1,000	7,000
1803 Large 3		90.00	120.00	200.00	475.00	850.00	6,000

HALF DOLLARS

1805, 5 over 4

1806, 6 over 5

Knobbed Top 6, Small Stars

Branch Stem through Claw

Pointed Top 6

Branch Stem not through Claw

	Quan. Minted	G-4	VG-8	F-12	VF-20	EF-40	MS-60
1805, 5 over 4 ...... }		$100.00	$130.00	$225.00	$500.00	$1,000	$6,250
1805 Normal date. }	211,722	80.00	95.00	150.00	400.00	750.00	5,500
1806 All kinds 839,576							
1806, 6 over 5		85.00	100.00	185.00	425.00	800.00	5,500
1806, 6 over inverted 6		90.00	115.00	200.00	475.00	875.00	6,000
1806 Knobbed 6, large stars (traces of overdate)		70.00	85.00	150.00	400.00	725.00	5,000
1806 Knobbed 6, small stars ...		70.00	85.00	150.00	400.00	725.00	5,000
1806 Knobbed 6, stem not through claw		Rare					
1806 Pointed 6, stem through claw*		70.00	85.00	150.00	400.00	725.00	5,000
1806 Pointed 6, stem not through claw		70.00	85.00	150.00	400.00	725.00	5,000
1807 301,076		70.00	85.00	150.00	400.00	725.00	5,000

*One variety shows E in STATES over A.

CAPPED BUST TYPE, Lettered Edge 1807-1836

John Reich designed this Capped Head concept of Liberty. The head of Liberty facing left was used on all U.S. coin denominations for the next thirty years. Reich was the first artist to consistently include the denomination on our gold and silver coins. He was from Germany and a bondman freed from servitude by a mint official.

G-4 GOOD— *Date and letters readable. Bust worn smooth with outline distinct.*

VG-8 VERY GOOD— *LIBERTY visible but faint. Legends distinguishable. Clasp at shoulder visible. Curl above it nearly smooth.*

F-12 FINE— *Clasp and adjacent curl clearly outlined with slight details.*

VF-20 VERY FINE— *Clasp at shoulder clear. Curl has wear only on highest point. Hair over brow distinguishable.*

EF-40 EXTREMELY FINE— *Clasp and adjacent curl fairly sharp. Brow and hair above distinct. Curls well defined.*

MS-60 UNCIRCULATED— *No trace of wear. Light blemishes.*

HALF DOLLARS

Designer John Reich; weight 13.48 grams; composition: .8924 silver, .1076 copper; approx. diameter 32.5 mm; edge varieties, 1807-1814: FIFTY CENTS OR HALF A DOLLAR; 1814-1831: star added between DOLLAR and FIFTY; 1832-1836: vertical lines added between words.

First style (Variety 1) 1807-1808

		1807 Small Stars	1807 Large Stars		1807, 50 over 20		
	Quan. Minted	G-4	VG-8	F-12	VF-20	EF-40	MS-60
1807 Small stars... ⎫		$45.00	$60.00	$125.00	$250.00	$550.00	$1,500
1807 Large stars... ⎬	750,500	40.00	50.00	100.00	175.00	400.00	1,400
1807 Same,							
50 over 20.... ⎭		35.00	45.00	75.00	150.00	300.00	1,300
1808, 8 over 7...... ⎫		35.00	45.00	70.00	110.00	200.00	1,000
1808 .... ⎬	1,368,600	30.00	42.50	50.00	80.00	150.00	900.00

Remodeled Portrait and Eagle 1809-1834

1809 Experimental edge
xxxx between words.

1809 Experimental edge
IIIII between words.

HALF DOLLARS

	Quan. Minted	G-4	VG-8	F-12	VF-20	EF-40	MS-60
1809 Normal	} 1,405,810	$30.00	$38.00	$45.00	$75.00	$125.00	$900.00
1809 xxxx edge		30.00	40.00	47.50	80.00	150.00	950.00
1809 iiiiii edge.....		30.00	38.00	45.00	75.00	125.00	900.00
1810	1,276,276	27.00	33.00	40.00	65.00	125.00	900.00

"Punctuated" Date 18.11

1811 Small 8

1811 Large 8

	Quan. Minted	G-4	VG-8	F-12	VF-20	EF-40	MS-60
1811 (18.11) 11 over 10....	} 1,203,644	30.00	35.00	60.00	100.00	200.00	950.00
1811 Small 8		27.00	32.00	37.50	60.00	135.00	900.00
1811 Large 8		27.00	32.00	37.50	60.00	135.00	875.00
1812, 2 over 1 small 8.......	} 1,628,059	30.00	35.00	60.00	100.00	200.00	875.00
1812, 2 over 1 large 8.......		85.00	125.00	250.00	400.00	850.00	——
1812 Normal		27.00	32.00	37.50	60.00	115.00	850.00

1812, 2 over 1, Small 8

1812, 2 over 1, Large 8

1813, 50C, over UNI

1814, 4 over 3

1814, E over A in STATES

	Quan. Minted	G-4	VG-8	F-12	VF-20	EF-40	MS-60
1813	} 1,241,903	27.00	32.00	37.50	60.00	115.00	825.00
1813, 50C over UNI		30.00	40.00	65.00	100.00	200.00	1,100
1814, 4 over 3......	} 1,039,075	27.00	35.00	45.00	70.00	125.00	825.00
1814 E over A in STATES		27.00	32.00	37.50	75.00	150.00	900.00
1814 Normal		27.00	32.00	37.50	60.00	115.00	825.00

1817, 7 over 3

1817, 7 over 4

1817 Punctuated Date

HALF DOLLARS

	Quan. Minted	G-4	VG-8	F-12	VF-20	EF-40	MS-60
1815, 5 over 2......... 47,150		$600.00	$800.00	$1,200	$1,600	$2,100	$5,000
1817, 7 over 3.....		50.00	75.00	200.00	300.00	650.00	1,750
1817, 7 over 4.....		V. Rare		3,000	6,000	——	
1817 dated 181.7...	1,215,567	27.00	35.00	50.00	75.00	150.00	900.00
1817 Normal		27.00	32.00	37.50	60.00	115.00	800.00

1818, 1st 8 Small, 2nd 8 over 7

1819, Small 9 over 8

1818, 1st 8 Large, 2nd 8 over 7

1819, Large 9 over 8

	Quan. Minted	G-4	VG-8	F-12	VF-20	EF-40	MS-60
1818, 8 over 7 small 8......		27.00	32.00	37.50	60.00	115.00	900.00
1818, 8 over 7 large 8......	1,960,322	27.00	32.00	37.50	60.00	115.00	900.00
1818 Normal		27.00	32.00	37.50	60.00	115.00	800.00
1819 Sm. 9 over 8		27.00	32.00	37.50	60.00	115.00	800.00
1819 Lg. 9 over 8	2,208,000	27.00	32.00	37.50	60.00	115.00	800.00
1819 Normal		27.00	32.00	37.50	60.00	115.00	800.00

1820, 20 over 19 Square Base 2

1820, 20 over 19 Curl Base 2

Curl Base, No Knob 2, Small Date

Square Base, Knob 2, Large Date

Square Base No Knob 2, Large Date

1822, 2 over 1

	Quan. Minted	G-4	VG-8	F-12	VF-20	EF-40	MS-60
1820 20 over 19 square 2		27.00	32.00	37.50	60.00	115.00	900.00
1820, 20 over 19 curl 2.........		27.00	32.00	37.50	60.00	115.00	900.00
1820 Curl base 2.... small date.....	751,122	27.00	32.00	37.50	60.00	115.00	900.00
1820 Sq. base knob 2, large date.....		27.00	32.00	37.50	60.00	115.00	900.00
1820 Sq. base no knob 2, lg. date		27.00	32.00	37.50	60.00	115.00	900.00

HALF DOLLARS

	Quan. Minted	G-4	VG-8	F-12	VF-20	EF-40	MS-60
1821	1,305,797	$27.00	$32.00	$37.50	$60.00	$115.00	$800.00
1822, 2 over 1......	} 1,559,573	45.00	60.00	90.00	110.00	180.00	1,200
1822		27.00	32.00	37.50	60.00	115.00	800.00

1823 Broken 3   **1823 Patched 3**   **1823 Ugly 3**

1823 Broken 3.....		42.00	55.00	80.00	100.00	175.00	900.00
1823 Patched 3....	} 1,694,200	42.00	55.00	80.00	100.00	175.00	900.00
1823 Ugly 3.......		27.00	32.00	37.50	60.00	115.00	800.00
1823 Normal......		27.00	32.00	37.50	60.00	115.00	775.00

"Various Dates"
(probably 4 over   **1824, 4 over 1**   **1824, 4 over 4**   **1824, 4 over 4**
2 over 0)

1824 over various dates		27.00	32.00	37.50	60.00	115.00	775.00
1824, 4 over 1......	} 3,504,954	27.00	32.00	37.50	60.00	115.00	775.00
1824, 4 over 4 (2 var.).......		27.00	32.00	37.50	60.00	115.00	900.00
1824 Normal......		27.00	32.00	37.50	60.00	115.00	800.00
1825	2,943,166	27.00	32.00	37.50	60.00	115.00	775.00
1826	4,004,180	27.00	32.00	37.50	60.00	115.00	775.00
1827, 7 over 6......		27.00	32.00	37.50	60.00	115.00	800.00
1827 Sq. base 2....	} 5,493,400	27.00	32.00	37.50	60.00	115.00	775.00
1827 Curl base 2....		27.00	32.00	37.50	60.00	115.00	800.00

1828 Curl Base, Knob 2   **1828 Square Base 2,**   **1828 Square Base 2,**
                              Large 8's   **Small 8's**

[144]

HALF DOLLARS

1828 Large Letters

1828 Small Letters

	Quan. Minted	G-4	VG-8	F-12	VF-20	EF-40	MS-60
1828 All kinds....	3,075,200						
1828 Curl base no knob 2		$27.00	$32.00	$37.50	$60.00	$115.00	$775.00
1828 Curl base knob 2		35.00	45.00	60.00	85.00	125.00	875.00
1828 Sq. base 2, lg. 8's		27.00	32.00	37.50	60.00	115.00	800.00
1828 Sq. base 2, sm. 8's, lg. let .		27.00	32.00	37.50	60.00	115.00	800.00
1828 Sq. base 2, sm. 8's & let ..		27.00	35.00	40.00	75.00	125.00	850.00
1829, 9 over 7.... }	3,712,156	27.00	32.00	37.50	60.00	115.00	800.00
1829		27.00	32.00	37.50	60.00	115.00	800.00

Raised segment lines to right, 1830

Raised segment lines to left, 1830-1831

1832 Large Letters Reverse.

Adopted edge 1830-1836

1830 Small 0 .... }	4,764,800	27.00	32.00	37.50	60.00	115.00	775.00
1830 Large 0 .. }		27.00	32.00	37.50	60.00	115.00	775.00
1831	5,873,660	27.00	32.00	37.50	60.00	115.00	775.00
1832 Normal .. }	4,797,000	27.00	32.00	37.50	60.00	115.00	775.00
1832 Large letters }		27.00	32.00	37.50	60.00	115.00	775.00
1833	5,206,000	27.00	32.00	37.50	60.00	115.00	775.00

1830 Small 0

1834 Large Date

1834 Small Date

1834 Lg. Letters Reverse   1834 Sm. Letters Reverse.   1836, 50 over 00

Portrait Modified Slightly 1834-1836

1834 Lg. date & let }		27.00	32.00	37.50	60.00	115.00	800.00
1834 Large date, small letters.. }	6,412,004	27.00	32.00	37.50	60.00	115.00	800.00
1834 Small date, stars, letters }		27.00	32.00	37.50	60.00	115.00	775.00
1835	5,352,006	27.00	32.00	37.50	60.00	115.00	775.00
1836 .... }	6,545,000	27.00	32.00	37.50	60.00	115.00	775.00
1836, 50 over 00 }		35.00	50.00	65.00	90.00	150.00	1,000

HALF DOLLARS
Variety 2 — Reeded Edge, Reverse "50 CENTS" 1836-1837

Designer Christian Gobrecht; weight 13.36 grams; composition: .900 silver, .100 copper; diameter 30 mm; reeded edge; mints: Philadelphia, New Orleans.

G-4 GOOD—*LIBERTY discernible on headband.*

VG-8 VERY GOOD—*Minimum of 3 letters in LIBERTY must be clear.*

F-12 FINE—*LIBERTY complete.*

VF-20 VERY FINE—*LIBERTY is sharp. Shoulder clasp is clear.*

EF-40 EXTREMELY FINE—*LIBERTY sharp and strong. Hair details show.*

MS-60 UNCIRCULATED—*No trace of wear. Light blemishes.*

	Quan. Minted	G-4	VG-8	F-12	VF-20	EF-40	MS-60
1836	1,200	$325.00	$450.00	$550.00	$1,000	$1,800	$4,250
1837	3,629,820	40.00	45.00	50.00	75.00	175.00	900.00

Variety 3 — Reeded Edge, Reverse "HALF DOL." 1838-1839

The 1838O was the first branch mint half dollar, though not mentioned in the Director's report. The New Orleans chief coiner stated that only 20 were struck. In 1838-39 the mint mark appears on the obverse; thereafter it is on the reverse through 1915.

	Quan. Minted	G-4	VG-8	F-12	VF-20	EF-40	MS-60
1838	3,546,000	40.00	45.00	50.00	85.00	175.00	900.00
1838O	(20)						50,000
1839	1,392,976	40.00	45.00	50.00	85.00	175.00	900.00
1839 Small letters reverse							
1839O	178,976	100.00	150.00	225.00	350.00	600.00	4,000

LIBERTY SEATED TYPE 1839-1891
Variety 1 — No Motto Above Eagle 1839-1853

Designer Christian Gobrecht; weight 13.36 grams; composition: .900 silver, .100 copper; diameter 30.6 mm; reeded edge; mints: Philadelphia, New Orleans.

G-4 GOOD—*Scant rim. LIBERTY on shield worn off. Date and letters readable.*

VG-8 VERY GOOD—*Rim fairly defined. At least 3 letters in LIBERTY are evident.*

F-12 FINE—*LIBERTY complete, but weak.*

VF-20 VERY FINE—*LIBERTY mostly sharp.*

EF-40 EXTREMELY FINE—*LIBERTY entirely sharp. Scroll edges and clasp distinct.*

MS-60 UNCIRCULATED—*No trace of wear. Light blemishes.*

| 1839 No drapery from elbow | | 30.00 | 50.00 | 80.00 | 225.00 | 600.00 | 6,000 |

HALF DOLLARS

Modified obverse, drapery from elbow. Small letters in legend
1839-1842.

**Drapery from Elbow
starting 1839**

**Small letters in
Legend 1839-41**

**1840 (only) with
Medium Letters, Large Eagle
(Style of 1838)**

	Quan. Minted	G-4	VG-8	F-12	VF-20	EF-40	MS-60
1839	1,972,400	$22.50	$27.50	$35.00	$50.00	$90.00	$600.00
1840 Sm. letters . . . }		18.00	25.00	30.00	40.00	75.00	600.00
1840 Med. letters }	1,435,008	30.00	40.00	70.00	125.00	225.00	——
1840O	855,100	20.00	27.50	35.00	50.00	90.00	650.00
1841	310,000	23.00	30.00	60.00	90.00	175.00	950.00
1841O	401,000	18.00	25.00	35.00	50.00	90.00	850.00
1842O Small date	203,000	300.00	600.00	900.00	1,750	3,000	——

Modified reverse with large letters in legend 1842-1853.

Small Date

Medium Date

Large Letter Reverse

		G-4	VG-8	F-12	VF-20	EF-40	MS-60
1842 Sm. date . . . . . }		20.00	30.00	35.00	50.00	85.00	750.00
1842 Med. date . . }	2,012,764	18.00	25.00	30.00	45.00	80.00	650.00
1842O Med. date	754,000	18.00	23.00	25.00	40.00	80.00	600.00
1843	3,844,000	18.00	23.00	25.00	35.00	75.00	575.00
1843O	2,268,000	18.00	23.00	25.00	35.00	75.00	575.00
1844	1,766,000	18.00	23.00	25.00	35.00	75.00	575.00
1844O . . . . }		18.00	23.00	25.00	35.00	75.00	575.00
1844O Double date }	2,005,000	25.00	40.00	60.00	125.00	325.00	1,000
1845	589,000	18.00	23.00	25.00	35.00	75.00	575.00
1845O . . . . }		18.00	23.00	25.00	35.00	75.00	650.00
1845O No drapery }	2,094,000	30.00	45.00	60.00	80.00	200.00	750.00

HALF DOLLARS

In 1846 date size was again enlarged. The 1846 medium date is approximately the size of the 1842 medium date shown. Tall date is similar to 1853.

	Quan. Minted	G-4	VG-8	F-12	VF-20	EF-40	MS-60
1846 Med. dt. All	2,210,000	$18.00	$23.00	$25.00	$35.00	$75.00	$575.00
1846 Tall date		18.00	23.00	25.00	35.00	75.00	575.00
1846 over horizontal 6 (error)..		40.00	60.00	90.00	150.00	300.00	1,100
1846O Med. date... ⎫		18.00	23.00	25.00	35.00	75.00	575.00
1846O Tall date.. ⎬	2,304,000	40.00	60.00	95.00	200.00	325.00	1,000
1847, 7 over 6 ..... ⎫		—	—	—	—	—	—
1847 Normal date ⎬	1,156,000	18.00	23.00	25.00	35.00	75.00	575.00
1847O...............	2,584,000	18.00	23.00	25.00	35.00	75.00	575.00
1848	580,000	30.00	40.00	60.00	90.00	150.00	850.00
1848O...............	3,180,000	18.00	23.00	25.00	35.00	75.00	575.00
1849	1,252,000	18.00	23.00	25.00	35.00	75.00	575.00
1849O...............	2,310,000	18.00	23.00	25.00	35.00	75.00	575.00
1850	227,000	40.00	60.00	95.00	150.00	250.00	1,100
1850O...............	2,456,000	18.00	23.00	25.00	35.00	75.00	575.00
1851	200,750	40.00	60.00	95.00	150.00	250.00	1,200
1851O...............	402,000	18.00	23.00	25.00	35.00	75.00	575.00
1852	77,130	75.00	125.00	200.00	350.00	500.00	1,500
1852O...............	144,000	40.00	60.00	95.00	150.00	250.00	1,100
1853O......................			—	24,000	40,000		

Variety 2 — Arrows at Date, Rays Around Eagle 1853 Only

Weight 12.44 grams; composition: .900 silver, .100 copper; diameter 30.6 mm; reeded edge; mints: Philadelphia, New Orleans, San Francisco.

1853	3,532,708	16.00	20.00	28.00	85.00	225.00	2,000
1853O All kinds	1,328,000	16.00	20.00	30.00	90.00	250.00	2,300

Variety 3 — Arrows at Date, No Rays 1854-1855

1854	2,982,000	16.00	19.00	24.00	43.00	90.00	900.00
1854O...............	5,240,000	16.00	19.00	24.00	43.00	90.00	900.00
1855 over 1854 .... ⎫			75.00	125.00	275.00	500.00	1,400
1855 Normal date ⎬	759,500	16.00	19.00	24.00	43.00	90.00	900.00
1855O.	3,688,000	16.00	19.00	24.00	43.00	90.00	900.00
1855S................	129,950	275.00	375.00	600.00	1,000	2,500	——

Variety 1 Design Resumed 1856-1866

1856	938,000	16.00	19.00	24.00	35.00	65.00	525.00
1856O...............	2,658,000	16.00	19.00	24.00	35.00	65.00	525.00
1856S................	211,000	22.00	25.00	35.00	85.00	200.00	1,300
1857	1,988,000	16.00	19.00	24.00	35.00	65.00	525.00
1857O................	818,000	18.00	22.00	27.00	37.50	75.00	575.00
1857S................	158,000	25.00	33.00	45.00	90.00	250.00	1,400

HALF DOLLARS

	Quan. Minted	G-4	VG-8	F-12	VF-20	EF-40	MS-60	Proof-63
1858	4,226,000	$16.00	$19.00	$24.00	$35.00	$65.00	$525.00	$2,750
1858O	7,294,000	16.00	19.00	24.00	35.00	65.00	525.00	
1858S	476,000	21.00	25.00	30.00	55.00	125.00	900.00	
1859 . . (800)	748,000	16.00	19.00	24.00	35.00	75.00	550.00	1,800
1859O	2,834,000	16.00	19.00	24.00	35.00	65.00	525.00	
1859S	566,000	21.00	25.00	30.00	55.00	125.00	900.00	
1860 (1,000)	303,700	21.00	25.00	27.50	45.00	90.00	850.00	1,400
1860O	1,290,000	16.00	19.00	24.00	35.00	65.00	525.00	
1860S	472,000	21.00	24.00	27.00	40.00	75.00	625.00	
1861 (1,000)	2,888,400	16.00	19.00	24.00	35.00	65.00	525.00	1,400
1861O	2,532,633	16.00	19.00	24.00	35.00	65.00	525.00	

The 1861O quantity includes 330,000 struck under the United States government; 1,240,000 for the State of Louisiana after it seceded from the Union; and 962,633 after Louisiana joined the Confederate States of America. As all these 1861O coins were struck from U.S. dies. It is impossible to distinguish one from another. They should not be confused with the very rare Confederate half dollar of 1861 (see pgs. 259-260) which has a distinctive reverse.

		G-4	VG-8	F-12	VF-20	EF-40	MS-60	Proof-63
1861S	939,500	16.00	19.00	24.00	35.00	65.00	525.00	
1862 . . (550)	253,550	22.50	30.00	35.00	70.00	100.00	800.00	1,400
1862S	1,352,000	16.00	19.00	24.00	35.00	65.00	525.00	
1863 . . (460)	503,660	21.00	24.00	27.00	45.00	75.00	700.00	1,400
1863S	916,000	16.00	19.00	24.00	35.00	65.00	525.00	
1864 . . (470)	379,570	21.00	24.00	27.00	45.00	75.00	700.00	1,400
1864S	658,000	16.00	19.00	24.00	35.00	70.00	525.00	
1865 . . (500)	511,900	21.00	24.00	27.00	45.00	75.00	700.00	1,400
1865S	675,000	16.00	19.00	24.00	35.00	70.00	525.00	
1866S No motto	60,000	45.00	75.00	135.00	225.00	350.00	4,500	
1866		(*Unique*—see similar quarter and dollar)						——

**Variety 4 —
Motto "In God We Trust"
Added Above Eagle
1866-1873**

		G-4	VG-8	F-12	VF-20	EF-40	MS-60	Proof-63
1866 . . (725)	745,625	15.00	18.00	22.00	30.00	60.00	525.00	1,300
1866S	994,000	15.00	18.00	22.00	30.00	60.00	550.00	
1867 . . (625)	449,925	17.00	20.00	25.00	35.00	80.00	700.00	1,300
1867S	1,196,000	15.00	18.00	22.00	30.00	60.00	550.00	
1868 . . (600)	418,200	15.00	18.00	22.00	30.00	60.00	525.00	1,300
1868S	1,160,000	15.00	18.00	22.00	30.00	60.00	550.00	
1869 . . (600)	795,900	15.00	18.00	22.00	30.00	60.00	525.00	1,300
1869S	656,000	15.00	18.00	22.00	30.00	60.00	550.00	
1870 (1,000)	634,900	15.00	18.00	22.00	30.00	60.00	525.00	1,300
1870CC	54,617	300.00	500.00	900.00	1,400	2,700	——	
1870S	1,004,000	15.00	18.00	22.00	30.00	75.00	575.00	
1871 . . (960)	1,204,560	15.00	18.00	22.00	30.00	65.00	550.00	1,300
1871CC	153,950	75.00	125.00	150.00	325.00	675.00	3,200	
1871S	2,178,000	15.00	21.00	27.50	35.00	65.00	550.00	

HALF DOLLARS

	Quan. Minted	G-4	VG-8	F-12	VF-20	EF-40	MS-60	Proof-63
1872 .. (950)	881,550	$20.00	$22.00	$27.50	$37.50	$80.00	$750.00	$1,300
1872CC	257,000	45.00	75.00	100.00	225.00	350.00	2,400	
1872S	580,000	15.00	20.00	30.00	40.00	75.00	575.00	
1873 Closed 3								
...... (600)	587,600	15.00	18.00	22.00	30.00	70.00	700.00	1,300
1873 Open 3	214,200				—	—		
1873CC	122,500	50.00	75.00	135.00	235.00	400.00	2,500	
1873S No arrows 5,000				Unknown in any collection.				

Variety 5 — Arrows at Date 1873-1874

Arrows were placed at the date to denote a change in weight from 12.44 to 12.50 grams.

Weight 12.50 grams; composition: .900 silver, .100 copper; diameter 30.6 mm; reeded edge; mints: Philadelphia, Carson City, San Francisco.

1873 .. (550)	1,815,700	20.00	25.00	30.00	75.00	175.00	1,000	2,500
1873CC	214,560	35.00	60.00	125.00	185.00	300.00	1,750	
1873S	228,000	30.00	35.00	60.00	100.00	200.00	1,200	
1874 .. (700)	2,360,300	20.00	25.00	30.00	75.00	175.00	1,000	2,500
1874CC	59,000	100.00	175.00	350.00	500.00	900.00	4,000	
1874S	394,000	30.00	35.00	60.00	100.00	200.00	1,400	

Variety 4 Resumed 1875-1891

1875 .. (700)	6,027,500	15.00	18.00	22.00	30.00	60.00	500.00	1,300
1875CC	1,008,000	17.00	20.00	25.00	45.00	75.00	550.00	
1875S	3,200,000	15.00	18.00	22.00	30.00	60.00	500.00	
1876 (1,150)	8,419,150	15.00	18.00	22.00	30.00	60.00	500.00	1,300
1876CC	1,956,000	17.00	20.00	25.00	45.00	75.00	625.00	
1876S	4,528,000	15.00	18.00	22.00	30.00	60.00	500.00	
1877 .. (510)	8,304,510	15.00	18.00	22.00	30.00	60.00	500.00	1,300
1877CC	1,420,000	17.00	20.00	25.00	45.00	75.00	625.00	
1877S	5,356,000	15.00	18.00	22.00	30.00	60.00	500.00	
1878 .. (800)	1,378,400	15.00	18.00	22.00	30.00	60.00	500.00	1,300
1878CC	62,000	150.00	225.00	350.00	600.00	950.00	2,400	
1878S	12,000	2,000	2,750	3,500	5,000	8,000	14,000	
1879 (1,100)	5,900	125.00	150.00	200.00	250.00	350.00	900.00	1,500
1880 (1,355)	9,755	110.00	135.00	180.00	225.00	300.00	800.00	1,500
1881 .. (975)	10,975	110.00	135.00	180.00	225.00	300.00	800.00	1,500
1882 (1,100)	5,500	125.00	150.00	200.00	250.00	350.00	900.00	1,500
1883 (1,039)	9,039	110.00	135.00	180.00	225.00	300.00	800.00	1,500
1884 .. (875)	5,275	125.00	150.00	200.00	250.00	350.00	950.00	1,500
1885 .. (930)	6,130	110.00	135.00	180.00	225.00	300.00	950.00	1,500
1886 .. (886)	5,886	110.00	135.00	180.00	225.00	300.00	950.00	1,500
1887 .. (710)	5,710	110.00	135.00	180.00	225.00	300.00	950.00	1,500
1888 .. (832)	12,833	100.00	125.00	150.00	200.00	275.00	800.00	1,500
1889 .. (711)	12,711	100.00	125.00	150.00	200.00	275.00	800.00	1,500
1890 .. (590)	12,590	100.00	125.00	150.00	200.00	275.00	800.00	1,500
1891 .. (600)	200,600	15.00	20.00	25.00	45.00	75.00	600.00	1,500

HALF DOLLARS
BARBER or LIBERTY HEAD TYPE 1892-1915

Like the dime and quarter dollar, this type was designed by Charles E. Barber, whose initial B is at the truncation of the neck.

G-4 GOOD—*Date and legends readable. LIBERTY worn off headband.*
VG-8 VERY GOOD—*Minimum of 3 letters readable in LIBERTY.*
F-12 FINE—*LIBERTY completely readable, but not sharp.*
VF-20 VERY FINE—*All letters in LIBERTY evenly plain.*
EF-40 EXTREMELY FINE—*LIBERTY bold, and its ribbon distinct.*
MS-60 UNCIRCULATED—*No trace of wear. Light blemishes.*

Designer Charles E. Barber; weight 12.50 grams; composition: .900 silver, .100 copper; diameter 30.6 mm; reeded edge; mints: Philadelphia, Denver, New Orleans, San Francisco.

Mint mark location on reverse below eagle.

	Quan. Minted	G-4	VG-8	F-12	VF-20	EF-40	MS-60	Proof-63
1892 (1,245)	935,245	$13.00	$20.00	$30.00	$50.00	$165.00	$575.00	$1,600
1892O*.......	390,000	100.00	125.00	150.00	275.00	400.00	1,000	
1892S......	1,029,028	100.00	125.00	150.00	275.00	400.00	1,100	
1893 .. (792)	1,826,792	10.00	16.00	25.00	45.00	175.00	575.00	1,600
1893O......	1,389,000	16.00	23.00	40.00	85.00	235.00	750.00	
1893S........	740,000	50.00	65.00	120.00	200.00	350.00	1,000	
1894 .. (972)	1,148,972	10.00	16.00	25.00	60.00	175.00	575.00	1,600
1894O......	2,138,000	9.00	15.00	30.00	60.00	210.00	650.00	
1894S......	4,048,690	8.00	11.00	25.00	55.00	195.00	600.00	
1895 .. (880)	1,835,218	8.00	11.00	22.00	52.00	175.00	575.00	1,600
1895O......	1,766,000	9.00	14.00	25.00	55.00	180.00	650.00	
1895S......	1,108,086	16.00	22.50	37.50	70.00	180.00	600.00	
1896 .. (762)	950,762	9.00	14.00	30.00	55.00	175.00	600.00	1,600
1896O........	924,000	16.00	25.00	40.00	100.00	250.00	1,000	
1896S......	1,140,948	50.00	60.00	80.00	175.00	325.00	1,150	
1897 .. (731)	2,480,731	5.50	7.00	20.00	40.00	130.00	575.00	1,600
1897O........	632,000	50.00	60.00	80.00	200.00	450.00	1,250	
1897S........	933,900	85.00	100.00	140.00	210.00	400.00	1,100	
1898 .. (735)	2,956,735	7.00	7.00	20.00	40.00	130.00	575.00	1,600
1898O........	874,000	15.00	24.00	37.50	80.00	235.00	750.00	
1898S......	2,358,550	8.00	11.00	25.00	55.00	165.00	625.00	
1899 .. (846)	5,538,846	5.50	7.00	20.00	40.00	130.00	575.00	1,600
1899O......	1,724,000	8.00	11.00	25.00	55.00	200.00	650.00	
1899S......	1,686,411	9.00	15.00	25.00	55.00	165.00	600.00	
1900 .. (912)	4,762,912	5.50	7.00	20.00	40.00	130.00	575.00	1,600
1900O......	2,744,000	8.00	11.00	25.00	55.00	200.00	750.00	
1900S......	2,560,322	8.00	11.00	23.00	45.00	165.00	600.00	
1901 .. (813)	4,268,813	5.50	7.00	20.00	50.00	140.00	575.00	1,600
1901O......	1,124,000	8.50	13.00	30.00	60.00	350.00	1,100	
1901S........	847,044	13.00	19.00	40.00	130.00	450.00	1,300	
1902 .. (777)	4,922,777	5.50	7.00	20.00	40.00	130.00	575.00	1,600
1902O......	2,526,000	8.00	11.00	22.00	45.00	170.00	750.00	

*Normal and "microscopic" mint mark varieties, see pages 59-60.

HALF DOLLARS

	Quan. Minted	G-4	VG-8	F-12	VF-20	EF-40	MS-60	Proof-63
1902S	1,460,670	$8.00	$10.00	$22.00	$50.00	$175.00	$650.00	
1903 . . (755)	2,278,755	5.50	7.00	20.00	40.00	150.00	575.00	$1,600
1903O	2,100,000	8.00	10.00	22.00	45.00	165.00	650.00	
1903S	1,920,772	8.00	10.00	22.00	45.00	175.00	650.00	
1904 . . (670)	2,992,670	5.50	7.00	20.00	40.00	130.00	575.00	1,600
1904O	1,117,600	10.00	13.00	30.00	65.00	250.00	1,100	
1904S	553,038	13.00	18.00	40.00	110.00	300.00	1,100	
1905 . . (727)	662,727	10.00	12.00	30.00	75.00	200.00	650.00	1,850
1905O	505,000	11.00	13.00	35.00	85.00	235.00	750.00	
1905S	2,494,000	8.00	10.00	22.00	45.00	170.00	650.00	
1906 . . (675)	2,638,675	5.50	7.00	20.00	40.00	130.00	575.00	1,600
1906D	4,028,000	5.50	8.50	22.00	40.00	140.00	575.00	
1906O	2,446,000	5.50	8.50	22.00	40.00	150.00	650.00	
1906S	1,740,154	5.50	8.50	22.00	45.00	175.00	650.00	
1907 . . (575)	2,598,575	5.50	7.00	20.00	40.00	130.00	575.00	1,600
1907D	3,856,000	5.50	8.50	22.00	40.00	140.00	575.00	
1907O	3,946,600	5.50	8.50	22.00	40.00	140.00	600.00	
1907S	1,250,000	8.00	11.00	25.00	45.00	180.00	650.00	
1908 . . (545)	1,354,545	5.50	7.00	20.00	40.00	130.00	575.00	1,600
1908D	3,280,000	5.50	7.00	20.00	40.00	130.00	575.00	
1908O	5,360,000	5.50	7.00	20.00	40.00	130.00	575.00	
1908S	1,644,828	5.50	9.00	22.00	45.00	175.00	625.00	
1909 . . (650)	2,368,650	5.50	7.00	20.00	40.00	130.00	575.00	1,600
1909O	925,400	5.50	10.00	25.00	60.00	225.00	800.00	
1909S	1,764,000	5.50	7.00	20.00	40.00	160.00	625.00	
1910 . . (551)	418,551	9.00	13.00	30.00	60.00	225.00	650.00	1,600
1910S	1,948,000	5.50	7.00	20.00	40.00	160.00	625.00	
1911 . . (543)	1,406,543	5.50	7.00	20.00	40.00	130.00	575.00	1,600
1911D	695,080	8.00	11.00	22.00	45.00	145.00	625.00	
1911S	1,272,000	5.50	7.00	20.00	40.00	150.00	625.00	
1912 . . (700)	1,550,700	5.50	7.00	20.00	40.00	130.00	575.00	1,600
1912D	2,300,800	5.50	7.00	20.00	40.00	130.00	575.00	
1912S	1,370,000	5.50	7.00	20.00	40.00	150.00	600.00	
1913 . . (627)	188,627	18.00	22.50	35.00	90.00	225.00	900.00	2,000
1913D	534,000	5.50	10.00	22.00	50.00	150.00	625.00	
1913S	604,000	5.50	10.00	22.00	60.00	175.00	625.00	
1914 . . (380)	124,610	25.00	27.50	55.00	145.00	275.00	900.00	2,200
1914S	992,000	5.50	9.00	22.00	45.00	165.00	625.00	
1915 . . (450)	138,450	18.00	25.00	40.00	100.00	225.00	850.00	2,100
1915D	1,170,400	5.50	7.00	20.00	40.00	130.00	575.00	
1915S	1,604,000	5.50	7.00	20.00	40.00	140.00	575.00	

LIBERTY WALKING TYPE 1916-1947

This type was designed by A. A. Weinman. The designer's monogram AAW appears under the tip of the wing feathers. On the 1916 coins and some of the 1917 coins the mint mark is located on the obverse below the motto.

G-4 GOOD—*Rims are defined. Motto IN GOD WE TRUST readable.*

VG-8 VERY GOOD—*Motto is distinct. About half of skirt lines at left are clear.*

F-12 FINE—*All skirt lines evident, but worn in spots. Details in sandal below motto are clear.*

VF-20 VERY FINE—*Skirt lines sharp including leg area. Little wear on breast and right arm.*

EF-40 EXTREMELY FINE—*All skirt lines bold.*

MS-60 UNCIRCULATED—*No trace of wear. Light blemishes.*

MS-65 CHOICE UNCIRCULATED—*No trace of wear. Barely noticeable blemishes.*

Designer Adolph A. Weinman; weight 12.50 grams; composition: .900 silver, .100 copper; diameter 30.6 mm; reeded edge; mints: Philadelphia, Denver, San Francisco. Net weight: .36169 oz. pure silver.

HALF DOLLARS

Location of mint mark.

Choice uncirculated, well struck specimens are worth more than values listed.

	Quan. Minted	G-4	VG-8	F-12	VF-20	EF-40	MS-60	Proof-65
1916	608,000	$18.00	$25.00	$50.00	$90.00	$175.00	$450.00	
1916D (Obv.)	1,014,400	15.00	20.00	25.00	60.00	150.00	400.00	
1916S (Obv.)	508,000	27.00	40.00	90.00	195.00	350.00	850.00	
1917	12,292,000	5.50	7.50	9.00	20.00	35.00	175.00	
1917D (Obv.)	765,400	14.00	20.00	30.00	85.00	175.00	550.00	
1917D. (Rev.)	1,940,000	9.00	12.00	25.00	50.00	150.00	575.00	
1917S (Obv.)	952,000	15.00	20.00	40.00	175.00	350.00	1,000	
1917S . (Rev.)	5,554,000	5.50	7.50	9.00	30.00	45.00	275.00	
1918	6,634,00	5.50	7.50	9.00	40.00	110.00	375.00	
1918D.	3,853,040	5.50	7.50	9.00	50.00	115.00	725.00	
1918S	10,282,000	5.50	7.50	9.00	30.00	40.00	325.00	
1919	962,000	10.00	15.00	30.00	100.00	325.00	1,150	
1919D.	1,165,000	10.00	11.00	30.00	150.00	375.00	2,200	
1919S	1,552,000	8.00	9.00	20.00	100.00	325.00	2,000	
1920	6,372,000	5.50	7.50	9.00	20.00	50.00	250.00	
1920D.	1,551,000	5.50	7.50	25.00	115.00	250.00	1,000	
1920S	4,624,000	5.50	7.50	20.00	40.00	125.00	950.00	
1921	246,000	55.00	90.00	160.00	425.00	950.00	2,200	
1921D.	208,000	85.00	125.00	270.00	525.00	1,100	2,500	
1921S	548,000	17.50	30.00	45.00	200.00	1,300	7,000	
1923S	2,178,000	*5.00*	*6.00*	9.00	40.00	125.00	900.00	
1927S	2,392,000	*5.00*	*6.00*	9.00	25.00	70.00	800.00	
1928S†	1,940,000	*5.00*	*6.00*	9.00	30.00	90.00	900.00	
1929D.	1,001,200	*5.00*	*6.00*	9.00	20.00	60.00	400.00	
1929S	1,902,000	*5.00*	*6.00*	9.00	20.00	65.00	375.00	
1933S	1,786,000	*5.00*	*6.00*	9.00	20.00	40.00	360.00	
1934	6,964,000	*4.50*	*4.50*	*5.00*	12.00	20.00	100.00	
1934D†	2,361,400	*4.50*	*4.50*	*5.00*	12.00	40.00	200.00	
1934S	3,652,000	*4.50*	*4.50*	*5.00*	12.00	25.00	350.00	
1935	9,162,000	*4.50*	*4.50*	*5.00*	12.00	16.00	70.00	
1935D.	3,003,800	*4.50*	*4.50*	*5.00*	12.00	40.00	200.00	
1935S	3,854,000	*4.50*	*4.50*	*5.00*	10.00	35.00	225.00	
1936 . (3,901)	12,617,901	*4.50*	*4.50*	*5.00*	10.00	16.00	65.00	$3,100
1936D.	4,252,400	*4.50*	*4.50*	*5.00*	10.00	30.00	125.00	
1936S	3,884,000	*4.50*	*4.50*	*5.00*	10.00	30.00	150.00	
1937 . (5,728)	9,527,728	*4.50*	*4.50*	*5.00*	10.00	16.00	70.00	2,000
1937D.	1,676,000	*4.50*	*4.50*	*5.00*	10.00	40.00	250.00	
1937S	2,090,000	*4.50*	*4.50*	*5.00*	10.00	35.00	175.00	
1938 . (8,152)	4,118,152	*4.50*	*4.50*	*5.00*	10.00	17.00	125.00	1,700
1938D.	491,600	24.00	27.00	30.00	40.00	90.00	450.00	

†Large and small mint mark varieties, see pages 59-60. Pieces dated 1928D are counterfeit.

HALF DOLLARS

	Quan. Minted	F-12	VF-20	EF-40	MS-60	MS-65	Proof-65
1939 . . . . . . (8,808)	6,820,808	$5.00	$10.00	$16.00	$90.00	$750.00	$1,500
1939D.	4,267,800	5.00	10.00	17.00	85.00	700.00	
1939S	2,552,000	5.00	10.00	20.00	125.00	825.00	
1940 . . . . . . (11,279)	9,167,279	4.50	6.00	12.00	55.00	525.00	1,300
1940S	4,550,000	4.50	6.00	15.00	100.00	1,000	
1941* . . . (15,412)	24,207,412	4.50	5.00	9.00	40.00	400.00	*1,200
1941D.	11,248,400	4.50	5.00	9.00	65.00	525.00	
1941S†	8,098,000	4.50	5.00	9.00	200.00	1,200	
1942 . . . . . . (21,120)	47,839,120	4.50	5.00	9.00	40.00	375.00	1,200
1942D. . . . . ⎫ 1942D, D over S . . . ⎬	10,973,800	4.50	5.00	9.00	70.00	500.00	
1942S†	12,708,000	4.50	5.00	9.00	110.00	800.00	
1943	53,190,000	4.50	5.00	9.00	40.00	350.00	
1943D.	11,346,000	4.50	5.00	9.00	75.00	525.00	
1943S	13,450,000	4.50	5.00	9.00	115.00	900.00	
1944	28,206,000	4.50	5.00	9.00	40.00	350.00	
1944D.	9,769,000	4.50	5.00	9.00	60.00	500.00	
1944S	8,904,000	4.50	5.00	9.00	75.00	800.00	
1945	31,502,000	4.50	5.00	9.00	40.00	350.00	
1945D.	9,966,800	4.50	5.00	9.00	60.00	500.00	
1945S	10,156,000	4.50	5.00	9.00	75.00	600.00	
1946	12,118,000	4.50	5.00	9.00	40.00	450.00	
1946D.	2,151,000	4.50	5.00	9.00	50.00	450.00	
1946S	3,724,000	4.50	5.00	9.00	75.00	600.00	
1947	4,094,000	4.50	5.00	9.00	75.00	600.00	
1947D.	3,900,600	4.50	5.00	9.00	75.00	600.00	

*Proofs struck with or without designer's initials.
†Large and small mint mark varieties, see pages 59-60.

FRANKLIN-LIBERTY BELL TYPE 1948-1963

The Benjamin Franklin half dollar and the Roosevelt dime were both designed by John R. Sinnock. His initials appear below the shoulder. The Liberty Bell is similar to that used by Sinnock on the 1926 Sesquicentennial commemorative half dollar modeled from a sketch by John Frederick Lewis.

VF-20 VERY FINE—*At least half of the lower and upper incused lines on the rim of the bell must show.*

EF-40 EXTREMELY FINE—*Wear spots appear at top of end curls and hair back of ears. On reverse, Liberty Bell will show wear at top and on lettering.*

MS-63 SELECT UNCIRCULATED—*No trace of wear. Light blemishes. Attractive mint luster.*

MS-65 CHOICE UNCIRCULATED—*No trace of wear. Barely noticeable blemishes.*

Designer John R. Sinnock; weight 12.50 grams; composition: .900 silver, .100 copper; diameter 30.6 mm; reeded edge; mints: Philadelphia, Denver, San Francisco. Net weight: .36169 oz. pure silver.

Mint mark location.

Choice, well struck uncirculated halves command higher prices.

	Quan. Minted	VF-20	EF-40	MS-63	MS-65	Proof-65
1948	3,006,814	$4.50	$5.00	$25.00	$50.00	
1948D.	4,028,600	4.50	5.00	23.00	45.00	

[154]

HALF DOLLARS

	Quan. Minted	VF-20	EF-40	MS-63	MS-65	Proof-65
1949	5,614,000	$4.50	$5.00	$80.00	$175.00	
1949D	4,120,600	4.50	5.00	75.00	175.00	
1949S	3,744,000	4.50	10.00	200.00	400.00	
1950 .... (51,386)	7,793,509	4.50	5.00	65.00	115.00	$625.00
1950D	8,031,600	4.50	5.00	40.00	90.00	
1951 .... (57,500)	16,859,602	4.50	5.00	25.00	50.00	350.00
1951D	9,475,200	4.50	5.00	60.00	165.00	
1951S	13,696,000	4.50	5.00	50.00	100.00	
1952 .... (81,980)	21,274,073	4.50	5.00	20.00	40.00	225.00
1952D	25,395,600	4.50	5.00	20.00	40.00	
1952S	5,526,000	4.50	5.00	45.00	120.00	
1953 .... (128,800)	2,796,920	4.50	6.00	40.00	90.00	175.00
1953D	20,900,400	4.50	5.00	18.00	35.00	
1953S	4,148,000	4.50	5.00	30.00	80.00	
1954 .... (233,300)	13,421,503	4.50	5.00	15.00	25.00	90.00
1954D	25,445,580	4.50	5.00	14.00	25.00	
1954S	4,993,400	4.50	5.00	20.00	60.00	
1955 .... (378,200)	2,876,381	4.50	6.00	17.00	25.00	80.00
1956 .... (669,384)	4,701,384	4.50	5.00	17.00	25.00	55.00
1957 ...... (1,247,952)	6,361,952	4.50	5.00	16.00	23.00	42.00
1957D	19,966,850	4.50	5.00	12.00	18.00	
1958 .... (875,652)	4,917,652	4.50	5.00	13.00	20.00	67.50
1958D	23,962,412	4.50	5.00	13.00	18.00	
1959 ...... (1,149,291)	7,349,291	4.50	5.00	13.00	20.00	45.00
1959D	13,053,750	4.50	5.00	14.00	18.00	
1960 ...... (1,691,602)	7,715,602	4.50	5.00	11.00	20.00	38.00
1960D	18,215,812	4.50	4.50	10.00	18.00	
1961 ...... (3,028,244)	11,318,244	4.50	4.50	10.00	18.00	38.00
1961D	20,276,442	4.50	4.50	9.50	18.00	
1962 ...... (3,218,019)	12,932,019	4.50	4.50	9.50	18.00	38.00
1962D	35,473,281	4.50	4.50	9.50	18.00	
1963 ...... (3,075,645)	25,239,645	4.50	4.50	8.00	18.00	38.00
1963D	67,069,292	4.50	4.50	8.00	18.00	

Note: Prices in italic are based on silver bullion valued at $8.00 per ounce.

KENNEDY TYPE 1964 to Date

Gilroy Roberts, former Chief Engraver of the Mint, designed the obverse of this coin. His stylized initials are on the truncation of the forceful bust of President John F. Kennedy. The reverse, which uses the presidential coat of arms for the motif, is the work of Chief Engraver Frank Gasparro. A few of the pieces dated 1971D and 1977D were struck in silver clad by error.

Designers Gilroy Roberts and Frank Gasparro. 1964: Standards same as previous issue; 1965-1970: weight 11.50 grams; composition: outer layers of .800 silver, .200 copper bonded to inner core of .209 silver, .791 copper; 1971: weight 11.34 grams; composition: outer layers of copper-nickel (.750 copper, .250 nickel) bonded to inner core of pure copper; diameter 30.6 mm; reeded edge. Net weight: 1964 .36169 oz. pure silver. 1965-1970 .1479 oz. pure silver.

HALF DOLLARS

1964
Mint
mark
location

1968
Mint
mark
location

Silver Coinage 1964

	Quan. Minted	MS-65	Proof-65			Quan Minted	MS-65	Proof-65
1964	(3,950,762)		$14.00		1965	65,879,366	$2.50	
	277,254,766	$7.00			1966	108,984,932	2.50	
1964D	156,205,446	7.00						

Silver Clad Coinage 1965-1970

	Quan. Minted	MS-65	Proof-65			Quan Minted	MS-65	Proof-65
1967	295,046,978	2.50			1969S Proof	(2,934,631)		$4.00
1968D	246,951,930	2.50			1970D (Issued only in			
1968S Proof	(3,041,506)		4.00		mint sets)	2,150,000	27.50	
1969D	129,881,800	2.50			1970S Proof	(2,632,810)		10.00

Copper-Nickel Clad Coinage — Modified Design 1971-

	Quan. Minted	MS-65	Proof-65			Quan. Minted	MS-65	Proof-65
1971	155,164,000	1.00			1980P	44,134,000	1.00	
1971D	302,097,424	1.00			1980D	33,456,449	1.00	
1971S Proof	(3,220,733)		3.00		1980S Proof	(3,554,806)		1.50
1972	153,180,000	1.00			1981P	29,544,000	1.00	
1972D	141,890,000	1.00			1981D	27,839,533	1.00	
1972S Proof	(3,260,996)		3.00		1981S Proof	(4,063,083)		2.00
1973	64,964,000	1.00			1982P	10,819,000	1.00	
1973D	83,171,400	1.00			1982D	13,140,102	1.00	
1973S Proof	(2,760,339)		2.50		1982S Proof	(3,857,479)		9.00
1974	201,596,000	1.00			1983P	34,139,000	1.00	
1974D	79,066,300	1.00			1983D	32,472,244	1.00	
1974S Proof	(2,612,568)		3.50		1983S Proof	(3,228,648)		9.00
1977	43,598,000	1.00			1984P	26,029,000	1.00	
1977D	31,449,106	1.00			1984D	26,262,158	1.00	
1977S Proof	(3,251,152)		1.50		1984S Proof			5.00
1978	14,350,000	1.50			1985P	18,706,962	1.00	
1978D	13,765,799	1.50			1985D	19,814,034	1.00	
1978S Proof	(3,127,781)		3.50		1985S Proof			5.00
1979	68,312,000	1.00			1986P		1.00	
1979D	15,815,422	1.00			1986D		1.00	
1979S Proof	(3,677,175)				1986S Proof			5.00
Filled S			2.50					
Clear S			20.00					

BICENTENNIAL COINAGE DATED 1776—1976

In an open contest for the selection of suitable designs for the special Bicentennial reverses of the quarter, half dollar and dollar, Seth G. Huntington's winning entry was featured on the half dollar. It shows Independence Hall in Philadelphia as the center device. The obverse was unchanged except for the dual dating 1776-1976. They were struck during 1975 and 1976 for general circulation as well as being included in proof and uncirculated sets.

HALF DOLLARS

Designers Gilroy Roberts and Seth Huntington. Silver clad: weight 11.50 grams; composition: outer layers of .800 silver, .200 copper bonded to inner core of .209 silver, .791 copper; copper-nickel clad: weight 11.34 grams; composition: outer layers of copper-nickel (.750 copper, .250 nickel) bonded to inner core of pure copper; diameter 30.6 mm; reeded edge. Net weight: silver clad coinage .14792 oz. pure silver.

	Quan. Minted	MS-65	Proof-65
1776-1976 Copper-nickel clad.	234,308,000	$1.00	
1776-1976D Copper-nickel clad	287,565,248	1.00	
1776-1976S Copper-nickel clad	(7,059,099)		$1.50
1776-1976S Silver clad.	*11,000,000	3.00	
1776-1976S Silver clad.	*(4,000,000)		5.50

*Approximate mintage.

BIBLIOGRAPHY

Beistle, M. L. *Register of United States Half Dollar Die Varieties and Sub-Varieties.* Shippensburg, Pa., 1929.

Haseltine, J. W. *Type Table of United States Dollars, Half Dollars and Quarter Dollars.* Philadelphia, 1881 (reprinted 1927, 1968).

Overton, Al C. *Early Half Dollar Die Varieties 1794-1836.* Colorado Springs, 1967. Revised edition, 1970.

SILVER DOLLARS — 1794 to Date

The silver dollar was authorized by Congress April 2, 1792. Weight and fineness were specified at 416 grains and 892.4 fine. The first issues appeared in 1794 and until 1804 all silver dollars had the value stamped on the edge: HUNDRED CENTS, ONE DOLLAR OR UNIT. After a lapse in coinage of the silver dollar during the period 1804 to 1835, coins were made with either plain or reeded edges and the value was placed on the reverse side.

The weight was changed by the law of January 18, 1837 to 412½ grains, fineness .900. The coinage was discontinued by the Act of February 12, 1873 and reauthorized by the Act of February 28, 1878. The dollar was again discontinued after 1935, and since then only the copper-nickel pieces first authorized in 1971 have been coined for circulation.

ORIGIN OF THE DOLLAR

The word Dollar evolves from German Taler, the name given to the first large-sized European silver coin. Designed as a substitute for the gold Florin, the coin originated in the Tyrol in 1484. So popular did these large silver coins become during the 16th century that many other countries struck similar pieces, giving them names derived from taler. In the Netherlands the coin was called Rijksdaalder, in Denmark Rigsdaler, in Italy Tallero, in Poland Talar, in France Jocandale, in Russia Jefimok. All these names are abbreviations of "Joachimsthaler." Until the discovery of the great silver deposits in Mexican and South American mines, the mint with the greatest output of large silver coins was that of Joachimsthal in the Bohemian Erzgebirge.

The Spanish Dollar, or piece-of-eight, was widely used and familiar to everyone in the English-American colonies. It was only natural therefore that the word "dollar" was adopted officially as the standard monetary unit of the United States by Congress on July 6, 1785. The Continental Dollar of 1776 is described on page 30.

SILVER DOLLARS

TYPE COIN VALUES

	G-4	F-12	EF-40	AU-50	MS-60	MS-63	MS-65	PF-60	PF-63	PF-65
Flowing Hair 1794-1795	900.00	1,800	4,500	12,000	32,000	40,000	55,000			
Drpd Bust, SE 1795-1798	700.00	1,400	3,200	6,500	13,000	22,500	50,000			
Drpd Bust, HE 1798-1804	325.00	500.00	1,250	3,000	8,500	15,000	35,000			
Lib Seat-NM 1840-1866	75.00	150.00	300.00	450.00	900.00	2,250	9,500	1,200	2,600	12,000
Lib. Seat-WM 1866-1873	75.00	150.00	300.00	475.00	1,200	2,350	9,800	1,200	2,500	11,000
U.S. Trade Dol 1873-1883	47.50	75.00	175.00	285.00	725.00	1,750	6,800	1,100	2,600	9,000
Morgan Dol 1878-1921	12.00	14.00	16.00	17.00	30.00	55.00	500.00	850.00	2,300	8,500
Peace Dol 1921-1935	12.00	14.00	16.00	17.00	32.00	65.00	475.00			

FLOWING HAIR TYPE 1794-1795

Varieties listed are those most significant to collectors, but numerous minor variations may be found because each of the early dies was individually made. Values of variations not listed in this guide depend on collector interest and demand. Values shown here for uncirculated pieces are for well struck, attractive coins with a minimum of surface marks.

AG-3 ABOUT GOOD—*Clear enough to identify.*

G-4 GOOD—*Date and letters readable. Main devices outlined, but lack details.*

VG-8 VERY GOOD—*Major details discernible. Letters well formed but worn.*

F-12 FINE—*Hair ends distinguishable. Top hairlines show, but otherwise worn smooth.*

VF-20 VERY FINE—*Hair in center shows some detail. Other details more bold.*

EF-40 EXTREMELY FINE—*Hair well defined but will show some wear.*

MS-60 UNCIRCULATED—*No trace of wear. Light blemishes.*

Designer Robert Scot; weight 26.96 grams; composition: .8924 silver, .1076 copper; approx. diameter 39-40 mm; edge: HUNDRED CENTS ONE DOLLAR OR UNIT with decorations between words.

	Quan. Minted	AG-3	G-4	VG-8	F-12	VF-20	EF-40	MS-60
1794	1,758	$4,000	$6,000	$9,000	$16,000	$25,000	$40,000	——

**Two Leaves Beneath
Each Wing (11 Varieties)**

**Three Leaves Beneath
Each Wing**

SILVER DOLLARS

	Quan. Minted	AG-3	G-4	VG-8	F-12	VF-20	EF-40	MS-60
1795 Two leaves .	⎱ 160,295	$500.00	$950.00	$1,200	$1,800	$2,750	$4,500	$32,000
1795 Three leaves.	⎰	500.00	950.00	1,200	1,800	2,750	4,500	32,000

DRAPED BUST TYPE, SMALL EAGLE REVERSE 1795-1798

AG-3 ABOUT GOOD—*Clear enough to identify.*
G-4 GOOD—*Bust outlined, no detail. Date readable, some leaves evident.*
VG-8 VERY GOOD—*Drapery worn except deepest folds. Hairlines smooth.*
F-12 FINE—*All drapery lines distinguishable. Hairlines near cheek and neck show some detail.*
VF-20 VERY FINE—*Left side of drapery worn smooth.*
EF-40 EXTREMELY FINE—*Drapery shows distinctly. Hair well outlined and detailed.*
MS-60 UNCIRCULATED—*No trace of wear. Light blemishes.*

1795 (2 varieties) ...	42,738	400.00	800.00	1,100	1,600	2,000	4,000	16,000

Small Date **Large Date**

Small Letters **Large Letters**

1796 Sm. dt. sm. let. (3 vars.)								
All kinds	72,920	300.00	700.00	1,000	1,400	1,800	3,200	13,000
1796 Sm. date, lg. let		300.00	700.00	1,000	1,400	1,800	3,200	13,000
1796 Lg. date, sm. let.		300.00	700.00	1,000	1,400	1,800	3,200	13,000
1797, 9 stars left, 7 right								
Sm. let. All kinds ...	7,776	625.00	1,200	1,700	2,200	3,300	——	——
1797, 9 stars l., 7 r., lg. let.		300.00	700.00	1,000	1,400	1,800	3,200	13,000
1797, 10 stars left, 6 right .		300.00	700.00	1,000	1,400	1,800	3,200	13,000
1798, 15 stars on obverse..		550.00	1,200	1,600	2,300	3,000	5,500	20,000
All kinds	327,536							
1798, 13 stars on obverse..		550.00	1,200	1,600	2,300	3,000	5,500	19,000

SILVER DOLLARS
HERALDIC EAGLE REVERSE 1798-1804

G-4 GOOD—*Letters and date readable. E PLURIBUS UNUM obliterated.*
VG-8 VERY GOOD—*Motto partially readable. Only deepest drapery details visible. All other lines smooth.*
F-12 FINE—*All drapery lines distinguishable. Hairlines near cheek and neck show some detail.*
VF-20 VERY FINE—*Left side of drapery worn smooth.*
EF-40 EXTREMELY FINE—*Drapery is distinct. Hair well detailed.*
MS-60 UNCIRCULATED—*No trace of wear. Light blemishes.*

	Quan. Minted	G-4	VG-8	F-12	VF-20	EF-40	MS-60
1798 Large heraldic eagle, knob 9...		$350.00	$450.00	$600.00	$850.00	$1,400	$9,500
1798 Lg. eagle, 10 arrows		325.00	400.00	550.00	800.00	1,250	8,500
1798 Close date...................		325.00	400.00	550.00	800.00	1,250	8,500
1798 Wide date, 13 arrows (11 var.) .		325.00	400.00	550.00	800.00	1,250	8,500

1799 over 98, Stars 7 and 6

Stars 8 and 5

1799 All kinds............	423,515						
1799 9 over 8 rev. with 15 stars		325.00	400.00	550.00	800.00	1,250	8,500
1799 9 over 8 rev. with 13 stars ..		350.00	450.00	600.00	850.00	1,400	9,500
1799 Irregular date, 15-star rev. ...		350.00	450.00	600.00	850.00	1,400	9,500
1799 Irregular date, 13-star rev. ...		325.00	400.00	550.00	800.00	1,250	8,500
1799 Normal date................		325.00	400.00	550.00	800.00	1,250	8,500
1799 Stars - 8 left, 5 right		350.00	450.00	600.00	850.00	1,400	9,500
1800 All kinds............	220,920	325.00	400.00	550.00	800.00	1,250	8,500
1800 Very wide date, low 8.......		325.00	400.00	550.00	800.00	1,250	8,500
1800 "Dotted date" from die breaks		325.00	400.00	550.00	800.00	1,250	8,500
1800 Only 12 arrows.............		325.00	400.00	550.00	800.00	1,250	8,500
1800 Only 10 arrows.............		325.00	400.00	550.00	800.00	1,250	8,500
1800 AMERICAI (2 varieties).......		325.00	400.00	550.00	800.00	1,250	8,500
1801 (4 varieties)	54,454	325.00	400.00	550.00	800.00	1,250	8,500
1801 Proof restrike (rev. struck from first die of 1804 dollar).						(Proof)	60,000

SILVER DOLLARS

1802 over 1

Small 3

Large 3

	Quan. Minted	G-4	VG-8	F-12	VF-20	EF-40	MS-60
1802 All kinds	41,650						
1802 2 over 1, narrow date		$325.00	$400.00	$550.00	$800.00	$1,250	$8,500
1802 2 over 1, wide date		325.00	400.00	550.00	800.00	1,250	8,500
1802 Narrow normal date		325.00	400.00	550.00	800.00	1,250	8,500
1802 Wide normal date............		325.00	400.00	500.00	800.00	1,250	8,500
1802 Proof restrike						(Proof)	60,000
1803 Small 3 (5 varieties)..⎫		350.00	450.00	550.00	850.00	1,400	9,500
1803 Large 3 (1 variety) ⎬	85,634	325.00	400.00	500.00	800.00	1,250	8,500
1803 Proof restrike ....⎭						(Proof)	60,000

THE 1804 DOLLAR

FIRST REVERSE

SECOND REVERSE

Note position of words
STATES OF
with relation to clouds.

Compare
with first
reverse.

1804 First reverse, Original (Dexter specimen sold for $280,000 in 1981.)
1804 Second reverse, Restrike (Idler-Buss specimen sold for $308,000 in 1985.)

This piece is one of the most publicized rarities in the United States series. There are specimens known as originals (first reverse), of which eight are known, and restrikes (second reverse), of which seven are known.

Numismatists have found that the 1804 "original" dollars were struck at the mint in the 1834-35 period, for use in presentation proof sets. The first known specimen, a proof, was obtained from a mint officer by Mr. Stickney on May 9, 1843, in exchange for an "Immune Columbia" piece in gold. Later, in 1859, the pieces known as restrikes were made at the mint to supply the needs of collectors who wanted specimens of these dollars.

Evidence that these pieces were struck during the later period is based on

[161]

SILVER DOLLARS

the fact that the 1804 dollars differ from issues of 1803 or earlier and conform more closely to those struck after 1836, their edges or borders having beaded segments and raised rim, not elongated denticles such as are found on the earlier dates.

Although the mint records state that 19,570 dollars were coined in 1804, in no place does it mention that they were dated 1804. It was the practice in those days to use old dies as long as they were serviceable with no regard in the annual reports for the dating of the coins. It is probable that the 1804 total for dollars actually covered coins that were dated 1803.

BIBLIOGRAPHY

Bolender, M. H. *The United States Early Silver Dollars from 1794 to 1803.* Freeport, Ill., 1950.
Newman, Eric P. and Bressett, Kenneth E. *The Fantastic 1804 Dollar.* Racine, Wis., 1962.
Haseltine, J. W. *Type Table of United States Dollars, Half Dollars and Quarter Dollars.* Philadelphia, 1881 (reprinted 1927, 1968).

GOBRECHT DOLLARS — 1836-1839

Suspension of silver dollar coinage was lifted in 1831; however, not until 1835 were steps taken to resume coinage. Late in that year Director R.M. Patterson ordered Engraver Christian Gobrecht to prepare a pair of dies from designs by Thomas Sully and Titian Peale. The first obverse die bore the seated figure of Liberty on the obverse with the inscription C. GOBRECHT F. (F. - FECIT - made it) below the base of Liberty. On the reverse was a large eagle flying left surrounded by twenty-six stars and the legend UNITED STATES OF AMEICA ONE DOLLAR. Public criticism forced Gobrecht's name to the base of Liberty on a new die and, with this, pieces were struck in late 1836 on the standard of 1792, 416 grains.

In early 1837 the weight was lowered to 412½ grains and pieces were struck on the new standard in March, 1837, using the dies of 1836. To distinguish the 1837 coinage from that of 1836, the reverse die was oriented in "medal" fashion.

Between 1855 and 1860 the Mint produced restrikes to satisfy collector demands. Mules (mismatched combinations of dies) were also struck in the 1850's and are rare. Restrikes and mules are seldom seen in worn condition.

Original die alignment using either "coin" ↑↓ or "medal" ↑↑ turn.

Die alignment of Restrikes ↑↘ .

Dollars issued for circulation in 1836 and 1839, and the patterns of 1836 (with name below base) and 1838 have dies oriented in normal "coin" alignment ↑↓ with the reverse inverted.

The special issue of 1837 (using dies of 1836 with name on base) have dies oriented in "medal" fashion ↑↑ with the reverse upright when turned.

SILVER DOLLARS

All circulating issues and patterns are positioned so that the eagle will be flying upright as shown in the illustration.

Restrikes incorporate both "medal" ↑↑ and "coin" ↑↓ turns, and use the same die combinations as originals, but with the eagle flying level when rotated (see illustration). Mules with wrong edge or die combinations also exist and are all rare.

CIRCULATION ISSUES AND PATTERNS

	VF-20	EF-40	Proof-60
1836 C. GOBRECHT F. below base. Rev. Eagle flying left amid stars. Plain edge ↑↓. Pattern			$35,000
1836 C. GOBRECHT F. on base. Rev. as above. Plain edge ↑↓. Circulation issue. 1,000 struck	$2,750	$4,200	7,000
1836 As above. Plain edge ↑↓. Circulation issue struck in 1837 on new standard. 600 struck	2,750	4,500	7,500

1838 Similar obv., designer's name omitted, stars added around border. Rev. Eagle flying in plain field. Reeded edge. ↑↓. Pattern	3,000	4,750	13,000
1839 As above. Reeded edge. ↑↓. Circulation issue, regular coinage. 300 struck	2,900	4,600	10,000

RESTRIKES

Restrikes were produced between 1855 and 1860 and are not official coins. All have reverse die orientation with eagle flying level when rotated.

1836 Name below base. Eagle in plain field. Plain edge		25,000
1836 Name on base. Plain or reeded edge		——
1838 Designer's name omitted. Plain or reeded edge		——
1839 Same as above. Plain or reeded edge.		——

SILVER DOLLARS
LIBERTY SEATED TYPE — HERALDIC EAGLE 1840-1873

Starting in 1840 silver dollars were issued for general circulation in larger quanties than before. The seated figure of Liberty device was adopted for the obverse, but the flying eagle design was rejected in favor of the more familiar form with olive branch and arrows used for the other silver denominations.

The 1866 proof quarter, half and dollar without motto are not mentioned in the Director's Report, and were not issued for circulation.

Mint mark location is on the reverse below eagle.

Designer Christian Gobrecht; weight 26.73 grams; composition: .900 silver, .100 copper; diameter 38.1 mm; reeded edge; mints: Philadelphia, New Orleans, Carson City, San Francisco. Net weight: .77344 oz. pure silver.

VG-8 VERY GOOD—*Any 3 letters of LIBERTY at least two-thirds complete.*

F-12 FINE—*All 7 letters of LIBERTY visible though weak.*

VF-20 VERY FINE—*LIBERTY is strong but its ribbon shows slight wear.*

EF-40 EXTREMELY FINE—*Horizontal lines of shield complete. Eagle's eye plain.*

MS-60 UNCIRCULATED—*No trace of wear. Light marks or blemishes.*

	Quan. Minted	VG-8	F-12	VF-20	EF-40	MS-60	Proof-60
1840	61,005	$110.00	$170.00	$220.00	$325.00	$1,100	$2,800
1841	173,000	100.00	150.00	200.00	300.00	950.00	2,800
1842	184,618	100.00	150.00	200.00	300.00	950.00	2,800
1843	165,100	100.00	150.00	200.00	300.00	950.00	2,800
1844	20,000	150.00	185.00	235.00	375.00	1,500	3,000
1845	24,500	150.00	185.00	235.00	375.00	1,500	3,000
1846	110,600	100.00	150.00	200.00	300.00	950.00	2,800
1846O	59,000	175.00	200.00	250.00	450.00	2,000	
1847	140,750	100.00	150.00	200.00	300.00	950.00	2,800
1848	15,000	150.00	200.00	250.00	450.00	1,500	3,000
1849	62,600	100.00	150.00	200.00	300.00	950.00	2,800
1850	7,500	150.00	185.00	250.00	400.00	3,000	5,500
1850O	40,000	170.00	225.00	325.00	550.00	2,750	
1851 Original, high date	1,300	1,200	1,500	2,300	3,900	12,000	12,000
1851 Restrike, date centered							10,000
1852 Original	1,100					10,000	
1852 Restrike							8,000
1853	46,110	100.00	150.00	200.00	300.00	1,400	4,500
1854	33,140	135.00	250.00	350.00	550.00	2,000	4,000
1855	26,000	250.00	350.00	500.00	700.00	2,000	5,600
1856	63,500	150.00	210.00	275.00	400.00	1,700	5,000
1857	94,000	125.00	175.00	235.00	350.00	1,700	3,250
1858	Estimated (80)						5,000

SILVER DOLLARS

	Quan. Minted	VG-8	F-12	VF-20	EF-40	MS-60	Proof-63
1859 .... (800)	256,500	$100.00	$150.00	$200.00	$300.00	$1,400	$2,600
1859O.........	360,000	100.00	150.00	200.00	300.00	900.00	
1859S.........	20,000	130.00	200.00	300.00	500.00	2,000	
1860 .. (1,330)	218,930	100.00	150.00	200.00	300.00	1,000	2,600
1860O.........	515,000	100.00	150.00	200.00	300.00	900.00	
1861 .. (1,000)	78,500	125.00	170.00	220.00	325.00	1,600	2,600
1862 .... (550)	12,090	225.00	325.00	500.00	650.00	2,300	2,600
1863 .... (460)	27,660	150.00	200.00	250.00	450.00	1,700	2,600
1864 .... (470)	31,170	150.00	200.00	250.00	450.00	1,700	2,600
1865 .... (500)	47,000	150.00	200.00	250.00	450.00	1,700	2,600
1866 (2 known)...							——

Motto "In God We Trust" Added to Reverse

1866 .... (725)	49,625	100.00	150.00	200.00	300.00	1,300	2,500
1867 .... (625)	47,525	100.00	150.00	200.00	300.00	1,300	2,500
1868 .... (600)	162,700	100.00	150.00	200.00	300.00	1,200	2,500
1869 .... (600)	424,300	100.00	150.00	200.00	300.00	1,200	2,500
1870 .. (1,000)	416,000	100.00	150.00	200.00	300.00	1,200	2,500
1870CC	12,462	150.00	225.00	325.00	600.00	2,200	
1870S..................				50,000	60,000	75,000	
1871 .... (960)	1,074,760	100.00	150.00	200.00	300.00	1,200	2,500
1871CC	1,376	625.00	875.00	1,300	2,200	8,000	
1872 .... (950)	1,106,450	100.00	150.00	200.00	300.00	1,200	2,500
1872CC	3,150	300.00	425.00	625.00	1,000	3,750	
1872S...........	9,000	150.00	225.00	350.00	750.00	2,750	
1873 .... (600)	293,600	100.00	150.00	200.00	300.00	1,200	2,500
1873CC	2,300	750.00	1,000	1,500	2,500	12,000	
1873S..............	700............................			Unknown in any collection.			

TRADE DOLLARS 1873-1885

This coin was issued for circulation in the Orient to compete with dollar-size coins of other countries. It weighed 420 grains compared to 412½ grains, the weight of the regular silver dollar.

Many of the pieces which circulated in the Orient were counterstamped with oriental characters, known as "chop marks". These are generally valued lower than normal pieces.

When first coined they were legal tender in the United States to the extent of $5.00, but with the decline in price of silver bullion Congress repealed the legal tender provision in 1876 and authorized the Treasury to limit coinage to export demand. In 1887 a law was passed authorizing the Treasury to redeem all Trade Dollars which were not mutilated.

The Trade Dollars of 1884 and 1885 were unknown to collectors generally

TRADE DOLLARS 1873 - 1885

until 1908. None is listed in the Director's report and numismatists believe that they are not a part of the regular mint issue. After 1878, strikings were specimen proofs only.

The law authorizing Trade Dollars was repealed in February, 1887.

VG-8 VERY GOOD— *About half of mottoes IN GOD WE TRUST and E PLURIBUS UNUM will show. Rim on both sides well defined.*

F-12 FINE— *Mottoes and LIBERTY readable but worn.*

EF-40 EXTREMELY FINE— *Mottoes and LIBERTY are sharp. Only slight wear on rims.*

MS-60 UNCIRCULATED— *No trace of wear. Light blemishes.*

Designer William Barber; weight 27.22 grams; composition: .900 silver, .100 copper; diameter 38.1 mm; reeded edge; mints: Philadelphia, Carson City, San Francisco.

1875S
S over CC

Mint mark location on reverse above letter "D" in dollar.

	Quan. Minted	VG-8	F-12	EF-40	MS-60	Proof-63
1873 . . . . (865)	397,500	$60.00	$75.00	$185.00	$800.00	$2,750
1873CC	124,500	65.00	85.00	185.00	1,200	
1873S	703,000	60.00	75.00	175.00	800.00	
1874 . . . . (700)	987,800	60.00	75.00	175.00	725.00	2,600
1874CC	1,373,200	65.00	80.00	185.00	1,100	
1874S	2,549,000	60.00	75.00	175.00	725.00	
1875 . . . . (700)	218,900	75.00	100.00	250.00	1,250	2,600
1875CC	1,573,700	65.00	80.00	185.00	850.00	
1875S . . . . }		60.00	75.00	175.00	725.00	
1875S, S over CC }	4,487,000	125.00	250.00	500.00	1,600	
1876 . . . . (1,150)	456,150	60.00	75.00	175.00	725.00	2,600
1876CC	509,000	65.00	80.00	185.00	950.00	
1876S	5,227,000	60.00	75.00	175.00	725.00	
1877 . . . . (510)	3,039,710	60.00	75.00	175.00	725.00	2,600
1877CC	534,000	75.00	100.00	200.00	1,200	
1877S	9,519,000	60.00	75.00	175.00	725.00	
1878 . . . . (900)	900					2,750
1878CC	*97,000	175.00	250.00	600.00	3,000	
1878S	4,162,000	60.00	75.00	175.00	725.00	
1879 . . . . (1,541)	1,541					2,750
1880 . . . . (1,987)	1,987					2,750
1881 . . . . (960)	960					2,750
1882 . . . . (1,097)	1,097					2,750
1883 . . . . (979)	979					2,750
1884 . . . . (10)	10					50,000
1885 . . . . (5)	5					110,000

*44,148 Trade Dollars were melted on July 19, 1878. Many of these may have been 1878CC.

BIBLIOGRAPHY

Willem, John M. *The United States Trade Dollar.* Second edition, Racine, Wis., 1965.

SILVER DOLLARS
LIBERTY HEAD OR MORGAN TYPE 1878-1921

The coinage law of 1873 made no provision for the standard silver dollar. During the lapse in coinage of this denomination the gold dollar became the unit coin and the trade dollar was used for our commercial transactions with the Orient.

The legal tender character was restored to the silver dollar by the Act of February 28, 1878, known as the Bland-Allison Act. The weight, 412½ grains and fineness .900 were to conform with the act of January 18, 1837.

George T. Morgan, formerly a pupil of Wyon in the Royal Mint in London, designed the new dollar. His initial M is found at the truncation of the neck, at the last tress. It also appears on the reverse on the left-hand loop of the ribbon.

Coinage of the silver dollar was suspended after 1904 when the bullion supply became exhausted. Under provisions of the Pittman Act of 1918, 270,232,722 silver dollars were melted and later, in 1921, coinage of the silver dollar was resumed. The Morgan design, with some slight refinements, was employed until the new Peace design was adopted later in that year.

Varieties listed are those most significant to collectors, but numerous other variations may be found. Values of variations not listed in this guide depend on collector interest and demand.

Sharply struck, "proof-like" coins have a highly reflective surface and are very scarce and usually command substantial premiums.

BIBLIOGRAPHY

Van Allen, Leroy C. and Mallis, A. George. *Comprehensive Catalogue and Encyclopedia of U.S. Morgan and Peace Silver Dollars.* New York. 1976.

Designer George T. Morgan; weight 26.73 grams; composition: .900 silver, .100 copper; diameter 38.1 mm; reeded edge; mints: Philadelphia, New Orleans, Carson City, Denver, San Francisco. Net weight: .77344 oz. pure silver.

Mint mark location is on reverse below wreath.

First Reverse

8 Tail Feathers, 1878 Philadelphia Only

Second Reverse

Third Reverse

Parallel top arrow feather,
concave breast.

Slanted top arrow feather,
convex breast.

SILVER DOLLARS

VF-20 VERY FINE—*Two-thirds of hairlines from top of forehead to ear must show. Ear well defined. Feathers on eagle's breast worn.*

EF-40 EXTREMELY FINE—*All hairlines strong and ear bold. Eagle's feathers all plain but slight wear on breast and wing tips.*

AU-50 ABOUT UNCIRCULATED—*Slight trace of wear. Most of mint luster is present although marred by bag marks.*

MS-60 UNCIRCULATED—*No trace of wear. Has full mint luster but may be noticeably marred by scuff marks or bag abrasions.*

MS-63 SELECT UNCIRCULATED—*No trace of wear, full mint luster, few noticeable surface marks.*

MS-65 CHOICE UNCIRCULATED—*No trace of wear, full mint luster and only minute surface marks.*

	Quan. Minted	VF-20	EF-40	AU-50	MS-60	MS-63	MS-65
1878, 8 tail feathers. (500)	750,000	$21.00	$25.00	$35.00	$75.00	$125.00	$1,400
1878, 7 tail feathers. (500)	9,759,550						
1878, 7 feathers, 2nd reverse		19.00	22.00	30.00	70.00	100.00	900.00
1878, 7 feathers, 3rd reverse........		21.00	28.00	53.00	80.00	130.00	1,000
1878, 7 over 8 feathers.............		24.00	33.00	45.00	85.00	150.00	1,300
1878CC 2,212,000		35.00	42.00	55.00	130.00	200.00	850.00
1878S.....................9,774,000		17.00	21.00	27.00	70.00	120.00	800.00
1879 .... (1,100) 14,807,100		17.00	21.00	25.00	55.00	100.00	1,000
1879CC‡ 756,000		75.00	225.00	450.00	900.00	1,500	8,000
1879O.....................2,887,000		17.00	21.00	25.00	65.00	160.00	1,600
1879S second reverse .. } 9,110,000		25.00	35.00	50.00	135.00	175.00	1,500
1879S third reverse ...		17.00	21.00	25.00	70.00	100.00	500.00
1880, 8 over 7* .... } 12,601,355		45.00	70.00	90.00	150.00	250.00	750.00
1880 .... (1,355)		17.00	21.00	25.00	60.00	180.00	700.00

1880CC, 80 over 79†   **1880CC, 8 over high 7***   **1880CC, 8 over low 7**

	Quan. Minted	VF-20	EF-40	AU-50	MS-60	MS-63	MS-65
1880CC all kinds............ 591,000							
1880CC, 80 over 79, 2nd rev.†.......		65.00	90.00	135.00	210.00	290.00	1,000
1880CC, 8 over 7, 2nd rev..........		65.00	90.00	135.00	210.00	290.00	1,000
1880CC, 8 over high 7, 3rd rev.*		60.00	80.00	130.00	210.00	290.00	1,000
1880CC, 8 over low 7, 3rd. rev.		60.00	80.00	130.00	210.00	290.00	1,000
1880CC third reverse		60.00	80.00	130.00	210.00	290.00	1,000
1880O, 8 over 7*........} 5,305,000		17.00	21.00	25.00	80.00	200.00	2,000
1880O..,.,...........		17.00	21.00	25.00	80.00	200.00	2,000
1880S, 8 over 7* ....} 8,900,000		17.00	21.00	25.00	70.00	100.00	500.00
1880S, 0 over 9		17.00	21.00	25.00	70.00	100.00	500.00
1880S..................		17.00	21.00	25.00	70.00	100.00	500.00
1881 .... (975) 9,163,975		17.00	21.00	25.00	60.00	110.00	750.00
1881CC 296,000		90.00	110.00	150.00	250.00	325.00	1,200
1881O.....................5,708,000		17.00	21.00	25.00	45.00	85.00	650.00
1881S................. 12,760,000		17.00	21.00	25.00	70.00	100.00	500.00
1882 .... (1,100) 11,101,100		17.00	21.00	25.00	55.00	85.00	650.00
1882CC 1,133,000		35.00	40.00	65.00	125.00	170.00	650.00
1882O................} 6,090,000		17.00	21.00	25.00	45.00	85.00	650.00
1882O, O over S*		17.00	21.00	25.00	65.00	95.00	650.00

* Several die varieties. Values shown are for the most common.
† 7 and 9 show within the 80, no tip below second 8.
‡ One variety shows mint mark broken or irregular at top. Clear mint mark is valued higher.
Proof Morgan Dollars where indicated in mintage record (quantity shown in parenthesis) are valued approximately as follows:
Proof-60 $850.00   **Proof-63 $2,300**   **Proof-65 $8,500**

SILVER DOLLARS

	Quan. Minted	VF-20	EF-40	AU-50	MS-60	MS-63	MS-65
1882S	9,250,000	$17.00	$21.00	$25.00	$70.00	$100.00	$550.00
1883	(1,039) 12,291,039	17.00	21.00	25.00	55.00	85.00	650.00
1883CC	1,204,000	35.00	40.00	65.00	125.00	170.00	650.00
1883O	8,725,000	17.00	21.00	25.00	45.00	70.00	550.00
1883S	6,250,000	25.00	30.00	125.00	475.00	900.00	4,000
1884	(875) 14,070,875	17.00	21.00	25.00	60.00	100.00	800.00
1884CC	1,136,000	35.00	40.00	65.00	125.00	170.00	650.00
1884O	9,730,000	17.00	21.00	25.00	45.00	70.00	550.00
1884S	3,200,000	25.00	40.00	225.00	1,400	3,500	16,000
1885	(930) 17,787,767	17.00	21.00	25.00	45.00	70.00	550.00
1885CC	228,000	170.00	180.00	190.00	260.00	310.00	1,200
1885O	9,185,000	17.00	21.00	25.00	45.00	70.00	550.00
1885S	1,497,000	17.00	21.00	50.00	125.00	225.00	1,500
1886	(886) 19,963,886	17.00	21.00	25.00	45.00	70.00	550.00
1886O	10,710,000	17.00	21.00	50.00	350.00	700.00	4,500
1886S	750,000	25.00	35.00	60.00	170.00	275.00	1,500
1887, 7 over 6	} (710) 20,290,710	20.00	25.00	40.00	80.00	125.00	600.00
1887		17.00	21.00	25.00	45.00	70.00	550.00
1887O, 7 over 6	} 11,550,000	22.00	30.00	45.00	90.00	135.00	1,500
1887O		17.00	21.00	25.00	60.00	110.00	1,350
1887S	1,771,000	17.00	21.00	25.00	80.00	200.00	1,350
1888	(832) 19,183,333	17.00	21.00	25.00	50.00	85.00	700.00
1888O	12,150,000	17.00	21.00	25.00	50.00	85.00	700.00
1888S	657,000	30.00	40.00	60.00	170.00	300.00	1,500
1889	(811) 21,726,811	17.00	21.00	25.00	50.00	80.00	850.00
1889CC	350,000	300.00	650.00	1,900	5,000	8,000	22,000
1889O	11,875,000	17.00	21.00	27.50	90.00	250.00	2,600
1889S	700,000	30.00	40.00	55.00	150.00	225.00	1,500
1890	(590) 16,802,590	17.00	21.00	25.00	50.00	100.00	1,000
1890CC	2,309,041	35.00	45.00	75.00	235.00	350.00	1,400
1890O	10,701,000	17.00	21.00	25.00	70.00	125.00	1,600
1890S	8,230,373	17.00	21.00	30.00	75.00	135.00	800.00
1891	(650) 8,694,206	17.00	21.00	35.00	85.00	150.00	1,700
1891CC	1,618,000	35.00	45.00	75.00	225.00	350.00	1,300
1891O	7,954,529	20.00	23.00	35.00	80.00	185.00	3,500
1891S	5,296,000	17.00	21.00	30.00	75.00	130.00	875.00
1892	(1,245) 1,037,245	19.00	25.00	45.00	150.00	335.00	2,200
1892CC	1,352,000	50.00	80.00	180.00	325.00	500.00	1,800
1892O	2,744,000	20.00	25.00	45.00	125.00	350.00	3,500
1892S	1,200,000	45.00	150.00	800.00	4,200	8,750	30,000
1893	(792) 389,792	50.00	100.00	175.00	300.00	600.00	2,600
1893CC	677,000	150.00	325.00	500.00	800.00	1,400	8,000
1893O	300,000	100.00	225.00	350.00	1,000	2,200	15,000
1893S	100,000	1,600	3,250	9,000	20,000	32,000	65,000
1894	(972) 110,972	325.00	425.00	600.00	950.00	1,600	9,000
1894O	1,723,000	23.00	33.00	75.00	450.00	1,100	13,000
1894S	1,260,000	40.00	85.00	160.00	350.00	700.00	3,000
1895†	(880) 12,880				† 15,000	20,000	35,000
1895O	450,000	110.00	260.00	500.00	2,000	5,250	32,500
1895S	400,000	150.00	360.00	550.00	875.00	1,600	8,000
1896	(762) 9,976,762	17.00	21.00	25.00	45.00	75.00	600.00
1896O	4,900,000	17.00	21.00	85.00	750.00	1,500	18,000
1896S	5,000,000	35.00	100.00	200.00	450.00	850.00	4,500
1897	(731) 2,822,731	17.00	21.00	25.00	50.00	80.00	600.00
1897O	4,004,000	17.00	21.00	50.00	400.00	1,100	8,000
1897S	5,825,000	17.00	21.00	30.00	80.00	150.00	800.00

†Beware of removed mint mark. Values are for Proofs; no others are known to exist.

SILVER DOLLARS

	Quan. Minted	VF-20	EF-40	AU-50	MS-60	MS-63	MS-65
1898 . . . . (735)	5,884,735	$17.00	$21.00	$25.00	$45.00	$80.00	$600.00
1898O	4,440,000	17.00	21.00	25.00	45.00	80.00	575.00
1898S	4,102,000	17.00	21.00	50.00	175.00	350.00	1,600
1899 . . . . (846)	330,846	42.00	55.00	70.00	100.00	175.00	1,000
1899O	12,290,000	17.00	21.00	25.00	50.00	85.00	600.00
1899S	2,562,000	18.00	22.00	60.00	160.00	330.00	1,500
1900 . . . . (912)	8,830,912	17.00	21.00	25.00	50.00	80.00	700.00
1900O . . . . }		17.00	21.00	25.00	50.00	80.00	575.00
1900O, O over CC* }	12,590,000	25.00	30.00	60.00	120.00	200.00	1,000
1900S	3,540,000	20.00	25.00	45.00	125.00	300.00	1,100
1901 . . . . (813)	6,962,813	35.00	50.00	225.00	850.00	2,200	18,000
1901O	13,320,000	17.00	21.00	25.00	50.00	85.00	700.00
1901S	2,284,000	25.00	35.00	65.00	275.00	550.00	3,500
1902 . . . . (777)	7,994,777	17.00	23.00	30.00	65.00	120.00	1,400
1902O	8,636,000	17.00	21.00	25.00	45.00	80.00	600.00
1902S	1,530,000	50.00	80.00	125.00	225.00	425.00	1,750
1903 . . . . (755)	4,652,755	18.00	22.00	30.00	60.00	125.00	800.00
1903O	4,450,000	175.00	200.00	220.00	260.00	350.00	1,100
1903S	1,241,000	45.00	150.00	575.00	1,650	3,000	10,000
1904 . . . . (650)	2,788,650	17.00	21.00	40.00	110.00	275.00	1,800
1904O	3,720,000	17.00	21.00	25.00	50.00	75.00	550.00
1904S	2,304,000	55.00	110.00	400.00	875.00	2,000	4,750
1921	44,690,000	15.00	16.00	17.00	30.00	55.00	650.00
1921D	20,345,000	15.00	16.00	18.00	45.00	90.00	1,100
1921S	21,695,000	15.00	16.00	18.00	35.00	100.00	1,400

*Several die varieties.
For Proof Morgan Dollar prices see Pg. 168.

PEACE TYPE 1921-1935

The dollar issued from 1921 to 1935 was a commemorative peace coin, which might easily have been a half dollar. The Peace Dollar, in fact, was issued without congressional sanction, under the terms of the Pittman Act, which referred to the bullion and in no way affected the design.

Anthony De Francisci, a medalist, designed this dollar. His monogram is located in the field of the coin under the neck of Liberty.

The new Peace Dollar was placed in circulation January 3, 1922. 1,006,473 pieces were struck in December, 1921.

The high relief of the 1921 design was found impractical for coinage and was slightly modified in 1922. The rare matte proof specimens of 1921 and 1922 are of the high relief style of 1921.

Designer Anthony De Francisci; weight 26.73 grams; composition: .900 silver, .100 copper; diameter 38.1 mm; reeded edge; mints: Philadelphia, Denver, San Francisco. Net weight: .77344 oz. pure silver.
Mint mark location is on reverse below ONE.

SILVER DOLLARS

Legislation dated August 3, 1964 authorized the coinage of 45 million silver dollars, and 316,076 dollars of the Peace design dated 1964 were struck at the Denver mint. Plans for completing this coinage were subsequently abandoned and all of these coins were melted. None were preserved or released for circulation.

VF-20 VERY FINE—*Hair over eye well worn. Some strands over ear well defined. Some eagle feathers on top and outside edge of right wing will show.*

EF-40 EXTREMELY FINE—*Hairlines over brow and ear are strong though slightly worn. Outside wing feathers at right and those at top are visible but faint.*

AU-50 ABOUT UNCIRCULATED—*Slight trace of wear. Most of mint luster is present although marred by contact marks.*

MS-60 UNCIRCULATED—*No trace of wear. Has full mint luster but may be noticeably marred by stains, surface marks or bag abrasions.*

MS-63 SELECT UNCIRCULATED—*No trace of wear, full mint luster, few noticeable surface marks.*

MS-65 CHOICE UNCIRCULATED—*No trace of wear, full mint luster, and only minute surface marks.*

Quan. Minted	VF-20	EF-40	AU-50	MS-60	MS-63	MS-65
1921 1,006,473	$35.00	$45.00	$70.00	$225.00	$400.00	$3,000
1922 51,737,000	15.00	16.00	17.00	32.00	65.00	475.00
1922D... 15,063,000	17.00	18.00	20.00	45.00	80.00	1,000
1922S... 17,475,000	17.00	18.00	20.00	50.00	110.00	1,050
1923 30,800,000	15.00	16.00	17.00	35.00	65.00	475.00
1923D.... 6,811,000	17.00	18.00	20.00	45.00	95.00	1,400
1923S... 19,020,000	17.00	18.00	20.00	50.00	125.00	1,500
1924 11,811,000	17.00	18.00	20.00	40.00	65.00	550.00
1924S.... 1,728,000	17.00	22.00	42.00	165.00	400.00	3,000
1925 10,198,000	17.00	18.00	20.00	45.00	75.00	500.00
1925S.... 1,610,000	17.00	20.00	30.00	135.00	300.00	2,100
1926 1,939,000	17.00	18.00	23.00	60.00	110.00	1,100
1926D.... 2,348,700	17.00	20.00	30.00	75.00	150.00	1,500
1926S.... 6,980,000	17.00	18.00	20.00	55.00	100.00	1,100
1927 848,000	20.00	25.00	35.00	115.00	215.00	1,750
1927D.... 1,268,900	19.00	26.00	85.00	235.00	550.00	4,000
1927S..... 866,000	19.00	25.00	50.00	200.00	325.00	1,750
1928 360,649	125.00	150.00	175.00	250.00	450.00	2,500
1928S* ... 1,632,000	18.00	25.00	45.00	150.00	350.00	2,200
1934 954,057	18.00	25.00	42.00	110.00	250.00	1,750
1934D* ... 1,569,500	18.00	22.00	45.00	125.00	325.00	2,400
1934S.... 1,011,000	40.00	160.00	450.00	1,350	2,250	8,000
1935 1,576,000	18.00	20.00	25.00	70.00	150.00	1,250
1935S† ... 1,964,000	18.00	20.00	45.00	175.00	400.00	2,300

*Large and small mint mark varieties, see pages 59-60.
†Varieties occur with either 3 or 4 rays below one.

EISENHOWER DOLLARS 1971-1978

Honoring both President Dwight D. Eisenhower and the first landing of man on the moon, this design is the work of Chief Engraver Frank Gasparro, whose initials are on the truncation and below the eagle. The reverse is an adaptation of the official Apollo 11 insignia. Collectors' coins were struck in 40% silver composition and the circulation issue is copper-nickel.

Since 1971, the dies for the Eisenhower dollar have been modified several times by changing the relief, strengthening the design and making the world above the eagle more clearly defined.

Low relief dies were used for all copper-nickel issues of 1971, all uncirculated silver of 1971, and most copper-nickel coins of 1972.

EISENHOWER DOLLARS

High relief dies were used for all proofs of 1971, all silver issues of 1972, and the reverse of some exceptional Philadelphia copper-nickel coins of 1972 (identified by round world and weakly defined continents).

Modified high relief reverse dies were used for late 1972 Philadelphia copper-nickel coins and for all subsequent issues. Modified high relief obverse dies were also used on all issues beginning in 1973.

A few 1974D and 1977D dollars in silver clad composition were made in error.

Designer Frank Gasparro. Silver issue: weight 24.59 grams; composition: outer layers of .800 silver, .200 copper bonded to inner core of .209 silver, .791 copper. Copper-nickel issue: weight 22.68 grams; composition: outer layers of .750 copper, .250 nickel bonded to inner core of pure copper. Diameter 38.1 mm; reeded edge. Net weight of silver issues: .3161 oz. pure silver.

Mint mark location is above the date.

| | Quan. Minted | | | |
	Proof	Regular	MS-65	Proof-65
1971 Copper-nickel clad		47,799,000	$2.25	
1971D Copper-nickel clad		68,587,424	2.25	
1971S Silver clad	(4,265,234)	6,868,530	7.00	$10.00
1972 Copper-nickel clad		75,890,000	2.25	
1972D Copper-nickel clad		92,548,511	2.25	
1972S Silver clad	(1,811,631)	2,193,056	10.00	13.00
1973 Copper-nickel clad		*2,000,056	10.00	
1973D Copper-nickel clad		*2,000,000	10.00	
1973S Copper-nickel clad	(2,760,339)			6.00
1973S Silver clad	(1,013,646)	1,883,140	12.00	80.00
1974 Copper-nickel clad		27,366,000	2.25	
1974D Copper-nickel clad		45,517,000	2.25	
1974S Copper-nickel clad	(2,612,568)			4.50
1974S Silver clad	(1,306,579)	1,900,000	10.00	25.00

*1,769,258 of each sold only in sets and not released for circulation. Unissued coins destroyed at mint.

BICENTENNIAL COINAGE DATED 1776-1976

The national significance of the Bicentennial of the United States was highlighted with the adoption of new reverse designs for the quarter, half dollar and dollar. Nearly a thousand entries were submitted after the Treasury announced in October of 1973 that an open contest was to be held for the selection of the new designs. After the field was narrowed down to twelve semifinalists, the judges chose the rendition of the Liberty Bell superimposed on the moon to appear on the dollar coins. This design is the work of Dennis R. Williams. The obverse remained unchanged except for the dual date 1776-1976, which appeared on all dollars made during 1975 and 1976. These dual-dated coins

BICENTENNIAL DOLLARS

were included in the various offerings of proof and uncirculated coins made by the Mint. They were also struck for general circulation.

The lettering was modified early in 1975 to produce a more attractive design.

Designers Frank Gasparro and Dennis R. Williams. Silver issue: weight 24.59 grams; composition: outer layers of .800 silver, .200 copper bonded to inner core of .209 silver, .791 copper. Copper-nickel issue: weight 22.68 grams; composition: outer layers of .750 copper, .250 nickel bonded to inner core of pure copper. Diameter 38.1 mm; reeded edge. Net weight of silver issues: .3161 oz. pure silver.

Obverse and Reverse Variety II   **Reverse Var. 1**

Variety I: Design in low relief, bold lettering on reverse. Variety II: Sharp design, delicate lettering on reverse.

	Quan. Minted	MS-65	Proof-65
1776-1976 Copper-nickel clad, variety I	4,019,000	$3.00	
1776-1976 Copper-nickel clad, variety II	113,318,000	2.25	
1776-1976D Copper-nickel clad, variety I	21,048,710	2.50	
1776-1976D Copper-nickel clad, variety II	82,179,564	2.25	
1776-1976S Copper-nickel clad, variety I	(2,845,450)		$6.00
1776-1976S Copper-nickel clad, variety II	(4,149,730)		5.00
1776-1976S Silver clad, variety I	* 11,000,000	8.00	
1776-1976S Silver clad, variety I	*(4,000,000)		10.00

*Approximate mintage.

EAGLE REVERSE RESUMED

1977 Copper-nickel clad	12,596,000	2.50	
1977D Copper-nickel clad	32,983,006	2.50	
1977S Copper-nickel clad	(3,251,152)		4.00
1978 Copper-nickel clad	25,702,000	2.25	
1978D Copper-nickel clad	33,012,890	2.25	
1978S Copper-nickel clad	(3,127,781)		7.00

SUSAN B. ANTHONY DOLLARS 1979 To 1981

Intended to honor this pioneer in women's rights, legislation dated October 10, 1978, provided for the issuance of the Susan B. Anthony dollar coin. Both obverse and reverse designs were the work of Chief Engraver of the U.S. Mint, Frank Gasparro. His initials FG are located below the portrait and the eagle.

Placement of Susan B. Anthony's likeness on the new dollar represented the first time that a woman, other than a mythical figure, has appeared on a circulating U.S. coin. The reverse design is the same as that used on the Eisenhower dollar. Mint marks P, D or S appear on the obverse, slightly above Anthony's right shoulder.

Because its small size often caused confusion with the quarter and half dollar coins in circulation, the Anthony dollar failed to gain widespread public acceptance and was discontinued in 1981.

Designer Frank Gasparro; weight 8.1 grams; composition: outer layers of copper-nickel (.750 copper, .250 nickel) bonded to inner core of pure copper; diameter 26.5 mm; reeded edge.

ANTHONY DOLLARS

Clear S **Filled S**

	Quan. Minted	MS-65	Proof-65		Quan. Minted	MS-65	Proof-65
1979P*	360,222,000	$1.50		1980D	41,628,708	$1.75	
1979D	288,015,744	1.50		1980S	20,422,000	3.00	
1979S	109,576,000	2.00		1980S Proof	(3,554,806)		$10.00
1979S Proof	(3,677,175)			1981P	3,000,000	6.00	
Filled S			$10.00	1981D	3,250,000	6.00	
Clear S			100.00	1981S	3,492,000	6.00	
1980P	27,610,000	1.75		1981S Proof	(4,063,083)		10.00

* The obverse design was modified in 1979 to widen the border rim. Late issues of 1979P and all subsequent issues have the wide rim. The 1979P with wide rim is very scarce.

GOLD

Gold has served as money or established the monetary value of currencies longer than any other material. The use of gold coins was widespread in Europe by the fourth century B.C.

The earliest coins circulated in the United States were foreign coins, mostly gold, brought from Europe. The Coinage Act in 1792 established an independent monetary system with the dollar as the basic United States monetary unit containing 24¾ grains of fine gold, based on the world price of $19.39 a troy ounce (480 grains). Congress changed the gold specification in 1834 and again in 1837, when it set the dollar price of gold at $20.67 an ounce.

In 1934, United States citizens were prohibited from holding monetary gold in this country; this was extended in 1961 to gold held abroad as well. The dollar price was then set at $35 per ounce. Use of gold in international trade was further restricted as the price rose. The government revalued it at $38 per ounce in 1972, then $42.22 in 1973. It has fluctuated boldly over the past few years. All restrictions on holding gold were removed in 1975.

GOLD DOLLARS 1849-1889

Coinage of the gold dollar was authorized by the Act of March 3, 1849. The weight was 25.8 grains, fineness .900. The first type, struck until 1854, is known as the Liberty Head or small-sized type.

In 1854 the piece was made larger in diameter and thinner. The design was changed to a feather headdress on a female, generally referred to as the Indian Head or large-sized type. In 1856 the type was changed slightly by enlarging the size of the head.

TYPE COIN VALUES

	F-12	VF-20	EF-40	AU-50	MS-60	MS-63	MS-65	PF-60	PF-63	PF-65
Liberty Hd 1849-1854	100.00	200.00	250.00	325.00	1,200	2,200	8,500			
Indian Hd Type II 1854-1856	150.00	350.00	600.00	1,700	5,500	16,500	30,000			
Indian Hd Type III 1856-1889	100.00	175.00	225.00	300.00	1,000	2,100	7,000	2,250	4,000	10,000

> Values of common gold coins have been based on a bullion price of $350.00 per Troy ounce, and may vary with the prevailing spot price of gold.
> The weight and content of these coins is stated in the introduction to each series, and may be used to recalculate bullion value.

LIBERTY HEAD TYPE 1849-1854

VF-20 VERY FINE— *LIBERTY on headband complete and readable. Knobs on coronet are defined.*

EF-40 EXTREMELY FINE— *Slight wear on Liberty's hair. Knobs on coronet sharp.*

AU-50 ABOUT UNCIRCULATED— *Trace of wear on headband. Nearly full luster.*

MS-60 UNCIRCULATED— *No trace of wear. Light marks and blemishes.*

Designer James B. Longacre; weight 1.672 grams; composition: .900 gold, .100 copper; diameter 13 mm; reeded edge. Net weight: .04837 oz. pure gold.

Type 1

With open or closed wreath.

Mint mark is below wreath.

	Quan. Minted	VF-20	EF-40	AU-50	MS-60
1849 Open wreath—All kinds*	688,567	$200.00	$250.00	$325.00	$1,200
1849 Closed wreath (ends closer to numeral)		200.00	250.00	325.00	1,200
1849C Closed wreath	} 11,634	325.00	650.00	1,100	3,000
1849C Open wreath (Ex. rare)		—	—	—	—
1849D Open wreath	21,588	300.00	500.00	750.00	2,600
1849O Open wreath	215,000	225.00	275.00	375.00	1,400
1850	481,953	200.00	250.00	325.00	1,200
1850C	6,966	400.00	600.00	1,000	3,000
1850D	8,382	350.00	575.00	900.00	2,500
1850O	14,000	300.00	475.00	600.00	1,600

*The variety with smaller head and no L on truncation is valued higher.

[175]

GOLD DOLLARS

	Quan. Minted	VF-20	EF-40	AU-50	MS-60	Proof-63
1851	3,317,671	$200.00	$250.00	$325.00	$1,200	
1851C	41,267	325.00	500.00	825.00	2,000	
1851D	9,882	350.00	575.00	850.00	2,250	
1851O	290,000	225.00	275.00	350.00	1,300	
1852	2,045,351	200.00	250.00	325.00	1,200	
1852C	9,434	300.00	500.00	850.00	2,400	
1852D	6,360	325.00	550.00	1,000	2,750	
1852O	140,000	225.00	275.00	350.00	900.00	
1853	4,076,051	200.00	250.00	325.00	1,200	
1853C	11,515	300.00	550.00	900.00	3,000	
1853D	6,583	325.00	600.00	1,000	3,000	
1853O	290,000	225.00	275.00	375.00	900.00	
1854	855,502	200.00	250.00	325.00	1,200	——
1854D	2,935	500.00	1,000	1,750	4,500	
1854S	14,632	300.00	500.00	800.00	2,200	

INDIAN HEAD TYPE, Small Head 1854-1856

Type 2

VF-20 VERY FINE— Feather curl tips outlined but details worn.

EF-40 EXTREMELY FINE— Slight wear on tips of feather curls on headdress.

AU-50 ABOUT UNCIRCULATED— Trace of wear on feathers, nearly full luster.

MS-60 UNCIRCULATED— No trace of wear. Light marks and blemishes.

Standards same as previous issue. Diameter changed to 15 mm.

		VF-20	EF-40	AU-50	MS-60	Proof-63
1854	783,943	350.00	600.00	1,700	5,500	——
1855	758,269	350.00	600.00	1,700	5,500	——
1855C	9,803	750.00	1,200	2,400	8,000	
1855D	1,811	2,750	5,000	8,000	20,000	
1855O	55,000	550.00	1,000	2,000	6,200	
1856S	24,600	500.00	950.00	1,800	6,000	

INDIAN HEAD TYPE, Large Head 1856-1889

Type 3

VF-20 VERY FINE— Curled feathers have slight detail. Details worn smooth at eyebrow, hair below headdress and behind ear and bottom curl.

EF-40 EXTREMELY FINE— Slight wear above and to right of eye and on top of curled feathers.

AU-50 ABOUT UNCIRCULATED— Trace of wear on feathers, nearly full luster.

MS-60 UNCIRCULATED— No trace of wear. Light marks and blemishes.

			VF-20	EF-40	AU-50	MS-60	Proof-63
1856 Upright 5		33,660	200.00	275.00	550.00	1,100	
1856 Slant 5		1,729,276	175.00	225.00	325.00	1,000	$7,250
1856D		1,460	3,000	4,750	6,500	18,500	
1857		774,789	175.00	225.00	325.00	1,000	7,250
1857C		13,280	450.00	600.00	950.00	2,750	
1857D		3,533	550.00	900.00	1,750	4,750	
1857S		10,000	300.00	400.00	700.00	2,500	
1858		117,995	175.00	225.00	325.00	1,000	7,250
1858D		3,477	800.00	1,100	2,000	6,000	
1858S		10,000	300.00	400.00	750.00	2,300	
1859	(80)	168,244	175.00	225.00	325.00	1,000	6,250
1859C		5,235	500.00	800.00	1,300	4,000	
1859D		4,952	500.00	850.00	1,500	4,600	
1859S		15,000	300.00	400.00	725.00	2,300	
1860	(154)	36,668	175.00	225.00	325.00	1,000	5,750
1860D		1,566	2,500	4,750	7,300	16,000	
1860S		13,000	300.00	425.00	750.00	2,300	
1861	(349)	527,499	175.00	225.00	325.00	1,000	5,750

GOLD DOLLARS

	Quan. Minted	VF-20	EF-40	AU-50	MS-60	Proof-63
1861D		$5,000	$8,000	$14,000	$28,000	
1862 (35)	1,361,390	175.00	225.00	325.00	1,000	$5,500
1863 (50)	6,250	450.00	650.00	1,000	3,500	10,000
1864 (50)	5,950	400.00	600.00	950.00	3,400	10,000
1865 (25)	3,725	400.00	600.00	950.00	3,500	10,000
1866 (30)	7,130	325.00	550.00	850.00	2,000	7,800
1867 (50)	5,250	350.00	600.00	900.00	2,200	7,800
1868 (25)	10,525	300.00	525.00	725.00	1,700	7,800
1869 (25)	5,925	325.00	550.00	800.00	1,800	7,800
1870 (35)	6,335	300.00	525.00	725.00	1,800	7,800
1870S	3,000	625.00	1,000	1,900	3,750	
1871 (30)	3,930	300.00	525.00	725.00	1,800	7,200
1872 (30)	3,530	300.00	525.00	725.00	1,800	7,200
1873 Closed 3 (25)	1,825	300.00	550.00	825.00	2,200	8,500
1873 Open 3	123,300	175.00	225.00	300.00	1,000	
1874 (20)	198,820	175.00	225.00	300.00	1,000	7,200
1875 (20)	420	2,200	3,200	4,500	8,000	25,000
1876 (45)	3,245	250.00	325.00	500.00	1,700	6,250
1877 (20)	3,920	275.00	350.00	450.00	1,800	6,250
1878 (20)	3,020	275.00	350.00	450.00	1,800	6,250
1879 (30)	3,030	275.00	350.00	450.00	1,750	6,250
1880 (36)	1,636	250.00	300.00	450.00	1,500	6,250
1881 (87)	7,707	225.00	275.00	350.00	1,100	5,750
1882 (125)	5,125	225.00	275.00	350.00	1,100	5,750
1883 (207)	11,007	225.00	275.00	350.00	1,100	5,750
1884 (1,006)	6,236	225.00	275.00	350.00	1,100	4,000
1885 (1,105)	12,261	225.00	275.00	350.00	1,100	4,000
1886 (1,016)	6,016	225.00	275.00	350.00	1,100	4,000
1887 (1,043)	8,543	225.00	275.00	350.00	1,100	4,000
1888 (1,079)	16,580	225.00	275.00	350.00	1,100	4,000
1889 (1,779)	30,729	225.00	275.00	350.00	1,100	4,000

BIBLIOGRAPHY

Akers, David W., *Gold Dollars.* Englewood, Ohio, 1975. (and other gold denominations)

Breen, Walter, *Major Varieties of U.S. Gold Dollars.* Chicago, 1964. (and other gold denominations)

Bowers, Q. David, *United States Gold Coins, An Illustrated History.* Wolfeboro, NH, 1982.

QUARTER EAGLES ($2.50 GOLD PIECES)—1796-1929

Authorized by the Act of April 2, 1792, they weighed 67.5 grains, 916 2/3 fine until the weight was changed to 64.5 grains, fineness 899.225, by the Act of June 28, 1834. The Act of January 18, 1837 established fineness at .900. Most dates before 1834 are rare. The first issue was struck in 1796, most of which had no stars on the obverse.

Proofs of some dates prior to 1855 are known to exist, and all are rare.

TYPE COIN VALUES									
	F-12	VF-20	EF-40	AU-50	MS-60	MS-63	MS-65	PF-60	PF-63	PF-65
Cap Bust Right-NS 1796	9,500	14,500	22,000	30,000	46,500	60,000				
Cap Bust Right 1796-1807	2,600	4,000	6,000	8,500	16,000	25,000	35,000			
Cap Bust Left-Lg. 1808	8,000	13,000	19,000	27,000	50,000	65,000				
Cap Bust Left-Sm. 1821-1827	3,200	4,500	6,750	9,000	17,000	20,000	30,000			
Cap. Bust Left-Sm. 1829-1834	2,600	3,600	5,500	8,500	13,500	16,500	25,000			
Classic Head 1834-1839	225.00	300.00	425.00	850.00	2,200	4,750	12,500			
Lib Coronet 1840-1907	100.00	200.00	240.00	325.00	1,100	2,000	5,000	2,750	6,000	12,000
Indian Head 1908-1929	100.00	185.00	225.00	250.00	500.00	1,200	5,000	3,750	7,000	14,000

CAPPED BUST TO RIGHT 1796-1807

F-12 FINE— *Hair worn smooth on high spots. E PLURIBUS UNUM weak but readable.*

VF-20 VERY FINE— *Some wear on high spots.*

EF-40 EXTREMELY FINE— *Only slight wear on hair and cheek.*

MS-60 UNCIRCULATED— *No trace of wear. Light blemishes.*

Designer Robert Scot; weight 4.37 grams; composition: .9167 gold, .0833 copper; approx. diameter 20 mm; reeded edge.

QUARTER EAGLES

No Stars on Obverse 1796 Only   **Stars on Obverse 1796-1807**

	Quan. Minted	F-12	VF-20	EF-40	MS-60
1796 No stars on obverse	963	$9,000	$14,500	$22,000	$46,500
1796 Stars on obverse	432	7,500	12,000	17,000	36,000
1797	427	5,500	8,000	12,000	20,000
1798	1,094	4,000	5,000	7,000	17,000
1802, 2 over 1	3,035	2,600	4,000	6,000	16,000
1804, 13-Star reverse	} 3,327	4,500	8,500	14,000	25,000
1804, 14-Star reverse		2,600	4,000	6,000	16,000
1805	1,781	2,600	4,000	6,000	16,000
1806, 6 over 4, stars 8 left, 5 right	1,136	2,600	4,000	6,000	16,000
1806, 6 over 5, stars 7 left, 6 right	480	3,500	5,500	7,500	18,000
1807	6,812	2,600	4,000	6,000	16,000

CAPPED BUST TO LEFT, Large Size 1808

F-12 FINE—*E PLURIBUS UNUM and LIBERTY on headband readable but weak.*

VF-20 VERY FINE—*Motto and LIBERTY clear.*

EF-40 EXTREMELY FINE—*All details of hair are plain.*

MS-60 UNCIRCULATED—*No trace of wear. Light blemishes.*

Designer John Reich. Standards same as previous issue.

1808	2,710	8,000	13,000	19,000	50,000

CAPPED HEAD TO LEFT 1821-1834

Those dated 1829 through 1834 are smaller in diameter than the 1821-1827 pieces. They also have smaller letters, dates and stars.

Standards same as previous issue. Diameter changed to approximately 18.5 mm.

1821	6,448	3,200	4,500	6,750	16,000
1824, 4 over 1	2,600	3,200	4,500	6,750	16,000
1825	4,434	3,200	4,500	6,750	16,000
1826, 6 over 5	760	4,500	6,000	9,000	30,000
1827	2,800	3,200	4,500	6,750	17,000

Reduced Size 1829-1834

1829	3,403	3,000	4,000	6,200	13,500
1830	4,540	2,600	3,600	5,500	13,500
1831	4,520	2,600	3,600	5,500	13,500
1832	4,400	2,600	3,600	5,500	13,500
1833	4,160	2,600	3,600	5,500	13,500
1834 (Motto)	4,000	6,000	9,000	14,000	28,000

QUARTER EAGLES
CLASSIC HEAD TYPE, No Motto on Reverse 1834-1839

In 1834 the quarter eagle was redesigned. A ribbon binding the hair, bearing the word LIBERTY, replaces the Liberty cap. The motto was omitted from the reverse. In 1840 a coronet and smaller head were designed to conform in appearance with that of the larger gold coins.

F-12 FINE—*LIBERTY readable and complete. Curl under ear outlined but no detail.*

VF-20 VERY FINE—*LIBERTY plain. Hair curl has detail.*

EF-40 EXTREMELY FINE—*Small amount of wear on top of hair and below L in LIBERTY. Wear evident on wing.*

AU-50 ABOUT UNCIRCULATED—*Trace of wear on coronet and hair above ear.*

MS-60 UNCIRCULATED—*No trace of wear. Light blemishes.*

Mint mark location.

Designer William Kneass; weight 4.18 grams; composition: .8992 gold, .1008 copper; diameter 18.2 mm; reeded edge.

	Quan. Minted	F-12	VF-20	EF-40	AU-50	MS-60
1834 No motto	112,234	$225.00	$300.00	$425.00	$850.00	$2,200
1835	131,402	225.00	300.00	425.00	850.00	2,200
1836	547,986	225.00	300.00	425.00	850.00	2,200
1837	45,080	225.00	325.00	475.00	900.00	2,750
1838	47,030	225.00	325.00	475.00	900.00	2,750
1838C	7,880	400.00	550.00	1,200	1,500	6,500
1839	27,021	225.00	325.00	475.00	900.00	2,750
1839C	18,140	375.00	525.00	1,000	1,400	6,000
1839D	13,674	400.00	550.00	1,200	1,500	5,200
1839O	17,781	300.00	400.00	600.00	1,100	4,500

1839, 9 over 8 varieties exist for P, C and D mints.

CORONET TYPE 1840-1907

Mint mark location.

Designer Christian Gobrecht; weight 4.18 grams; composition: .900 gold, .100 copper; diameter 18 mm; reeded edge. Net weight: .12094 oz. pure gold.

	Quan. Minted	VF-20	EF-40	AU-50	MS-60
1840	18,859	$275.00	$325.00	$450.00	$1,300
1840C	12,822	450.00	750.00	1,100	3,000
1840D	3,532	1,000	2,000	3,000	6,000
1840O	33,580	250.00	300.00	450.00	1,500
1841 Proofs only		15,000	30,000	40,000	60,000
1841C	10,281	425.00	750.00	1,100	2,250
1841D	4,164	750.00	1,400	2,500	4,750
1842	2,823	500.00	800.00	1,200	3,000
1842C	6,729	500.00	800.00	1,200	2,600
1842D	4,643	650.00	1,200	2,000	4,250
1842O	19,800	275.00	500.00	1,000	2,000
1843	100,546	250.00	275.00	375.00	1,200
1843C Small date, crosslet 4	2,988	1,300	2,500	3,500	5,000
1843C Large date, plain 4	23,076	450.00	800.00	1,100	2,300
1843D Small date, crosslet 4	36,209	450.00	850.00	1,200	2,750
1843O Small date, crosslet 4	288,002	250.00	275.00	400.00	1,250
1843O Large date, plain 4	76,000	250.00	275.00	400.00	1,250

QUARTER EAGLES

	Quan. Minted	VF-20	EF-40	AU-50	MS-60
1844	6,784	$300.00	$500.00	$1,000	$2,000
1844C	11,622	375.00	550.00	1,100	2,750
1844D	17,332	500.00	750.00	1,200	3,000
1845	91,051	225.00	250.00	375.00	1,200
1845D	19,460	450.00	750.00	1,200	3,000
1845O	4,000	950.00	1,500	2,500	9,000
1846	21,598	250.00	400.00	600.00	1,300
1846C	4,808	600.00	1,000	1,600	3,750
1846D	19,303	500.00	800.00	1,300	3,000
1846O	62,000	225.00	250.00	450.00	1,250
1847	29,814	225.00	250.00	400.00	1,200
1847C	23,226	375.00	450.00	900.00	2,500
1847D	15,784	500.00	800.00	1,100	2,750
1847O	124,000	225.00	300.00	500.00	1,250
1848	7,497	425.00	650.00	1,000	2,500

CAL. Above Eagle on Reverse

California Gold Quarter Eagle

In 1848 about two hundred and thirty ounces of gold were sent to Secretary of War Marcy by Col. R. B. Mason, Military Governor of California. The gold was turned over to the mint and made into quarter eagles. The distinguishing mark "CAL." was punched above the eagle on the reverse side, while the coins were in the die. Two specimens with proof surface are known.

	Quan. Minted	VF-20	EF-40	AU-50	MS-60
1848 CAL. above eagle	1,389	4,500	7,000	12,500	30,000
1848C	16,788	400.00	600.00	1,000	2,300
1848D	13,771	500.00	700.00	1,100	2,500
1849	23,294	250.00	300.00	500.00	1,200
1849C	10,220	450.00	700.00	1,100	2,400
1849D	10,945	500.00	900.00	1,300	2,750
1850	252,923	200.00	240.00	375.00	1,200
1850C	9,148	450.00	700.00	1,000	2,200
1850D	12,148	450.00	850.00	1,350	2,500
1850O	84,000	225.00	250.00	600.00	1,200
1851	1,372,748	200.00	240.00	325.00	1,100
1851C	14,923	450.00	700.00	1,000	2,200
1851D	11,264	450.00	800.00	1,350	2,500
1851O	148,000	225.00	240.00	400.00	1,100
1852	1,159,681	200.00	240.00	325.00	1,100
1852C	9,772	350.00	700.00	1,000	2,300
1852D	4,078	550.00	1,000	2,000	3,750
1852O	140,000	225.00	240.00	400.00	1,300
1853	1,404,668	200.00	240.00	325.00	1,100
1853D	3,178	600.00	1,200	2,000	3,750
1854	596,258	200.00	240.00	325.00	1,100
1854C	7,295	450.00	700.00	1,100	2,400
1854D	1,760	2,200	3,600	4,800	9,500
1854O	153,000	200.00	240.00	375.00	1,200
1854S	246		20,000	40,000	—
1855	235,480	200.00	240.00	325.00	1,100
1855C	3,677	750.00	1,300	2,350	4,500
1855D	1,123	2,500	4,000	5,250	15,000
1856	384,240	200.00	240.00	300.00	1,100
1856C	7,913	500.00	700.00	1,100	2,750

QUARTER EAGLES

	Quan. Minted	VF-20	EF-40	AU-50	MS-60	Proof-63
1856D	874	$3,200	$8,000	$11,000	$20,000	
1856O	21,100	250.00	300.00	500.00	1,300	
1856S	72,120	235.00	275.00	475.00	1,200	
1857	214,130	200.00	240.00	325.00	1,100	$15,000
1857D	2,364	650.00	1,000	1,900	4,000	
1857O	34,000	235.00	275.00	450.00	1,200	
1857S	69,200	235.00	300.00	500.00	1,400	
1858	47,377	225.00	250.00	400.00	900.00	14,000
1858C	9,056	400.00	600.00	1,000	2,500	

A modified reverse design (smaller letters and arrowheads) was used on all Philadelphia issues from 1859 through 1907, and on San Francisco issues of 1877 through 1879.

	Quan. Minted	VF-20	EF-40	AU-50	MS-60	Proof-63
1859 .... (80)	39,444	225.00	240.00	325.00	825.00	10,000
1859D	2,244	600.00	900.00	2,000	4,000	
1859S	15,200	225.00	325.00	450.00	1,200	
1860 .... (112)	22,675	225.00	240.00	375.00	1,000	7,000
1860C	7,469	400.00	700.00	1,100	2,500	
1860S	35,600	235.00	300.00	450.00	1,100	

1862, 2 over 1

	Quan. Minted	VF-20	EF-40	AU-50	MS-60	Proof-63
1861 .... (90)	1,283,878	200.00	240.00	325.00	1,100	7,000
1861S	24,000	250.00	300.00	600.00	1,200	
1862, 2 over 1 .... }		900.00	1,500	3,000	——	
1862 .... (35) }	98,543	225.00	250.00	375.00	1,150	8,000
1862S	8,000	450.00	800.00	1,000	2,200	
1863 Proofs only .... (30)	30					40,000
1863S	10,800	300.00	500.00	800.00	1,900	
1864 .... (50)	2,874	1,000	1,750	2,800	5,500	12,000
1865 .... (25)	1,545	1,000	1,750	2,800	5,500	13,000
1865S	23,376	250.00	350.00	550.00	1,300	
1866 .... (30)	3,110	350.00	500.00	900.00	1,900	9,000
1866S	38,960	250.00	350.00	550.00	1,400	
1867 .... (50)	3,250	300.00	500.00	800.00	1,800	8,000
1867S	28,000	250.00	300.00	550.00	1,300	
1868 .... (25)	3,625	275.00	375.00	650.00	1,500	8,000
1868S	34,000	225.00	300.00	500.00	1,300	
1869 .... (25)	4,345	275.00	325.00	600.00	1,300	8,000
1869S	29,500	225.00	300.00	500.00	1,300	
1870 .... (35)	4,555	275.00	350.00	600.00	1,400	8,000
1870S	16,000	250.00	325.00	425.00	1,400	
1871 .... (30)	5,350	275.00	350.00	500.00	1,400	8,000
1871S	22,000	200.00	240.00	375.00	1,200	
1872 .... (30)	3,030	300.00	400.00	600.00	1,400	8,000
1872S	18,000	200.00	250.00	375.00	1,100	
1873 Closed 3 .... (25)	55,225	200.00	240.00	325.00	1,100	8,000
1873 Open 3	122,800	200.00	240.00	325.00	1,100	
1873S	27,000	250.00	300.00	425.00	1,200	
1874 .... (20)	3,940	275.00	350.00	600.00	1,200	9,000
1875 .... (20)	420	1,900	4,000	6,000	9,500	22,500
1875S	11,600	250.00	300.00	450.00	850.00	
1876 .... (45)	4,221	250.00	350.00	600.00	1,400	8,000
1876S	5,000	250.00	325.00	450.00	1,250	
1877 .... (20)	1,652	450.00	650.00	850.00	1,900	9,000

QUARTER EAGLES

	Quan. Minted	VF-20	EF-40	AU-50	MS-60	Proof-63
1877S	35,400	$200.00	$240.00	$325.00	$1,100	
1878 .... (20)	286,260	200.00	240.00	325.00	1,100	$9,000
1878S	178,000	200.00	240.00	325.00	1,100	
1879 .... (30)	88,990	200.00	240.00	325.00	1,100	8,000
1879S	43,500	200.00	240.00	325.00	1,100	
1880 .... (36)	2,996	250.00	325.00	400.00	1,300	8,000
1881 .... (51)	691	900.00	1,500	2,750	4,000	9,500
1882 .... (67)	4,067	250.00	300.00	400.00	1,300	7,500
1883 .... (82)	2,002	275.00	350.00	425.00	1,400	7,500
1884 .... (73)	2,023	275.00	350.00	425.00	1,400	7,500
1885 .... (87)	887	750.00	1,100	2,000	3,000	8,750
1886 .... (88)	4,088	250.00	300.00	400.00	1,200	7,500
1887 .... (122)	6,282	235.00	250.00	375.00	1,200	7,000
1888 .... (97)	16,098	200.00	240.00	325.00	1,100	7,000
1889 .... (48)	17,648	200.00	240.00	325.00	1,100	7,000
1890 .... (93)	8,813	250.00	275.00	350.00	1,200	7,000
1891 .... (80)	11,040	250.00	275.00	350.00	1,200	7,000
1892 .... (105)	2,545	275.00	375.00	500.00	1,200	6,750
1893 .... (106)	30,106	200.00	240.00	325.00	1,100	6,750
1894 .... (122)	4,122	250.00	300.00	400.00	900.00	6,500
1895 .... (119)	6,119	200.00	250.00	350.00	1,150	6,500
1896 .... (132)	19,202	200.00	240.00	325.00	1,100	6,500
1897 .... (136)	29,904	200.00	240.00	325.00	1,100	6,500
1898 .... (165)	24,165	200.00	240.00	325.00	1,100	6,500
1899 .... (150)	27,350	200.00	240.00	325.00	1,100	6,000
1900 .... (205)	67,205	200.00	240.00	325.00	1,100	6,000
1901 .... (223)	91,323	200.00	240.00	325.00	1,100	6,000
1902 .... (193)	133,733	200.00	240.00	325.00	1,100	6,000
1903 .... (197)	201,257	200.00	240.00	325.00	1,100	6,000
1904 .... (170)	160,960	200.00	240.00	325.00	1,100	6,000
1905* .... (144)	217,944	200.00	240.00	325.00	1,100	6,000
1906 .... (160)	176,490	200.00	240.00	325.00	1,100	6,000
1907 .... (154)	336,448	200.00	240.00	325.00	1,100	6,000

*Pieces dated 1905S are counterfeit.

Values of common gold coins have been based on a bullion price of $350. per Troy ounce, and may vary with the prevailing spot price of gold.

INDIAN HEAD TYPE 1908-1929

The new type represents a departure from all preceding coin types in the United States series. Bela Lyon Pratt was the designer of this and the half eagle piece. The coin has no raised milling and the main devices and legends are incuse.

Designer Bela Lyon Pratt; weight 4.18 grams; composition: .900 gold, .100 copper; diameter 18 mm; reeded edge. Net weight: .12094 oz. pure gold.

VF-20 VERY FINE—*Hair cord knot distinct. Feathers at top of head clear. Cheekbone worn.*

EF-40 EXTREMELY FINE—*Cheekbone, war bonnet and head-band feathers slightly worn.*

AU-50 ABOUT UNCIRCULATED—*Trace of wear on cheekbone and headdress.*

MS-60 UNCIRCULATED—*No trace of wear. Light blemishes.*

Mint mark location is on reverse left of arrows.

	Quan. Minted	VF-20	EF-40	AU-50	MS-60	Matte Proof-63
1908 .... (236)	565,057	$185.00	$225.00	$250.00	$500.00	$7,000
1909 .... (139)	441,899	185.00	225.00	250.00	500.00	7,000

QUARTER EAGLES

	Quan. Minted	VF-20	EF-40	AU-50	MS-60	Matte Proof-63
1910 .... (682)	492,682	$185.00	$225.00	$250.00	$500.00	$7,000
1911 .... (191)	704,191	185.00	225.00	250.00	500.00	7,000
1911D........................	55,680	750.00	1,000	1,700	3,500	
1912 .... (197)	616,197	185.00	225.00	250.00	500.00	7,000
1913 .... (165)	722,165	185.00	225.00	250.00	500.00	7,000
1914 .... (117)	240,117	185.00	225.00	250.00	500.00	7,000
1914D........................	448,000	185.00	225.00	250.00	500.00	
1915 .... (100)	606,100	185.00	225.00	250.00	500.00	7,000
1925D........................	578,000	185.00	225.00	250.00	500.00	
1926	446,000	185.00	225.00	250.00	500.00	
1927	388,000	185.00	225.00	250.00	500.00	
1928	416,000	185.00	225.00	250.00	500.00	
1929	532,000	185.00	225.00	250.00	500.00	

THREE DOLLAR GOLD PIECES — 1854-1889

The three dollar gold piece was authorized by the Act of February 21, 1853. The coin was first struck in 1854. It was never popular and saw very little circulation.

The coin weighs 77.4 grains, .900 fine. The head on the obverse represents an Indian princess with hair tightly curling over the neck, head crowned with a circle of feathers, the band of which is inscribed LIBERTY. A wreath of tobacco, wheat, corn and cotton occupies the field of the reverse, with the denomination and date within it.

Restrikes of some years were made at the Mint; particularly 1873 and 1876.

In the year 1854 only, the word DOLLARS is in much smaller letters than in years 1855 through 1889. The 1856 proof has DOLLARS in large letters cut over the same word in small letters.

TYPE COIN VALUES

	F-12	VF-20	EF-40	AU-50	MS-60	MS-63	MS-65	PF-60	PF-63	PF-65
Indian Head 1854-1889	375.00	625.00	900.00	1,400	5,200	9,500	15,000	6,000	11,000	24,000

Designer James B. Longacre, weight 5.015 grams; composition: .900 gold, .100 copper; diameter 20.5 mm; reeded edge. Net weight: .14512 oz. pure gold.

VF-20 VERY FINE—*Eyebrow, hair about forehead and ear and bottom curl are worn smooth. Curled feather-ends have faint details showing.*

EF-40 EXTREMELY FINE—*Light wear above and to right of eye. and on top of curled feathers.*

AU-50 ABOUT UNCIRCULATED—*Trace of wear on top of curled feathers and in hair above and to right of eye.*

MS-60 UNCIRCULATED—*No trace of wear. Light blemishes.*

Mint mark location is on reverse below wreath.

	Quan. Minted	VF-20	EF-40	AU-50	MS-60	Proof-63
1854	138,618	$625.00	$900.00	$1,400	$5,200	$25,000
1854D........................	1,120	6,500	1,000	18,000	——	
1854O........................	24,000	625.00	900.00	1,500	5,500	
1855	50,555	625.00	900.00	1,400	5,200	30,000
1855S........................	6,600	825.00	1,300	2,000	8,500	
1856	26,010	625.00	900.00	1,400	5,200	22,000
1856S*........................	34,500	725.00	1,200	1,600	5,750	
1857	20,891	625.00	900.00	1,400	5,500	20,000
1857S........................	14,250	750.00	1,200	1,600	5,750	
1858	2,133	800.00	1,300	1,700	6,000	18,000
1859 .... (80)	15,638	625.00	900.00	1,400	5,500	16,000

*Small and medium S varieties exist.

THREE DOLLAR GOLD PIECES

	Quan. Minted	VF-20	EF-40	AU-50	MS-60	Proof-63
1860 .... (119)	7,155	$725.00	$1,200	$1,400	$5,500	$14,000
1860S . (2,592 melted at Mint)	7,000	800.00	1,400	1,700	——	
1861 .... (113)	6,072	725.00	1,200	1,400	5,500	14,000
1862 .... (35)	5,785	725.00	1,200	1,400	5,500	14,000
1863 .... (39)	5,039	775.00	1,300	1,500	5,500	14,000
1864 .... (50)	2,680	775.00	1,300	1,500	5,200	14,000
1865 .... (25)	1,165	950.00	1,500	2,000	6,500	18,000
1866 .... (30)	4,030	775.00	1,300	1,500	5,500	14,000
1867 .... (50)	2,650	775.00	1,300	1,500	5,500	14,000
1868 .... (25)	4,875	775.00	1,300	1,500	5,500	14,000
1869 .... (25)	2,525	775.00	1,300	1,500	5,500	14,000
1870 .... (35)	3,535	775.00	1,300	1,500	5,500	14,000
1870S *(Unique)*	1	687,500	U.S. Gold Sale, 1982			
1871 .... (30)	1,330	850.00	1,350	1,600	5,750	14,000
1872 .... (30)	2,030	775.00	1,300	1,500	5,200	14,000
1873 Closed 3........................		2,500	4,000	5,000	9,000	20,000
1873 Open 3 (Original) ... (25)	25					30,000
1874 .... (20)	41,820	625.00	850.00	1,200	5,200	17,500
1875 Proofs only .... (20)	20			Carter Sale, 1984		121,000
1876 Proofs only .... (45)	45			Carter Sale, 1984		35,200
1877 .... (20)	1,488	950.00	1,750	2,100	6,500	18,000
1878 .... (20)	82,324	625.00	900.00	1,300	5,200	17,500
1879 .... (30)	3,030	775.00	1,300	1,500	5,500	14,000
1880 .... (36)	1,036	850.00	1,300	1,600	5,500	14,000
1881 .... (54)	554	1,000	1,700	2,100	6,500	15,000
1882 .... (76)	1,576	775.00	1,300	1,500	5,500	12,000
1883 .... (89)	989	850.00	1,300	1,600	5,600	12,000
1884 .... (106)	1,106	850.00	1,300	1,600	5,500	11,000
1885 .... (109)	910	900.00	1,400	1,700	5,500	11,000
1886 .... (142)	1,142	775.00	1,300	1,600	5,600	11,000
1887 .... (160)	6,160	700.00	1,100	1,400	5,200	11,000
1888 .... (291)	5,291	700.00	1,100	1,400	5,200	11,000
1889 .... (129)	2,429	700.00	1,100	1,400	5,200	11,000

FOUR DOLLAR GOLD OR "STELLA"

These pattern coins were first suggested by the Hon. John A. Kasson, then U.S. Minister to Austria; and it was through the efforts of Dr. W. W. Hubbell, who patented the goloid metal used in making the goloid metric dollars, that we have these beautiful and interesting pieces.

There are two distinct types in both years of issue. Charles E. Barber designed the flowing hair type, and George T. Morgan the coiled hair. They were struck in gold, aluminum, copper and white metal. Only those struck in gold are listed.

	Quan. Minted	EF-40	Proof-65
1879 Flowing hair	(415)	$20,000	$55,000
1879 Coiled hair	(10)		100,000
1880 Flowing hair	(15)		75,000
1880 Coiled Hair........................	(10)		115,000

HALF EAGLES — 1795-1929

($5.00 GOLD PIECES)

The half eagle was the first gold coin actually struck for the United States. The $5.00 piece was authorized to be coined by the Act of April 2, 1792, and the first type weighed 135 grains, 916 2/3 fine. The Act of June 28, 1834 changed the weight to 129 grains, 899.225 fine. Fineness became .900 by the Act of January 18, 1837.

There are many varieties among the early dates caused by changes in the number of stars, style of eagle, overdates, and differences in the size of figures in the dates. Those dated prior to 1807 do not bear any mark of value. The 1822 half eagle is considered the most valuable regular issue coin of the entire United States series. Proofs of some dates prior to 1855 are known to exist, and all are rare. The half eagle was the only U.S. denomination struck in each of the seven mints.

TYPE COIN VALUES

	F-12	VF-20	EF-40	AU-50	MS-60	MS-63	MS-65	PF-60	PF-63	PF-65
Cap Bust-Sm. Eag. 1795-1798	5,000	8,000	11,000	14,000	27,500	35,000	50,000			
Cap Bust-Lg. Eag. 1795-1807	1,100	1,750	2,750	4,250	10,000	17,500	25,000			
Cap Draped Bust 1807-1812	1,100	1,600	2,400	3,850	9,500	16,500	23,000			
Cap Head 1813-1834	1,500	2,000	3,000	5,000	12,000	20,000	28,000			
Classic Head 1834-1838	225.00	300.00	450.00	950.00	2,500	5,500	13,500			
Lib Coronet-NM 1839-1866	150.00	200.00	250.00	350.00	1,700	5,000	14,000	7,500	13,000	21,000
Lib. Coronet 1866-1908	150.00	175.00	200.00	250.00	400.00	1,200	7,000	3,750	8,500	17,000
Indian Head 1908-1929	175.00	260.00	285.00	375.00	1,500	3,000	8,000	6,000	11,000	19,000

CAPPED BUST TO RIGHT, SMALL EAGLE 1795-1798

This type was struck from mid-1795 to early 1798, when the small eagle reverse was changed to the large or "heraldic" eagle. Note that the 1795 and 1797 dates exist for both types, but the heraldic reverses of these dates were probably struck under emergency conditions in late 1798.

Designer Robert Scot; weight 8.75 grams; composition: .9167 gold, .0833 copper; approx. diameter 25 mm; reeded edge.

F-12 FINE—*Hair worn smooth but with distinct outline. For heraldic type, E PLURIBUS UNUM is faint but readable.*

VF-20 VERY FINE—*Slight to noticeable wear on high spots such as hair, turban, eagle's head and wings.*

EF-40 EXTREMELY FINE—*Slight wear on hair and highest part of cheek.*

MS-60 UNCIRCULATED—*No trace of wear. Light blemishes.*

	Quan. Minted	F-12	VF-20	EF-40	MS-60
1795 Small eagle*	8,707	$5,000	$8,000	$11,000	$27,500

*One variety has final S in STATES over D.

1796, 6 over 5	**1797, 15 Stars**	**1797, 16 Stars**

1796, 6 over 5	6,196	5,000	8,000	11,000	27,500

[185]

HALF EAGLES

	Quan. Minted	F-12	VF-20	EF-40	MS-60
1797, 15 stars	} 3,609	$7,000	$10,000	$15,000	$30,000
1797, 16 stars		7,500	11,000	16,000	32,000
1798 Small eagle *(7 known)*		——	75,000	100,000	——

CAPPED BUST TO RIGHT, HERALDIC EAGLE 1795-1807

		F-12	VF-20	EF-40	MS-60
1795 Heraldic eagle*		6,000	9,000	14,500	32,000
1797, 7 over 5*		5,250	8,000	12,000	23,000
1797, 16 star obverse* *(Unique)*		——			
1798 Small 8		1,100	1,750	2,750	10,000
1798 Large 8, 13 star reverse	} 24,867	1,100	1,750	2,750	11,000
1798 Large 8, 14 star reverse		1,500	2,500	3,500	14,000
1799	7,451	1,100	1,750	2,750	10,000

*These three pieces are thought to have been struck in 1798 and included in the mintage figure for that year.

1802 over 1	**1803 over 2**	**Small 8 over Large 8**

		F-12	VF-20	EF-40	MS-60
1800	37,628	1,100	1,750	2,750	10,000
1802, 2 over 1	53,176	1,100	1,750	2,750	10,000
1803, 3 over 2	33,506	1,100	1,750	2,750	10,000
1804 Small 8	} 30,475	1,100	1,750	2,750	10,000
1804 Small 8 over large 8		1,100	1,750	2,750	10,000
1805	33,183	1,100	1,750	2,750	10,000

Pointed 6, 8 and 5 Stars	**Round Top 6, 7 and 6 Stars**

		F-12	VF-20	EF-40	MS-60
1806 Pointed top 6	9,676	1,100	1,750	3,000	11,000
1806 Round top 6	54,417	1,100	1,750	2,750	10,000
1807	32,488	1,100	1,750	2,750	10,000

HALF EAGLES
CAPPED DRAPED BUST TO LEFT 1807-1812

Designer John Reich. Standards same as previous issue.

F-12 FINE— *LIBERTY readable but partly weak.*

VF-20 VERY FINE— *Headband edges slightly worn. LIBERTY is bold.*

EF-40 EXTREMELY FINE— *Slight wear on highest portions of hair. 80% of major curls are plain.*

MS-60 UNCIRCULATED— *No trace of wear. Light blemishes.*

	Quan. Minted	F-12	VF-20	EF-40	MS-60
1807	51,605	$1,100	$1,600	$2,500	$9,750

1808, 8 over 7   **Normal Date**   **1809, 9 over 8**

		F-12	VF-20	EF-40	MS-60
1808, 8 over 7 .... ⎫		1,100	1,600	2,400	9,500
1808 .... ⎬	55,578	1,100	1,600	2,400	9,500
1809, 9 over 8	33,875	1,100	1,600	2,400	9,500

Small Date **Large Date**		**Large 5**		**Tall 5**	
1810 Small date, small 5............. ⎫		3,000	4,500	9,000	
1810 Small date, tall 5 .... ⎬		1,100	1,600	2,400	9,500
1810 Large date, small 5 .... ⎬	100,287	1,250	2,500	4,000	11,000
1810 Large date, large 5............. ⎭		1,100	1,600	2,400	9,500
1811 Small 5 .... ⎫		1,100	1,600	2,400	9,500
1811 Tall 5 .... ⎬	99,581	1,100	1,600	2,400	9,500
1812	58,087	1,100	1,600	2,400	9,500

CAPPED HEAD TO LEFT (large diameter) 1813-1829

		F-12	VF-20	EF-40	MS-60
1813	95,428	1,500	2,000	3,000	12,000
1814, 4 over 3	15,454	1,750	2,800	4,000	15,000
1815	635			55,000	150,000
1818 Normal dies.................... ⎫		1,500	2,000	3,000	12,000
1818 STATESOF one word........... ⎬	48,588	1,500	2,000	3,000	12,000
1818, 5D over 50.................... ⎭		1,500	2,000	3,000	13,000
1819 .... ⎫				30,000	50,000
1819, 5D over 50.................... ⎬	51,723			30,000	50,000

[187]

HALF EAGLES

Curved Base 2   **Square Base 2**   **Small Letters**   **Large Letters**

	Quan. Minted	F-12	VF-20	EF-40	MS-60
1820 Curved-base 2, small letters.....	⎫	$1,500	$2,000	$3,200	$13,000
1820 Curved-base 2, large letters.....	⎬ 263,806	1,500	2,000	3,200	13,000
1820 Square-base 2.................	⎭	1,500	2,000	3,200	13,000
1821	34,641	3,000	6,500	9,000	25,000

1825, 5 over 1

1825, 5 over 4

1822 *(3 known)*........................	17,796				
1823	14,485	2,300	3,300	4,300	18,000
1824	17,340	5,500	9,000	18,000	33,000
1825, 5 over 1 .... ⎫		3,000	4,500	7,500	22,500
1825, 5 over 4 *(2 known)*.......... ⎬	29,060			140,000	220,000
1826	18,069		6,500	9,500	27,500
1827	24,913		9,000	19,000	35,000

Note: In the 1822 row the value **687,500** appears under EF-40 with dashes on either side.

Large Date

Small Date

1828, 8 over 7 .... ⎫		5,000	7,000	16,500	35,000
1828 .... ⎬	28,029	6,500	9,500	21,000	35,000
1829 Large date	57,442	—	—	—	50,000

The half eagles dated 1829 (small date) through 1834 are smaller in diameter than the earlier pieces. They also have smaller letters, dates and stars.

HALF EAGLES
CAPPED HEAD TO LEFT (reduced diameter) 1829-1834

	Large 5D	Small 5D	13 Stars Square Base 2		
	Quan. Minted	*F-12*	*VF-20*	*EF-40*	*MS-60*
1829 Small date .... inc. above			$20,000	$30,000	$65,000
1830 Small or large 5 D 126,351		$2,200	3,750	5,250	16,000
1831 Small or large 5 D 140,594		2,200	3,750	5,250	16,000
1832 Curved-base 2, 12 stars *(6 known)*	157,487	—	—	45,000	—
1832 Square-base 2, 13 stars		4,750	6,750	10,000	21,000
1833 Large date	193,630	2,200	3,750	5,250	16,000
1833 Small date		2,200	3,750	6,750	17,000

4 Plain 4   **4** Crosslet 4

1834 Plain 4........................	50,141	2,200	3,750	5,250	15,000
1834 Crosslet 4		2,200	3,750	5,250	15,000

CLASSIC HEAD TYPE 1834-1838

As on the quarter eagle of 1834, the motto E PLURIBUS UNUM was omitted from the new, reduced size half eagle in 1834, to distinguish the old coins which had become worth more than face value.

Designer William Kneass; weight 8.36 grams; composition: .8992 gold, .1008 copper; diameter 22.5 mm; reeded edge.

1834 Plain 4........................	657,460	225.00	300.00	450.00	2,500
1834 Crosslet 4		275.00	375.00	800.00	4,750
1835	371,534	225.00	300.00	450.00	2,500
1836	553,147	225.00	300.00	450.00	2,500
1837	207,121	225.00	300.00	550.00	2,750
1838	286,588	225.00	300.00	450.00	2,500
1838C................................	17,179	825.00	1,200	2,500	7,750
1838D................................	20,583	825.00	1,200	2,500	7,750

HALF EAGLES
CORONET TYPE, No Motto Above Eagle 1839-1866

Designer Christian Gobrecht; weight 8.359 grams; composition: .900 gold, .100 copper; diameter (1839-40) 22.5 mm. (1840-1929) 21.6 mm; reeded edge. Net weight: .24187 oz. pure gold.

VF-20 VERY FINE—*LIBERTY bold. Major lines show in neck hair.*

EF-40 EXTREMELY FINE—*Neck hair details clear. Slight wear on top and lower part of coronet, and hair.*

AU-50 ABOUT UNCIRCULATED—*Trace of wear on coronet and hair above eye.*

MS-60 UNCIRCULATED—*No trace of wear. Light blemishes.*

Mint mark above date 1839 only, below eagle 1840-1908.

	Quan. Minted	VF-20	EF-40	AU-50	MS-60
1839	118,143	$250.00	$375.00	$700.00	$2,000
1839C	17,205	500.00	900.00	1,300	3,300
1839D	18,939	500.00	900.00	1,300	3,300
1840*	137,382	225.00	275.00	800.00	2,100
1840C*	18,992	450.00	850.00	1,350	3,250
1840D*	22,896	550.00	900.00	1,700	3,400
1840O*	40,120	400.00	650.00	1,100	2,500
1841	15,833	325.00	450.00	850.00	2,250
1841C	21,467	450.00	750.00	1,400	3,500
1841D	29,392	475.00	850.00	1,500	3,500
1841O (Unconfirmed in any collection)	50				

*Scarce varieties of the 1840 coins have the large diameter and wide rims of the 1839 issues.

1842 Large Date	**Large Letters**	**Small Letters**	**Extra 7 at borders**

	Quan. Minted	VF-20	EF-40	AU-50	MS-60
1842 Small letters	⎫ 27,578	250.00	450.00	675.00	2,000
1842 Large letters	⎭	250.00	450.00	675.00	2,000
1842C Small date	⎫ 27,432	1,000	1,400	2,500	5,000
1842C Large date	⎭	425.00	700.00	1,000	3,200
1842D Small date	⎫ 59,608	500.00	800.00	1,100	3,300
1842D Large date	⎭	550.00	850.00	1,500	3,700
1842O	16,400	325.00	650.00	900.00	2,300
1843	611,205	200.00	250.00	350.00	1,700
1843C	44,277	425.00	700.00	10,000	2,500
1843D	98,452	425.00	800.00	12,000	3,500
1843O Small letters	19,075	300.00	500.00	800.00	2,500
1843O Large letters	82,000	300.00	500.00	700.00	2,200
1844	340,330	200.00	250.00	350.00	1,700
1844C	23,631	450.00	750.00	1,100	3,500
1844D	88,982	425.00	700.00	1,000	3,400
1844O	364,600	275.00	400.00	725.00	2,100
1845	417,099	200.00	250.00	350.00	1,700
1845D	90,629	425.00	650.00	1,000	3,000
1845O	41,000	350.00	500.00	900.00	2,300

HALF EAGLES

	Quan. Minted	VF-20	EF-40	AU-50	MS-60	Proof-63
1846	395,942	$200.00	$250.00	$350.00	$1,700	
1846C	12,995	600.00	975.00	1,450	3,500	
1846D	} 80,294	475.00	725.00	1,100	2,800	
1846D high second D over D		500.00	800.00	1,500	3,200	
1846O	58,000	350.00	500.00	1,000	2,300	
1847	915,981	200.00	250.00	350.00	1,700	
1847, top of extra very low 7 at border	——	——				
1847C	84,151	425.00	750.00	1,000	3,000	
1847D	64,405	425.00	750.00	1,000	3,000	
1847O	12,000	475.00	900.00	1,300	3,000	
1848	260,775	200.00	250.00	350.00	1,700	
1848C	64,472	500.00	800.00	1,100	2,750	
1848D	47,465	500.00	800.00	1,100	3,000	
1849	133,070	200.00	250.00	350.00	1,800	
1849C	64,823	500.00	800.00	1,100	3,000	
1849D	39,036	500.00	800.00	1,200	3,200	
1850	64,491	200.00	250.00	350.00	1,700	
1850C	63,591	500.00	800.00	1,100	3,000	
1850D	43,984	500.00	800.00	1,200	3,200	
1851	377,505	200.00	250.00	350.00	1,700	
1851C	49,176	500.00	800.00	1,100	3,000	
1851D	62,710	500.00	800.00	1,100	3,000	
1851O	41,000	350.00	500.00	800.00	2,100	
1852	573,901	200.00	250.00	350.00	1,700	
1852C	72,574	500.00	800.00	1,100	3,000	
1852D	91,584	500.00	800.00	1,100	3,000	
1853	305,770	200.00	250.00	350.00	1,700	
1853C	65,571	500.00	800.00	1,100	3,000	
1853D	89,678	500.00	800.00	1,100	3,000	
1854	160,675	200.00	250.00	350.00	1,700	
1854C	39,283	500.00	800.00	1,100	3,000	
1854D	56,413	500.00	800.00	1,100	3,000	
1854O	46,000	300.00	500.00	855.00	2,500	
1854S	268		——	187,000	——	
1855	117,098	200.00	250.00	350.00	1,700	——
1855C	39,788	500.00	800.00	1,100	3,000	
1855D	22,432	500.00	800.00	1,100	3,000	
1855O	11,100	500.00	800.00	1,200	3,250	
1855S	61,000	300.00	450.00	500.00	2,000	
1856	197,990	200.00	250.00	350.00	1,700	——
1856C	28,457	500.00	800.00	1,100	3,000	
1856D	19,786	500.00	800.00	1,100	3,000	
1856O	10,000	550.00	950.00	1,400	3,500	
1856S	105,100	200.00	250.00	350.00	1,700	
1857	98,188	200.00	250.00	350.00	1,700	——
1857C	31,360	500.00	800.00	1,100	3,000	
1857D	17,046	500.00	800.00	1,100	3,000	
1857O	13,000	500.00	800.00	1,100	3,000	
1857S	87,000	200.00	250.00	350.00	1,700	
1858	15,136	250.00	375.00	550.00	2,000	——
1858C	38,856	500.00	800.00	1,100	3,000	
1858D	15,362	500.00	800.00	1,100	3,000	
1858S	18,600	400.00	750.00	900.00	2,200	
1859	(80) 16,814	300.00	500.00	800.00	2,100	$15,000
1859C	31,847	500.00	800.00	1,100	3,000	
1859D	10,366	500.00	900.00	1,500	3,500	
1859S	13,220	300.00	500.00	900.00	2,200	

HALF EAGLES

	Quan. Minted	VF-20	EF-40	AU-50	MS-60	Proof-63
1860 .... (62)	19,825	$300.00	$500.00	$900.00	$2,200	$14,000
1860C	14,813	500.00	800.00	1,100	3,000	
1860D	14,635	500.00	900.00	1,600	3,600	
1860S	21,200	400.00	900.00	2,000	——	
1861 .... (66)	688,150	200.00	250.00	350.00	1,700	13,000
1861C	6,879	1,200	2,100	3,750	8,000	
1861D	1,597	4,000	7,000	10,000	22,000	
1861S	18,000	350.00	800.00	1,500	——	
1862 .... (35)	4,465	350.00	800.00	1,500	——	13,000
1862S	9,500	500.00	1,000	2,000	——	
1863 .... (30)	2,472	600.00	900.00	1,500	3,300	13,000
1863S	17,000	400.00	750.00	1,000	3,000	
1864 .... (50)	4,220	425.00	650.00	1,300	4,000	13,000
1864S	3,888	1,000	2,200	3,000	——	
1865 .... (25)	1,295	850.00	1,200	2,000	——	13,000
1865S	27,612	500.00	1,000	2,000	——	
1866S	9,000	500.00	1,100	2,100	——	

Variety 2 — Motto Above Eagle 1866-1908

Designer Christian Gobrecht; weight 8.359 grams; composition: .900 gold, .100 copper; diameter 21.6 mm; reeded edge. Net weight: .24187 oz. pure gold.

VF-20 VERY FINE—*Half of hairlines above coronet missing. Hair curls under ear evident, but worn. Motto and its ribbon sharp.*

EF-40 EXTREMELY FINE—*Small amount of wear on top of hair and below L in LIBERTY. Wear evident on wing tips and neck of eagle.*

AU-50 ABOUT UNCIRCULATED—*Trace of wear on tip of coronet and hair above eye.*

MS-60 UNCIRCULATED—*No trace of wear. Light blemishes.*

	Quan. Minted	VF-20	EF-40	AU-50	MS-60	Proof-63
1866 .... (30)	6,730	350.00	550.00	850.00	2,000	12,000
1866S	34,920	325.00	550.00	850.00	1,600	
1867 .... (50)	6,920	350.00	600.00	900.00	2,000	12,000
1867S	29,000	300.00	550.00	900.00	——	
1868 .... (25)	5,725	350.00	550.00	900.00	2,000	12,000
1868S	52,000	275.00	500.00	900.00	——	
1869 .... (25)	1,785	650.00	800.00	1,300	2,750	12,000
1869S	31,000	250.00	400.00	600.00	1,400	
1870 .... (35)	4,035	350.00	650.00	900.00	1,700	12,000
1870CC	7,675	2,400	4,000	6,000		
1870S	17,000	300.00	550.00	1,000	——	
1871 .... (30)	3,230	400.00	650.00	1,100	——	12,000
1871CC	20,770	700.00	1,000	1,500	3,350	
1871S	25,000	250.00	450.00	800.00	1,600	
1872 .... (30)	1,690	600.00	850.00	1,100	2,500	12,000
1872CC	16,980	650.00	1,000	1,500	3,350	
1872S	36,400	250.00	400.00	650.00	1,200	
1873 Closed 3 .... (25) ⎰	112,505	175.00	200.00	300.00	750.00	12,000
1873 Open 3 .... ⎱		175.00	200.00	275.00	600.00	
1873CC	7,416	700.00	1,100	1,700	3,700	
1873S	31,000	400.00	800.00	1,200	2,000	
1874 .... (20)	3,508	450.00	850.00	1,300	2,100	12,000
1874CC	21,198	425.00	700.00	950.00	2,500	
1874S	16,000	250.00	500.00	800.00	——	
1875 .... (20)	220	——	——	——	——	——
1875CC	11,828	550.00	1,000	1,600	2,800	
1875S	9,000	375.00	900.00	1,200	2,500	

HALF EAGLES

	Quan. Minted	VF-20	EF-40	AU-50	MS-60	Proof-63
1876 .... (45)	1,477	$600.00	$950.00	$1,500	$2,600	$11,000
1876CC	6,887	600.00	900.00	1,500	3,100	
1876S.........................	4,000	800.00	1,500	2,000	3,000	
1877 .... (20)	1,152	600.00	1,000	1,700	3,500	12,000
1877CC	8,680	600.00	1,000	1,500	3,100	
1877S.........................	26,700	175.00	275.00	350.00	800.00	
1878 .... (20)	131,740	175.00	200.00	250.00	450.00	12,000
1878CC	9,054	1,500	2,700	3,700		
1878S.........................	144,700	175.00	200.00	250.00	450.00	
1879 .... (30)	301,950	175.00	200.00	250.00	400.00	11,000
1879CC	17,281	375.00	550.00	950.00	2,000	
1879S.........................	426,200	175.00	200.00	250.00	400.00	
1880 .... (36)	3,166,436	175.00	200.00	250.00	400.00	10,000
1880CC	51,017	350.00	650.00	750.00	1,500	
1880S.........................	1,348,900	175.00	200.00	250.00	400.00	
1881, 1 over 0 ....⎫		——	——	——	——	
1881 .... (42) ⎬	5,708,802	175.00	200.00	250.00	400.00	9,500
1881CC	13,886	400.00	600.00	950.00	1,900	
1881S.........................	969,000	175.00	200.00	250.00	400.00	
1882 .... (48)	2,514,568	175.00	200.00	250.00	400.00	9,500
1882CC	82,817	275.00	325.00	500.00	1,200	
1882S.........................	969,000	175.00	200.00	250.00	400.00	
1883 .... (61)	233,461	175.00	200.00	250.00	400.00	9,500
1883CC	12,958	375.00	650.00	950.00	1,400	
1883S.........................	83,200	175.00	200.00	250.00	400.00	
1884 .... (48)	191,078	175.00	200.00	250.00	400.00	9,500
1884CC	16,402	375.00	650.00	950.00	1,400	
1884S.........................	177,000	175.00	200.00	250.00	400.00	
1885 .... (66)	601,506	175.00	200.00	250.00	400.00	9,500
1885S.........................	1,211,500	175.00	200.00	250.00	400.00	
1886 .... (72)	388,432	175.00	200.00	250.00	400.00	9,500
1886S.........................	3,268,000	175.00	200.00	250.00	400.00	
1887 Proofs only....... (87)	87					20,000
1887S.........................	1,912,000	175.00	200.00	250.00	400.00	
1888 .... (95)	18,296	175.00	250.00	300.00	500.00	9,000
1888S.........................	293,900	175.00	200.00	250.00	400.00	
1889 .... (45)	7,565	275.00	450.00	575.00	1,300	9,000
1890 .... (88)	4,328	300.00	600.00	825.00	1,500	9,000
1890CC	53,800	225.00	300.00	500.00	900.00	
1891 .... (53)	61,413	175.00	200.00	250.00	450.00	9,000
1891CC	208,000	225.00	250.00	400.00	850.00	
1892 .... (92)	753,572	175.00	200.00	250.00	400.00	9,000
1892CC	82,968	225.00	275.00	400.00	850.00	
1892O.........................	10,000	650.00	850.00	1,350	3,000	
1892S.........................	298,400	175.00	200.00	250.00	450.00	
1893 .... (77)	1,528,197	175.00	200.00	250.00	400.00	9,000
1893CC	60,000	225.00	275.00	450.00	1,200	
1893O.........................	110,000	225.00	275.00	475.00	1,200	
1893S.........................	224,000	175.00	200.00	250.00	425.00	
1894 .... (75)	957,955	175.00	200.00	250.00	400.00	9,000
1894O.........................	16,600	250.00	350.00	450.00	950.00	
1894S.........................	55,900	175.00	200.00	250.00	475.00	
1895 .... (81)	1,345,936	175.00	200.00	250.00	400.00	9,000
1895S.........................	112,000	175.00	200.00	250.00	450.00	
1896 .... (103)	59,063	175.00	200.00	250.00	450.00	9,000
1896S.........................	155,400	175.00	200.00	250.00	450.00	
1897 .... (83)	867,883	175.00	200.00	250.00	400.00	9,000
1897S.........................	354,000	175.00	200.00	250.00	400.00	

HALF EAGLES

	Quan. Minted	VF-20	EF-40	AU-50	MS-60	Proof-63
1898 .... (75)	633,495	$175.00	$200.00	$250.00	$400.00	$9,000
1898S	1,397,400	175.00	200.00	250.00	400.00	
1899 .... (99)	1,710,729	175.00	200.00	250.00	400.00	9,000
1899S	1,545,000	175.00	200.00	250.00	400.00	
1900 .... (230)	1,405,730	175.00	200.00	250.00	400.00	8,500
1900S	329,000	175.00	200.00	250.00	400.00	
1901 .... (140)	616,040	175.00	200.00	250.00	400.00	8,500
1901S, 1 over 0		175.00	225.00	325.00	500.00	
1901S	3,648,000	175.00	200.00	250.00	400.00	
1902 .... (162)	172,562	175.00	200.00	250.00	400.00	8,500
1902S	939,000	175.00	200.00	250.00	400.00	
1903 .... (154)	227,024	175.00	200.00	250.00	400.00	8,500
1903S	1,855,000	175.00	200.00	250.00	400.00	
1904 .... (136)	392,136	175.00	200.00	250.00	400.00	8,500
1904S	97,000	175.00	200.00	250.00	400.00	
1905 .... (108)	302,308	175.00	200.00	250.00	400.00	8,500
1905S	880,700	175.00	200.00	250.00	400.00	
1906 .... (85)	348,820	175.00	200.00	250.00	400.00	8,500
1906D	320,000	175.00	200.00	250.00	400.00	
1906S	598,000	175.00	200.00	250.00	400.00	
1907 .... (92)	626,192	175.00	200.00	250.00	400.00	8,500
1907D	888,000	175.00	200.00	250.00	400.00	
1908	421,874	175.00	200.00	250.00	400.00	

> Values of common gold coins have been based on a bullion price of $350. per Troy ounce, and may vary with the prevailing spot price of gold.

INDIAN HEAD TYPE 1908-1929

This type conforms to the quarter eagle of the same date. The incuse designs and lettering make this a unique series, along with the quarter eagle, in our United States coinage.

Designer Bela Lyon Pratt; weight 8.359 grams; composition: .900 gold, .100 copper; diameter 21.6 mm; reeded edge. Net weight: .24187 oz. pure gold.

Mint mark location.

VF-20 VERY FINE— *Noticeable wear on large middle feathers and tip of eagle's wing.*
EF-40 EXTREMELY FINE— *Cheekbone, war bonnet and headband feathers slightly worn. Feathers on eagle's upper wing show considerable wear.*
AU-50 ABOUT UNCIRCULATED— *Trace of wear on cheekbone and headdress.*
MS-60 UNCIRCULATED— *No trace of wear. Light blemishes.*

Scarcer coins with well struck mint marks command higher prices.

						Matte Proof-63
1908 .... (167)	578,012	260.00	285.00	375.00	1,500	$11,000
1908D	148,000	260.00	285.00	375.00	1,500	
1908S	82,000	300.00	450.00	750.00	2,750	
1909 .... (78)	627,138	260.00	285.00	375.00	1,500	11,000
1909D	3,423,560	260.00	285.00	375.00	1,500	
1909O*	34,200	600.00	1,000	1,750	6,500	
1909S	297,200	260.00	300.00	550.00	2,000	
1910 .... (250)	604,250	260.00	285.00	375.00	1,500	11,000

*Beware spurious "O" mint mark.

HALF EAGLES

	Quan. Minted	VF-20	EF-40	AU-50	MS-60	Matte Proof-63
1910D	193,600	$260.00	$285.00	$375.00	$1,600	
1910S	770,200	260.00	285.00	400.00	2,100	
1911 .... (139)	915,139	260.00	285.00	400.00	1,500	11,000
1911D	72,500	350.00	400.00	800.00	4,750	
1911S	1,416,000	260.00	300.00	400.00	1,750	
1912 .... (144)	790,144	260.00	285.00	400.00	1,500	11,000
1912S	392,000	260.00	300.00	500.00	2,100	
1913 .... (99)	916,000	260.00	285.00	400.00	1,500	11,000
1913S	408,000	275.00	325.00	550.00	3,500	
1914 .... (125)	247,125	260.00	285.00	400.00	1,500	11,000
1914D	247,000	260.00	285.00	400.00	1,500	
1914S	263,000	260.00	285.00	400.00	1,750	
1915* .... (75)	588,075	260.00	285.00	375.00	1,500	12,000
1915S	164,000	275.00	300.00	450.00	2,500	
1916S	240,000	260.00	285.00	425.00	1,750	
1929	662,000	2,500	3,000	4,500	6,500	

*Pieces dated 1915D are counterfeit.

EAGLES ($10.00 Gold Pieces) — 1795-1933

Coinage authority including specified weights and fineness of the eagle conforms to that of the half eagle. The small eagle reverse was used until 1797 when the large, heraldic eagle replaced it. The early dates have variations in the number of stars, the rarest date being 1798. Many of these early pieces show file scratches from the mint's practice of adjusting weight. No eagles were struck dated 1805 to 1837. Proofs of some dates prior to 1855 are known to exist, and all are rare.

TYPE COIN VALUES

	F-12	VF-20	EF-40	AU-50	MS-60	MS-63	MS-65	PF-60	PF-63	PF-65
Cap Bust-Sm. Eag. 1795-1797	6,000	8,000	12,000	19,000	30,000	45,000	60,000			
Cap Bust-Lg. Eag. 1797-1804	2,250	3,200	4,500	7,500	15,000	20,000	35,000			
Lib Coronet-NM 1838-1866	200.00	300.00	375.00	550.00	2,400	6,000	18,000	10,500	20,000	26,000
Lib. Coronet 1866-1907	200.00	275.00	300.00	325.00	550.00	2,000	8,000	5,000	11,000	22,000
Indian Head-NM 1907-1908	250.00	550.00	600.00	700.00	1,700	3,000	8,500	10,000	20,000	28,000
Indian Head 1908-1933	225.00	500.00	525.00	575.00	1,500	2,500	7,000	7,500	15,000	26,000

CAPPED BUST TO RIGHT, SMALL EAGLE 1795-1797

Designer Robert Scot; weight 17.50 grams; composition: .9167 gold, .0833 copper; approx. diameter 33 mm; reeded edge.

F-12 FINE—Details on turban and head obliterated.

VF-20 VERY FINE—Neck hairlines and details under turban and over forehead are worn but distinguishable.

EF-40 EXTREMELY FINE—Definite wear on hair to left of eye and strand of hair across and around turban, also on eagle's wing tips.

MS-60 UNCIRCULATED—No trace of wear. Light blemishes.

	Quan. Minted	F-12	VF-20	EF-40	MS-60
1795 9 leaves below eagle	}	$6,500	$8,500	$12,500	$32,000
1795 13 leaves below eagle	5,583	6,000	8,000	12,000	30,000
1796	4,146	6,000	8,000	12,000	32,000
1797 Small eagle	3,615	6,000	8,000	12,000	32,000

[195]

EAGLES
CAPPED BUST TO RIGHT, HERALDIC EAGLE 1797-1804

	Quan. Minted	F-12	VF-20	EF-40	MS-60
1797 Large eagle	10,940	$2,250	$3,500	$5,000	$18,000
1798, 8 over 7, 9 stars left, 4 right	900	4,500	7,500	12,000	25,000
1798, 8 over 7, 7 stars left, 6 right	842	10,000	22,000	—	—
1799	37,449	2,250	3,200	4,500	15,000
1800	5,999	2,250	3,200	4,500	17,000

	Quan. Minted	F-12	VF-20	EF-40	MS-60
1801	44,344	2,250	3,200	4,500	15,000
1803	15,017	2,250	3,200	4,500	17,000
1804	3,757	3,000	4,500	7,500	23,000
1804 Plain 4. Proof. (4 known)					40,000

CORONET TYPE, No Motto Above Eagle 1838-1866

In 1838 the weight and diameter of the eagle were reduced and the obverse and reverse were redesigned. Liberty now faces left and the word LIBERTY is placed on the coronet. A more natural appearing eagle is used on the reverse. The value, TEN D., is shown for the first time on this denomination.

Designer Christian Gobrecht; weight 16.718 grams; composition: .900 gold, .100 copper, diameter 27 mm; reeded edge. Net weight: .48375 oz. pure gold.

VF-20 VERY FINE— Hairlines above coronet partly worn. Curls under ear worn but defined.

EF-40 EXTREMELY FINE— Small amount of wear on top of hair and below L in LIBERTY. Wear evident on wing tips and neck of eagle.

AU-50 ABOUT UNCIRCULATED— Trace of wear on tip of coronet and hair above eye.

MS-60 UNCIRCULATED— No trace of wear. Light blemishes.

Mint mark location on reverse below eagle.

EAGLES

	Quan. Minted	VF-20	EF-40	AU-50	MS-60	Proof-63
1838	7,200	$850.00	$ 1,750	$3,000	$9,000	
1839 Large letters	25,801	550.00	1,000	2,400	7,000	

The Liberty head style of 1838 and 1839 (large letters) differs from that used for subsequent issues.

	Quan. Minted	VF-20	EF-40	AU-50	MS-60	Proof-63
1839 Small letters	12,447	800.00	1,450	2,500	7,000	
1840	47,338	350.00	450.00	650.00	3,500	
1841	63,131	350.00	450.00	650.00	3,500	
1841O	2,500	600.00	1,250	1,900	6,500	
1842 Small date	18,623	350.00	450.00	650.00	3,250	
1842 Large date	62,884	350.00	450.00	650.00	3,250	
1842O	27,400	350.00	450.00	750.00	4,500	
1843	75,462	350.00	450.00	650.00	3,000	
1843O	175,162	325.00	425.00	700.00	2,750	
1844	6,361	500.00	900.00	1,250	4,000	
1844O	118,700	325.00	425.00	700.00	2,750	
1845	26,153	350.00	450.00	750.00	3,250	
1845O	47,500	350.00	500.00	700.00	2,800	
1846	20,095	350.00	450.00	650.00	2,800	
1846O	81,780	350.00	500.00	750.00	2,800	
1847	862,258	300.00	375.00	550.00	2,400	
1847O	571,500	325.00	400.00	650.00	2,500	
1848	145,484	300.00	375.00	550.00	2,400	
1848O	35,850	350.00	500.00	750.00	2,800	
1849	653,618	300.00	375.00	550.00	2,400	
1849O	23,900	350.00	500.00	750.00	2,800	
1850 Large date	291,451	300.00	375.00	550.00	2,400	
1850 Small date		350.00	600.00	——		
1850O	57,500	350.00	500.00	750.00	2,800	
1851	176,328	325.00	400.00	650.00	2,200	
1851O	263,000	325.00	400.00	650.00	2,500	
1852	263,106	300.00	375.00	550.00	2,400	
1852O	18,000	400.00	575.00	800.00	2,800	

1853,
3 over 2

	Quan. Minted	VF-20	EF-40	AU-50	MS-60	Proof-63
1853, 3 over 2	201,253	400.00	800.00			
1853		300.00	375.00	550.00	2,400	
1853O	51,000	350.00	500.00	750.00	2,750	
1854	54,250	325.00	450.00	750.00	2,500	
1854O Large or small date	52,500	325.00	425.00	750.00	2,950	
1854S	123,826	325.00	425.00	725.00	2,500	
1855	121,701	300.00	375.00	550.00	2,400	——
1855O	18,000	400.00	550.00	800.00	2,800	
1855S	9,000	700.00	1,300	1,600	4,500	——
1856	60,490	300.00	375.00	600.00	2,600	
1856O	14,500	400.00	550.00	800.00	3,000	
1856S	68,000	325.00	450.00	650.00	2,500	

EAGLES

	Quan. Minted	VF-20	EF-40	AU-50	MS-60	Proof-63
1857	16,606	$350.00	$450.00	$700.00	$2,600	——
1857O	5,500	900.00	1,400	2,000	5,500	
1857S	26,000	325.00	450.00	650.00	2,600	
1858*	2,521	3,500	6,000	8,000	22,000	——
1858O	20,000	350.00	450.00	675.00	3,400	
1858S	11,800	375.00	550.00	700.00	3,400	
1859	(80) 16,093	350.00	450.00	650.00	3,250	$24,000
1859O	2,300	1,250	2,500	3,600	6,000	
1859S	7,000	750.00	1,350	1,900	3,500	
1860	(50) 15,105	325.00	425.00	600.00	3,000	20,000
1860O	11,100	375.00	600.00	750.00	4,250	
1860S	5,000	750.00	1,250	1,900	5,000	
1861	(69) 113,233	300.00	375.00	550.00	2,400	20,000
1861S	15,500	325.00	425.00	750.00	2,800	
1862	(35) 10,995	325.00	425.00	750.00	2,800	20,000
1862S	12,500	325.00	425.00	750.00	2,800	
1863	(30) 1,248	2,500	4,500	6,000	8,000	27,500
1863S	10,000	425.00	850.00	1,150	3,300	
1864	(50) 3,580	850.00	1,350	1,850	4,250	25,000
1864S	2,500	1,800	3,250			
1865	(25) 4,005	775.00	1,150	1,550	4,500	24,000
1865S	} 16,700	775.00	1,150	1,550	4,500	
1865S, 865 over inverted 186		950.00	1,500			
1866S	8,500	1,000	1,700	2,400	5,000	

*Beware removed mint mark.

Variety 2 — Motto Above Eagle 1866-1907

Mint mark location is on reverse below the eagle.

VF-20 VERY FINE— *Half of hairlines over coronet visible. Curls under ear worn but defined. IN GOD WE TRUST and its ribbon are sharp.*

EF-40 EXTREMELY FINE— *Small amount of wear on top of hair and below L in LIBERTY. Wear evident on wing tips and neck of eagle.*

AU-50 ABOUT UNCIRCULATED— *Trace of wear on hair above eye and on coronet.*

MS-60 UNCIRCULATED— *No trace of wear. Light blemishes.*

1866	(30) 3,780	475.00	650.00	900.00	2,100	18,000
1866S	11,500	425.00	600.00	750.00	2,000	
1867	(50) 3,140	475.00	650.00	900.00	2,100	15,000
1867S	9,000	450.00	650.00	850.00	1,700	
1868	(25) 10,655	425.00	600.00	750.00	1,400	15,000
1868S	13,500	425.00	600.00	750.00	1,400	
1869	(25) 1,855	750.00	1,500	2,000	2,500	15,000
1869S	6,430	450.00	700.00	900.00	1,700	
1870	(35) 4,025	450.00	700.00	900.00	2,100	15,000
1870CC	5,908	1,200	3,500	5,500		
1870S	8,000	450.00	700.00	900.00	1,800	
1871	(30) 1,820	700.00	1,200	1,900	4,500	15,000
1871CC	8,085	750.00	1,400	2,200		
1871S	16,500	375.00	550.00	700.00	1,400	

EAGLES

	Quan. Minted	VF-20	EF-40	AU-50	MS-60	Proof-63
1872 .... (30)	1,650	$900.00	$1,600	$2,250	$3,700	$14,000
1872CC	4,600	600.00	1,000	1,300	3,800	
1872S	17,300	375.00	550.00	700.00	1,400	
1873 .... (25)	825	1,250	2,800	4,000	8,000	22,000
1873CC	4,543	1,050	1,750	3,000	6,000	
1873S	12,000	375.00	550.00	700.00	1,400	
1874 .... (20)	53,160	300.00	350.00	500.00	700.00	18,000
1874CC	16,767	425.00	600.00	750.00	2,000	
1874S	10,000	400.00	525.00	675.00	1,300	
1875 .... (20)	120					———
1875CC	7,715	600.00	900.00	1,300	2,800	
1876 .... (45)	732	1,250	2,800	4,300	7,800	18,000
1876CC	4,696	800.00	1,250	1,850	3,600	
1876S	5,000	500.00	750.00	1,100	2,200	
1877 .... (20)	817	1,600	3,000	4,200	9,000	22,000
1877CC	3,332	1,000	1,600	2,200	3,900	
1877S	17,000	325.00	450.00	650.00	900.00	
1878 .... (20)	73,800	300.00	325.00	400.00	700.00	16,000
1878CC	3,244	1,100	1,700	2,750	4,200	
1878S	26,100	300.00	400.00	500.00	700.00	
1879 .... (30)	384,770	275.00	300.00	325.00	550.00	15,000
1879CC	1,762	2,500	4,500	7,500	12,000	
1879O	1,500	1,200	2,100	3,200	7,500	
1879S	224,000	275.00	300.00	325.00	550.00	
1880 .... (36)	1,644,876	275.00	300.00	325.00	550.00	14,000
1880CC	11,190	350.00	500.00	700.00	1,200	
1880O	9,200	350.00	500.00	800.00	1,200	
1880S	506,250	275.00	300.00	325.00	550.00	
1881 .... (40)	3,877,260	275.00	300.00	325.00	550.00	14,000
1881CC	24,015	325.00	450.00	650.00	1,100	
1881O	8,350	350.00	475.00	700.00	1,350	
1881S	970,000	275.00	300.00	325.00	550.00	
1882 .... (40)	2,324,480	275.00	300.00	325.00	550.00	14,000
1882CC	6,764	350.00	500.00	750.00	1,600	
1882O	10,820	325.00	475.00	675.00	900.00	
1882S	132,000	275.00	300.00	325.00	550.00	
1883 .... (40)	208,740	275.00	300.00	325.00	550.00	14,000
1883CC	12,000	350.00	500.00	800.00	1,400	
1883O	800	2,100	3,400	5,750	12,000	
1883S	38,000	275.00	300.00	325.00	550.00	
1884 .... (45)	76,905	275.00	300.00	325.00	550.00	21,000
1884CC	9,925	400.00	600.00	900.00	1,400	
1884S	124,250	275.00	300.00	325.00	550.00	
1885 .... (65)	253,527	275.00	300.00	325.00	550.00	13,000
1885S	228,000	275.00	300.00	325.00	550.00	
1886 .... (60)	236,160	275.00	300.00	325.00	550.00	13,000
1886S	826,000	275.00	300.00	325.00	550.00	
1887 .... (80)	53,680	275.00	300.00	325.00	550.00	13,000
1887S	817,000	275.00	300.00	325.00	550.00	
1888 .... (75)	132,996	275.00	300.00	325.00	550.00	13,000
1888O	21,335	275.00	300.00	350.00	425.00	775.00
1888S	648,700	275.00	300.00	325.00	550.00	
1889 .... (45)	4,485	425.00	600.00	950.00	1,500	14,000
1889S	425,400	275.00	300.00	325.00	550.00	
1890 .... (63)	58,043	275.00	300.00	425.00	800.00	12,000
1890CC	17,500	350.00	375.00	500.00	900.00	
1891 .... (48)	91,868	275.00	300.00	325.00	450.00	12,000
1891CC	103,732	275.00	300.00	400.00	850.00	

EAGLES

	Quan. Minted	VF-20	EF-40	AU-50	MS-60	Proof-63
1892 .... (72)	797,552	$275.00	$300.00	$325.00	$550.00	$12,000
1892CC	40,000	325.00	450.00	650.00	1,200	
1892O.........................	28,688	275.00	300.00	400.00	700.00	
1892S.........................	115,500	275.00	300.00	325.00	550.00	
1893 .... (55)	1,840,895	275.00	300.00	325.00	550.00	12,000
1893CC	14,000	400.00	550.00	750.00	1,300	
1893O.........................	17,000	325.00	425.00	550.00	850.00	
1893S.........................	141,350	275.00	300.00	325.00	550.00	
1894 .... (43)	2,470,778	275.00	300.00	325.00	550.00	12,000
1894O.........................	107,500	275.00	300.00	325.00	550.00	
1894S.........................	25,000	275.00	300.00	325.00	600.00	
1895 .... (56)	567,826	275.00	300.00	325.00	550.00	12,000
1895O.........................	98,000	275.00	300.00	325.00	550.00	
1895S.........................	49,000	275.00	300.00	400.00	1,200	
1896 .... (78)	76,348	275.00	300.00	325.00	550.00	12,000
1896S.........................	123,750	275.00	300.00	325.00	550.00	
1897 .... (69)	1,000,159	275.00	300.00	325.00	550.00	12,000
1897O.........................	42,500	275.00	300.00	325.00	550.00	
1897S.........................	234,750	275.00	300.00	325.00	550.00	
1898 .... (67)	812,197	275.00	300.00	325.00	550.00	12,000
1898S.........................	473,600	275.00	300.00	325.00	550.00	
1899 .... (86)	1,262,305	275.00	300.00	325.00	550.00	11,000
1899O.........................	37,047	275.00	300.00	325.00	550.00	
1899S.........................	841,000	275.00	300.00	325.00	550.00	
1900 .... (120)	293,960	275.00	300.00	325.00	550.00	11,000
1900S.........................	81,000	275.00	300.00	325.00	550.00	
1901 .... (85)	1,718,825	275.00	300.00	325.00	550.00	11,000
1901O.........................	72,041	275.00	300.00	325.00	550.00	
1901S.........................	2,812,750	275.00	300.00	325.00	550.00	
1902 .... (113)	82,513	275.00	300.00	325.00	550.00	11,000
1902S.........................	469,500	275.00	300.00	325.00	550.00	
1903 .... (96)	125,926	275.00	300.00	325.00	550.00	11,000
1903O.........................	112,771	275.00	300.00	325.00	550.00	
1903S.........................	538,000	275.00	300.00	325.00	550.00	
1904 .... (108)	162,038	275.00	300.00	325.00	550.00	11,000
1904O.........................	108,950	275.00	300.00	325.00	550.00	
1905 .... (86)	201,078	275.00	300.00	325.00	550.00	11,000
1905S.........................	369,250	275.00	300.00	325.00	550.00	
1906 .... (77)	165,497	275.00	300.00	325.00	550.00	11,000
1906D.........................	981,000	275.00	300.00	325.00	550.00	
1906O.........................	86,895	274.00	300.00	325.00	550.00	
1906S.........................	457,000	275.00	300.00	325.00	550.00	
1907 .... (74)	1,203,973	275.00	300.00	325.00	550.00	11,000
1907D.........................	1,030,000	275.00	300.00	325.00	550.00	
1907S.........................	210,500	275.00	300.00	325.00	550.00	

Values of common gold coins have been based on a bullion price of $350. per Troy ounce, and may vary with the prevailing spot price of gold.

INDIAN HEAD TYPE 1907-1933

Augustus Saint-Gaudens, considered by many the greatest of modern sculptors introduced a new high standard of art in United States coins evidenced by his eagle and double eagle types of 1907. The obverse of the eagle shows the head of Liberty crowned with an Indian war bonnet while an impressively majestic eagle dominates the reverse side. A departure from older standards is found on the edge of the piece, where 46 raised stars are arranged signifying the

EAGLES

states of the Union, instead of a lettered or reeded edge. (48 stars 1912 and later.)

The first eagles struck had no motto IN GOD WE TRUST as did the later issues starting in 1908. President Theodore Roosevelt personally objected to the use of the Deity's name on coins. The motto was restored to the coins by an Act of Congress in 1908.

VF-20 VERY FINE— *Bonnet feathers worn near band. Hair high points show wear.*

EF-40 EXTREMELY FINE— *Slight wear on cheekbone and headdress feathers. Eagle's eye and left wing will show slight wear.*

AU-50 ABOUT UNCIRCULATED— *Trace of wear on hair above eye and on forehead.*

MS-60 UNCIRCULATED-- *No trace of wear. Light blemishes.*

Designer Augustus Saint-Gaudens. Standards same as previous issue. Edge 1907-1911: 46 raised stars; 1912-1933: 48 raised stars. Net weight: .48375 oz. pure gold.

Variety 1 — No Motto on Reverse 1907-1908

No Motto

Mint mark location is above left tip of branch on 1908-D no motto, and at left of arrow points thereafter.

Choice uncirculated (MS-65) coins are rare and worth substantial premiums.

	Quan. Minted	VF-20	EF-40	AU-50	MS-60	Proof-63
1907 "Wire edge" (rim), periods.....	500			$6,500	$12,000	$20,000
1907 Rounded edge, periods before and after •E•PLURIBUS•UNUM•	*42				30,000	——
1907 No periods	239,406	$550.00	$600.00	700.00	1,700	
1908 No motto..................	33,500	600.00	650.00	800.00	1,900	
1908D No motto	210,000	550.00	600.00	750.00	1,750	

*19,958 melted at Mint.

Variety 2 — Motto on Reverse 1908-1933

With Motto
IN GOD WE TRUST

						Matte Proof-63
1908 .... (116)	341,486	500.00	525.00	575.00	1,600	$15,000
1908D........................	836,500	500.00	525.00	575.00	1,700	
1908S........................	59,850	500.00	525.00	800.00	3,500	
1909 .... (74)	184,863	500.00	525.00	575.00	1,500	15,000
1909D........................	121,540	500.00	525.00	575.00	1,700	
1909S........................	292,350	500.00	525.00	575.00	2,000	
1910 .... (204)	318,704	500.00	525.00	575.00	1,500	15,000

EAGLES

	Quan. Minted	VF-20	EF-40	AU-50	MS-60	Matte Proof-63
1910D	2,356,640	$500.00	$525.00	$575.00	$1,500	
1910S	811,000	500.00	525.00	575.00	2,000	
1911 .... (95)	505,595	500.00	525.00	575.00	1,500	$15,000
1911D	30,100	550.00	750.00	1,150	5,000	
1911S	51,000	500.00	525.00	600.00	2,250	
1912 .... (83)	405,083	500.00	525.00	575.00	1,500	15,000
1912S	300,000	500.00	525.00	575.00	2,200	
1913 .... (71)	442,071	500.00	525.00	575.00	1,500	15,000
1913S	66,000	475.00	750.00	1,250	10,000	
1914 .... (50)	151,050	500.00	525.00	575.00	1,500	17,500
1914D	343,500	500.00	525.00	575.00	1,600	
1914S	208,000	500.00	525.00	575.00	2,100	
1915 .... (75)	351,075	500.00	525.00	575.00	1,500	17,500
1915S	59,000	500.00	525.00	650.00	2,750	
1916S	138,500	500.00	525.00	600.00	1,800	
1920S	126,500	4,500	7,500	12,000	20,000	
1926	1,014,000	500.00	525.00	600.00	1,500	
1930S	96,000	3,000	4,500	7,500	13,000	
1932	4,463,000	500.00	525.00	575.00	1,500	
1933	312,500				70,000	

DOUBLE EAGLES ($20.00 Gold Pieces) — 1849-1933

This largest denomination of all regular United States issues was authorized to be coined by the Act of March 3, 1849. Its weight was 516 grains, .900 fine. The 1849 double eagle is a unique pattern and reposes in the Smithsonian. The rarest date obtainable is 1883. The 1861 reverse design by Anthony C. Paquet was withdrawn soon after striking. Very few specimens are known.

TYPE COIN VALUES

	F-12	VF-20	EF-40	AU-50	MS-60	MS-63	MS-65	PF-60	PF-63	PF-65
Lib Coronet-NM 1849-1866	400.00	575.00	650.00	800.00	1,600	4,000	15,000	15,000	22,000	38,000
Lib (Twenty D.) 1866-1876	400.00	550.00	600.00	650.00	850.00	2,300	8,000	15,000	20,000	36,000
Lib 1877-1907	400.00	500.00	550.00	600.00	700.00	1,500	6,000	7,000	16,000	32,000
Saint-Gaudens-RN, HR 1907	2,750	3,500	5,000	6,500	11,000	16,000	27,000			
Saint-Gaudens 1907-1932	400.00	575.00	625.00	650.00	800.00	1,500	4,000	14,000	23,000	38,000

VF-20 VERY FINE—*LIBERTY is bold. Jewels on crown defined. Lower half worn flat. Hair worn about ear.*
EF-40 EXTREMELY FINE—*Trace of wear on rounded prongs of crown and down hair curls. Minor bag marks.*
AU-50 ABOUT UNCIRCULATED—*Trace of wear on hair over eye and on coronet.*
MS-60 UNCIRCULATED—*No trace of wear. Light blemishes.*

Designer James B. Longacre; weight 33.436 grams; composition: .900 gold, .100 copper; diameter 34 mm; reeded edge. Net weight: .96750 oz. pure gold.

Mint mark location is below the eagle.   1861S Paquet Reverse

DOUBLE EAGLES
Without Motto on Reverse 1849-1866

	Quan. Minted	VF-20	EF-40	AU-50	MS-60	Proof-63
1849	1			Smithsonian collection		
1850	1,170,261	$575.00	$650.00	$800.00	$2,500	
1850O	141,000	700.00	850.00	1,000	3,750	
1851	2,087,155	575.00	650.00	800.00	1,800	
1851O	315,000	700.00	850.00	1,000	3,750	
1852	2,053,026	575.00	650.00	800.00	1,800	
1852O	190,000	700.00	850.00	1,000	3,750	

1853,
3 over 2

	Quan. Minted	VF-20	EF-40	AU-50	MS-60	Proof-63
1853, 3 over 2	} 1,261,326	—	—	800.00	—	
1853		575.00	650.00	800.00	1,800	
1853O		675.00	800.00	1,200	4,400	
1854	757,899	575.00	650.00	800.00	1,800	
1854O	3,250	20,000	33,000	50,000		
1854S	141,468	575.00	650.00	800.00	3,350	
1855	364,666	575.00	650.00	800.00	1,600	
1855O	8,000	2,000	3,500	5,500	—	
1855S	879,675	575.00	650.00	800.00	1,800	
1856	329,878	575.00	650.00	800.00	1,800	
1856O	2,250	25,000	35,000	57,000		
1856S	1,189,750	575.00	650.00	800.00	1,800	
1857	439,375	575.00	650.00	800.00	1,800	
1857O	30,000	700.00	850.00	1,300	4,700	
1857S	970,500	575.00	650.00	800.00	1,800	
1858	211,714	575.00	650.00	800.00	2,000	
1858O	35,250	700.00	850.00	1,800	5,750	
1858S	846,710	575.00	650.00	800.00	1,800	
1859	(80) 43,597	575.00	650.00	800.00	3,200	—
1859O	9,100	1,650	2,750	4,750	8,500	
1859S	636,445	575.00	650.00	800.00	1,600	
1860	(59) 577,670	575.00	650.00	800.00	1,600	—
1860O	6,600	2,200	3,500	5,000	9,000	
1860S	544,950	575.00	650.00	800.00	1,800	
1861	(66) 2,976,453	575.00	650.00	800.00	1,600	$30,000
1861O	17,741	1,200	2,300	3,400	7,700	
1861S	768,000	575.00	650.00	800.00	1,600	
1861 — A.C. Paquet rev. (Tall letters)				(Ex. Rare)		—
1861S—A.C. Paquet rev. (Tall letters)		5,000	6,750	9,000	—	
1862	(35) 92,133	575.00	650.00	800.00	4,000	24,000
1862S	854,173	575.00	650.00	800.00	1,900	
1863	(30) 142,790	575.00	650.00	800.00	4,200	22,000
1863S	966,570	575.00	650.00	800.00	1,900	
1864	(50) 204,285	575.00	650.00	800.00	2,600	22,000
1864S	793,660	575.00	650.00	800.00	1,900	
1865	(25) 351,200	575.00	650.00	800.00	2,000	24,000
1865S	1,042,500	575.00	650.00	800.00	1,900	
1866S	incl. below	675.00	800.00	1,350	4,500	

DOUBLE EAGLES
Motto Above Eagle, Value TWENTY D. 1866-1876

	Quan. Minted	VF-20	EF-40	AU-50	MS-60	Proof-63
1866 . . . . (30)	698,775	$550.00	$600.00	$650.00	$2,000	$20,000
1866S	842,250	550.00	600.00	650.00	1,900	
1867 . . . . (50)	251,065	550.00	600.00	650.00	1,900	20,000
1867S	920,750	550.00	600.00	650.00	1,900	
1868 . . . . (25)	98,600	550.00	600.00	650.00	2,100	20,000
1868S	837,500	550.00	600.00	650.00	1,900	
1869 . . . . (25)	175,155	550.00	600.00	650.00	1,900	20,000
1869S	686,750	550.00	600.00	650.00	1,750	
1870 . . . . (35)	155,185	550.00	600.00	650.00	1,750	20,000
1870CC 3,789		15,000	27,500	——	——	
1870S	982,000	550.00	600.00	650.00	1,700	
1871 . . . . (30)	80,150	550.00	600.00	650.00	1,800	20,000
1871CC 17,387		1,400	2,500	3,500		
1871S	928,000	550.00	600.00	650.00	1,500	
1872 . . . . (30)	251,880	550.00	600.00	650.00	1,300	20,000
1872CC 26,900		775.00	1,000	1,500	3,300	
1872S	780,000	550.00	600.00	650.00	850.00	
1873 Closed 3 . . . . (25) ⎫		650.00	750.00	950.00	1,800	20,000
1873 Open 3 . . . . ⎬	1,709,825	550.00	600.00	650.00	850.00	
1873CC Closed 3 22,410		750.00	850.00	1,300	2,750	
1873S 1,040,600		550.00	600.00	650.00	850.00	
1874 . . . . (20)	366,800	550.00	600.00	650.00	850.00	22,000
1874CC 115,085		675.00	800.00	1,100	2,000	
1874S 1,214,000		550.00	600.00	650.00	850.00	
1875 . . . . (20)	295,740	550.00	600.00	650.00	850.00	——
1875CC 111,151		675.00	800.00	1,100	1,800	
1875S 1,230,000		550.00	600.00	650.00	850.00	
1876 . . . . (45)	583,905	550.00	600.00	650.00	850.00	20,000
1876CC 138,441		675.00	750.00	900.00	1,800	
1876S 1,597,000		550.00	600.00	650.00	850.00	

TWENTY DOLLARS 1877-1907

DOUBLE EAGLES

	Quan. Minted	VF-20	EF-40	AU-50	MS-60	Proof-63
1877 .... (20)	397,670	$500.00	$550.00	$600.00	$700.00	$18,000
1877CC	42,565	750.00	800.00	1,000	1,800	
1877S	1,735,000	500.00	550.00	600.00	700.00	
1878 .... (20)	543,645	500.00	550.00	600.00	700.00	18,000
1878CC	13,180	750.00	900.00	1,350	3,000	
1878S	1,739,000	500.00	550.00	600.00	700.00	
1879 .... (30)	207,630	500.00	550.00	600.00	700.00	17,500
1879CC	10,708	850.00	1,500	2,100	4,250	
1879O	2,325	2,500	3,750	5,500	12,000	
1879S	1,223,800	500.00	550.00	600.00	700.00	
1880 .... (36)	51,456	500.00	575.00	625.00	1,000	17,500
1880S	836,000	500.00	550.00	600.00	700.00	
1881 .... (61)	2,260	2,250	4,500	7,250	10,500	25,000
1881S	727,000	500.00	550.00	600.00	700.00	
1882 .... (59)	630	3,500	9,000	15,000	30,000	40,000
1882CC	39,140	700.00	800.00	950.00	1,600	
1882S	1,125,000	500.00	550.00	600.00	700.00	
1883 Proofs only .... (92)	92					——
1883CC	59,962	700.00	800.00	950.00	1,600	
1883S	1,189,000	500.00	550.00	600.00	700.00	
1884 Proofs only .... (71)	71					——
1884CC	81,139	700.00	800.00	950.00	1,600	
1884S	916,000	500.00	550.00	600.00	700.00	
1885 .... (77)	828	3,500	8,000	12,500	21,000	32,500
1885CC	9,450	900.00	1,300	2,000	3,500	
1885S	683,500	500.00	550.00	600.00	700.00	
1886 .... (106)	1,106	4,000	9,000	13,500	22,500	40,000
1887 Proofs only ...... (121)	121					42,500
1887S	283,000	500.00	550.00	600.00	700.00	
1888 .... (105)	226,266	500.00	550.00	600.00	700.00	17,000
1888S	859,600	500.00	550.00	600.00	700.00	
1889 .... (41)	44,111	500.00	550.00	600.00	750.00	17,000
1889CC	30,945	650.00	750.00	900.00	1,850	
1889S	774,700	500.00	550.00	600.00	700.00	
1890 .... (55)	75,995	500.00	550.00	600.00	700.00	17,000
1890CC	91,209	650.00	750.00	800.00	1,500	
1890S	802,750	500.00	550.00	600.00	700.00	
1891 .... (52)	1,442	1,250	2,750	4,250	8,500	18,000
1891CC	5,000	1,200	2,200	3,000	5,500	
1891S	1,288,125	500.00	550.00	600.00	700.00	
1892 .... (93)	4,523	1,000	1,850	2,350	5,000	18,000
1892CC	27,265	650.00	800.00	1,200	2,000	
1892S	930,150	500.00	550.00	600.00	700.00	
1893 .... (59)	344,339	500.00	550.00	600.00	700.00	16,000
1893CC	18,402	675.00	825.00	1,300	2,500	
1893S	996,175	500.00	550.00	600.00	700.00	
1894 .... (50)	1,368,990	500.00	550.00	600.00	700.00	16,000
1894S	1,048,550	500.00	550.00	600.00	700.00	
1895 .... (51)	1,114,656	500.00	550.00	600.00	700.00	16,000
1895S	1,143,500	500.00	550.00	600.00	700.00	
1896 .... (128)	792,663	500.00	550.00	600.00	750.00	16,000
1896S	1,403,925	500.00	550.00	600.00	700.00	
1897 .... (86)	1,383,261	500.00	550.00	600.00	700.00	16,000
1897S	1,470,250	500.00	550.00	600.00	700.00	
1898 .... (75)	170,470	500.00	550.00	600.00	800.00	16,000
1898S	2,575,175	500.00	550.00	600.00	700.00	
1899 .... (84)	1,669,384	500.00	550.00	600.00	700.00	16,000

DOUBLE EAGLES

	Quan. Minted	VF-20	EF-40	AU-50	MS-60	Proof-63
1899S	2,010,300	$500.00	$550.00	$600.00	$700.00	
1900 (124)	1,874,584	500.00	550.00	600.00	700.00	$16,000
1900S	2,459,500	500.00	550.00	600.00	700.00	
1901 (96)	111,526	500.00	550.00	600.00	750.00	16,000
1901S	1,596,000	500.00	550.00	600.00	700.00	
1902 (114)	31,254	500.00	550.00	600.00	800.00	16,000
1902S	1,753,625	500.00	550.00	600.00	700.00	
1903 (158)	287,428	500.00	550.00	600.00	700.00	16,000
1903S	954,000	500.00	550.00	600.00	725.00	
1904 (98)	6,256,797	500.00	550.00	600.00	700.00	16,000
1904S	5,134,175	500.00	550.00	600.00	700.00	
1905 (92)	59,011	500.00	550.00	600.00	800.00	16,000
1905S	1,813,000	500.00	550.00	600.00	700.00	
1906 (94)	69,690	500.00	550.00	600.00	775.00	16,000
1906D	620,250	500.00	550.00	600.00	750.00	
1906S	2,065,750	500.00	550.00	600.00	700.00	
1907 (78)	1,451,864	500.00	550.00	600.00	700.00	16,000
1907D	842,250	500.00	550.00	600.00	750.00	
1907S	2,165,800	500.00	550.00	600.00	700.00	

Values of common gold coins are based on a bullion price of $350. per Troy ounce, and may vary with the prevailing spot price of gold.

SAINT-GAUDENS TYPE 1907-1933

The $20 gold piece designed by Augustus Saint-Gaudens is considered to be the most beautiful United States coin. The first coins issued were 11,250 high relief pieces struck for general circulation. The relief is much higher than later issues and the date 1907 is in Roman numerals. A few of the proof coins were made using the lettered edge collar from the extremely high relief version. These can be distinguished by a pronounced bottom left serif on the N in UNUM, and other minor differences. Flat-relief double eagles were issued later in 1907 with Arabic numerals, and continued through 1933.

The field of the rare extremely high relief experimental pieces is excessively concave and connects directly with the edge without any border, giving it a sharp knifelike appearance; Liberty's skirt shows two folds on the side of her right leg; the Capitol building in the background at left is very small; the sun, on the reverse side, has 14 rays, as opposed to the regular high relief coins that have only 13 rays extending from the sun. High relief proofs are trial or experimental pieces.

Designer Augustus Saint-Gaudens. Standards same as previous issue. Edge: E. PLURIBUS UNUM with words divided by stars. One specimen of the high relief variety with plain edge is known.

VF-20 VERY FINE—*Minor wear on legs and toes. Eagle's left wing and breast feathers worn.*
EF-40 EXTREMELY FINE—*Drapery lines on chest visible. Wear on left breast, knee and below. Eagle's feathers on breast and right wing are bold.*
MS-60 UNCIRCULATED—*No trace of wear. Light marks or blemishes.*

	Proof
1907 Ex. high relief, plain edge (*Unique*)	——
1907 Ex. high relief, lettered edge	$225,000

DOUBLE EAGLES

	Quan. Minted	VF-20	EF-40	AU-50	MS-60	Proof
1907 High relief, Roman numerals (MCMVII), wire rim	}11,250	$3,500	$5,000	$6,500	$11,000	——
1907 Same, flat rim		3,500	5,000	6,500	11,000	——

Arabic Numerals

No Motto

		VF-20	EF-40	AU-50	MS-60
1907 Arabic numerals..........	361,667	700.00	850.00	900.00	1,000
1908	4,271,551	575.00	650.00	725.00	850.00
1908D.......................	663,750	575.00	650.00	725.00	900.00

With Motto IN GOD WE TRUST, 1908-1933

Mint mark location on obverse above date.

						Matte Proof-63
1908 .... (101)	156,359	575.00	625.00	700.00	850.00	$25,000
1908D..........................	349,500	575.00	625.00	700.00	900.00	
1908S..........................	22,000	750.00	950.00	1,200	3,700	

[207]

DOUBLE EAGLES

Double eagles from 1907 to 1911 have 46 stars on the obverse and 48 stars from 1912 to 1933.

1909, 9 over 8

	Quan. Minted	VF-20	EF-40	AU-50	MS-60	Matte Proof-63
1909, 9 over 8	⎫	$600.00	$750.00	$800.00	$1,000	
1909 . . . . (67)	⎬ 161,282	600.00	750.00	800.00	1,100	$25,000
1909D 52,500		650.00	800.00	1,000	2,700	
1909S 2,774,925		575.00	625.00	650.00	800.00	
1910 . . . . (167)	482,167	575.00	625.00	650.00	800.00	23,000
1910D 429,000		575.00	625.00	650.00	800.00	
1910S 2,128,250		575.00	625.00	650.00	800.00	
1911 . . . . (100)	197,350	575.00	625.00	650.00	800.00	23,000
1911D 846,500		575.00	625.00	650.00	800.00	
1911S 775,750		575.00	625.00	650.00	800.00	
1912 . . . . (74)	149,824	575.00	700.00	800.00	900.00	23,000
1913 . . . . (58)	168,838	575.00	625.00	650.00	800.00	23,000
1913D 393,500		575.00	625.00	650.00	800.00	
1913S 34,000		600.00	700.00	900.00	1,200	
1914 . . . . (70)	95,320	575.00	625.00	650.00	800.00	23,000
1914D 453,000		575.00	625.00	650.00	800.00	
1914S 1,498,000		575.00	625.00	650.00	800.00	
1915 . . . . (50)	152,050	575.00	625.00	650.00	800.00	25,000
1915S 567,500		575.00	625.00	650.00	800.00	
1916S 796,000		575.00	625.00	650.00	900.00	
1920 228,250		575.00	625.00	650.00	800.00	
1920S 558,000		6,500	9,500	12,000	17,500	
1921 528,500		8,000	13,000	16,000	25,000	
1922 1,375,500		575.00	625.00	650.00	800.00	
1922S 2,658,000		575.00	700.00	900.00	1,300	
1923 566,000		575.00	625.00	650.00	800.00	
1923D 1,702,250		575.00	625.00	650.00	800.00	
1924 4,323,500		575.00	625.00	650.00	800.00	
1924D 3,049,500		800.00	1,200	1,500	2,250	
1924S 2,927,500		800.00	1,200	1,500	2,100	
1925 2,831,750		575.00	625.00	650.00	800.00	
1925D 2,938,500		800.00	1,200	1,500	2,200	
1925S 3,776,500		800.00	1,200	1,500	2,400	
1926 816,750		575.00	625.00	650.00	800.00	
1926D 481,000		900.00	1,200	1,600	2,700	
1926S 2,041,500		750.00	1,000	1,200	1,900	
1927 2,946,750		575.00	625.00	650.00	800.00	
1927D 180,000					200,000	
1927S 3,107,000			4,200	6,000	10,000	
1928 8,816,000		575.00	625.00	650.00	800.00	
1929 1,779,750			4,500	6,000	9,000	
1930S 74,000			10,000	13,000	18,000	
1931 2,938,250			8,000	10,000	14,000	
1931D 106,500			9,000	12,000	16,000	
1932 1,101,750			10,000	13,000	18,000	
1933 445,500			None placed in circulation			

COMMEMORATIVE COINS

Commemorative coins have been popular since the days of the Greeks and Romans. In the beginning they served to record and honor important events and in the absence of newspapers they proved highly useful in passing along news of the day.

Many modern nations have issued commemorative coins and such pieces are highly esteemed by collectors. Yet no nation has surpassed our own country when it comes to commemorative coins and in this we have reason to be proud.

The unique position occupied by commemoratives in United States coinage is largely due to the fact that with few exceptions they are the only coins that have a real historical significance. The progress and advance of people in the New World are presented in an interesting and instructive manner on the commemorative issues. Such a record of facts artistically presented on our gold and silver memorial issues appeals strongly to the collector who favors the historical side of numismatics. It is the historical features of the commemoratives, in fact, which create interest among many people who would otherwise have little interest in coins.

Commemorative issues are considered for coinage by two committees of Congress — The Committee on Banking, Housing and Urban Affairs, and the Committee on Banking and Currency of the House. Congress is guided to a great extent by the reports of these committees when passing upon bills authorizing commemorative coins.

These special coins are usually issued either to commemorate events or to help pay for monuments or celebrations that commemorate historical persons, places or things. The commemorative coins are offered in most instances by a commission in charge of the event to be commemorated, and sold at a price in advance of the face value of the piece. All are of the standard weight and fineness of traditional gold and silver coins, and all are legal tender.

Commemorative coins are popularly collected either by major types or in sets with mint mark varieties. In many years no special commemorative coins were issued. Some regular coins such as the Lincoln cent of 1909, Washington quarter of 1932, and Bicentennial issues of 1976 are also considered to be commemoratives.

Unless otherwise stated, the coinage figures given represent the total outstanding coinage. In many cases, larger quantities were minted but were not all sold. The unsold coins were usually returned to the mint and melted, although some were placed in circulation at face value.

Note: The Commemorative section following is arranged alphabetically.

Perfect brilliant uncirculated commemoratives (MS-65) are worth far more than the uncirculated (MS-60) pieces which are often dull, cleaned, or blemished by contact marks.

A limited number of proof strikings or presentation pieces were made for some of these issues. All very rare and valuable.

COMMEMORATIVE SILVER — Isabella Quarter, Alabama, Albany

ISABELLA QUARTER DOLLAR

In 1893 the Board of Lady Managers of the Columbian Exposition petitioned for a souvenir quarter dollar. Authority was granted March 3, 1893. The coin known as the Isabella quarter was designed by C. E. Barber. These souvenir quarters were sold for $1.00. The obverse has the crowned bust of Queen Isabella of Spain. The kneeling female on the reverse with distaff and spindle is emblematic of women's industry.

	Quan. Issued	AU-50	MS-60	MS-63	MS-65
1893 Columbian Exposition, Chicago.....	24,214	$250.00	$600.00	$1,000	$5,000

ALABAMA CENTENNIAL

The Alabama half dollars were authorized in 1920 for the centennial which was celebrated in 1919, but they were not struck until 1921. The coins, designed by Laura Gardin Fraser, were offered first during President Harding's visit to Birmingham, October 26, 1921. The St. Andrews cross, an emblem on the state flag, appears on a part of the issue between the figures 22 indicating the twenty-second state of the Union. The obverse has busts of W. W. Bibb, first governor of Alabama, and T. E. Kilby, governor at the time of the centennial. This is the first instance of the use of a living person's portrait on a United States coin.

2 x 2 in Field

1921 Alabama Centennial, with 2 x 2 in field of obverse 6,006	175.00	375.00	700.00	4,000
1921 Alabama Centennial, no 2 x 2 59,038	100.00	325.00	600.00	3,700

ALBANY, NEW YORK CHARTER

The 250th anniversary of the granting of a charter to the city of Albany was the occasion for a commemorative half dollar. The reverse design shows Governor Dongan, Peter Schuyler and Robert Livingston. The obverse has a beaver gnawing on a maple branch. Gertrude K. Lathrop of Albany was the designer.

1936 Albany, New York 17,671	250.00	300.00	425.00	1,200

COMMEMORATIVE SILVER — Antietam, Arkansas

BATTLE OF ANTIETAM

A souvenir half dollar was designed by William Marks Simpson and struck in 1937 to commemorate the seventy-fifth anniversary of the famous Civil War battle to thwart Lee's invasion of Maryland. The opposing generals McClellan and Lee are featured on the obverse while the Burnside Bridge, an important tactical objective, is shown on the reverse. The Battle of Antietam, on September 17, 1862, was one of the bloodiest single-day battles of the war with total losses of about 25,000 men.

	Quan. Minted	AU-50	MS-60	MS-63	MS-65
1937 Battle of Antietam 1862-1937.......	18,028	$275.00	$425.00	$525.00	$1,300

ARKANSAS CENTENNIAL

This souvenir issue marked the one hundredth anniversary of the admission of Arkansas into the Union. Edward Everett Burr designed the piece and models were prepared by Emily Bates of Arkansas. Although 1936 was the centennial year the first of several issues was brought out in 1935 from all three mints. During 1936 a new design was authorized by Congress. The late Senator Joseph T. Robinson consented to have his portrait placed on the obverse side of the coins which were struck in January 1937 at the Philadelphia Mint. The 1937 and 1938 issues were the same as those of 1935 except for the dates. They were sold by the distributors at $8.75 per set of three coins. The obverse shows accolated heads of an Indian chief of 1836 and an American girl of 1936.

		Quan. Issued		MS-60	MS-63	MS-65
1935	Arkansas Centennial	13,012				
1935D	Same type D mint	5,505	Set	$275.00	$375.00	$2,600
1935S	Same type S mint...................	5,506				
1936	Arkansas Centennial, same as 1935—					
	date 1936 on rev	9,660				
1936D	Same type D mint	9,660	Set	275.00	375.00	2,600
1936S	Same type S mint...................	9,662				
1937	Arkansas Centennial (same as 1935)..	5,505				
1937D	Same type D mint	5,505	Set	300.00	400.00	3,200
1937S	Same type S mint...................	5,506				
1938	Arkansas Centennial (same as 1935)..	3,156				
1938D	Same type D mint	3,155	Set	525.00	800.00	4,500
1938S	Same type S mint...................	3,156				
1939	Arkansas Centennial (same as 1935)..	2,104				
1939D	Same type D mint	2,104	Set	1,000	1,300	7,000
1939S	Same type S mint...................	2,105				
	Single, type coin .... Abt. Unc.	$80.00		100.00	150.00	850.00

COMMEMORATIVE SILVER — Bay Bridge, Boone

BAY BRIDGE SAN FRANCISCO-OAKLAND

The opening of the San Francisco Bay Bridge was the occasion for a special souvenir fifty-cent piece. The designs were the work of Jacques Schnier, a San Francisco artist. A California grizzly bear dominates the obverse. The famous bridge is shown on the reverse. The coins were struck at the San Francisco Mint in November 1936. The bear depicted was Monarch II.

	Quan. Issued	AU-50	MS-60	MS-63	MS-65
1936S San Francisco-Oakland Bay Bridge	71,424	$85.00	$140.00	$180.00	$800.00

DANIEL BOONE BICENTENNIAL

Date Added in Field

This coin, issues for which covered several dates, was struck to commemorate the two hundredth anniversary of the famous frontiersman's birth. The commemorative date, 1934, was removed after the first issue. The change of date to 1935 for the next year's coinage brought about the addition of 1934 above the words PIONEER YEAR. Coinage covered several years similar to the schedule for the Texas issues. The models for this coin were prepared by Augustus Lukeman. The obverse bears a portrait of Daniel Boone. The reverse shows Boone with Chief Black Fish.

	Quan. Issued		MS-60	MS-63	MS-65
1934 Daniel Boone Bicentennial	10,007		$125.00	$175.00	$625.00
1935 Same type	10,010				
1935D Same type D mint	5,005	Set	350.00	500.00	1,800
1935S Same type S mint	5,005				
1935 Daniel Boone same as 1934 sm. 1934 on rev	10,008				
1935D Same type D mint	2,003	Set	1,000	1,500	3,500
1935S Same type S mint	2,004				
1936 Daniel Boone (same as 1934)	12,012				
1936D Same type D mint	5,005	Set	325.00	500.00	1,800
1936S Same type S mint	5,006				
1937 Daniel Boone (same as 1934)	9,810				
1937D Same type D mint	2,506	Set	650.00	1,000	2,400
1937S Same type S mint	2,506				
1938 Daniel Boone (same as 1934)	2,100				
1938D Same type D mint	2,100	Set	1,400	1,700	2,800
1938S Same type S mint	2,100				
Single, type coin	Abt. Unc.	$95.00	125.00	175.00	625.00

COMMEMORATIVE SILVER — Bridgeport, California, Cincinnati

BRIDGEPORT, CONNECTICUT CENTENNIAL

In commemoration of the one hundredth anniversary of the incorporation of the city of Bridgeport a special fifty-cent piece was authorized May 15, 1936. Henry Kreiss designed this coin which somewhat resembles the Connecticut Tercentenary issue. The head of P. T. Barnum, who was Bridgeport's best known citizen, occupies the obverse. An ultra-modernistic eagle dominates the reverse.

	Quan. Issued	AU-50	MS-60	MS-63	MS-65
1936 Bridgeport, Conn., Centennial	25,015	$125.00	$175.00	$250.00	$1,300

CALIFORNIA DIAMOND JUBILEE

The California half dollar was designed by Jo Mora, a noted California sculptor. The obverse bears a kneeling figure of a forty-niner. The reverse shows a walking grizzly bear, the state emblem. The celebration for which these coins were struck marked the seventy-fifth anniversary of the admission of California into the Union. The jubilee was held in 1925.

1925S California Diamond Jubilee	86,594	85.00	160.00	280.00	1,150

CINCINNATI MUSIC CENTER

Although the head of Stephen Foster, "America's Troubadour," dominates the obverse of this special issue the anniversary celebrated bears no relation to him. The coins, designed by Constance Ortmayer of Washington, D. C., were struck to commemorate the fiftieth anniversary in 1936 of Cincinnati as a center of music. The coins were struck at the three mints and were sold only in sets at $7.75, the highest initial cost of a new type.

1936 Cincinnati Music Center	5,005 ⎫				
1936D Same type D	5,005 ⎬ Set	900.00	1,250	7,000	
1936S Same type S	5,006 ⎭				
Single, type coin		250.00	325.00	450.00	2,400

COMMEMORATIVE SILVER — Cleveland, Columbia, South Carolina, Columbian

CLEVELAND GREAT LAKES EXPOSITION

A special coinage of fifty-cent pieces was authorized in commemoration of the centennial celebration of Cleveland, Ohio on the occasion of the Great Lakes Exposition held there in 1936. The designs were prepared by Brenda Putnam. Although half the coinage was struck in 1937 all were dated 1936. The obverse has a bust of Moses Cleaveland and the reverse displays a map of the Great Lakes region with a compass pointed at Cleveland. Nine Great Lakes cities are marked by stars.

	Quan. Issued	AU-50	MS-60	MS-63	MS-65
1936 Cleveland, Great Lakes Exposition	50,030	$65.00	$115.00	$150.00	$775.00

COLUMBIA, SOUTH CAROLINA SESQUICENTENNIAL

Souvenir half dollars were authorized to help finance the extensive celebrations marking the sesquicentennial of the founding of Columbia in 1786. A. Wolfe Davidson designed the coin which was struck at all three mints and sold only in sets. The obverse bears the figure of Justice with sword and scales. At the left is the Capital of 1786 and at the right the Capital of 1936. A palmetto tree, the state emblem, is the reverse device.

	Quan. Issued		MS-60	MS-63	MS-65
1936 Columbia, S.C., Sesquicentennial	9,007				
1936D Same type D mint	8,009	Set 1,000	1,200		2,600
1936S Same type S mint	8,007				
Single, type coin		215.00	350.00	400.00	900.00

COLUMBIAN EXPOSITION HALF DOLLAR

The first United States commemorative coin was the Columbian half dollar. C. E. Barber designed the obverse showing the bust of Columbus; and G. T. Morgan designed the reverse having a representation of Columbus' flagship the Santa Maria above two hemispheres. The coins were sold for $1.00 each at the World's Columbian Exposition in Chicago during 1893. A great many remained unsold and a substantial quantity was later released for circulation at face value. Approximately 100 brilliant proofs were struck for each date.

1892 Columbian Exp. Chicago	950,000	20.00	70.00	125.00	800.00
1893 Same type	1,550,405	20.00	70.00	125.00	800.00

COMMEMORATIVE SILVER — Connecticut, Delaware, Elgin

CONNECTICUT TERCENTENARY

In commemoration of the three hundredth anniversary of the founding of the Colony of Connecticut a souvenir half dollar was struck. Henry Kreiss designed the coin. The famous "Charter Oak" is the main device on the obverse. According to tradition the Royal Charter was secreted in the tree during the reign of James II who wished to revoke it. The Charter was produced after the king's overthrow in 1688 and the Colony continued under its protection.

	Quan. Issued	AU-50	MS-60	MS-63	MS-65
1935 Connecticut Tercentenary	25,018	$200.00	$275.00	$375.00	$1,500

DELAWARE TERCENTENARY

The three hundredth anniversary of the landing of the Swedes in Delaware was the occasion for a souvenir issue of half dollars. The colonists landed on a spot which is now Wilmington and established a church which is the

oldest Protestant church still used for worship. Their ship "Kalmar Nyckel" is shown on the reverse of the coin and the Old Swedes Church is on the obverse. Designs were chosen from a competition which was won by Carl L. Schmitz. This coin was authorized in 1936, struck in 1937 and dated 1938 on the reverse and 1936 on the obverse. The anniversary was celebrated in 1938 both in Sweden and America. A two kronor coin was issued in Sweden to commemorate the same event.

1936 Delaware Tercentenary	20,993	210.00	270.00	340.00	1,700

ELGIN, ILLINOIS CENTENNIAL

The one hundredth anniversary of the founding of Elgin was marked by a special issue of half dollars in 1936. The proceeds were devoted to financing a Pioneer Memorial statue, which is depicted on the reverse of the coin. The year 1673 bears no relation to the event but refers to the year in which Joliet and Marquette entered Illinois Territory. The designs were prepared by Trygve Rovelstad who also designed the Memorial.

1936 Elgin, Illinois, Centennial	20,015	200.00	225.00	375.00	1,300

COMMEMORATIVE SILVER — Gettysburg, Grant, Hawaiian

BATTLE OF GETTYSBURG

On June 16, 1936 Congress authorized a coinage of fifty-cent pieces in commemoration of the Battle of Gettysburg. The models were prepared by Frank Vittor, a Philadelphia sculptor. Portraits of a Union and a Confederate veteran are shown on the obverse. Two shields representing the Union and Confederate armies separated by a double-bladed fasces are on the reverse.

	Quan. Issued	AU-50	MS-60	MS-63	MS-65
1936 Battle of Gettysburg 1863-1938.....	26,928	$210.00	$260.00	$365.00	$1,100

GRANT MEMORIAL

This coin was struck during 1922 as a centenary souvenir of Ulysses S. Grant's birth. A star which appeared on the first issues was later removed, creating a second variety. The star has no particular significance. Laura Gardin Fraser designed both the Grant half dollar and gold dollar. The reverse shows a log cabin in Point Pleasant, Ohio, where Grant lived as a boy.

Star in obv. field

(Fake stars have flattened spot on reverse.)

1922 Grant Memorial. Star in obv. field...	4,256	350.00	825.00	1,800	7,500
1922 Same, no star	67,405	55.00	130.00	225.00	1,300

HAWAIIAN SESQUICENTENNIAL

This small issue was struck to commemorate the 150th anniversary of the rediscovery of the Hawaiian Islands by Captain James Cook in 1778. The design was sketched by Juliette May Fraser of Honolulu and executed by Chester Beach. Captain Cook is shown on the obverse and a native chief on the reverse. The coins were distributed in 1928 and sold for $2.00 each, the highest initial sale price up to that time.

1928 Hawaiian Sesquicentennial..........	9,958	750.00	900.00	1,500	5,500
1928 Hawaiian Sesquicentennial — sandblast proof presentation piece......	50				—

COMMEMORATIVE SILVER — Hudson, Huguenot, Illinois

HUDSON, NEW YORK SESQUICENTENNIAL

This souvenir half dollar marked the one hundred and fiftieth anniversary of the founding of Hudson, New York, which was named after the explorer Hendrik Hudson. The designs by Chester Beach show Hudson's flagship the "Half Moon" on the obverse and the seal of the City of Hudson on the reverse. Details of the seal include representations of Neptune with trident on a spouting whale and a mermaid blowing a conch shell.

	Quan. Issued	AU-50	MS-60	MS-63	MS-65
1935 Hudson, N.Y. Sesquicentennial.....	10,008	$450.00	$650.00	$900.00	$2,900

HUGUENOT-WALLOON TERCENTENARY

Settling of the Huguenots and Walloons in the New World was the occasion commemorated by this issue. New Netherlands, now New York, was founded in 1624 by a group of Dutch colonists. The persons represented on the obverse were not directly concerned with the occasion, however. They are Admiral Coligny and William the Silent. The reverse shows the vessel "Nieu Nederland." G. T. Morgan prepared the models for this coin.

1924 Huguenot-Walloon Tercentenary..	142,080	70.00	135.00	250.00	1,000

ILLINOIS CENTENNIAL

The obverse was designed by G. T. Morgan and the reverse by J. R. Sinnock. The obverse shows the head of Lincoln taken from the statue by Andrew O'Connor in Springfield, Illinois. The reverse is based on the Illinois State Seal. This coin was authorized to commemorate the one hundredth anniversary of the admission of Illinois into the Union, the first souvenir piece for such an event.

1918 Illinois Centennial................	100,058	65.00	150.00	250.00	1,100

COMMEMORATIVE SILVER — Iowa, Lexington, Long Island

IOWA CENTENNIAL

This half dollar, commemorating the one hundredth anniversary of Iowa's statehood, was designed by Adam Pietz of Philadelphia. The obverse shows the Iowa state seal and the reverse has the first stone capitol building at Iowa City. This issue was sold first to the residents of Iowa and only a small remainder to others. The entire issue was disposed of in a few weeks.

	Quan. Issued	AU-50	MS-60	MS-63	MS-65
1946 Iowa Centennial..................	100,057	$80.00	$110.00	$160.00	$475.00

LEXINGTON-CONCORD SESQUICENTENNIAL

The two famous battles fought in 1775 are commemorated on this coin. A statue of the familiar Minute Man is depicted on the obverse, and the old Belfry at Lexington is the reverse device. Chester Beach designed the coin. The famous statue by Daniel Chester French located in Concord was used for the design.

1925 Lexington-Concord					
Sesquicentennial	162,013	35.00	60.00	130.00	950.00

LONG ISLAND TERCENTENARY

This souvenir issue was authorized to commemorate the three hundredth anniversary of the first white settlement on Long Island which was at Jamaica Bay by Dutch colonists. The design was prepared by Howard Kenneth Weinman, son of the sculptor A. A. Weinman who designed the regular Liberty walking type half dollar. Accolated heads depicting a Dutch settler and an Indian are shown on the obverse, while a Dutch sailing vessel is the reverse device. This was the first issue for which a date was specified (1936) irrespective of the year minted or issued.

| 1936 Long Island Tercentenary.......... | 81,826 | 70.00 | 110.00 | 150.00 | 800.00 |

COMMEMORATIVE SILVER — Lynchburg, Maine, Maryland

LYNCHBURG, VIRGINIA SESQUICENTENNIAL

The issuance of a charter to the city of Lynchburg in 1786 was commemorated in 1936 by a special coinage of half dollars. The models for the coin were prepared by Charles Keck. The obverse bears a portrait of Senator Carter Glass, a native of Lynchburg and former Secretary of the Treasury, who objected to the idea of using portraits of living men on coins. Despite his protests his likeness was incorporated on the coin. The reverse shows Liberty standing, with the old Lynchburg courthouse in the background.

	Quan. Issued	AU-50	MS-60	MS-63	MS-65
1936 Lynchburg, Va., Sesquicentennial...	20,013	$190.00	$250.00	$310.00	$1,300

MAINE CENTENNIAL

Congress authorized the Maine Centennial half dollar May 10, 1920, to be sold at the Centennial celebration at Portland. They were received too late for this event and were sold by the state Treasurer until all

were sold. Anthony de Francisci modeled this coin according to specifications furnished him. The latin word DIRIGO means: I direct. The obverse device is the arms of the state of Maine.

1920 Maine Centennial	50,028	80.00	170.00	270.00	1,500

MARYLAND TERCENTENARY

The three hundredth anniversary of the founding of the Maryland Colony by Cecil Calvert (known as Lord Baltimore) was the occasion for this special coin. The profits from the sale of this issue were used to finance the celebration in Baltimore during 1934. Hans Schuler designed the coin which shows the facing head of Lord Baltimore on the obverse and the arms of Maryland on the reverse, reminiscent of the Maryland colonial pieces.

1934 Maryland Tercentenary............	25,015	115.00	160.00	230.00	1,500

COMMEMORATIVE SILVER — Missouri, Monroe, New Rochelle

MISSOURI CENTENNIAL

The one hundredth anniversary of the admission of Missouri to the Union was celebrated at Sedalia during August, 1921. To mark the occasion Congress authorized the coinage of a fifty-cent piece. Robert Aitken designed the piece which shows the bust of a frontiersman on the obverse, and another frontiersman and Indian on the reverse. The first coins struck show 2★4 incused, indicating that Missouri was the twenty-fourth star in the flag. The type without the star was struck later, but was the first to be sold.

2 ★ 4 in field

	Quan. Issued	AU-50	MS-60	MS-63	MS-65
1921 Missouri Centennial 2★4 in field	5,000	$250.00	$600.00	$1,050	$5,000
1921 Missouri Centennial, no 2★4	15,428	225.00	575.00	1,000	4,800

MONROE DOCTRINE CENTENNIAL

The motion picture industry promoted this issue in conjunction with a motion picture exposition in June 1923. The obverse shows the heads of James Monroe and John Quincy Adams who were identified with the Monroe Doctrine. The Western Hemisphere is portrayed on the reverse by two female figures. Chester Beach prepared the models for this coin.

1923S Monroe Doctrine Centennial..... 274,077	27.50	75.00	150.00	1,300

NEW ROCHELLE, NEW YORK

To observe the founding of New Rochelle in 1688 by French Huguenots, a special half dollar was issued in 1938. The title to the land which the Huguenots purchased from John Pell provided that a fattened calf be given away every year on June 20th. This will explain the appearance of the calf and figure representing John Pell on the obverse of the coin. The fleur-de-lis which is shown on the reverse is adopted from the Seal of the city. Both sides of the coin were designed by Gertrude K. Lathrop.

1938 New Rochelle, N.Y. 1688-1938 15,266	375.00	450.00	575.00	1,400

COMMEMORATIVE SILVER — Norfolk, Oregon

NORFOLK, VIRGINIA, BICENTENNIAL

To provide funds for the celebration of Norfolk's anniversary of its growth from a township in 1682 to a royal borough in 1736, Congress first passed a law for the striking of medals. The proponents, however, being dissatisfied finally succeeded in winning authority for half dollars commemorating the 300th anniversary of the original Norfolk land grant and the 200th anniversary of the establishment of the borough. William Marks Simpson and his wife Marjorie Emory Simpson designed the piece. The obverse shows the Seal of the City of Norfolk with a three-masted ship as the central device. The reverse features the Royal Mace of Norfolk presented by Lieutenant Governor Dinwiddie in 1753.

	Quan. Issued	AU-50	MS-60	MS-63	MS-65
1936 Norfolk, Va., Bicentennial	16,936	$375.00	$425.00	$500.00	$1,000

OREGON TRAIL MEMORIAL

This memorial coin was struck in commemoration of the Oregon trail and in memory of the pioneers, many of whom lie buried along the famous 2,000 mile highway of history. James Earle Fraser and his wife, Laura Gardin Fraser, prepared the designs. The original issue was struck at Philadelphia and San Francisco in 1926. The coin was reissued in 1928 (released in 1933), 1933, 1934, 1936, and 1938. The 1933 half dollar was the first commemorative coin struck at the Denver Mint.

		Quan. Issued	AU-50	MS-60	MS-63	MS-65
1926	Oregon Trail Memorial	47,955	100.00	130.00	175.00	700.00
1926S	Same type S mint	83,055	100.00	130.00	175.00	700.00
1928	Oregon Trail Mem. (same as 1926)	6,028	125.00	280.00	400.00	900.00
1933D	Oregon Trail Memorial, same D mint	5,008	175.00	310.00	425.00	1,075
1934D	Oregon Trail Memorial, same D mint	7,006	110.00	230.00	350.00	950.00
1936	Oregon Trail Mem. (same as 1926)	10,006	110.00	175.00	300.00	850.00
1936S	Same type S mint	5,006	130.00	270.00	375.00	1,100
1937D	Oregon Trail Memorial D mint	12,008	100.00	160.00	240.00	725.00
1938	Oregon Trail Memorial (same as 1926)	6,006				
1938D	Same type D mint	6,005	Set	650.00	850.00	1,900
1938S	Same type S mint	6,006				
1939	Oregon Trail (same as 1926)	3,004				
1939D	Same type D mint	3,004	Set	1,300	1,700	3,400
1939S	Same type S mint	3,005				
	Single, type coin		100.00	130.00	175.00	700.00

COMMEMORATIVE SILVER — Panama-Pacific, Pilgrim

PANAMA-PACIFIC EXPOSITION

This half dollar was designed by C. E. Barber. The exposition held in San Francisco in 1915 celebrated the opening of the Panama Canal. The coins were struck at the San Francisco Mint and were sold at $1.00 each during the exposition. The Panama-Pacific coins have the distinction of being the first commemorative coins to carry the motto. IN GOD WE TRUST appears above the eagle. A representation of Columbia with the golden gate in the background is the principal feature of the obverse.

	Quan. Issued	AU-50	MS-60	MS-63	MS-65
1915S Panama-Pacific Exposition........	27,134	$225.00	$575.00	$975.00	$5,300

PILGRIM TERCENTENARY

To commemorate the landing of the Pilgrims at Plymouth, Massachusetts in 1620, Congress authorized a special half dollar May 12, 1920. Cyrus E. Dallin, a Boston sculptor, executed the designs furnished him by the Commission. The obverse has a portrait of Governor Bradford. The reverse shows the "Mayflower." The first issue had no date on the obverse. The coins struck in 1921 show that date in addition to 1620-1920. There was a large coinage of both issues and not all were sold. A total of 128,000 were returned to the mint and melted.

1920 Pilgrim Tercentenary.............	152,112	40.00	70.00	140.00	700.00

With 1921 Date
Added in Field on Obverse.

1921 Same type.......................	20,053	90.00	180.00	270.00	1,500

COMMEMORATIVE SILVER — Rhode Island, Roanoke, Robinson

RHODE ISLAND TERCENTENARY PROVIDENCE

The three hundredth anniversary of Roger Williams' founding of Providence was the occasion for this special half dollar in 1935. The designs were the work of Arthur Graham Carey and John Howard Benson. The obverse shows Roger Williams in a canoe being welcomed by an Indian. The reverse has the anchor of Hope with a shield and mantling in the background. Although the founding of Providence was being celebrated, no mention of the city is to be found on the coin.

	Quan. Issued	AU-50	MS-60	MS-63	MS-65
1936 Rhode Island Tercentenary	20,013				
1936D Same type D mint...........	15,010	Set	$375.00	$575.00	$2,800
1936S Same type S mint	15,011				
Single, type coin		$95.00	135.00	200.00	950.00

ROANOKE ISLAND, NORTH CAROLINA

A celebration was held in Old Fort Raleigh in 1937 to commemorate the 350th anniversary of Sir Walter Raleigh's "Lost Colony" and the birth of Virginia Dare, the first white child born on the American continent. A special half dollar for the occasion was designed by William Marks Simpson of Baltimore. The obverse bears a portrait of Sir Walter Raleigh and the reverse has a figure representing Eleanor Dare holding the child Virginia Dare.

1937 Roanoke Island, N.C., 1587-1937 ...	29,030	160.00	230.00	325.00	1,100

ROBINSON-ARKANSAS CENTENNIAL

A new obverse design for the Arkansas Centennial coin was authorized by the Act of June 26, 1936. Senator Joseph T. Robinson is the subject for the new issue designed by Henry Kreiss. The reverse, designed by Everett Burr, was unchanged. The law specified a change in the reverse, because of the fact that the obverse side is that

which bears the date. From a numismatic viewpoint, however, the side which has the portrait is usually considered the obverse. Thus in this instance, the side with the eagle device is considered the reverse.

1936 Arkansas Centennial (Robinson) ...	25,265	100.00	130.00	175.00	825.00

[223]

COMMEMORATIVE SILVER — San Diego, Sesquicentennial, Old Spanish Trail

SAN DIEGO-CALIFORNIA-PACIFIC EXPOSITION

Congress approved the coinage of souvenir half dollars for the exposition May 3, 1935. Robert Aitken designed the coin which was struck at the San Francisco Mint. The same type with date 1936 was struck at the Denver Mint, under authority of the special Recoinage Act of May 6, 1936, which specified that 180,000 pieces could be recoined with the date 1936 irrespective of the year of issue. The obverse displays a seated female with spear and a bear in the left background. The reverse shows the observation tower and the State of California building at the Exposition.

	Quan. Issued	AU-50	MS-60	MS-63	MS-65
1935S San Diego, California-Pacific Exp. S mint	70,132	$75.00	$125.00	$175.00	$550.00
1936D San Diego, California-Pacific Exposition D mint (same as 1935)	30,092	80.00	150.00	200.00	600.00

SESQUICENTENNIAL OF AMERICAN INDEPENDENCE

The one hundred and fiftieth anniversary of the signing of the Declaration of Independence was the occasion for an International Fair held in Philadelphia in 1926. To help raise funds for financing the fair special issues of half dollars and quarter-eagles were authorized by Congress. For the first time a portrait of a president appeared on a coin struck during his lifetime. President Coolidge and Washington are depicted on the obverse of the half dollar. The reverse bears an accurate model of the Liberty Bell. John R. Sinnock, Chief Engraver of the United States mint, designed the sesquicentennial coins. The dies were in very low relief causing much loss of detail in the coin.

1926 Sesquicentennial of American Independence	141,120	30.00	60.00	125.00	1,400

OLD SPANISH TRAIL

This coin commemorated the four hundredth anniversary of the overland trek of the Cabeza de Vaca Expedition through the gulf states in 1535. L. W. Hoffecker designed the coin models which were prepared by Edmund J. Senn.

COMMEMORATIVE SILVER — Old Spanish Trail,
Statue of Liberty, Stone Mountain

The explorer's name literally translated means "head of a cow;" therefore this device was chosen for the obverse. The reverse bears a yucca tree and a map showing the Old Spanish Trail.

	Quan. Issued	AU-50	MS-60	MS-63	MS-65
1935 Old Spanish Trail 1535-1935.......	10,008	$625.00	$825.00	$1,050	$2,200

STATUE OF LIBERTY

The first clad half dollar commemorative depicts this country's heritage as a nation of immigrants. The obverse, designed by Edgar Steever, pictures a ship of immigrants steaming into New York harbor, with the Statue of Liberty greeting them in the foreground and the New York skyline in the distance. The reverse, designed by Sherl Joseph Winter, has a scene of an immigrant family with their belongings on the threshold of America.

	MS-65	Proof-65
1986D Statue of Liberty....................................	$7.00	
1986S Same type S mint		$8.50

STONE MOUNTAIN MEMORIAL

The models for this coin were prepared by Gutzon Borglum. The first coins were struck at Philadelphia January 21, 1925, General Thomas "Stonewall" Jackson's birthday. General Robert E. Lee and Jackson, mounted, are shown on the obverse. The reverse has an eagle and the words MEMORIAL TO THE VALOR OF THE SOLDIER OF THE SOUTH. The funds received from the sale of this large issue of half dollars were devoted to the expense of carving figures of Confederate leaders and soldiers on Stone Mountain in Georgia. The carving was completed and dedicated in 1970.

1925 Stone Mountain Memorial 1,314,709	25.00	50.00	130.00	450.00

COMMEMORATIVE SILVER — Texas, Vancouver, Vermont

TEXAS CENTENNIAL

This issue commemorated the independence of Texas. The first of several dates was offered in 1934. The later dates were struck at all three mints. The models were prepared by Pompeo Coppini. The reverse shows the kneeling figure of winged Victory, and on each side, medallions with portraits of General Sam Houston and Stephen Austin, founders of the Republic and State of Texas. The large five-pointed star behind the eagle on the obverse carries out the "Lone star" tradition.

	Quan. Issued	AU-50	MS-60	MS-63	MS-65
1934 Texas Centennial	61,463		$170.00	$250.00	$550.00
1935 Texas Centennial (same as 1934)	9,996				
1935D Same type D mint	10,007	Set	450.00	725.00	1,600
1935S Same type S mint	10,008				
1936 Texas Centennial (same as 1934)	8,911				
1936D Same type D mint	9,039	Set	450.00	725.00	1,600
1936S Same type S mint	9,055				
1937 Texas Centennial (same as 1934)	6,571				
1937D Same type D mint	6,605	Set	450.00	725.00	1,700
1937S Same type S mint	6,637				
1938 Texas Centennial (same as 1934)	3,780				
1938D Same type D mint	3,775	Set	725.00	1,100	2,000
1938S Same type S mint	3,814				
Single, type coin		125.00	170.00	250.00	550.00

FORT VANCOUVER CENTENNIAL

Dr. John McLaughlin, shown on the obverse of this coin, built Fort Vancouver on the Columbia River in 1825. The sale of the coins at $1.00 each helped to finance the pageant staged for the celebration. Laura Gardin Fraser prepared the models for this coin which was minted in San Francisco. The S Mint mark was omitted. The reverse has a pioneer settler in buckskin suit with a musket in his hands. Fort Vancouver is in the background.

1925 Fort Vancouver Centennial	14,994	300.00	475.00	625.00	1,750

VERMONT SESQUICENTENNIAL

This souvenir issue commemorates the 150th Anniversary of the Battle of Bennington and the Independence of Vermont. Authorized in 1925, it was not coined until 1927. The models were prepared by Charles Keck. The obverse shows the head of Ira Allen, founder of Vermont. The reverse bears a catamount on a pedestal.

COMMEMORATIVE SILVER — Vermont, B. T. Washington, Washington-Carver

		Quan. Issued	AU-50	MS-60	MS-63	MS-65
1927	Vermont Sesquicentennial (Bennington).....................	28,142	$150.00	$275.00	$425.00	$1,500

BOOKER T. WASHINGTON MEMORIAL

This commemorative coin was issued to perpetuate the ideals and teachings of Booker T. Washington and to construct memorials to his memory. Issued from all mints, it received wide distribution from the start. The reverse has the legend FROM SLAVE CABIN TO HALL OF FAME. His log cabin birthplace is shown beneath. Designed by Isaac Scott Hathaway, as was the Washington-Carver half dollar issued under the same authority.

		Quan. Issued		MS-60	MS-63	MS-65
1946	Booker T. Washington............	*1,000,546				
1946D	Same type D mint	200,113	Set	$40.00	$48.00	$300.00
1946S	Same type S mint...................	500,279				
1947	Same type as 1946	100,017				
1947D	Same type D mint	100,017	Set	60.00	75.00	425.00
1947S	Same type S mint...................	100,017				
1948	Same type as 1946	8,005				
1948D	Same type D mint	8,005	Set	140.00	160.00	725.00
1948S	Same type S mint...................	8,005				
1949	Same type as 1946	6,004				
1949D	Same type D mint	6,004	Set	180.00	240.00	1,100
1949S	Same type S mint...................	6,004				
1950	Same type as 1946	6,004				
1950D	Same type D mint	6,004	Set	160.00	210.00	925.00
1950S	Same type S mint...................	512,091				
1951	Same type as 1946	510,082				
1951D	Same type D mint	7,004	Set	100.00	150.00	680.00
1951S	Same type S mint...................	7,004				
	Single, type coin			13.00	16.00	100.00

*Minted; quantity melted unknown.

WASHINGTON-CARVER

Designed by Isaac Scott Hathaway, this coin shows the conjoined busts of two prominent black Americans. Booker T. Washington was a lecturer, educator,

COMMEMORATIVE SILVER — Washington-Carver, Washington, Wisconsin

and principal of Tuskegee Institute. He urged training to advance independence and efficiency for his race. George Washington Carver was an agricultural chemist who worked to improve the economy of the south. He spent his life teaching crop improvement and new uses for soybeans, peanuts, sweet potatoes and cotton waste.

Money obtained from the sale of these commemoratives was to be used "to oppose the spread of communism among Negroes in the interest of national defense."

		Quan. Minted	MS-60	MS-63	MS-65
1951	Washington-Carver	110,018			
1951D	Same type D mint	10,004	Set $100.00	$130.00	$650.00
1951S	Same type S mint	10,004			
1952	Same type as 1951	2,006,292			
1952D	Same type D mint	8,006	Set 125.00	175.00	800.00
1952S	Same type S mint	8,006			
1953	Same type as 1951	8,003			
1953D	Same type D mint	8,003	Set 150.00	240.00	825.00
1953S	Same type S mint	108,020			
1954	Same type as 1951	12,006			
1954D	Same type D mint	12,006	Set 100.00	130.00	650.00
1954S	Same type S mint	122,024			
	Single, type coin		13.00	16.00	100.00

GEORGE WASHINGTON

This coin, the first commemorative half dollar issued since 1954, commemorates the 250th anniversary of the birth of George Washington. It is also the first 90% silver coin produced by the U.S. Mint since 1964. Designed by Elizabeth Jones, Chief Sculptor and Engraver of the United States, the obverse features George Washington astride a horse. The reverse depicts the eastern facade of Mount Vernon. The uncirculated version was struck at Denver and the proof at San Francisco.

		MS-65	Proof-65
1982D	Geo. Washington-250th Anniversary	$14.00	
1982S	Same		$16.00

WISCONSIN TERRITORIAL CENTENNIAL

The one hundredth anniversary of the Wisconsin Territorial government was the occasion for a special half dollar issue. The original design was made by David Parsons, a University of Wisconsin student. Benjamin Hawkins, a

COMMEMORATIVE SILVER — Wisconsin, York, Lafayette Dollar

New York artist, made changes to conform with technical requirements. The reverse has the Territorial Seal, which includes a forearm holding a pickaxe over a mound of lead ore, and the inscription 4th DAY OF JULY ANNO DOMINI 1836. The obverse shows a badger on a log typifying the early fur trade, and the state emblem.

	Quan. Issued	AU-50	MS-60	MS-63	MS-65
1936 Wisconsin Centennial	25,015	$225.00	$260.00	$350.00	$1,050

YORK COUNTY, MAINE TERCENTENARY

A souvenir half dollar was authorized by Congress upon the three hundredth anniversary of the founding of York County, Maine. Brown's Garrison on the Saco River was the site of a town which was settled in 1636. The designs were made by Walter H. Rich of Portland. The obverse design shows a stockade and the reverse has an adaptation of the York County seal.

1936 York County, Maine Tercentenary	25,015	200.00	250.00	325.00	975.00

LAFAYETTE DOLLAR

The heads of Washington and Lafayette appear on this commemorative issue, which was the first commemorative coin of one dollar denomination, and the first authorized United States coin to bear a portrait of one of our presidents. The dies were prepared by C. E. Barber. The statue on the reverse is similar to the monument of General Lafayette which was erected in Paris as a gift of the American people. The coins were sold by the Lafayette Memorial Commission for $2.00 each.

1900 Lafayette Dollar	36,026	400.00	1,100	2,500	10,000

LOS ANGELES XXIII OLYMPIAD

Three distinctive coins were issued to commemorate the 1984 Los Angeles Summer Olympic Games. The silver dollar dated 1983 was designed by Elizabeth Jones, Chief Engraver of the Mint. On the obverse is a representation of the traditional Greek discus thrower inspired by the ancient work of the sculptor Myron. The reverse depicts the head and upper body of an American eagle.

	Quan. Issued	MS-65	Proof-65
1983P Discus Thrower Silver Dollar	294,543	$45.00	
1983D Same type D mint	174,014	47.50	
1983S Same type S mint (1,577,025)	174,014	47.50	$45.00

The 1984 Olympic silver dollar was designed by Robert Graham, an American sculptor who created the sculpture placed at the entrance to the Los Angeles Memorial Coliseum. The obverse depicts Graham's sculpture with the Coliseum in the background. The reverse features an American eagle.

1984P Olympic Coliseum Silver Dollar	217,954	45.00	
1984D Same type D mint	116,675	57.50	
1984S Same type S mint (1,801,210)	116,675	57.50	45.00

COMMEMORATIVE SILVER — Statue of Liberty
STATUE OF LIBERTY

Designed by Mint artist John Mercanti, this .900 fine silver dollar commemorates Ellis Island as the "Gateway to America." The obverse features a classic pose of Liberty in the foreground, with the Ellis Island Immigration Center standing behind her. On the reverse is a silhouette of Liberty's torch, along with the words "Give me your tired, your poor, your huddled masses yearning to breathe free."

	MS-65	Proof-65
1986P Statue of Liberty Dollar	$23.00	
1986S Same type S mint		$25.00

COMMEMORATIVE GOLD — Grant, Lewis & Clark
GRANT MEMORIAL GOLD DOLLARS

Like the half-dollar commemorative coins the gold dollars were issued first with a star which was removed for the later issues. The designs by Laura Gardin Fraser are the same as for the half-dollar coinage.

		Quan. Issued	AU-50	MS-60	MS-63	MS-65
1922	Grant Memorial Dollar with star..	5,016	$625.00	$1,250	$2,200	$5,000
1922	Grand Memorial Dollar no star ...	5,000	625.00	1,250	2,200	5,000

LEWIS AND CLARK EXPOSITION

The Lewis and Clark Centennial Exposition was held in Portland, Oregon in 1905. A souvenir issue of gold dollars was struck to mark the event with the dates 1904 and 1905. The two famous explorers are represented on each side of the coin which was designed by C. E. Barber. A bronze memorial of the Indian guide, Sacagawea, who assisted in the famous expedition, was erected in Portland, Oregon and financed by the sale of these coins.

COMMEMORATIVE GOLD — Lewis & Clark, Los Angeles, Louisiana Purchase, McKinley,

		Quan. Issued	AU-50	MS-60	MS-63	MS-65
1904	Lewis and Clark Dollar........	10,025	$575.00	$1,250	$2,300	$6,500
1905	Lewis and Clark Dollar........	10,041	575.00	1,250	2,300	6,500

LOS ANGELES XXIII OLYMPIAD

Mintage of a commemorative gold coin for the 1984 Olympics was the first U.S. gold piece issued in over 50 years. The weight, size and fineness are the same as the last ten dollar coin issued in 1933. It is the first coin ever to bear the W mint mark for West Point.

The obverse depicts two runners bearing the Olympic torch aloft, and was designed by John Mercanti from a concept by James Peed, an artist at the Mint. The eagle on the reverse is modeled after the Great Seal.

		Quan. Issued	MS-65	Proof-65
1984P	Olympic Gold Eagle.............	(33,309).............		$750.00
1984D	Olympic Gold Eagle.............	(34,533).............		650.00
1984S	Olympic Gold Eagle.............	(48,551).............		600.00
1984W	Olympic Gold Eagle...........	(381,085)....... 75,886	$400.00	385.00

LOUISIANA PURCHASE EXPOSITION

The first souvenir gold coins were authorized for the Louisiana Purchase Exposition held in St. Louis in 1904. There are two varieties of gold dollars — one with the head of Jefferson who was president when the Louisiana Territory was purchased from France; and the other President William McKinley who sanctioned the Exposition. The reverse is the same for each variety. The designs were by C. E. Barber.

		Quan Issued	AU-50	MS-60	MS-63	MS-65
*1903	Louisiana Pur. Jefferson Dol......	17,500	$400.00	$700.00	$1,200	$4,000
*1903	Louisiana Pur. McKinley Dol	17,500	400.00	700.00	1,200	4,000

*Proofs exist of each type

McKINLEY MEMORIAL GOLD DOLLARS

The sale of the McKinley dollars aided in paying for a memorial building at Niles, Ohio, the martyred president's birthplace. The obverse showing a profile

COMMEMORATIVE GOLD — McKinley,
Panama-Pacific

of McKinley was designed by C. E. Barber; the reverse with the memorial building was designed by G. T. Morgan.

	Quan. Issued	AU-50	MS-60	MS-63	MS-65
1916 McKinley Memorial Dollar	9,977	$350.00	$800.00	$1,050	$4,500
1917 McKinley Memorial Dollar	10,000	375.00	850.00	1,250	4,750

PANAMA-PACIFIC EXPOSITION

Charles Keck designed the gold dollar, the obverse of which has the head of a man representing a Panama Canal laborer. Two dolphins encircle ONE DOLLAR on the reverse.

The quarter-eagle was the work of Charles E. Barber and George T. Morgan. It was the first commemorative coin of this denomination. The obverse shows Columbia with a caduceus in her left hand seated on a hippocampus typifying the use of the Panama Canal. An American eagle with raised wings is shown on the reverse.

The fifty-dollar gold piece was designed by Robert Aitken and was issued in round and octagonal form. The obverse bears the helmeted head of Minerva; the owl, symbol of wisdom, is on the reverse. The octagonal issue has eight dolphins in the angles on both sides. The devices are smaller on the octagonal variety.

1915S Panama-Pacific Exposition Dollar..	15,000	375.00	775.00	1,100	3,600
1915S Panama-Pacific Exposition $2.50...	6,749	800.00	1,900	3,000	7,500

1915S Panama-Pacific $50 Round.............	483	22,000	31,000	37,500	47,500

COMMEMORATIVE GOLD — Panama-Pacific, United States Sesquicentennial, Statue of Liberty

	Quan. Issued	AU-50	MS-60	MS-63	MS-65
1915S Panama-Pacific $50 Octagonal	645	$17,000	$25,000	$28,000	$37,500

UNITED STATES SESQUICENTENNIAL—QUARTER EAGLES

The obverse of this special gold issue has a standing female figure symbolic of Liberty, holding in one hand a scroll representing the Declaration of Independence and in the other the Torch of Freedom. The reverse bears a representation of Independence Hall in Philadelphia. The coin was designed by J. R. Sinnock.

1926 United States Sesquicent. $2.50	46,019	350.00	650.00	900.00	4,200

STATUE OF LIBERTY

The first commemorative half eagle is also the first of this denomination to be minted in over fifty years. Standards for weight and size are the same as previous gold coins. The design is the creation of the Mint's chief engraver, Elizabeth Jones. The obverse features an unusual close-up view of Liberty's face in sharp relief with the inscription 1986 LIBERTY. An eagle in flight adorns the reverse. All were minted at West Point and bear the W mint mark.

	MS-65	Proof-65
1986W Statue of Liberty five dollar gold	$175.00	$185.00

BIBLIOGRAPHY

Bullowa, David M. *The Commemorative Coinage of the United States 1892-1938.* New York, 1938.
Mosher, Stuart. *United States Commemorative Coins 1892-1939.* New York, 1940.
Slabaugh, Arlie. *United States Commemorative Coinage.* Racine, 1975.
Swiatek, Anthony and Breen, Walter. *The Encyclopedia of United States Silver and Gold Commemorative Coins 1892-1954,* New York, 1981.
Taxay, Don. *An Illustrated History of U.S. Commemorative Coinage.* New York, 1967.

UNITED STATES BULLION COINS

American citizens regained the right to gold ownership on December 31, 1974, yet no such coins were issued to satisfy the publics desire for gold bullion in a convenient form. Would be investors have mostly purchased Krugerrands, Maple Leafs and to some extent older United States and foreign gold pieces. That is now changing, and by the end of 1986 United States gold bullion coins will be available for sale to everyone.

Sometime after October 1, 1986, the U.S. Treasury will issue a legal tender one ounce gold coin whose price will be pegged to the value of gold bullion. It will also issue three fractional gold coins containing ½, ¼ and 1/10 of an ounce of gold, all with legal tender status.

Under the legislation, each of the four coins is given a face value far lower than the market value of the gold that the coins will contain. The face values will be $50 for the one ounce coin, $25 for the half ounce, $10.00 for the quarter ounce and $5 for the one-tenth ounce. The pieces will be made in the traditional fineness of U.S. gold coins and contain 90% pure gold.

Also similar to other U.S. coins, these pieces will each be required to display the denomination and date of issue, along with the inscriptions: LIBERTY, IN GOD WE TRUST, UNITED STATES OF AMERICA and E PLURIBUS UNUM. Unlike other standard coins, these pieces will also show the weight and gold fineness.

It is expected that the coins will be marketed directly by the Treasury and also through a network of dealers. It is also expected that their prices will be competitive with those of other bullion coins. Like the Krugerrand, the Maple Leaf and other competing pieces, the new U.S. coins will fluctuate in price according to the value of the gold they contain. This price will reflect the value of the metal plus a surcharge to cover the cost of production and distribution.

The one ounce coin will carry a design "symbolic of Liberty" on the obverse. The reverse will bear a design "representing a family of eagles with the male carring an olive branch and flying above a nest containing a female eagle and hatchlings." The designs of the three smaller coins has not yet been announced.

Congress has also authorized a similar one ounce U.S. silver bullion coin. Issuance of the silver "Liberty Coin" was provided for as part of the same legislation that cleared the way for the new Statue of Liberty commemoratives. Like the gold bullion coins, the silver ounces will not be issued until after October 1, 1986, so as not to interfere with sales of the Statue of Liberty commemoratives.

The silver bullion coin will have a face value of one dollar and will be legal tender for that amount. Its actual value and its issue price will be substantially higher and based on the fluctuating "spot metal" price of silver.

At current bullion metal prices the one ounce silver Liberty dollar might be expected to sell for around $7.00, and the one ounce $50 gold coin for perhaps $375.00. The premiums on the smaller denomination gold coins would be somewhat higher, as the cost of production and distribution would be greater in relation to the value of the coin's precious metal content.

All of these coins will be listed and illustrated in future editions of the Guide Book. Because of the unique nature of these special bullion pieces, they will be placed in a separate section apart from the regular issue gold and silver coins of the past.

PRIVATE OR TERRITORIAL GOLD COINS

The words "Private Gold," used with reference to coins struck outside of the United States Mint, are a general term. In the sense that no state or territory had authority to coin money, private gold simply refers to those interesting necessity pieces of various shapes, denominations and degrees of intrinsic worth which were circulated in isolated areas of our country by individuals, assayers, bankers, etc. Some will use the words "Territorial" and "State" to cover certain issues because they were coined and circulat-ed in a territory or state. While the state of California properly sanctioned the ingots stamped by F. D. Kohler as state assayer, in no instance were any of the gold pieces struck by authority of any of the territorial governments.

The stamped ingots put out by Augustus Humbert, the United States assayer of gold, were not recognized at the United States Mint as an official issue of coins, but simply as ingots, though Humbert placed the value and fineness on the pieces as an official agent of the federal government.

Private coins were circulated in most instances because of a shortage of regular coinage. In the western states particularly, money became so scarce that the very commodity which the pioneers had come so far to acquire was converted into a local medium of exchange.

Ephraim Brasher's New York doubloon of 1787 described on page 40 also falls into this class.

BIBLIOGRAPHY

Adams, Edgar H. *Private Gold Coinage of California 1849-1855.* Brooklyn, N.Y., 1913.
Adams, Edgar H. *Official Premium Lists of Private and Territorial Gold Coins.* Brooklyn, N.Y., 1909.
Bowers, Q. David. *The History of United States Coinage as Illustrated by the Garrett Collection.* Los Angeles, Cal., 1979.
Clifford, Henry H. *Pioneer Gold Coinage in the West- 1848-1861.* Reprint from "The Westerners Brand Book- Book Nine." Los Angeles Corral, 1961.
Griffin, Clarence. *The Bechtlers and Bechtler Coinage and Gold Mining in North Carolina 1814-1830.* Spindale, N.C., 1929.
Kagin Donald H. *Private Gold Coins and Patterns of the United States,* New York, 1981.
Lee, Kenneth W. *California Gold — Dollars, Half Dollars, Quarter Dollars.* Santa Ana, Cal., 1979.
Seymour, Dexter C. *The 1830 Coinage of Templeton Reid.* American Numismatic Society Museum Notes No. 22. New York, 1977.

TEMPLETON REID
Georgia 1830

The first private gold coinage under the Constitution was struck by Templeton Reid, a jeweler and gunsmith, in Milledgeville, Georgia in July, 1830. To be closer to the mines, he moved to Gainesville where most of his coins were made. Although weights were accurate, Reid's assays were not and his coins were slightly short of claimed value. Accordingly, he was severely attacked in the newspapers and soon lost the public's confidence. He closed his mint before the end of October, 1830 and his output amounted only to about 1,600 coins. Denominations struck were $2.50, $5.00 and $10.00.

1830 $2.50	....	V.F.	$12,000
1830 $5.00	....	V.F.	65,000

TEMPLETON REID — GEORGIA

1830 TEN DOLLARS	V.G.	$50,000
(No date) TEN DOLLARS	V.G.	30,000

TEMPLETON REID
"California Gold 1849"

The enigmatic later issues of Templeton Reid were probably made from California gold. Reid, who never went to California, was then a cotton gin maker in Columbus, Georgia, where he died in 1851. The coins were in denominations of ten and twenty-five dollars. Struck copies of both exist in various metals.

The only specimen known of the $25 piece was stolen from the Cabinet of the U.S. Mint on August 16, 1858. It was never recovered.

1849 TEN DOLLAR CALIFORNIA GOLD (Smithsonian Collection)	*Unique*
1849 TWENTY-FIVE DOLLARS CALIFORNIA GOLD	*Unknown*

THE BECHTLERS
Rutherford County, N. C. 1830-1852

Two skilled German metallurgists, Christopher Bechtler and his son August, and later Christopher Bechtler, Junior, a nephew of Christopher the elder, operated a "private" mint at Rutherfordton, North Carolina. Rutherford county in which Rutherfordton is located was the principal source of the nation's gold supply from 1790 to 1840.

The coins minted by the Bechtlers were of only three denominations, but they cover a wide variety of weights and sizes.

THE BECHTLERS

The Bechtlers have the distinction of producing the first gold dollar in the United States. The government mint did not release the first regular series until 1849.

The inscription "Aug. 1, 1834" on one variety of the five-dollar piece has a special significance. The Secretary of the Treasury recommended to the Director of the Mint that the gold coins of the reduced weight bear the date "Aug. 1, 1834." Instead of this, however, a new U.S. gold design was used (the motto was omitted). Christopher Bechtler evidently acted on the official recommendation to avoid any difficulty with Treasury authorities.

CHRISTOPHER BECHTLER

	V. Fine	E. Fine	Unc.
ONE DOLLAR CAROLINA, 28 gr. N reversed	$750.00	$1,000	$2,500
ONE DOLLAR N. CAROLINA, 28 gr. centered, no star ...	1,500	2,500	6,000
ONE DOLLAR N. CAROLINA, 28 gr. high, no star	4,500	6,000	9,000

ONE DOLLAR N. CAROLINA, 30 gr....................	1,000	1,800	3,500
$2.50 CAROLINA, 67 gr. 21 carats	1,500	2,500	5,000

$2.50 CAROLINA, 70 gr. 20 carats	1,800	2,750	5,500
$2.50 GEORGIA, 64 gr. 22 carats	2,000	3,000	6,000
$2.50 GEORGIA, 64 gr. 22 carats — even 22.........	2,250	3,500	6,500

$2.50 NORTH CAROLINA, 75 gr. 20 carats.			
RUTHERFORD in a circle. Border of lg. beads	4,250	6,000	9,000
$2.50 NORTH CAROLINA, without 75 G..............	4,000	5,750	8,500

THE BECHTLERS

	V. Fine	E. Fine	Unc.
$2.50 NORTH CAROLINA, without 75 G, CAROLINA above 250 instead of GOLD			*(Unique)*
$2.50 NORTH CAROLINA, 20 carats on obv. 75 gr. on rev. Border finely serrated	$4,250	$6,500	——

5 DOLLARS CAROLINA, RUTHERFORD, 140 gr. 20 carats. Date August 1, 1834.			
Plain edge	2,500	3,300	$7,000
Reeded edge	3,100	5,000	7,500
5 DOLLARS CAROLINA, 134 gr. 21 carats, with star	2,000	3,300	7,000
5 DOLLARS CAROLINA, 134 gr. 21 carats, no star, ...	——		

(Reverse of A. Bechtler shown on page 240)

5 DOLLARS GEORGIA, RUTHERFORD, 128 gr. 22 carats	3,500	5,000	7,500
Similar. Colon before 22 and after 128 G.	——	——	
5 DOLLARS GEORGIA, RUTHERF. 128 gr. 22 carats	2,600	3,800	6,500
5 DOLLARS CAROLINA, RUTHERF. 140 gr. 20 carats. Date August 1, 1834	2,600	3,800	6,500
Similar. 20 distant from carats.	5,000	8,500	——

Without
150 G

5 DOLLARS NORTH CAROLINA, 150 gr. 20 carats	3,250	5,500	13,000
5 DOLLARS. Same as last variety without 150 G	4,000	6,000	14,000

THE BECHTLERS
AUGUST BECHTLER
1842-1852

	V. Fine	E. Fine	Unc.
1 DOLLAR CAROLINA, 27 gr. 21 carats...............	$700.00	$1,000	$2,500
5 DOLLARS CAROLINA, 134 gr. 21 carats.............	2,000	3,250	6,000

5 DOLLARS CAROLINA, 128 gr. 22 carats.............	3,500	5,000	10,000
5 DOLLARS CAROLINA, 141 gr. 20 carats.............	3,250	5,000	10,000

(Restrikes in "proof" exist from original dies.)

NORRIS, GREGG & NORRIS
San Francisco 1849

Edgar H. Adams considered this piece the first of the California private gold coins. A newspaper account dated May 31, 1849, described a five-dollar gold coin, struck at Benicia City, though with the imprint San Francisco. It mentioned the private stamp of Norris, Gregg and Norris. The initials N. G. and N. were not identified until 1902 when the coins of Augustus Humbert were sold.

	Fine	V. Fine	E. Fine	Unc.
1849 HALF EAGLE — Plain edge	$2,500	$3,400	$6,250	$20,000
1849 HALF EAGLE — Reeded edge	2,500	3,500	7,000	22,000
1850 HALF EAGLE with STOCKTON beneath date				(Unique)

MOFFAT & CO.
San Francisco 1849-1853

The firm of Moffat and Company was perhaps the most important of the California private coiners. The assay office they conducted was semi-official in character. The successors to this firm, Curtis, Perry and Ward, later established the United States Branch mint of San Francisco.

In June or July, 1849, Moffat & Co. began to issue small rectangular pieces of gold owing to lack of coin in the locality, in values from $9.43 to $264. The $9.43, $14.25 and $16.00 varieties are the only types known today.

The only specimen known of the $9.43 ingot is in the National Coin Collection in the Smithsonian.

$9.43 Ingot (*Unique*)		——
$14.25 Ingot (*Unique*)		——
$16.00 Ingot	E.F.	$20,000

The dies for the $10 piece were cut by a Bavarian, Albert Kuner. The words MOFFAT & CO. appear on the coronet of Liberty instead of the word LIBERTY as in regular United States issues.

	Fine	V. Fine	E. Fine	Unc.
1849 FIVE DOL. (All varieties)	$650.00	$1,000	$1,750	$6,000
1850 FIVE DOL. (All varieties)	650.00	1,000	1,750	6,500
1849 TEN DOL.	1,600	2,100	4,750	10,000
1849 TEN D.	1,750	2,750	5,000	

United States Assay Office
AUGUSTUS HUMBERT
U. S. Assayer 1851

Augustus Humbert, a New York watchcase maker, was appointed United States Assayer, and he placed his name and the government stamp on the ingots of gold issued by Moffat & Co. The assay office, a Provisional Government Mint, was a temporary expedient to accommodate the Californians until the establishment of a permanent branch mint.

The fifty-dollar gold piece was accepted as legal tender on a par with standard U.S. gold coins and was known variously as a slug, quintuple eagle or five-eagle piece. It was officially termed an ingot.

MOFFAT — HUMBERT

LETTERED EDGE VARIETIES

	Fine	V. Fine	E. Fine	A. Unc.
1851 50 D C 880 THOUS., no 50 on Reverse. Sunk in edge: AUGUSTUS HUMBERT UNITED STATES ASSAYER OF GOLD CALIFORNIA 1851..................	$7,000	$9,000	$17,500	$24,000

Reverse, Rays from Central Star

	Fine	V. Fine	E. Fine	A. Unc.
1851 50 D C Similar to last variety, but 50 on Reverse	8,000	10,000	——	——
1851 Similar to last variety, but 887 THOUS.......................	7,500	9,500	——	——
1851 50 D C 887 THOUS., no 50 on Reverse.........................	——	——	——	
1851 50 D C 880 THOUS. Rev. Rays from central star (*Unique*)				——

MOFFAT — HUMBERT

REEDED EDGE VARIETIES

	Fine	V. Fine	E. Fine	A. Unc	Unc.
1851 FIFTY DOLLS 880 THOUS. "Target" Reverse	$5,500	$7,500	$13,000	$18,000	$30,000
1851 FIFTY DOLLS 887 THOUS. "Target" Reverse	5,500	7,500	13,000	18,000	30,000
1852 FIFTY DOLLS. 887 THOUS.	6,000	8,200	14,000	19,000	36,000

A unique proof specimen of the 1851 with 887 THOUS. was sold at the Garrett II auction in 1980 for $500,000.

The withdrawal of the discredited private coins of $5, $10 and $20 denominations as a result of the new U.S. Assay operations caused a new turn of affairs for Californians.

The fractional currency coins of almost every nation were pressed into service by the Californians, but the supply was too small to help to any extent. Moffat & Co. proceeded in January, 1852 to issue a new ten-dollar piece bearing the stamp MOFFAT & CO.

1852 TEN D. MOFFAT & CO. (Close date)	2,200	3,500	6,000	9,000	——
1852 TEN D. MOFFAT & CO. (Wide date)	2,200	3,500	6,000	8,700	——

MOFFAT — HUMBERT

	Fine	V. Fine	E. Fine	A. Unc	Unc.
1852 TWENTY DOLS. 1852, 2 over 1.	$2,700	$4,000	$6,000	$8,500	——

1852 TEN DOLS. 1852, 2 over 1.....	1,500	2,250	3,500	5,750	——
1852 TEN DOLS.	1,000	1,800	2,700	5,000	$7,500

UNITED STATES ASSAY OFFICE OF GOLD

1852

The firm of Moffat & Co. dissolved and a new reorganized company known as the United States Assay Office of Gold, composed of Curtis, Perry and Ward took over the contract.

1852 FIFTY DOLLS. 887 THOUS.	5,000	7,000	11,000	18,000	28,000
1852 FIFTY DOLLS. 900 THOUS.	5,000	8,000	12,500	20,000	30,000

UNITED STATES ASSAY OFFICE

	Fine	V. Fine	E. Fine	A. Unc	Unc.
1852 TEN DOLS 884 THOUS.	$800.00	$1,400	$2,200	$3,500	$7,500

| 1853 TEN D. 884 THOUS. . . . . | 3,500 | 6,000 | 10,000 | 13,000 | —— |
| 1853 TEN D. 900 THOUS. . . . . | 2,000 | 3,500 | 5,500 | 7,000 | —— |

| 1853 TWENTY D. 884 THOUS. . . . . . . | 5,500 | 9,000 | 12,000 | 17,000 | 21,000 |

| 1853 TWENTY D. 900 THOUS. . . . . . . | 1,200 | 2,000 | 3,500 | 6,000 | 10,000 |

U. S. ASSAY — MOFFAT

The last Moffat issue was the 1853 twenty dollar piece which is very similar to the U.S. double eagle of that period. It was struck after the retirement of Mr. Moffat from the Assay Office.

	Fine	V. Fine	E. Fine	Unc.
1853 TWENTY D.	$2,000	$3,500	$5,000	$10,000

CINCINNATI MINING & TRADING CO.

The origin and location of this company are unknown.

	E. Fine	Unc.
1849 FIVE DOLLARS	Unique	
1849 TEN DOLLARS — Garrett Sale, 1980	$270,000	——

(Beware of spurious specimens cast in base metal with word TRACING in place of TRADING.)

MASSACHUSETTS AND CALIFORNIA COMPANY
San Francisco 1849

This company was believed to have been organized in Northampton, Mass. in May 1849.

	Fine	Proof
1849 FIVE D.	$35,000	$100,000

MINERS' BANK
San Francisco 1849

The institution of Wright & Co., exchange brokers located in Portsmouth Square, San Francisco, was known as the Miners' Bank.

A ten dollar piece was issued in the autumn of 1849, but the coins were not readily accepted because they were worth less than face value. The firm dissolved January 14, 1850. Unlike most issues, the gold in these coins was alloyed with copper.

	V. Fine	E. Fine	Unc.
(1849) TEN. D.	$7,500	$11,000	$33,000

(Specimen sold in Garrett sale, 1980 — MS-65, $135,000)

J. S. ORMSBY
Sacramento 1849

The initials J. S. O. which appear on certain issues of California privately coined gold pieces represent the firm of J. S. Ormsby & Co. They struck both five and ten dollar denominations, all undated.

	V. Fine
(1849) 5 DOLLS. (*Unique*)	—
(1849) 10 DOLLS. — Garrett Sale, 1980	$100,000

PACIFIC COMPANY
San Francisco 1849

The origin of the Pacific Co. is very uncertain. All data regarding the firm is based on conjecture.

Edgar H. Adams wrote that he believed that the coins bearing the stamp of the Pacific Company were produced by the coining firm of Broderick and Kohler. The coins were probably handstruck, with the aid of a sledgehammer.

PACIFIC COMPANY

1849 5 DOLLARS
Coles Sale, 1983
Ex. Fine................ $57,500

1849 10 DOLLARS
A. Unc.......... $132,000

F. D. KOHLER
California State Assayer 1850

The State Assay Office was authorized April 12, 1850. Governor Burnett appointed F. D. Kohler that year who thereupon sold his assaying business to Baldwin & Co. He served at both San Francisco and Sacramento Offices. The State Assay Offices were discontinued at the time the U. S. Assay Office was established Feb. 1, 1851.

Ingots issued ranged from $36.55 to $150. An Ex. F. specimen sold in the Garrett Sale, 1980 for $200,000.

$36.55 Sacramento	——
$47.71 Sacramento	——
$37.31 San Francisco	——
$40.07 San Francisco	——
Note: $40.07 stolen from the Mint Cabinet in 1858 and was never recovered.	
$41.68 San Francisco	——
$45.34 San Francisco	——
$50.00 San Francisco Ex.F	$200,000
$54.09 San Francisco	——

DUBOSQ & COMPANY
San Francisco 1850

Theodore Dubosq, a Philadelphia jeweler, took melting and coining machinery to San Francisco in 1849.

	V. Fine
1850 FIVE D...........	$40,000
1850 TEN D.	50,000

BALDWIN & COMPANY
San Francisco 1850

George C. Baldwin and Thomas S. Holman were in the jewelry business in San Francisco and were known as Baldwin & Co. They were the successors to F. D. Kohler & Co., taking over their machinery and other equipment in May, 1850.

	Fine	V. Fine	E. Fine	Unc.
1850 FIVE DOL..........................	$2,750	$4,750	$7,500	$18,000
1850 TEN DOLLARS — Horseman type.....	12,000	19,000	29,000	——

1851 TEN D.............................	6,000	9,000	18,000	——

The Baldwin & Co. $20 piece was the first of that denomination issued in California.

Baldwin coins were believed to have contained about twenty-thousandths copper alloy.

1851 TWENTY D..	60,000	——

Beware of spurious specimens cast in base metal.

SHULTZ & COMPANY
San Francisco 1851

The firm located in back of Baldwin's establishment operated a brass foundry beginning in 1851. Judge G. W. Shultz and William T. Garratt were partners in the enterprise.

	Fine	V. Fine	A. Unc
1851 FIVE D	$12,000	$20,000	$37,500

DUNBAR & COMPANY
San Francisco 1851

Edward E. Dunbar operated the California Bank in San Francisco. Mr. Dunbar later returned to New York and organized the famous Continental Bank Note Co.

	E. Fine
1851 FIVE D.	$60,000

WASS, MOLITOR & COMPANY
San Francisco 1852-1855

The gold smelting and assaying plant of Wass, Molitor & Co. was operated by two Hungarian patriots, Count S. C. Wass and A. P. Molitor. They maintained an excellent laboratory and complete apparatus for analysis and coinage of gold.

Large Head, Pointed Bust

	Fine	V. Fine	E. Fine	Unc.
1852 FIVE DOLLARS. Small head with rounded bust	$2,000	$3,500	$6,000	$16,000
1852 FIVE DOLLARS. Large head with pointed bust	2,200	3,750	6,000	16,000

WASS, MOLITOR & COMPANY

The company struck five, ten, twenty and fifty dollar coins. In 1852 they produced a ten dollar piece similar in design to the five dollar denomination. The difference is in the reverse legend which reads: s.m.v. (Standard Mint Value) CALIFORNIA GOLD TEN D.

No pieces were coined in 1853 or 1854, but they brought out the twenty dollar and fifty dollar pieces in 1855. A considerable number of the fifty dollar coins were made. There was a ten dollar piece issued in 1855 also, with the Liberty head and small close date.

Large Head   **Small Head**

Small Date

	Fine	V. Fine	E. Fine	Unc.
1852 TEN D. Large head	$1,500	$3,000	$4,500	——
1852 TEN D. Small head	3,000	4,500	8,000	——
1852 TEN D. Small close date.............		(Ex. Rare)		
1855 TEN D............................	6,500	12,000	16,500	——

Large Head   **Small Head**

1855 TWENTY DOL. Large head		——	40,000	——
1855 TWENTY DOL. Small head	6,000	11,000	15,000	——

[251]

WASS, MOLITOR & COMPANY

	Fine	V. Fine	E. Fine	Unc.
1855 50 DOLLARS......................	$11,000	$15,000	$25,000	$120,000

KELLOGG & COMPANY
San Francisco 1854-1855

John G. Kellogg came to San Francisco October 12, 1849, from Auburn, New York. At first he was employed by Moffat and Company, and remained with that organization when control passed to Curtis, Perry and Ward. When the United States Assay Office was discontinued December 14, 1853, Mr. Kellogg became associated with G. F. Richter, who had been an assayer in the government assay office. These two set up business as Kellogg & Richter December 19, 1853.

When the U. S. Assay Office ceased operations a period ensued during which no private firm was striking gold. The new San Francisco branch mint did not produce coins for some months after Curtis & Perry took the contract for the government. The lack of coin was again keenly felt by businessmen who petitioned Kellogg & Richter to "supply the vacuum" by issuing private coin.

Their plea was soon answered, for on February 9, 1854, Kellogg & Co. placed their first twenty-dollar piece in circulation.

1854 TWENTY D........................	1,500	2,000	3,500	8,000

The 1855 twenty-dollar piece is similar to that dated 1854. The letters on the reverse side are larger and the arrows longer on one 1854 variety. There are several die varieties of both issues.

KELLOGG & COMPANY

	Fine	V. Fine	E. Fine	Unc.
1855 TWENTY D.........................	$1,400	$2,000	$3,500	$12,000

The firm dissolved late in 1854 and reorganized as Kellogg & Humbert. The latter partner was Augustus Humbert, for some time identified as U.S. Assayer.

Regardless of the fact that the branch mint was then producing coins, Kellogg & Humbert issued coins in 1855 in a quantity greater than before.

	Proof
1855 FIFTY DOLLS. — Carter Sale 1984	$154,000

OREGON EXCHANGE COMPANY
Oregon City, 1849
THE BEAVER COINS OF OREGON

Upon the discovery of gold in California there was a great exodus of settlers who joined in the hunt for the precious metal. Soon returning gold seekers offered their gold dust, which became the accepted medium of exchange. As in other western areas of that time the uncertain qualities of the gold and weighing devices tended to irk the tradespeople and petitions were made to the legislature for a standard gold coin issue.

On February 16, 1849, the legislature passed an act providing for a mint and specified five- and ten-dollar gold coins without alloy. Oregon City, the largest city in the territory with a population of about 1000, was designated as the location for the mint. At the time this act was passed Oregon had been brought into the United States as a territory by act of Congress. When the new governor arrived March second, he declared the coinage act unconstitutional.

The public-spirited people, however, continued to work for a convenient

OREGON EXCHANGE COMPANY

medium of exchange and soon took matters into their own hands by starting a private mint. Eight men of affairs whose names were Kilborne, Magruder, Taylor, Abernethy, Willson, Rector, Campbell and Smith set up the Oregon Exchange Company.

The coins struck were of virgin gold as specified in the original act. Ten-dollar dies were made later, and were of finer design and workmanship.

	Fine	V. Fine	E. Fine	Unc.
1849 5 D .... (6,000 minted)	$6,500	$12,500	$17,000	——

	Fine	V. Fine	E. Fine	Unc.
1849 TEN D .... (2,850 minted)	20,000	32,500	45,000	——

MORMON GOLD PIECES
Salt Lake City, Utah 1849-1860

The first name given to the organized Mormon Territory was the "State of Deseret," the last word meaning "honey bee." The beehive, which is shown on the reverse of the five-dollar 1860 piece, was a favorite device of the followers of Joseph Smith and Brigham Young. The clasped hands appear on most Mormon coins and exemplify strength in unity. "Holiness to the Lord" was an inscription frequently used.

Brigham Young was the instigator of the coinage system and personally supervised the mint which was housed in a little adobe building in Salt Lake City.

The mint was inaugurated late in 1849 as a public convenience.

	Fine	V. Fine	E. Fine	Unc.
1849 TWO AND HALF DO................	$2,750	$4,500	$7,000	
1849 FIVE DOLLARS	2,200	3,500	5,000	$11,000

MORMON GOLD PIECES

	Fine
1849 TEN DOLLARS	$75,000

	Fine	*V. Fine*
1849 TWENTY DOLLARS	$20,000	$35,000

The Mormon twenty-dollar piece was the first of that denomination to be coined in this country.

1850 FIVE DOLLARS

Fine	$2,500
V. Fine	3,500
Ex. Fine	5,750
Unc.	———

1860 5D

Fine	$5,500
V. Fine	8,500
Ex. Fine	12,500
Unc.	23,000

COLORADO GOLD PIECES
Clark, Gruber & Co. — Denver 1860-1861

Clark, Gruber and Co. was a well-known private minting firm in Denver, Colo. in the early sixties.

COLORADO GOLD PIECES

	Fine	V. Fine	E. Fine	Unc.
1860 2½ D............................	$750.00	$1,250	$1,750	$7,500
1860 5D.............................	1,000	1,600	3,000	10,000

1860 TEN D...........................	3,000	4,000	7,000	16,000
1860 TWENTY D.......................	10,000	15,000	25,000	———

The $2.50 and five-dollar pieces of 1861 follow closely the designs of the 1860 issues. The main difference is found in the legends. The reverse side now has CLARK GRUBER & CO. DENVER. PIKES PEAK is on the coronet of Liberty.

1861 2½ D............................	850.00	1,250	2,500	7,500
1861 FIVE D..........................	1,200	1,750	2,750	8,500
1861 TEN D...........................	1,500	2,000	3,500	10,000

1861 TWENTY D.......................	4,500	7,000	16,000	———

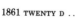

JOHN PARSONS & COMPANY
Tarryall Mines — Colorado 1861

Very little is known regarding the mint of John Parsons and Co., although it is reasonably certain that it operated in the South Park of Colorado, near the original town of Tarryall, in the summer of 1861.

PIKES PEAK GOLD

		V. Fine
(1861) Undated 2½ D..		$35,000
(1861) Undated FIVE D.......................................		50,000

J. J. CONWAY & COMPANY
Georgia Gulch, Colorado, 1861

Records show that the Conway Mint operated for a short while in 1861. As in all gold mining areas the value of gold dust caused disagreement among the merchants and the miners. The firm of J. J. Conway & Co. solved this difficulty by bringing out its gold pieces in August, 1861.

(1861) Undated 2½ DOLL'S..	35,000
(1861) Undated FIVE DOLLARS	60,000
(1861) Undated FIVE DOLLARS, Similar.	
Variety without numeral 5 on reverse	40,000

(1861) Undated
    TEN DOLLARS....

CALIFORNIA SMALL DENOMINATION GOLD

There was a scarcity of small coins during the California gold rush and starting in 1852, quarter, half and dollar pieces were privately minted from native gold to alleviate the shortage. The need and acceptability of these pieces declined

CALIFORNIA SMALL DENOMINATION GOLD

after 1856 and they then became popular as souvenirs. Private coinage became illegal with passage of the Act of 1864, but production continued until 1882 before the law was enforced.

The designs of the early issues were similar to those of the larger territorials. Later issues showed greater variety, had lower intrinsic value, and were often struck from highly polished dies giving prooflike surfaces. In contrast to the tokens which lack the denomination and were often back dated, California small denomination gold was mostly made in the year indicated. Authentic pieces all have CENTS, DOLLAR, or an abbreviation thereof on the reverse.

A total of about 10,000 pieces still exist; of these nearly 500 different varieties have been identified, many of them very rare. Although some of the early pieces are machine made with reeded edges, most are hand struck and have crude designs and incomplete features. Many bear the maker's initials: D, DN, N, NR, L, H, G, GG, FD, or DERI. Major types are listed below; values are for the commonest varieties of each type. The tokens are much less valuable. Modern restrikes and replicas have no numismatic value.

Values are only for genuine coins with the denomination on the reverse expressed as: CENTS, DOL., DOLL., *or* DOLLAR.

	EF-40	AU-50	MS-60
25c Octagonal: Large Liberty head/Wreath	$80.00	$135.00	$210.00
Small Liberty head/Wreath	80.00	135.00	210.00
Liberty head/Beaded circle	115.00	185.00	275.00
Small Liberty head/Shield and wreath	115.00	200.00	300.00
Large Indian head/Wreath	115.00	185.00	275.00
Small Indian head/Wreath	175.00	250.00	350.00
Washington head/Wreath	375.00	600.00	825.00
25c Round: Large Liberty head/Wreath	100.00	150.00	250.00
Small Liberty head/Wreath	100.00	150.00	225.00
Small Liberty head/Shield and wreath	175.00	300.00	400.00
Large Indian head/Wreath	110.00	175.00	275.00
Small Indian head/Wreath	150.00	225.00	350.00
Washington head/Wreath	550.00	850.00	1,100
50c Octagonal: Liberty head/Wreath	110.00	175.00	250.00
Liberty head/Legend and wreath	150.00	225.00	350.00
Liberty head/Beaded circle	150.00	200.00	275.00
Liberty head/Eagle	800.00	950.00	1,700
Large Indian head/Wreath	250.00	375.00	550.00
Small Indian head/Wreath	300.00	475.00	700.00
50c Round: Liberty head/Wreath	125.00	175.00	250.00
Liberty head/Legend and wreath	150.00	200.00	300.00
Large Indian head/Wreath	200.00	275.00	400.00
Small Indian head/Wreath	225.00	350.00	500.00
$1.00 Octagonal: Liberty head/Legend and wreath	250.00	375.00	550.00
Liberty head/Eagle	1,500	2,000	3,200
Liberty head/Beaded circle	250.00	375.00	550.00
Indian head/Legend and wreath	500.00	600.00	900.00
Small Indian head/Wreath	500.00	600.00	900.00
$1.00 Round: Liberty head/Legend and wreath	1,200	1,500	2,200
Indian head/Legend and wreath	1,300	1,750	2,500

See bibliography on page 236.

CIVIL WAR TOKENS — 1861-1864

Civil War Tokens are generally divided into two groups: tradesmen's tokens, and anonymously issued pieces with political or patriotic themes. They came into existence only because of the scarcity of government coins and disappeared as soon as the bronze coins of 1864 met the public demand for small copper change.

From the outset of the Civil War, government cents were insufficient in number, widely hoarded and worth a premium over all other currencies. As a result of this scarcity of cent pieces, private copper coins were issued by many individuals. Their wide circulation was made possible by the scarcity of copper-nickel cents and the public dislike of fractional paper money.

The tradesmen's tokens were issued by various firms to provide change and advertise the dealers' wares. They usually bore an implied or an explicit promise of redemption in goods or money. The second type was simply unauthorized substitutes for government coins, produced at a profit by private manufacturers and put into general circulation through various agencies.

These tokens are of great variety in composition and design. A number were more or less faithful imitations of the copper-nickel cent. A few of this type have the word "NOT" in very small letters above the words "ONE CENT."

Many pieces, especially of the tradesmen token type, were individual in device and size, representing any caprice of design or slogan that appealed to the maker. Some were political or patriotic in character, carrying the likeness of some military leader such as McClellan or bearing such inscriptions as "Millions for contractors, not one cent for the widows." An estimated 50,000,000 or more of these pieces were issued. Approximately 10,000 different varieties have been recorded.

The legal status of the Civil War Tokens was uncertain. Mint Director Pollock thought they were illegal; however, there was no law prohibiting the issue of tradesmen's tokens or of private coins not in imitation of United States coins. A law was passed April 22, 1864 prohibiting the issue of any one or two-cent coins, tokens, or devices for use as money, and on June 8 another law was passed which abolished private coinage of every kind.

	Fine	V. Fine	Unc.
Copper or Brass Tokens	$2.50	$4.00	$24.00
Nickel or German Silver Tokens	20.00	30.00	60.00
White Metal Tokens	20.00	30.00	60.00
Copper-Nickel Tokens	35.00	50.00	90.00
Silver Tokens	60.00	100.00	150.00

CONFEDERATE STATES OF AMERICA
CONFEDERATE 1861 HALF DOLLAR

The half dollar struck by the Confederacy was unknown to collectors until 1879. A specimen of the coin and both dies were found in the possession of Dr. B. F. Taylor of New Orleans. Mr. E. Mason, Jr. of Philadelphia purchased Dr. Taylor's specimen and the reverse die and later sold them to J. W. Scott and Company of New York.

CONFEDERATE STATES OF AMERICA — 1861

Five hundred genuine 1861 half dollars from the New Orleans mint were acquired by J. W. Scott and Company. The reverses were planed off and then restamped with the Confederate die. These are known as restrikes. The restrikes have flattened obverses.

According to records only four originals were struck. These were made on a hand press. Original silver half dollar planchets were used, as well as the original obverse die. One of the coins was given to the Secretary of the Confederacy Memminger who passed it on to President Jefferson Davis for his approval. Another was given to Prof. J. L. Riddell of the University of Louisiana. Dr. E. Ames of New Orleans received a third specimen, the last being kept by Chief Coiner B. F. Taylor, who sold it later as mentioned above.

Lack of bullion prevented the Confederate government from proceeding with any coinage plans that might have been made.

J. W. Scott struck some tokens in white metal using the Confederate reverse die and a special die bearing the inscription:

4 ORIGINALS STRUCK BY ORDER OF C. S. A. IN NEW ORLEANS 1861 ******* REV. SAME AS U.S. (FROM ORIGINAL DIE SCOTT)

Confederate Reverse   **Scott Obverse**

	Quan. Minted	V. Fine	Unc.
1861 HALF DOL. (Ex. Rare)	4	—	—
1861 HALF DOL. Restrike	500	$850.00	$2,000
1861 Scott Token obverse. Confederate reverse	500	175.00	550.00

THE CONFEDERATE CENT

An order to make cents for the Confederacy was placed with Mr. Robert Lovett Jr., an engraver and die-sinker of Philadelphia, through a jewelry firm of that city. Fearing arrest by the United States government for giving assistance to the enemy, Mr. Lovett decided against delivering the coins to the Confederate government and hid the coins and dies in his cellar.

The original dies were later purchased by Capt. John W. Haseltine who made restrikes from the dies.

		Proof
1861 Cent Original (copper-nickel) — Garrett sale, 1981 E. Fine	12	$12,500
1861 Cent Restrike (copper) — Garrett sale, 1981	55	3,000
1861 Cent Restrike (gold) — Stack's Sale, 1979	7	10,000
1861 Cent Restrike (silver) — Garrett Sale, 1981	12	5,000

LESHER REFERENDUM DOLLARS

Coined by Joseph Lesher in 1900 and 1901 at Victor, Colorado. Used in trade to some extent, and stocked by various merchants who redeemed them in goods. Coins were numbered and a blank space left at bottom of 1901 issues, in which were stamped names of businessmen who bought them. All are quite rare, many varieties extremely rare. Composition is .950 fine silver alloyed with copper.

	V.Fine	Unc.
1900 First Type, no business name	$650.00	$1,500
1900 A.B. Bumstead, with or without scrolls	575.00	1,400
1900 Bank Type (9 known)	—	—
1901 Imprint Type, no name	600.00	1,500
1901 Imprint Type, various names	$600-$3,500	$1,500-$6,000

FEUCHTWANGER CENT 1837

Dr. Lewis Feuchtwanger produced a metal which was really a variety of German silver consisting of nickel, copper and some zinc. He suggested as early as 1837 to Congress that his metal be substituted for copper, and made one-cent and three-cent trial pieces.

One Cent.. Fine $22.00   Ex. Fine $90.00
Three-Cent piece... V. Scarce

HARD TIMES

TOKENS

1834-1844

In addition to the coins issued by the United States government, numismatists include in their collections the Hard Times and Civil War tokens which circulated as money during two periods in this country's history when nearly all the minor coin was hoarded.

The Hard Times tokens were issued in the period 1834-1844 and are the size of the large U. S. cent. They were generally struck in copper and are of two general groups: political tokens whose theme centered around President Jackson's fight against the United States Bank, and those issued by merchants (tradesmen's cards). Many different varieties exist. The most common pieces are generally valued $2.75 Good to $20.00 Ex. Fine.

COINS AND TOKENS OF HAWAII

The first official coins of Hawaii were the copper cents of 1847 issued by King Kamehameha III. The five cent piece of 1881 and the eighth dollar piece of 1883 are patterns. In 1883 Kalakaua I issued silver dimes, quarters, halves and dollars bearing his bust and showing the Hawaiian coat of arms on the reverse. By 1937 most of these silver coins had been withdrawn and melted. The plantation tokens listed here were all used as small change on the Islands.

One Cent 1847   **Ten Cents 1883**

	Quan. Minted	Fine	V. Fine	E. Fine	MS-60	MS-65	Proof
1847 Cent	100,000	$175.00	$250.00	$400.00	$800.00	$2,250	
1881 Five Cents		2,250	3,000	4,000	5,000	7,000	$8,000
1883 Ten Cents	250,000	30.00	60.00	250.00	1,250	3,000	12,500
1883 Eighth Dollar (12½ c)							35,000
1883 Quarter Dollar	500,000	30.00	45.00	100.00	325.00	500.00	12,500
1883 Half Dollar	700,000	75.00	100.00	250.00	1,250	3,500	12,500
1883 Dollar	500,000	200.00	250.00	7,500	5,000	15,000	17,500

HAWAIIAN TOKENS

Thomas Hobron token 1879

Haiku Plantation 1882

Wailuku Plantation 1880

Wailuku Plantation 1871

	Fine	V. Fine	E. Fine
Waterhouse Token 1862. Bust of Kamehameha IV	$400.00	$600.00	$850.00
Wailuku Plantation Token 1871	125.00	225.00	350.00
Wailuku Plantation Token 1880	150.00	250.00	450.00
Wailuku Plantation Token, Half Real 1880	250.00	350.00	500.00
Thomas Hobron Token 1879	75.00	100.00	200.00
Haiku Plantation Token	100.00	150.00	250.00
Grove Ranch Plantation Token 1886	125.00	175.00	300.00
Grove Ranch Plantation Token 1887	150.00	200.00	350.00

ALASKA RURAL REHABILITATION CORPORATION
TOKENS OF 1935

These tokens were issued by the U. S. Government for the use of the colonists of the Matanuska Valley Colonization Project to supply them with much needed Federal aid. They were redeemable only at the ARRC stores. The "Bingles," as they were called, were in use only about six months during 1935-1936 after which they were redeemed for regular U. S. money and destroyed. They were issued on a basis of family dependents. Each token is the size of the corresponding U. S. coin with the exception of the one cent piece which is octagonal. The design is the same on both sides of each denomination.

Aluminum				**Quan. Mtd.**	**V. Fine**	**Unc.**
Quan. Minted	**V. Fine**	**Unc.**	50c 2,500		$30.00	$50.00
1c 5,000	$12.50	$25.00	$1.00....... 2,500		40.00	75.00
5c 5,000	12.50	25.00		**Brass**		
10c 5,000	12.50	25.00	$5.00....... 1,000		65.00	100.00
25c 3,000	17.50	35.00	$10.00 1,000		75.00	125.00

PHILIPPINES UNDER SOVEREIGNTY OF THE U.S.

The 1903-19 issues were struck at Philadelphia and San Francisco. 1920 and after were struck at Manila. Because of World War II the 1944-45 coins were minted at Philadelphia, Denver and San Francisco.

Bronze

	E.Fine	Unc.
½ Centavo 1903-08........	$2.00	$14.00
1 Centavo 1903-36........	2.50	13.00

PHILIPPINES UNDER SOVEREIGNTY OF THE U.S.

Copper Nickel

		E. Fine	Unc.
5	Centavos 1903-28...	$2.00	$16.00
5	Centavos 1918		
	Rev. of 20 Centavos		
	(Mule) Fine $150.00	350.00	950.00

Reduced Size

5	Centavos 1930-35...	3.50	30.00

Silver

10	Centavos 1903-06...	3.00	20.00
20	Centavos 1903-06...	4.50	30.00
50	Centavos 1903-06...	15.00	85.00
1	Peso 1903-06.......	20.00	85.00

Size Reduced

10	Centavos 1907-35...	2.50	21.00
20	Centavos 1907-29...	3.50	22.00
20	Centavos 1928		
	Rev. of 5 Centavos		
	(Mule).............	50.00	300.00
50	Centavos 1907-21	8.00	35.00
1	Peso 1907-12.......	14.00	60.00

COMMONWEALTH ISSUES

Bronze

1	Centavo 1937-44....	.20	1.25

Copper-Nickel

		E. Fine	Unc.
5	Centavos 1937-41...	$2.25	$9.00

Copper-Nickel-Zinc
Same Type as Cop.-Nic.

5	Centavos 1944-45...	.20	1.00

Silver

10	Centavos 1937-45...	.75	1.50
20	Centavos 1937-45...	1.25	3.00
50	Centavos 1944-45...	4.00	6.00

COMMEMORATIVE ISSUES

Establishment of the
Commonwealth

Quezon and Murphy

50	Centavos 1936	40.00	80.00
1	Peso 1936..........	100.00	175.00

Roosevelt and Quezon

1	Peso 1936..........	100.00	175.00

MISSTRUCK COINS

With the production of millions of coins each year, it is natural that a few abnormal pieces escape inspection and are inadvertently released for circulation, usually in original bags or rolls of new coins. Once generally unappreciated, today these pieces are eagerly sought for the information they shed on minting techniques, and as a variation from normal date and mint series collecting.

Nearly every misstruck coin is unique in some way, and prices may vary from coin to coin. They may all be classified in general groups related to the kind of manufacturing malfunction involved. Collectors value these pieces according to the scarcity of each kind of error for each type of coin.

The following listings show current average values for the most frequently encountered kinds of errors, in uncirculated condition for modern issues and extremely fine for obsolete types, when unmarred by serious marks or scratches. Exceptions are valued higher or lower. Rare date errors generally do not command a premium beyond their normal values.

1. CLIPPED PLANCHET: An incomplete coin, missing 10-25% of the metal.
2. LAMINATION: A flaw of less than 25% peeled off the coin's surface.
3. WRONG PLANCHET: A coin struck on a blank intended for another denomination.
4. DEFECTIVE DIE: Coin shows raised metal from a large die crack or small rim break.
5. BLANK PLANCHET: A blank of metal intended for coinage but not struck.
6. OFF CENTER: Approximately 10-20% of design missing from obsolete type coins; 20-60% missing from modern coins.
7. BROCKAGE: Mirror image of one coin impressed on another.
8. MULTIPLE STRIKE: Coin has additional image from being struck again approximately 80% off center. Value increases with number of strikes.

For more inclusive information, please refer to pages 242-250 in the 1980 edition of this Guide.

	1	2	3	4	5	6	7	8
Large Cent	$50.	$15.		$15.	$30.	$100.	$175.	$250.
Indian 1c	20.	2.	$500.-$975.	5.	1.	50.	100.	150.
Lincoln 1c	1.	1.	75.-150.	3.	1.	2.	30.	12.
Steel 1c	10.	35.	150.-400.	5.	10.	50.	150.	150.
Liberty 5c	25.	10.	250.-600.	30.	30.	70.		200.
Buffalo 5c	10.	4.	250.-550.	10.	3.	40.		250.
Jefferson 5c	2.	2.	20.-100.	5.	3.	4.	35.	25.
Wartime 5c	10.	3.	200.-300.	10.	150.	50.		75.
Barber 10c	20.	10.			10.	65.		
Mercury 10c	6.	3.		10.	10.	20.		165.
Roosevelt 10c (S)	5.	3.		8.	10.	15.		50.
Roosevelt 10c (C)	2.	8.		5.	3.	4.	25.	20.
Washington 25c (S)	9.	7.	50.- 125.		30.	60.		150.
Washington 25c (C)	3.	10.	15.- 90.	5.	4.	15.	50.	50.
Bicentennial 25c	15.	25.	250.-750.	50.	4.	50.	———	200.
Franklin 50c	50.	15.	150.-500.		40.	300.		
Kennedy 50c (S)	18.	16.	150.-300.		40.	200.		175.
Kennedy 50c (C)	8.	15.	125.-500.	5.	8.	50.		75.
Bicentennial 50c	25.	25.	300.-750.	75.	8.	100.	———	250.
Silver $1	75.	35.			250.	1000.		
Eisenhower $1	10.	30.	1000.-2000.		20.	300.		450.
Bicentennial $1	30.	50.	1500.-2500.	———	20.	350.	———	
Anthony $1	40.	25.	600.- 1500.	350.	100.	500.	———	———

BULLION VALUE OF SILVER COINS

Silver Bullion	Wartime Nickel .05626 oz.	Dime .07234 oz.	Quarter .18084 oz.	Half Dollar .36169 oz.	Silver Clad Half Dollar .14792 oz.	Silver Dollar .77344 oz.
$ 4.00	$ .23	$ .29	$ .72	$ 1.45	$ .59	$ 3.10
4.50	.25	.32	.81	1.63	.66	3.48
5.00	.28	.36	.90	1.81	.74	3.87
5.50	.31	.40	1.00	1.99	.81	4.26
6.00	.34	.44	1.09	2.17	.89	4.64
6.50	.36	.47	1.18	2.35	.96	5.03
7.00	.40	.51	1.27	2.53	1.04	5.42
7.50	.42	.55	1.36	2.72	1.11	5.80
8.00	.45	.58	1.45	2.90	1.19	6.19
8.50	.48	.62	1.54	3.08	1.26	6.58
9.00	.50	.65	1.63	3.26	1.33	6.96
9.50	.53	.69	1.72	3.44	1.42	7.35
10.00	.56	.72	1.81	3.62	1.48	7.73
11.00	.62	.80	1.99	3.98	1.63	8.51
12.00	.68	.87	2.17	4.34	1.78	9.28
13.00	.73	.94	2.35	4.70	1.92	10.05
14.00	.79	1.01	2.53	5.06	2.07	10.83
15.00	.84	1.09	2.71	5.43	2.22	11.60

BULLION VALUE OF GOLD COINS

Price Per Ounce	$5.00 Liberty Head 1839-1908 Indian Head 1908-1929	$10.00 Liberty Head 1838-1907 Indian Head 1907-1933	$20.00 1849-1933
$ 200.00	$ 48.37	$ 96.75	$ 193.50
225.00	54.42	108.85	217.69
250.00	60.47	120.94	241.88
275.00	66.52	133.03	266.07
300.00	72.50	145.13	290.25
325.00	78.60	157.22	314.44
350.00	84.65	169.31	338.63
375.00	90.70	181.40	362.81
400.00	96.75	193.50	387.00
425.00	102.80	205.60	411.19
450.00	108.84	217.69	435.38
475.00	114.89	229.78	459.56
500.00	120.94	241.87	483.75
525.00	126.98	253.97	507.94
550.00	133.03	266.06	532.13
575.00	139.08	278.16	556.31
600.00	145.12	290.25	580.50

INDEX

INDEX — *Continued*

INDEX — *Continued*

The following numismatic magazines are obtainable by subscription. They are published monthly or as indicated below. Information or sample copies may be obtained by writing to the individual publisher.

The Numismatist
Published by the American
Numismatic Association
P.O. Box 2366
Colorado Springs, Colo.   80901

Numismatic News Weekly
Iola, Wisconsin   54990

Coins Magazine
Iola Wisconsin   54990

Coin World (Weekly)
P.O. Box 150
Sidney, Ohio   45367

The Canadian Numismatic Journal
Published by the Canadian
Numismatic Association
P.O. Box 226
Barrie, Ontario, Canada

Hobbies Magazine
1106 S. Michigan Ave.
Chicago, Ill.   60605
(Has a coin section)

COINage Magazine
2660 E. Main St.
Ventura, California   93003

*Providing Coin Collector's with
Quality Hobby Supplies for
over 40 years.*

For more information on available
WHITMAN Coin Products write:

WHITMAN Coin Products M.S. 438R
Western Publishing Company, Inc.
1220 Mound Avenue
Racine, WI 53404

LIMITED EDITION, COMMEMORATIVE MEDALLION

Now in celebration of Whitman's *A Guide Book of United States Coins* ("Red Book") 40th Anniversary of publication, Whitman Coin Products is issuing a limited edition, proof-like, one ounce silver medallion to commemorate the occasion. This collector's medallion was exclusively designed and struck for Whitman. It is comprised of one ounce of .999 pure silver in an attractive collector's case.

Your Whitman limited edition *A Guide Book of United States Coins* ("Red Book") medallion will be complemented later this year by the issuance of the Whitman's *Handbook of United States Coins* ("Blue Book") medallion. The two medallions will complete your limited edition set, so be sure to watch for further details in the 1987 Edition Blue Book available in August.

To receive your limited edition Red Book medallion, and free display holder, order now while the supplies last.

To order, fill in and mail the order blank below with check or money order for $9.95 (plus sales tax where applicable) plus the proof of purchase label from the front cover of this book for a Red Book medallion with case.

I understand I may return the medallion within 14 days and receive a full refund if not completely satisfied.

Mail To:
Whitman Coin Department
Western Publishing Company, Inc.
P.O. Box 700, M.S. #438
Racine, WI 53401

| Place Proof of Purchase Label Here |

NAME _____
Please Print

ADDRESS _____

CITY _____ STATE _____ ZIP _____

PLACE OF PURCHASE _____

cut along line